TUMULTUOUS DECADE

Empire, Society, and Diplomacy in 1930s Japan

The 1930s was a dark period in international affairs. The Great Depression affected the economic and social circumstances of the world's major powers, contributing to armed conflicts such as the Spanish Civil War and the Second World War. This volume focuses exclusively on Japan, which witnessed a flurry of progressive activities in this period, activities that served both domestic and international society during the "tumultuous decade."

Featuring an interdisciplinary and international group of scholars, *Tumultuous Decade* examines Japanese domestic and foreign affairs between 1931 and 1941. It looks at Japan in the context of changing approaches to global governance, the rise of the League of Nations, and attempts to understand the Japanese worldview as it stood in the 1930s, a crucial period for Japan and the wider world. The editors argue that, like many other emerging powers at the time, Japan experienced a national identity crisis during this period and that this crisis is what ultimately precipitated Japan's role in the Second World War as well as the global order that took shape in its aftermath.

(Japan and Global Society)

MASATO KIMURA is director of the Shibusawa Eiichi Memorial Foundation.

TOSH MINOHARA is a professor in the Graduate School of Law at Kobe University.

JAPAN AND GLOBAL SOCIETY

Editors: Akira Iriye, *Harvard University*; Masato Kimura, *Shibusawa Eiichi Memorial Foundation*; David A. Welch, *Balsillie School of International Affairs, University of Waterloo*

How has Japan shaped, and been shaped by, globalization – politically, economically, socially, and culturally? How has its identity, and how have its objectives, changed? *Japan and Global Society* explores Japan's past, present, and future interactions with the Asia Pacific and the world from a wide variety of disciplinary and interdisciplinary perspectives and through diverse paradigmatic lenses. Titles in this series are intended to showcase international scholarship on Japan and its regional neighbours that will appeal to scholars in disciplines both in the humanities and the social sciences.

   Japan and Global Society is supported by generous grants from the Shibusawa Eiichi Memorial Foundation and the University of Missouri–St Louis.

Editorial Advisory Board

For a list of books published in the series, see page 299.

Tumultuous Decade

Empire, Society, and Diplomacy in 1930s Japan

EDITED BY MASATO KIMURA
AND TOSH MINOHARA

UNIVERSITY OF TORONTO PRESS
Toronto Buffalo London

© University of Toronto Press 2013
Toronto Buffalo London
www.utppublishing.com
Printed in the U.S.A.

ISBN 978-1-4426-4386-4 (cloth)
ISBN 978-1-4426-1234-1 (paper)

Printed on acid-free paper

Library and Archives Canada Cataloguing in Publication

Tumultuous decade : empire, society, and diplomacy in 1930s Japan / edited by Masato Kimura and Tosh Minohara.

(Japan and global society)
Includes bibliographical references and index.
ISBN 978-1-4426-4386-4 (bound). – ISBN 978-1-4426-1234-1 (pbk.)

1. Japan – Foreign relations – 1912–1945.   2. Japan – Politics and government – 1926–1945.   3. Japan – Social conditions – 1912–1945.
4. Japan – Economic conditions – 1918–1945.   5. National characteristics, Japanese.   I. Kimura, Masato, 1952–   II. Minohara, Tosh, 1971–
III. Series: Japan and global society series

DS889.5.T84 2013   327.5209'043   C2012-908471-9

University of Toronto Press acknowledges the financial assistance to its publishing program of the Canada Council for the Arts and the Ontario Arts Council.

University of Toronto Press acknowledges the financial support of the Government of Canada through the Canada Book Fund for its publishing activities.

Contents

Preface

University of Toronto Press, in cooperation with the University of Missouri–St Louis and the Shibusawa Eiichi Memorial Foundation of Tokyo, is launching an ambitious new series, "Japan and Global Society." The volumes in the series will explore how Japan has defined its identities and objectives in the larger region of Asia and the Pacific and, at the same time, how the global community has been shaped by Japan and its interactions with other countries.

The dual focus on Japan and on global society reflects the series editors' and publishers' commitment to globalizing national studies. Scholars and readers have become increasingly aware that it makes little sense to treat a country in isolation. All countries are interdependent and shaped by cross-national forces so that mono-national studies, those that examine a country's past and present in isolation, are never satisfactory. Such awareness has grown during the past few decades when global, transnational phenomena and forces have gained prominence. In the age of globalization, no country retains complete autonomy or freedom of action. Yet nations continue to act in pursuit of their respective national interests, which frequently results in international tensions. Financial, social, and educational policies continue to be defined domestically, with national communities as units. But transnational economic, environmental, and cultural forces always infringe upon national entities, transforming them in subtle and sometimes even violent ways. Global society, consisting of billions of individuals and their organizations, evolves and shapes national communities even as the latter contributes to defining the overall human community.

Japan provides a particularly pertinent instance of such interaction, but this series is not limited to studies of that country alone. Indeed, the books published in the series will show that there is little unique about Japan, whose history has been shaped by interactions with China, Korea, the United States, and many other countries. For this reason, forthcoming volumes will deal with countries in the Asia-Pacific region and compare their respective developments and shared destinies. At the same time, it is expected that some studies in the series will transcend national frameworks and discuss more transnational themes, such as humanitarianism, migrations, and diseases, documenting how these phenomena affect Japan and other countries and how, at the same time, they contribute to the making of a more interdependent global society.

Lastly, we hope these studies will help to promote an understanding of non-national entities, such as regions, religions, and civilizations. Modern history continues to be examined in terms of nations as the key units of analysis, and yet these other entities have their own vibrant histories, which do not necessarily coincide with nation-centred narratives. To look at Japan, or for that matter any other country, and to examine its past and present in these alternative frameworks will enrich our understanding of modern world history and of the contemporary global civilization.

Akira Iriye

Acknowledgments

Putting together what in the end became a nearly decade-long international project required herculean stamina as well as incredible patience. Despite the countless hours of labour that the editors and contributors have put into this project, its successful completion would not have come about had it not been for the generous amount of outside help we received over the years. We therefore would like to take this opportunity to express our deepest gratitude to our benefactors, who have continuously extended their strong support for this project. First and foremost among these are the Shibusawa Eiichi Memorial Foundation and the University of Missouri–St Louis (UMSL), without whose generous financial and logistical support this project would never have gotten off the ground in the first place. We particularly would like to give our personal thanks to Mr Masahide Shibusawa, president of the Shibusawa Eiichi Memorial Foundation, and Dr Joel Glassman, director of the UMSL's Center for International Studies.

In its early stages, this project also benefited enormously from the generosity of the Reischauer Institute of Japanese Studies, Harvard University, through its Research Grants program, which provided financial support for collaborative research projects between the visiting scholars and then graduate students at Harvard. Indeed, this project would not have seen the light of day had it not been for the fact that all the editors and contributors were affiliated with Harvard in some capacity during 2000 and 2001. By getting to know each other through numerous discussions at research seminars and other intellectual exchanges, we came to appreciate our differences in our approach to the study of history. We also realized very clearly that, if we combined our research interests, we could create a multidisciplinary work that would illuminate pre-war Japan in a completely different light. As a wave of post-modernism was sweeping across the history departments in the United States during that time, the encounter between young Japanese and American scholars reaffirmed our belief in the importance of diversity in academia. Thus it was a natural step that scholars from both sides of the Pacific would work together and launch a project devoted to a re-examination of Japan during the tumultuous decade of the 1930s.

With the blessing and encouragement of Professors Akira Iriye and Andrew Gordon, in 2002 the editors formally organized the project that eventually would culminate in this volume. Beginning in Cambridge, Massachusetts, the group met at least once a year during annual conferences of the Association for Asian Studies and convened special research seminars in such places as Harvard University, Kobe University, International House in Tokyo, Japan Center for International Exchange, and the University of California, Berkeley. Every meeting became an intellectual dojo whose synergy not only stimulated one's own research, but also made the entire volume a much better one. Each chapter is thus very much a collaborative piece in that it has received input and advice from other project members.

Many people read the manuscript, in whole or in part, and offered helpful comments and suggestions. Two anonymous readers, who read the entire manuscript thoroughly, provided sharp but warranted criticisms alongside a very positive review as a whole. Reflecting these comments during the revision process has made the volume much better in the end, for which the editors are extremely grateful. Other individuals contributed to the volume by providing valuable insight by sharing their knowledge of the 1930s or by providing access to their research facilities. Among these many scholars we would like to give special mention to Professors Thomas Gold, Iguchi Haruo, Iokibe Makoto, Liu Jie, Kagotani Nato, Kato Yoko, Gil Latz, Tak Matsukata, and Genzo Yamamoto.

Finally, at the publication stage, special mention must be made of Stephen Kotowych, Daniel Quinlan, and Wayne Herrington, editors at the University of Toronto Press, who were not only extremely supportive, but also generous in providing their wisdom and expertise. In particular, we have learned to appreciate their tremendous patience, as putting the volume together took much longer than anticipated.

Using international sources requires adopting a few standard conventions, and for purposes of this English-language edition we decided to incorporate Romanized transliterations for non-Western names, words, phrases, and titles, rather than use Japanese, Chinese, or Korean characters. We also adopted the traditional Japanese practice of putting family or surnames first, except for individuals who regularly use the Western name format or are better known in the West by that format. For Korean names, it is generally acceptable either to hyphenate personal names or to capitalize them, and we have allowed the contributors to use either format. To conserve space, Asian-language sources cited have not been translated; instead, Romanized versions of the original titles have been used.

We would like to end with the standard disclaimer that the opinions expressed in this volume, and any errors, are the sole responsibility of the authors alone, and not those of the organizations or individuals who have supported our work. As editors, we are of course keen to learn of any errors the volume may contain, so that they may be addressed in future revisions.

Masato Kimura and Tosh Minohara

Introduction

MASATO KIMURA
TOSH MINOHARA

This book analyses the pivotal decade of 1931–41 from the distinct vantage points of Japan's empire, society, and diplomacy, to shed new light on and to provide new insight into that "tumultuous decade." Specifically, the times are examined through a multi-disciplinary lens based on an international history approach. The broad scope of the book can be seen in the wide range of topics, encompassing politics, diplomacy, economy, sociology, technology, philosophy, psychology, eugenics, and cultural studies, to name a few. By applying this framework, it is possible to revise the commonly accepted image of the ten years from 1931 until 1941 as a "dark period," one that epitomizes the bleak world of the aftermath of Black Thursday of 1929, which heralded the Great Depression. As history clearly shows us, this seminal event paved the path leading to armed conflicts across the world – the civil war in Spain, Italy's invasion of Ethiopia, Germany's invasion of the Sudetenland, and Japan's military expansion into Manchuria and China proper. It is now widely accepted that these regional conflicts eventually culminated in the Second World War, an event that unmistakably served to define the twentieth century. In the chapters to follow, however, the arc of history, so described, is enlarged on and reconsidered.

A Brief Chronology of the History of the Tumultuous Decade

To provide a reconsidered view of East Asia in the 1930s, the first step is to introduce the chronology of events of the tumultuous decade from 1931 to 1941. The Manchurian Incident, a conflict that erupted on 18 September 1931, shocked the Washington order that had served as the basic framework for the Asia-Pacific region during the 1920s. At the end of the 1920s and into the early 1930s, the faction in Japan opposed to the Washington order, centred on the military and right-wingers, was growing in power. After the Japanese government concluded the Naval Disarmament Treaty in London in 1930, the opposition party and the army drove Foreign Minister Shidehara Kijurō into a corner, arguing that he had violated the "prerogative of supreme command." At this time, and in anticipation of elections, gamesmanship and double dealing were rampant in the political world, despite the deep concerns of the common people, the press, and the military.

At the global financial level, the 1930s unfolded in direct response to the financial panic of 1929, and the resulting economic chaos advanced not only on Japan, but also on Manchuria and the northeast region of China, a territory occupied by Japan that had presented a number of challenges since victory in the Russo-Japanese War of 1904–05. The sudden and sharp decline of stock prices on Wall Street on Thursday, 29 October 1929, devalued the price of Japanese silk in the U.S. market by 25 per cent, hitting the Japanese economy hard. The unemployment rate increased, and Japanese farmers suffered extreme poverty. In their distress, the "haves" such as the United States, Britain, and France started to form self-sufficient economic blocs and to take self-centred protective measures. In response, Japanese gradually became more sympathetic towards the reforms proposed by the military and right wingers under the slogans of *Dai Ajia Shugi* (Greater Asia) and *Showa Ishin* (Showa Restoration). It was under these circumstances that the militarist general Ishiwara Kanji and the Kwantung Army roused themselves to action in Manchuria (via the Ryujo Lake Incident), and the puppet state of Manchukuo was established, with Pu-yi, the last emperor of the Chin dynasty, placed in charge.

These developments redefined the direction of domestic and international affairs in East Asia. In Japan, neither the Hamaguchi Osachi nor the Inukai Tsuyoshi cabinets could stop the Kwantung Army's aggressive activities in Manchuria. Moreover, a series of assassinations by right wingers and young military officers threatened Japanese political and business leaders. On 15 May 1930, young navy officers shot Inukai to death in the prime minister's own residence in response to his cabinet's reluctance to recognize Manchukuo. Similarly, neither the Washington Treaty nor the League of Nations, both of which had been established to resolve nation-state disputes, was able to curb Japan's aggressive military actions by specifying sanctions to be taken against a treaty signatory.

All of the Great Powers were aware that, if the Manchurian Incident was not managed carefully, it could lead to the collapse of the Versailles-Washington international order. The inability to act in response to Japan can be attributed to various reasons. Britain could not afford to interfere with Japan's military activities because of its own economic difficulties related to the 1929 depression and its retreat from the gold standard in September 1931. In the United States, the Hoover administration relied upon Japanese cabinet members and politicians such as Prime Minister Hamaguchi and Finance Minister Inoue Jun'nosuke, who, notwithstanding their liberal orientation and strong relationships with private American bankers such as Thomas Lamont, were unable to balance the conservative and nationalistic trends unfolding in Japan. Ultimately, in 1932, Japan's navy attacked Shanghai and landed marines there, forcing the United States and Britain to change their policy towards Japan. On 7 January 1932, U.S. Secretary of State Henry Stimson proclaimed the doctrine that the United States could not condone Japan's military activities in Manchuria and China.

Japan withdrew from the League of Nations in March 1933. Despite this setback, both the United States and Japan tried to maintain a positive relationship in the economic arena. For Japan, maintaining good relationships with the United States was an important strategy to avoid being isolated and to explore how to create a new political order in Asia that could protect her interests and access to strategic resources. Despite the complicated situation in China at the time, the United States, Britain, and Japan exchanged business missions from 1934 to 1937 in an effort to strengthen bilateral and multilateral economic relationships. Such national "ambassadors" as Charlie Chaplin and "Babe" Ruth visited Japan to promote cultural exchanges. Japan also invited cultural events to its cities: the General Conference of International Chambers of Commerce was to have been held in Tokyo in 1939, Tokyo was the intended site of the 1940 Olympic Summer Games, and Osaka planned an International Exposition in the 1940s, each in support of maintaining Japan's global relationships.

Unfortunately, all those events were cancelled when conflict broke out between China and Japan in 1937. Beginning with smaller battles near the Marco Polo Bridge in the suburbs of Beijing in July 1937, the conflict developed into full-scale war. Initially, the Japanese and Chinese governments tried to compromise, but they were unsuccessful, and the Pacific theatre of the Second World War became a major battlefield until Japan's surrender on 15 August 1945.

Between 1937 and 1945, the region in effect experienced a second Sino-Japanese War that brought together Chiang Kai-shek, leader of the Kuomintang, and Mao Ze-dong, leader of the Chinese Communist Party, under the pretext of opposing the Japanese invasion of China. The two armies were odd bedfellows, to be sure, having fought since the 1920s in a contest pitting two totally different visions of China's future. The United States and Britain were cautious in coping with this conflict, for two reasons. First, both U.S. president Franklin D. Roosevelt and British prime minister Neville Chamberlain were more worried about the growing power of Adolf Hitler and Benito Mussolini, whose totalitarian states had become a great menace to liberal democracy and academic freedom in Europe. Second, an isolationist U.S. Congress strongly opposed any involvement by the United States in global conflicts. Indeed, the United States was not itself a formal member of the League of Nations even though President Woodrow Wilson had proposed the idea at the Versailles Conference in 1919.

After losing several opportunities to stop the war against China and as relationships with Britain and the United States continued to worsen, Japan turned in the 1930s to strengthening its partnerships with Germany and Italy. Hitler's prediction of war with Britain and France once Germany invaded Czechoslovakia and Poland also led to Germany's reconsidering Japan as an important ally that could attack Britain and France in Southeast Asia as well as menace the Soviet Union. Japan welcomed the establishment of amicable treaties with Germany and Italy in its own right to defend against the influx of communism from the Soviet Union. After annexing Czechoslovakia, Germany invaded Poland on 1 September 1939. Britain and France immediately declared war. A series of swift German victories in 1940 encouraged Japan to conclude a tripartite treaty with Germany and Italy in Berlin on 27 September, although many pro-Western Japanese politicians, admirals, diplomats such as Yoshida Shigeru, and business leaders opposed it. Japan's foreign minister Matsuoka Yōsuke, who negotiated the treaty, had a unique idea at the time that collaboration among Japan, Germany, Italy, and the Soviet Union could strengthen Japan's position in negotiating with the United States. For their part, the United States and Britain, concluding that Hitler was the most dangerous menace, viewed the Japan-German-Italy alliance in negative terms, transforming Japan into a clear enemy.

In the midst of these developments, the possibility of war between the United States and Japan could not be ignored. When the Japanese army invaded northern French Indo-China in September 1940, U.S. Secretary of State Cordell Hull initiated an embargo of strategic materials and in August 1941 a total embargo of crude oil and pig iron. These actions led Japan to perceive itself as being encircled by an American, British, Chinese, and Dutch net – the so-called ABCDs. In October 1941, Hull sent a note to Japan describing the necessary conditions under which the United States would lift the embargo; as they included the Japanese army's retreating from the whole of its Chinese territories, Japan rejected the "Hull Note." Japan initiated war against the United States, Britain, France, and the Netherlands in December 1941 by attacking several important strategic bases such as Pearl Harbor in Hawaii, the British naval base in Singapore, and strategic airfields in the Philippines.

A Reconsideration of the Tumultuous Decade: 1930s Japan

This volume takes the position that the events stemming from 1929, while often portrayed as presaging the "dark years" to come, nonetheless provide only a partial view of the complex chain of events that took place during the 1930s. The decade also witnessed several notable accomplishments, such as the advent of the global movement espousing liberal and progressive ideals, as epitomized by the creation of numerous non-governmental organizations. Despite the depression, several large private foundations, such as the Mitsui, Hattori, and Asahigarasu Foundations, were established by major Japanese companies to facilitate large research projects on advanced technology and medical treatment. Furthermore, one cannot discount the immense contributions by intellectual and business leaders who endeavoured to lay the foundations for the establishment of international business that went beyond culture and diplomacy. For example, we can point to the active role of world business leaders at the International Chamber of Commerce (ICC) after the London International Economic Conference adopted a resolution (although one that proved to be incomplete) for multinational cooperation for rapid economic recovery. The ICC, established by world business leaders in 1919 in Paris to promote world trade and the free flow of capital for sustainable economic development, became one of the few venues where world business leaders could have relatively free discussions about the state of the world economy.

For Japan, in particular, the period witnessed a flurry of progressive activities that functioned to serve both domestic and international society. After Japan's withdrawal from the League of Nations in 1932, and even after the turmoil of the China-Japanese War in 1937, Japanese diplomats, business leaders, and intellectuals continued to participate in world organizations. We can find similar phenomena in the cultural world. As Akira Iriye has pointed out, "the Paris-based International Institute of Cultural Cooperation became even more active in the early 1930s than earlier."[1] The Institute of Pacific Relations, established in 1925 in Honolulu, organized one of the most important intellectual conferences on peaceful Pacific relations in the 1930s, and Japanese intellectuals participated and shared their ideas. Notions of modernity assumed greater importance at this time; in Japan's case, since the early Meiji era "to be modern" – to balance Japanese and Western thought – had been one of the most important challenges for Japanese society. Such movements and activities had seen in various fields, such as the management of hygiene, eugenics, and immunology in both domestic and colonial areas, since the late nineteenth century. It can be argued that such movements, from the perspective of international history, displayed certain qualities that transcended the nation-state system and national identities.

As for the domestic elements of Japan's internationalism, we should touch upon the so-called Taisho Democracy and its effect on Japanese society during the 1930s. The Taisho era was a fifteen-year period (1912–26), positioned between the Meiji (1868–1912) and Showa (1926–89). Despite its limited duration, in the Taisho era Japan came to embrace ample and diversified thoughts and ideas such as liberal democracy, internationalism, idealism, fascism, communism, and even anarchism and eroticism. Many who were influenced by such circumstances continued to espouse liberal positions even as the atmosphere of Japanese society gradually became darker due to intermittent financial panics in the early Showa period, a time of greater conservatism and nationalism after the Manchurian Incident.

By combining such additional insights about the 1930s with traditional and multi-archival analysis of major Japanese foreign ministers of that decade, we can describe the evolving in Japan of the 1930s an alternative internationalism that is more aggressive, dynamic, and diversified than presented in other histories of the period. In other words, it becomes possible to take a series of initial but important steps to present a grand design based on a comprehensive framework for analysing the 1930s and the complex concepts and events shaping it.

Organization of the Volume

With this in mind, the volume is composed of three sections: "Economics, Culture, Society, and Identity," "The Empire and Imperial Concerns," and "High Diplomacy and the Statesmen." Each chapter in these sections represents an original attempt to illuminate the Japanese view of the world and the activities that occurred during the tumultuous decade of the 1930s. In particular, Japan's challenge to create an alternative international system is emphasized to examine how the country departed from the path of international cooperation with the major powers – the so-called Shidehara Diplomacy — to follow one of international friction and conflict.

In Chapter 1, Masato Kimura focuses on the Japanese business community's perception of the United States. With respect to the changing dynamics of world trade and its accompanying rules in the 1930s, the United States is a case in point. Although reluctant to become involved directly in global politics due to its preoccupation with domestic economic matters, the United States, given its huge natural resource base, nevertheless was destined to have tremendous influence on the rules governing trading nations. The severe impact of the Great Depression on the U.S. economy and the slowness of the recovery gave rise to fundamental questions about American capitalism, which was based on market mechanisms and strongly relied on entrepreneurs and free competition. The implications for Japan in the 1930s were clear: as an emerging empire in East Asia, it would take a more autonomous position in fashioning ideas and systems for governing both itself and its colonies.

In Chapter 2, Jessamyn Abel analyses the *Kokusai Bunka Shinkokai* (KBS), founded in 1934, the precursor of the present-day Japan Foundation. The KBS not only gave shape to Japan's international cultural activities; it also illustrated through such activities the evolving relationship between nationalists and internationalists during the 1930s. After classifying the concepts of "internationalism," Abel points out that the gap between rhetoric and reality characterizing internationalism was apparent in the Japanese formulation of regional internationalism in the 1930s and 1940s.

In Chapter 3, Cemil Aydin offers an interpretation of Japanese pan-Asianism as a proactive attempt to frame an alternative modernity: comparing pan-Islamic and anti-Western solidarity as illustrative of

Japan's alternative internationalism after the Manchurian Incident. Such comparative approaches to world history clarify not only the influence of Pan-Asianism and Pan-Islamism on Japanese and Turkish nationalism; they also demonstrate how differences between each were products of late-nineteenth-century tensions between imperialism and globalization, as well as the corresponding impact on the thinking of intellectuals in the 1930s.

Chapter 4, by Sumiko Otsubo, provides an analysis of the debate over the National Eugenics Law of 1940. Several movements and disputes concurrent with the passing of this law revealed serious domestic disagreements about how Japan ought to define itself as a modern nation. Otsubo points out the difficult choices between the modern and the traditional, science and nature, rationalism and spiritualism, that continue to be the basis of contemporary debate.

The second section consists of three chapters relating to aspects of empire and colonization. Given Japan's alternative internationalism, the country faced important decisions about how to govern its colonies in Taiwan, Korea, and other areas.

In Chapter 5, Evan Dawley introduces the case study of the rapid modernization of Jilong, a small port city in northern Taiwan. There, the practice of *shakai jigyo* ("social work") during the 1920s and 1930s became an essential part of Japan's expanding colonial control, becoming more scientifically constructed and centrally directed – in essence, more modern.

In Chapter 6, Jun Uchida focuses on neighbourhood groups created in colonial Korea to support Japan's war in China, despite severe anti-Japanese movements not only in Korea but also among overseas Koreans. Although Japan tried to extinguish all forms of Korean culture, Uchida shows that, once Japan was defeated in August 1945, the Koreans swiftly cast off such oppressive policies.

Chapter 7, by Yuka Fujioka, is an analysis of the Japanese government efforts to explain Japan's foreign policies to Japanese immigrants in the United States, as part of a covert attempt to gain support for Japan's invasion of China after the Manchurian Incident. Through this chapter, one is confronted with a new image of Japanese immigrants who are less passive and less isolated in their support of Japan's foreign policy towards Asia.

The third and final section consists of four chapters examining the key Japanese foreign ministers during the period, based on multi-archival and traditional diplomatic history methodologies. The four chapters clarify in chronological order how each foreign minister responded to the challenges presented by the international system.

In Chapter 8, Rustin Gates sheds lights on Foreign Minister Uchida Ya-suya – not as the reformist in the early Showa who had been impressed by the so-called new diplomacy and Taisho democracy, but as the last spokesman for internationalism in the context of Meiji imperialism. In effect, Gates argues, Uchida, as a representative of an older generation, attempted to justify Japan's invasion of Manchuria in 1931 with the diplomatic principles of the imperial age before the First World War.

In Chapter 9, Satoshi Hattori analyses and clarifies a series of controversial decisions that Foreign Minister Matsuoka Yōsuke made in the spring of 1941 as he attempted to construct an alternative world order by forging allied relations among Germany, Italy, the Soviet Union, and Japan. Matsuoka's decision and position became important turning points for U.S.-Japanese relations as the United States subsequently abandoned hope for Japan's return to the world democratic community.

In Chapter 10, Peter Mauch sheds light on the positions taken by Toyoda Teijirō, who was both an admiral in the Imperial Japanese Navy and foreign minister in the summer and early fall of 1941, a period coinciding with the critical stage of United States-Japan negotiations before Pearl Harbor. His successor, Tōgō Shigenori, was obliged to select his policy as a means of balancing domestic pressure in support of a strong challenge to the international system and U.S. pressure to maintain the status quo.

Finally, in Chapter 11, Tosh Minohara looks at the final stage of U.S.-Japanese negotiations between Foreign Minister Tōgō Shigenori and U.S. Secretary of State Cordell Hull during late fall 1941, and reveals a startlingly original interpretation of this critical moment in twentieth-century U.S.-Japanese history. Minohara argues that the famous "Hull Note" was not the last straw that prompted Japan's decision to go to war, and confirms the remarkable fact that, contrary to conclusions of previous historians, on 20 November 1941 the Japanese government intercepted a cable from the Chinese Embassy in Washington to the Chungking government concerning the United States' tentative response to Tōgō's plan.

Taken as a whole, the chapters in this volume demonstrate Japan's attempt to create an alternative internationalism in the 1930s, one that included adjustments and reactions to the rapidly changing international order of the time. The analysis further confirms that the resulting

tension between Japan and the world created a certain degree of ambivalence in Japan's emerging leadership. It seems to us that Japan started
to explore its new status and leadership in the global community in the
1930s based on its comparatively strong military and economic power
in the Asia Pacific region. Since the Meiji Restoration in the middle of
the nineteenth century, Japanese leaders had been struggling with how
to embrace Western thought and technology and harmonize it with
traditional thinking and Japan's social system, while also cultivating
Japan's military power and rapid economic development. After its remarkable victories in the Sino-Japanese War, the Russo-Japanese War,
and the First World War, Japan became, along with the United States,
Britain, France, and Italy, one of the five Great Powers. Through their
participation in multinational conferences during the 1920s, Japanese
leaders shared the common feeling that the emerging international society could decide the future of Japan, for better or for worse. In other
words, Japan began to understand the difficulty of maintaining its status and power independent of collaboration with other countries.

The collapse of the European and U.S. financial systems in 1929 gave
Japan the opportunity to communicate its alternative internationalism
more widely. This helps to explain the pendulum-like swing from pan-
Asianism to internationalism, bringing to the surface the complex issues of national identity and nationalism facing Japan. The arc of this
pendulum, over time, was determined by changing definitions of the
appropriate roles of government and non-government actors in the political, business, and academic communities. Ultimately, Japan's internal debate collided with an evolving international order, precipitating
the clash at Pearl Harbor. Still, as this volume makes clear, in tracing
the origins of this tragedy to the tumultuous decade between 1931 and
1941, we can also identify new, creative, and at times progressive contributions that government leaders and others chose to make in the formulation of what ultimately came to be described as the post–Second
World War global system.

NOTE

1 Akira Iriye, *The Cambridge History of American Foreign Relations*, vol. 3, *The
  Globalizing of America, 1913–1945* (Cambridge: Cambridge University Press,
  1993), p. 130.

East Asia

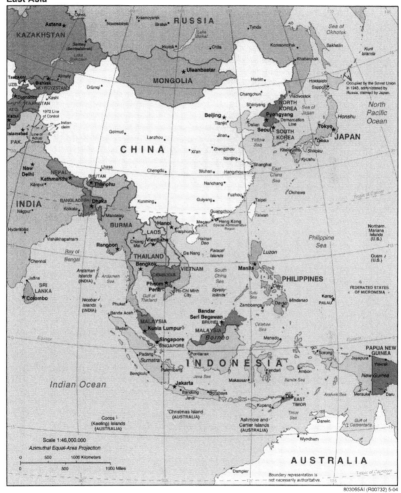

PART ONE

Economics, Culture, Society, and Identity

1 The *Zaikai*'s Perception of and Orientation towards the United States in the 1930s

MASATO KIMURA

The purpose of this chapter is to introduce and shed light on the changing perception of the United States by Japan's business elite, the *Zaikai* (literally, business circle), in the 1930s, based on the reports of travellers and senior officers who had dealings with the United States and the British Empire. I focus on examples from Tokyo and Osaka, areas representative of almost all major Japanese industries at the time.[1]

The term *Zaikai* has broad meaning. Ogata Sadako writes that the *Zaikai* "are generally regarded as a power elite who represented the interests of the business community as a whole rather than of individual businessmen."[2] Masataka Matsuura refers to a further definition of the *Zaikai* from the inter-war period: "a very narrow business circle of the elite connected to political power"[3] and "the core group in the business society which lasted between the two World Wars."[4] In sum, the major business circles in the inter-war period in Japan included the *Zaikai* as well as several powerful local and national associations such as the chambers of commerce in the major cities. With this in mind, in this chapter I refer to the *Zaikai* as major business groups and leaders who regularly expressed their opinions on political and economic issues and who sought to influence Japanese policy from the beginning of the 1920s until the outbreak of the Sino-Japanese War in 1937.

U.S. and European business leaders had a notable impact on international relations in the inter-war period as reconstructing the world economy, especially that of Europe, was high on the agenda. U.S. business leaders in particular participated in decision-making to develop economic policy at home and in the League of Nations. The impact of Japanese business leaders on the international relations of the period, however, is less well understood.[5] Previous research on the *Zaikai*'s

contributions to Japanese business diplomacy has focused on two important economic missions in the inter-war period: the *Eibei Hōmon Jitsugyo-
dan* (Japanese Businessmen's Mission to Britain and the United States)
in 1921–22, and the *Ōbei Hōmon Keizai Shisetsudan* (Japanese Economic
Mission to Europe and the United States) in 1937. Analysis of these two
missions can provide insight into the *Zaikai*'s views on international relations as well as into some important aspects of the *Zaikai*'s influence
on Japan's foreign relations and the relationship between government
and business. Regarding the 1930s, previous research on the *Ōbei Hōmon
Keizai Shisetsudan* sets the stage for the discussion to follow.[6]

   The 1930s are often described as a "dark period" – the aftermath of
"Black Thursday," which led to the Great Depression, armed conflicts
such as the Spanish Civil War and Japan's invasion of Manchuria and
China, and the path to the Second World War. This picture, though correct, is incomplete. The 1930s also witnessed international movements
and conferences associated with the League of Nations and business
leaders' activities on the international stage, both of which aided the re-
establishment of the international business and diplomatic community
after the Second World War. In presenting an initial analysis that supports this perspective of the 1930s, one might also find, in passing, some
indications as to why the *Zaikai* would not and could not prevent war
with the United States.[7]

Factors Influencing the *Zaikai*'s Perception of the United States

The Great Depression

The Great Depression transformed the *Zaikai*'s attitude towards the
United States in that most Japanese business leaders became pessimistic about its future. The Depression's damage to the U.S. economy and
society went far beyond the *Zaikai*'s initial estimates. Early reactions of
both the U.S. and Japanese governments to "Black Monday" had been
optimistic – it was expected that stock prices on Wall Street would re-
bound quickly – but the situation soon evolved into a serious crisis as
wholesale prices plummeted in the United States.

   The catastrophe of October 1929 contributed to a dramatic decline
in the value of Japanese exports to the United States, mainly due to
the price of silk, which in 1930 fell to one-third that of the previous
year. That and similar price trends triggered a worldwide financial crisis. The condition of Japan's economy, already hit by financial panic

in 1927, now became critical due not only to the panic of 1929 but also to the Hamaguchi cabinet's resolute decision to put Japan back on the gold standard. One consequence was that farm villages in areas such as the Tohoku region (northeastern Japan) fell into poverty.

The crisis in the United States was much more severe than in Japan, and the monthly magazines of the major Japanese chambers of commerce focused on economic and social conditions there. In doing so, they both reflected and shaped the common perception among Japanese leaders of serious U.S. economic decline. As the extent of the effect of the Depression on U.S. society became clear, the *Zaikai*'s economic worldview and orientation swung towards East Asia.

Private bankers and financial officers had great influence over Japan's monetary practice and policy, and over the *Zaikai*. Given the influence, in turn, of U.S. private banks on the Japanese financial market, the Japanese finance ministry and Japanese financiers paid close attention to reform of the banking system during the Roosevelt administration. Central to their attention was whether or not the U.S. federal government could restrict the activities of U.S. private bankers, particularly in light of their tremendous contribution to the world economy since the Great War. For example, Thomas Lamont, director of J.P. Morgan & Company, and Arthur Young, director of the First National Bank, participated in several important economic conferences organized by the League of Nations and the International Chamber of Commerce, where they introduced serious initiatives to rebuild European economies through their financial groups. They also increased bank loans to develop the Japanese economy, cooperated with Japan to rebuild the metropolitan areas of Tokyo destroyed by the 1923 Kanto earthquake, and aided in the reconstruction of the Chinese railroad and telegraphic communication infrastructure in the 1920s.

International financier Yutaro Tomita pointed out, however, that the Roosevelt administration's 1933 prohibition of collusion between investment and commercial banking had undermined the influence of bankers on U.S. monetary policy.[8] Wall Street's influence on U.S. economic policy and diplomacy had also declined as the U.S. government claimed greater decision-making initiative in the 1930s. As a result, there was increased U.S. government scrutiny over lending to other countries. The Roosevelt administration's cautious attitude towards lending to Japan following the beginning of Japanese military activities in Manchuria in September 1931 was an important factor in Japanese financial sectors' changing perception of the United States in this period.

Before the Great Depression, the United States had been the model for Japanese businesses. Indeed, American capitalism had been an ideal of Japanese businessmen since the late nineteenth century. Through the Meiji and Taisho periods, many Japanese had been influenced by such famous Americans as George Washington, Thomas Edison, Benjamin Franklin, and Abraham Lincoln. Through their lives and accomplishments, Japanese businessmen learned about the spirit of American capitalism and its values, including freedom, liberalism, democracy, efficiency, and frugality. Japanese companies introduced the mass-production system pioneered by the Ford automobile factory as well as elements of American-style management and innovations in quality control. Japanese business leaders often visited the United States to learn the ways of American business and society. They sent their sons to prestigious American universities such as Harvard, Yale, and Columbia to study economics, law, and technology, and to build personal networks with American power elites on the East Coast. Iwasaki Yatarō, the founder of Mitsubishi Zaibatsu, sent his younger brother, Yanosuke, and his son, Koyata, to the United States. Dan Takuma studied mining at the Massachusetts Institute of Technology. Shigeyoshi Ikeda, who served as chief executive officer of Mitsui Bank in the 1920s, was a Harvard graduate.

The decline of the U.S. economy in the 1930s, however, caused the Japanese business community to question the credibility of the American business model. In the wake of the Great Depression, strong and positive images of the U.S. economy and American society gradually faded as Japanese became more aware of its dark side, as represented by the struggle between organized crime and the federal government precipitated by the Volstead Act of 1919. Moreover, the large numbers of unemployed made American society appear disorderly. Although the Hoover and the Roosevelt administrations attempted to jump-start the economy in the first half of the 1930s, there was no clear indication of recovery until late in the decade. Unemployment hovered around 20 per cent. Newspaper reports covered desperate workers committing suicide, Wall Street in despair, devastated farms, and harsh protests by labour unions. Large sections of the Japanese business community concluded that American democracy and its economy were facing a crisis that appeared difficult to rectify through capitalist principles.

Many Japanese business leaders who had previously been impressed by the United States began to focus their attention on the weaknesses perceived to be inherent in American democracy and capitalism. Many criticized the so-called Gilded Age for its excessive focus on money. Put differently, Japanese business leaders believed money and profit were necessary for capitalism, but were not almighty. Morimura Ichizaemon, owner of Morimura-gumi, one of the *Zaibatsu* (financial combines) that exported Japanese porcelain to the United States, wrote, in essence, that it was ridiculous for American millionaires to spend a lot of money just to have a crazy party in New York; he also mentioned that Japanese businessmen should pursue capitalism based on morality.[9]

Taken together, these changing perceptions led the *Zaikai* to re-think the economic role of government. In general, and consistent with capitalist principles, the Japanese government's role in the economy since the nineteenth century had been limited. But in the wake of the Great Depression, distinguished economists, including John Maynard Keynes, had been urging that governments should and could do many things to raise effective demand in society. The Roosevelt administration was indeed carrying out such macroeconomic policies – including the famous Tennessee Valley Authority development project – full economic recovery would be many years off. Germany, however, presented a different model, to which the attention of the *Zaikai* increasingly turned. In Germany, the application of policy control mechanisms in the late 1930s had led to impressive growth – although Japanese business leaders were more likely to keep their economic activities free of centralized control.

Some exceptional Japanese leaders and companies, of course, maintained a balanced perspective of the United States. Ayukawa Yoshisuke, founder of Nissan Motors Company, maintained close relations with the United States and tried to build a joint-venture auto manufacturing plant in Manchuria that would have combined U.S. and Japanese capital and technology.[10] Ayukawa is noteworthy for his domestic and international thinking, given the Ministry of Commerce and Industry's encouragement of the domestic production of automobiles, a policy that Toyota followed. Ayukawa continued to explore possibilities for technical cooperation with American automobile companies even as Nissan tried to promote "domesticization" in line with Japanese government policy.

Tensions between Japan and the West

As Japan's invasion of Manchuria and China accelerated, the U.S. business community's attitude towards Japan rapidly worsened. How did the *Zaikai* perceive this change? First and foremost, they attributed the deteriorating situation to the effect of Chinese propaganda, exacerbated by a lack of concrete information about Japanese military activities in China. In fact, Chinese propaganda was so effective that many American businesses and people became pro-Chinese. Most Japanese business leaders, on the other hand, supported Japan's special interests in Manchuria and the establishment of the new state of Manchukuo in 1932. Their support appears to have been based on two factors: lack of information on Japanese military activities in China and, after the coup of 26 February 1936, reluctance to criticize the military. After the Marco Polo Bridge Incident in June 1937, however, few Japanese business leaders opposed Japan's attacks on China.

Some Japanese, living abroad, objectively understood Japan's position in the world. Kano Hisa'akira, director of the London branch of the Yokohama Specie Bank, stood out for his criticism of Japan's aggressive policy towards China. Kano wrote directly to Koichi Kido, a leader with influence on the Japanese government, pointing out that the Sino-Japanese War was unwise, as it isolated Japan from the mainstream of the world's thinking. To avoid such isolation, he argued, Japan should cease its invasion of China as soon as possible.[11]

Differing perceptions of the right to exercise control over "spheres of influence" played a particularly important role in the deterioration of U.S.-Japanese relations. Japanese businessmen often pointed out the gap and contradictions inherent in both the United States' Open Door Policy and the Monroe Doctrine. John Hay, secretary of state in the McKinley administration, had declared the Open Door Policy in 1899, under which the United States would not permit any country to dominate and close China's market, which was to be open to the world. Japan's aggression in China thus was criticized by American businessmen who had been expanding their activities in China since the early twentieth century. At the same time, the United States, invoking the Monroe Doctrine, refused to allow other countries to intervene in the Americas. The Monroe Doctrine concerned itself with military affairs, but it seemed to Japanese business leaders that it was often applied to business as well, reflecting self-serving U.S. strategy. For many Japanese, there was a large gap between America's ideal of free trade and its protectionism. Although the United States continued to provide access to its huge domestic market, most Japanese business people felt it embraced a double standard in its foreign policy and international business relations.

By the beginning of the 1930s, Japan was recovering from the financial shock caused by the meltdown of 1929. The dramatic decline of the relative value of the yen became an export advantage and an encouragement for import-substituting industries, and from 1932 increased exports fuelled a gradual recovery of the Japanese economy.[12] Japanese companies were so efficient that their products soon swamped the world market. European countries — in particular, Britain and the Netherlands — criticized Japan's export-oriented activities as a form of social dumping.

In view of Japan's withdrawal from the League of Nations and the failure of the 1933 World Economic Conference in London, the *Zaikai* were eager to mend economic relations with the United States, Britain, France, and Germany. They also began to attach more importance to the International Chamber of Commerce (ICC). The Japanese government and the *Zaikai* explored with the United States and Britain new means for cooperative bilateral relations. One of their experiments was the exchange of economic and business missions among the three countries. The exchanges included three large missions: a British one in 1934 led by Lord Barnby, a US mission in 1935 led by Cameron Forbes, and a Japanese mission in 1937 led by Kadono Chokuro. It is interesting to note how the *Zaikai* compared U.S. and British responses to Japanese actions in Manchuria. In his 1934 visit, Lord Barnby made amicable speeches that encouraged the misperception that the British business community would recognize Japan's special interests in Manchuria and the establishment of Manchukuo. In fact, while the British understood Japan's interests in Manchuria, they were reluctant to permit Manchukuo to cooperate with Japanese businesses in the Chinese market.

Most Japanese business leaders believed that maintaining good relations with the developed Western countries – in particular, the United States and Britain – was a life and death matter for the Japanese economy. To maintain these relationships, it was necessary to prevent any trend towards economic nationalism or autarky. Kushida Manzō, director general of Mitsubishi Bank and chairman of the Japanese National Committee, uttered a grave warning against autarky and economic nationalism: "every country is today more nationalistic in its commercial policy than ever before. This economic nationalism is indeed a menace to the recovery of world trade; and this strong trend, if it is not checked in time, will inevitably tend to engender international ill will and may even threaten international political stability."[13] He continued: "This is, perhaps, a very strong statement but we ought to take it as a warning, because economic nationalism would, in the least, reduce the volume of world trade to a minimum."[14] Kushida concluded: "If expansion of international trade is the right road to world prosperity, as we believe it assuredly is, and the interdependence of commercial countries is fully recognized, then the time must come when commercial policy will be so modified that international exchange of commodities will be far less restricted than it is today."[15]

The Zaikai Engage the West: The Economic Mission of 1937

In 1937, the *Zaikai* sent an economic mission to the United States and Europe to allow business leaders to exchange views and to participate in the general congress of the ICC in Berlin. The purpose of the mission was fourfold: a) to promote personal exchanges among influential politicians and business leaders; b) to reciprocate the 1934 Barnby and 1935 Forbes missions; c) to discuss bilateral economic issues between Japan and the United States and Britain; and d) to propose at the Berlin congress that Japan was willing to host the next general congress of the ICC in Tokyo in 1939.[16] The cabinet of the Japanese prime minister, Hayashi Senjurō, strongly backed this mission to improve relations with Britain and the United States.

Kadono Chokurō, vice president of Ōkura-gumi and participant in the Japanese Businessmen's Mission of 1921–22, was nominated the representative of the 1937 mission.[17] Before attending the Berlin congress, the mission visited the United States, where it was welcomed by business leaders in San Francisco, Los Angeles, Dallas, Chicago, and New York, resulting in an exchange between Japanese and American business leaders on such issues such as cotton, textiles, and automobiles. Discussions generally went well on bilateral trade issues, as the focus remained on free trade and the two countries did not have serious economic conflicts.[18] For American businessmen, the Japanese mission was also an opportunity to exchange views on the political and economic situation in East Asia,[19] but little progress was made on bridging the gap on the "China problem."

While in the United States, the Japanese mission asked American business leaders to endorse Japan's invitation to host the ICC general congress in Tokyo in 1939. Winthrop W. Aldrich, president of the Chase National Bank, received a letter from Yoshida Hatsujirō, in the New York office of Mitsui & Company, asking him to support Japan's proposal. In his letter Yoshida stated, "Japan has already received assurances of sympathetic reaction to her proposal from British, German, Belgian and Australian National Committees."[20] Aldrich replied that he approved of the invitation and asked Thomas J. Watson, president of the ICC, to accept it. Thomas Lamont and other American business leaders also supported it.[21] For its part, the Japanese government endorsed hosting the ICC general congress, which it saw as an opportunity to introduce Japan to foreign businesses and to showcase the country as the best business partner for Western nations in Asia, as Asia's most civilized nation, and as the proposed site of the 1940 Olympic Summer Games.[22]

The Japanese mission next visited Berlin. There, at the 9th Congress of the ICC, discussions focused on world economic reconstruction and growing trade blocks and bilateralism. The congress's keynote theme was "world peace through world trade." Thomas J. Watson, the newly elected president of the ICC, enthusiastically led the discussion to find new approaches to realize this key concept.[23] Watson, president of IBM, was well known as a staunch supporter of Cordell Hull's trade policy. Hull's vision was that "[g]overnments will serve the best who can check the drift into bilateralism and restore the machinery of multilateral trade."[24] Japanese business leaders participated in almost all the sessions of the congress and explained Japan's views on each problem and the current situation of the Japanese economy. They also appealed to others who shared Japan's stance on maintaining a sustainable free trade system. The congress wound up on 27 June 1937 with its participants formally accepting Japan's invitation to hold the next one.

The Japanese delegation next visited London and Liverpool, where, between 5 July and 27 July, British cabinet members, including the foreign minister and the trade minister, members of the London Chamber of Commerce, and Japanese and British business leaders held discussions on Anglo-Japanese political relations, industrial competition between Britain and Japan, trade control, specific trade issues such as import quotas and protective trade policy, and the China problem, including the possibility of Anglo-Japanese cooperation in the Chinese market.[25] While both sides recognized the importance of bilateral cooperation, the gap between the two countries was not appreciably narrowed.

The Sino-Japanese War, which commenced in July 1937, forced the ICC to rescind Japan's invitation.[26] Japanese business leaders were shocked, as they had expected a rapid resolution to the war. Many, moreover, were reluctant to disagree with the positions of the United States and European countries. They understood Japan could not survive without their trade – indeed, the U.S. and the British Empire, in particular, were thought to hold the power of life and death over the Japanese economy, since almost all of Japan's strategic goods were imported from these countries. Since the coup of 26 February 1936, however, the military had controlled freedom of speech in Japan, and business leaders had to keep their opinions to themselves. Had the ICC general congress taken place in Tokyo in 1939, over a thousand business leaders and their families would have visited the city. It would have had a positive effect not only on Japanese businesses but also on political and military circles. Sadly, this was not to happen.

The Zaikai's Views on U.S.-Japanese Relations

Despite their increasingly pessimistic views on the recovery of American economy from the Great Depression, the *Zaikai* had a generally optimistic view of U.S.-Japanese relations as they anticipated deepening interdependence in the world economy. Two main issues contributed, however, to the deterioration of relations. First, trade frictions became more pronounced, as illustrated by the exchange of cotton-textile goods between the two countries. The *Zaikai* thought such frictions could be resolved because the basic structure of the bilateral trade was complementary and not overly competitive. Japan was a good customer for the United States, buying raw materials such as cotton, pig iron, crude oil, and machinery. And although it had declined since the early 1930s, the United States provided a domestic market for Japanese silk and textile goods. Simply put, the understanding was that Japan was a good trade partner for the United States and that war between the two countries was irrational. The *Zaikai* thought that the real competitor for Japanese textile exports was Britain, and they underestimated the strong Anglo-American intention to "maintain the pre-depression status quo in their commercial spheres of influence and largely succeeded."[27]

A second and more important issue was Japan's military invasion of China – in particular, Manchuria. Although the independence of Manchukuo was not recognized by the League of Nations, and Japan withdrew from the League in 1933, the *Zaikai* optimistically thought that the United States might invest in both Manchukuo and Japan, thus pacifying U.S. opposition to Japanese militarism.[28] But the United States and Britain refused to recognize Japan's invasion of China, even though neither country could become directly involved because of the imminent threat from Nazi Germany.

At the same time, the *Zaikai*'s view of the United States was naive. The U.S. East Coast was the focus of their attention, and limited information sources did not allow for a comprehensive understanding of the breadth of domestic U.S. power or the diversity of U.S. public opinion. In contrast to this simple and superficial understanding, several business leaders in the mid-1930s, such as Shibusawa Eiichi, Dan Takuma, Inoue Jun'nosuke, and Takahashi Korekiyo, showed greater insight into American thinking about the economic crisis and the deterioration of U.S.-Japanese relations. As a result of their respective experiences in the United States, these men had a more sophisticated understanding, for example, about how American society was sensitive to both the profit motive and the principles and rules emanating from a democratic political system.[29] Even so, most Japanese business leaders could not understand the logic of such thinking, and their tacit support for the emerging military government betrayed their underestimation of American democracy's potential. Some business leaders tried to improve the bilateral relationship through business cooperation. While the Sino-Japanese War dragged on, Ayukawa Yoshisuke supported several secret missions to the United States to reestablish the amicable relationships that had existed between Japan and the United States and Britain. But these missions, not fully supported by the *Zaikai*, were unsuccessful.

Once there was consensus among Japanese business leaders that the crucial problem facing the world was how to emerge from the Depression and reconstruct the world economy, the *Zaikai* began to pay more attention to the ICC as a means to achieve that end. The murder of distinguished leaders such as Inoue Jun'nosuke, Dan Takuma, and Takahashi Korekiyo, however, weakened the *Zaikai*'s power in the Japanese political and economic world.[30] Only those who, like Kano Hisa'akira, lived abroad felt able to express their opinions frankly, and the political leadership paid little attention to them. The 1937 Japanese Economic Mission proved the last chance for the *Zaikai* to rebuild relationships with the United States and the European countries. Although the mission's purposes were not realized in the short run, the human networks it established and reinforced proved most useful for Japan's return to the international business community after the Second World War.

Conclusion

An analysis of the Japanese business community's changing perceptions of the United States in the 1930s can shed light on the meaning of that tumultuous decade in modern Japanese history. Despite the efforts of the *Zaikai*, Japanese leaders held conflicted and incomplete thoughts on the dynamic mechanism of America's political economy. While Japan maintained a strong interest in American capitalism as a driving force in the world economy, it also became fascinated by German power – its military, technology, and economic growth – and concluded that Germany could become a partner in helping Japan to cope with frictions associated with its relations with the Anglo-American and Soviet powers. The result was the ill-fated tripartite alliance between Germany, Italy, and Japan.

Japan lacked the experience, knowledge, and analytical tools to comprehend the complex evolution of the United States' domestic and external international relationships. Japan, of course, was not unique in its inability to comprehend that complexity. The young and idealistic United States was both self serving and pragmatic, and many Japanese, including the *Zaikai*, were confused by a dual and simultaneous capacity of the United States to embrace both realism and idealism.[31] This confusion manifested itself in the late 1930s in a number of unexpected ways, the ultimate consequence of which was Pearl Harbor.

NOTES

1 During the 1930s, both Tokyo and Osaka played a dominant role in the Japanese economy. There have been few studies on U.S.-Japanese economic and business relations. A notable exception is Hosoya Chihiro, Saito Makoto, Imai Sei'ichi, and Royama Michio, eds., *US-Japanese Relations: Ten Years to the Outbreak of the War, 1931–1941*, vol. 3 (Tokyo: University of Tokyo Press, 1971).

2 Sadako Ogata, "Business Community and Japanese Foreign Policy," in *The Foreign Policy of Modern Japan*, ed. Robert A. Scalapino (Berkeley: University of California Press, 1977), 180.

3 Masataka Matsuura, "Analyzing Relationships between Business and Politics in Pre-War Japan: Some Thoughts on the *Zaikai*," Discussion Paper JS/00/381 (London: London School of Economics and Political Science, Suntory and Toyota International Centres for Economics and Related Disciplines, February 2000), 25.

4 Ibid., 26.

5 For discussion of the *Zaikai*'s effectiveness within decision-making for national trade policy, see William M. Fletcher, *The Japanese Business*

Community and National Trade Policy, 1920–1942 (Chapel Hill: University of North Carolina Press, 1989).

6 See Kimura Masato, "The Return of Japanese Businesses to the World Community: The International Chamber of Commerce after the Second World War," *Journal of Shibusawa Studies* 14 (October 2001); and idem, "The Contribution and Limitation of Japanese Business Diplomacy in the Interwar Period: Case Studies of Two Major Economic Missions," Discussion Paper JS/02/429 (London: London School of Economics and Political Science, Suntory and Toyota International Centres for Economics and Related Disciplines, March 2002).

7 I do not mean to suggest that the purpose of this chapter is to analyse the causes of the Pacific War.

8 The impact of the Great Depression on U.S. investment banks was tremendous; see Ron Chernow, *The Touse of Morgan: An American Banking Dynasty and the Rise of Modern Finance* (New York: Atlantic Monthly Press, 1990).

9 Wakamiya Unosuke, *Morimura Ichizaemon Genkoroku* (Tokyo: Morimura Homeikai, 1929), 176.

10 For Ayukawa's achievements, see Iguchi Haruo, *Unfinished Business: Ayukawa Yoshisuke and U.S.-Japan Relations, 1937–1953* (Cambridge, MA: Harvard University Asia Center, 2001).

11 *Kido Koichi Kankei Bunsho* (Tokyo: University of Tokyo Press, 1966), 157.

12 For the impact of the Great Depression on the Japanese economy, see Osamu Ishii, *Cotton-Textile Diplomacy: Japan, Great Britain, and the United States, 1930–1936* (New York: Arno Press, 1981).

13 Manzō Kushida, "Japan's Position in World Commerce," *World Trade* 8 (March 1936), 6.

14 Ibid.

15 Ibid.

16 See Takashima Seiichi, ed., *Ōbei Hōmon Keizai Shisetsudan hokokusho* (Tokyo: Nihon Keizai Renmeikai, 1938), 1.

17 For this mission, see Takashima, *Ōbei Hōmon Keizai Shisetsudan*; and idem, *Honpojin no kaigai shisatsu ryoko kankei zakken*, Archives of the Ministry of Foreign Affairs, Japan (hereafter cited as AMFAJ), K.2.1.0.4-1-2.

18 For Japanese-U.S. trade relations during the 1930s, see Ueyama Kazuo and Sakata Yasuo, eds., *Tairitsu to Dakyo: 1930 nendai no Nichi Bei tsusho kankei* (Tokyo: Daiichi Hoki,1994).

19 Ibid.

20 Letter, Yoshida to Aldrich, 20 April 1937, Winthrop W. Aldrich Collection, Baker Library, Harvard Business School (SF 6/2/66, Box 42).

21 Letter, Aldrich to Yoshida, 27 April 1937, Winthrop W. Aldrich Collection, Baker Library, Harvard Business School (SF 6/2/66, Box 42).
22 For details of the 1940 Tokyo Olympics, see Masaru Ikei, "'Tokyo Olympic' in 1940," in *Japan's Diplomacy in the Interwar Period*, edited by Akira Iriye and Sadashi Aruga (Tokyo: University of Tokyo Press, 1984).
23 *World Trade* 6 (June 1937).
24 Ridgeway, *Merchants of Peace*, 132.
25 Takashima, *Ōbei Hōmon Keizai Shisetsudan hokokusho*, 39–47.
26 See *Tokyo Sokai Shimatsuki*, vol. 2, 38.
27 See Ishii, *Cotton-Textile Diplomacy*, 477.
28 See Iguchi, *Unfinished Business*, 120–1.
29 Takahashi Korekiyo spent two years as a teenager in San Francisco as menial labourer. Shibusawa Eiichi visited the United States four times between 1902 and 1922 and visited almost all of its major cities, while Takuma, as noted, studied mining at the Massachusetts Institute of Technology.
30 On the effect of these assassinations on the power of the *Zaikai*, see Hugh Byas, *Government by Assassination* (New York: Routledge, 1942).
31 Japan's perception of the United States and the identification of appropriate bilateral policies for the relationship comprise not only a historical question but a contemporary one. In the broader field of international relations, the relationship has global implications.

2 Cultural Internationalism and Japan's Wartime Empire: The Turns of the *Kokusai Bunka Shinkōkai*

JESSAMYN R. ABEL

In February 1933 the Japanese representative to the League of Nations, Matsuoka Yōsuke, stood and led his delegation out of the hall of the General Assembly. This dramatic moment, a protest against the League's decision on the Manchurian dispute and a prelude to Japan's official withdrawal, appeared to mark a reversal of the Japanese government's policies of international cooperation. But neither withdrawal from the League nor the expansion of empire and escalation of war completely expunged internationalist principles from either the practice or the rhetoric of Japan's foreign policy. Foreign affairs specialists continued to view multilateral cooperation as essential to international relations, and internationalists sought to compensate for the loss of League membership by developing cultural avenues of international cooperation. Such efforts were eventually appropriated by the state to form what might be called "imperialist internationalism," as advocates of imperial expansion twisted internationalist activities and rhetoric to promote Japanese domination in Asia.

One example of such supposedly apolitical internationalism may be found in the establishment of the *Kokusai Bunka Shinkōkai* (KBS, or Society for International Cultural Relations), a national organization for international cultural exchange. The historical turns of the KBS show how internationalist rhetoric persisted as the lingua franca of foreign relations, even during the years of rampant nationalism and global war. Recognizing the persistence of internationalism through this period provides a key to understanding the range of practices to which internationalism has been attached, and might shed light on recent applications of similar rhetoric. The case of the KBS is significant because its history displays how the supposedly benign and apolitical can be made to serve imperialist goals. Its return to more beneficent aims in the post-war period serve to remind us that the lofty rhetoric of internationalism always has within it the potential to be harnessed for all manner of political ends, some quite admirable, others more dubious.

The word "internationalism" can be used with reference to imperialist activity because the concept is a complex rhetorical device that can be directed towards conflicting, often opposing, political goals. At its most basic level, internationalism refers to the conviction that strengthening international institutions and other cooperative ties, such as exchange and communication, promotes peace and security.[1] It is not a static concept, but a process, shaped and transformed by people and events, so that its practical meaning changes as competing interests promote their own notions of what constitutes an international community and how it should be structured.[2] Internationalism generally has a positive connotation, and many, if not all, incarnations emphasize aspirations for some combination of peace, security, progress, and prosperity. Yet, not all of the many contending versions are inherently good.[3] It is precisely because of the nobility of its central tenets that internationalism has so often been used as a disguise for more questionable goals such as war or the pursuit of empire.[4] Although internationalism and nationalism are often seen as opposed, they are, in fact, closely related. Internationalists are often the staunchest patriots, seeking to advance national interests through multilateral cooperation, while internationalism is often promoted in nationalistic terms.[5] The trans-war history of the KBS exhibits both sides of this duality. Internationalist rhetoric does not admit to *openly* imperialist visions of regional or global unity under a single hegemon, while imperialism differs most starkly from internationalism in its *explicit* domination of one nation by another. Yet the rhetoric of internationalism has been integral to imperialism in the twentieth century. The term "imperialist internationalism" refers to the justification and promotion of imperialist actions and goals through the rhetoric of internationalism, including the pretense of national independence and equality. It is this rhetoric and its almost perversely flexible usage that is examined in this chapter, rather than the reality of cooperation or domination.

The flexibility of internationalism made it useful for promoting a broad range of foreign policies over time. After Japan's withdrawal from the League, internationalists emphasized alternative, "non-political" kinds of international cooperation; the KBS was conceived as an internationalist institution seeking to promote peace and security through the promotion of cultural exchange on a global scale. After the escalation of the war with China in 1937, the KBS increasingly limited its activities to Asia and pursued imperialist internationalism as a supporting structure of Japan's regional domination, while the construction of a "cultural nation" as part of Japan's post-war democratization saw the KBS return to its original aims.

The Foundation of the KBS

The quest for alternative methods of international cooperation following Japan's split with the League of Nations included a shift towards cultural internationalism, embodied in the development of non-governmental – and hence, it was suggested, apolitical – avenues for diplomacy. The KBS was founded in April 1934 to develop "mutual understanding" with the other nations of the world through cultural exchange. The semi-public organization operated under the aegis of the foreign ministry's Cultural Activities Bureau, but private individuals carried out its activities. Emerging just after Japan's withdrawal from the League of Nations, the KBS can be seen as part of the struggle to redefine international cooperation in light of new diplomatic realities.

The KBS concentrated on international activities founded on a solid base of nationalist sentiment and pride in Japanese culture. Such cultural pride might well have characterized what one contemporary Westerner in Japan called "enlightened" nationalism, "which embodies a desire to attract and interest the foreigner," as opposed to one that "seeks to repel him."[6] But this nationalist core, however enlightened, made the organization susceptible to appropriation – without dramatic alteration of its stated mission – by "national" interests as defined by a government bent on imperialist expansion. As the war expanded and intensified after 1937, exigencies of the day and the combination of people interested in international cultural cooperation led the KBS to shift the emphasis of its activities. It turned from international public relations – the promotion of mutual knowledge and understanding on a global scale – to propagandistic support of Japanese military advances in Greater East Asia, without abandoning its rhetoric of peaceful cultural exchange. As total mobilization for war permeated Japanese society, the internationalism of the KBS gradually shifted from an effort to improve Japan's foreign relations through the promotion of its culture abroad to the malign internationalism of a cog in the imperialist machine.

Introducing Japan

Ideas of cultural internationalism and the belief in the importance of cultural communication and exchange as a means to world peace were widespread in the years after the First World War. Organizations were founded to promote cooperation in all areas of cultural endeavour, the most prominent being the League of Nations Committee on Intellectual Cooperation, which was linked to intellectual cooperation committees in many countries, including Japan. The rise of cultural internationalism coincided with a growing awareness among its Western proponents that internationalism could not be limited to Europe and the United States. This realization prompted the broadening of cultural interaction beyond the West and increased the scholarly study of non-Western societies.[7] The foundation of the KBS was part of a larger Japanese response to these developments: the foreign ministry had a Cultural Activities Bureau while the army engaged in cultural activities as part of its invasion of China. By the late 1930s, culture was a central theme of Japanese foreign policy.[8]

In this atmosphere, two related goals inspired the establishment of the KBS. On the one hand, its founders expressed the internationalist aims of compensating for Japan's withdrawal from the League and contributing to world peace through cultural exchange. On the other hand, they exhibited nationalist sentiments of growing pride in Japanese culture and a desire to improve their country's international standing. These goals were embodied in the organization's philosophy of international cooperation for "mutual benefit." At its founding in 1934, the Society was not, however, an overt instrument of national policy. In a typical pattern for Japanese semi-official organizations, KBS leaders sought government cooperation, and representatives of the relevant ministries sat on the board of directors, but the Society's operations were conducted by private individuals. The nationalism imbuing the KBS also incorporated a broader pan-Asian perspective, even if in claiming to represent "Eastern culture" the Society focused on introducing Japanese culture under that name to Western audiences.

At the time of its establishment, the Society proposed to implement ten kinds of activities: 1) publishing books, collections, and translations; 2) instituting lecture series and sending lecturers abroad; 3) holding lecture meetings, exhibits, and concerts; 4) presenting and exchanging cultural materials; 5) inviting eminent foreigners to Japan; 6) facilitating research on Eastern culture by foreign scholars; 7) sending students abroad and coordinating student exchanges; 8) maintaining contact with groups and individuals abroad concerned with cultural activities; 9) producing films and supporting their production; and 10) opening and managing institutes, libraries, and research facilities.[9] In practice, their activities can be divided into three categories: support for Japanese cultural ambassadors abroad, support for foreign researchers in Japan, and the production and distribution of "cultural materials."

In the first few years of operation, the KBS concentrated geographically on Europe and the United States and thematically on traditional Japanese art and literature. In the fiscal year ending 31 March 1936, the Society sent its chairman, Kabayama Aisuke, and managing directors Dan Inō and Anesaki Masaharu on a tour of the United States and Europe to introduce the KBS and promote Japanese culture. They also sent representatives to Central and South America, China and Manchuria, Australia and the Soviet Union. In addition, they sponsored lectures on art and other aspects of Japanese culture in England, the United States, and India, and organized a lecturer exchange between Japan and Italy. In addition to people, the Society sent objects, contributing works of art to an international art exhibit in Sydney, Australia, and assisting with an exhibit of ancient Japanese art in Boston. In support of foreign researchers of Japanese culture in Japan, the KBS instituted the *Kokusai Bunka Shinkōkai* Fellowship and held a seminar and regular lecture meetings. They invited eminent scholars to Japan from the United States and Hungary, assisted visits by a Siamese dance troupe and more than one hundred members of the American Garden Club studying the Japanese garden, and provided facilities for participants in the Pan-Pacific New Education Conference in Tokyo. In addition, foreign researchers used the Society's growing library. Finally, in terms of cultural materials, the KBS produced an English translation of its *Bibliography of Modern Japanese Literature*, completed an English-language map of Japan in progress since the previous year, published as pamphlets the lectures sponsored by the Society (over twenty in all), and conducted research and preparation for the production of movies, slides, photographs, and other materials to be used for the introduction of Japanese culture.[10]

The KBS conducted similar activities in subsequent years. By the start of the Society's third year, General Secretary Aoki Setsuichi announced that "now we are in contact with every part of the world in a lasting bond of cultural friendship."[11] They had established permanent liaisons in Paris, Geneva, Berlin, Melbourne, Buenos Aires, Rome, and New York, later adding Beijing, Rio de Janeiro, and Lima, though by

1941 the war had made contact with all but the Beijing office impossible. In 1937, the organization established a branch office in Kyoto to organize activities and assist foreign researchers in the Kansai region.

The founding of the KBS was based on three basic goals: to compensate, to some extent, for the loss of the League of Nations as a forum for international cooperation; to improve Japan's position in the international community by fostering "understanding" of Japan; and, more broadly, to contribute to world culture. The establishment of the organization was, most immediately, a response to Japan's withdrawal from the League – indeed, preparatory discussions for the establishment of the KBS began on 8 June 1933, less than three months after the official announcement of Japan's withdrawal.[12]

Several of the founders of the Society had been members of the League's International Committee on Intellectual Cooperation, including Marquis Tokugawa Yorisada (a member of the House of Peers who had studied in England), Count Kabayama Aisuke (a businessman, politician, vice president of the America Japan Society, and graduate of Amherst College in Massachusetts), Count Kuroda Kiyoshi (a member of the House of Peers who had studied in France), Viscount Okabe Nagakage (a bureaucrat and politician who served as the first director of the foreign ministry's Cultural Bureau and in 1943 would become minister of education), Dr Anesaki Masaharu (professor emeritus of Tokyo Imperial University, who continued as Japan's representative to the Committee until 1938), Baron Dan Inō (a former professor of art at Tokyo Imperial University who had studied at Harvard and the University of Lyons), and Yamada Saburō (a former professor of international law at Tokyo Imperial University then serving as president of Keijō Imperial University in Seoul, Korea). KBS General Secretary Aoki had been the director of the Tokyo Office of the League of Nations.[13]

The founders of the KBS hoped the organization would accomplish some of the functions that the League had performed for Japan. The Society's prospectus, published in April 1934, cited the Imperial Rescript on the withdrawal from the League of Nations to support the notion that Japan's departure increased the importance of establishing other ways of contributing to the international community: "Even though we withdrew from the League of Nations on a political level, activities that utilize our country's strength for the sake of world culture and human welfare have actually become increasingly numerous, and the Rescript made it entirely clear that, on this point, the mission of the Japanese people must be given more importance."[14] The proponents of international cooperation thus used the Imperial Rescript – which could be construed as announcing the end of Japan's multilateral participation – to bolster their own efforts to continue and expand such activities. Some of the energy expended towards international cooperation, now prevented from operating in the political sphere, shifted to the realm of culture.

The Society's emphasis on contributing to "world culture and human welfare" reflected the cultural internationalists' belief that the "apolitical" nature of international cultural exchange could partially replace the League's political multilateralism. In December 1938, a month after the Japanese government announced it would end all cooperation with the non-political activities of the League,[15] the KBS Board of Directors decided to continue the work of the now-defunct Japanese committee of the League's International Committee on Intellectual Cooperation, stating "this Society will, as much as possible, continue to carry out appropriate activities of the Committee."[16] Mitsui Takaharu, a businessman from the powerful Mitsui family closely involved with the KBS, likewise pointed out the advantages of international cultural exchange in times of crisis. As late as March 1940, he argued, "the active implementation of cultural activities between two states whose relations are not normal … can compensate for insufficiencies in political activities."[17] According to Mitsui's logic, the activities proposed by the KBS should not be hindered by Japan's political disputes with other nations but, on the contrary, were necessitated by them.

The explicit goal underlying the founding of the KBS was the promotion of "mutual understanding" among peoples of various nations through cultural exchange. In the wake of the Lytton Report, which named Japan as the aggressor in Manchuria, international understanding of Japan – particularly Western understanding and acceptance of the state of Manchukuo – became urgent. One scholar has suggested that the KBS's establishment was inspired by the hope of easing Great Power criticism of Japan's foreign policy in the wake of the withdrawal from the League of Nations. According to this interpretation, Japanese internationalists believed that cultural exchanges could have a positive influence on political relations with the Western powers.[18] The national aim of gaining Great Power recognition of Japan's continental empire was almost invariably couched in what had already become the entrenched internationalist language of peace and humanity. At the time of the Society's establishment, its president, Prince Takamatsu Nobuhito (the emperor's younger brother and second in line to the throne), grandly stated its *raison d'être*: "[E]xtolling Japanese culture abroad will not only prevent mutual misunderstanding and contribute to mutual understanding, but [will] also proclaim the dignity of the state and contribute to the welfare of global humanity."[19] Takamatsu's reference to "mutual understanding" reflected the cacophony of Japanese voices blaming the League's decision on a lack of understanding of Japan. Takamatsu also sounded other typical themes when suggesting that the introduction of Japanese culture abroad would not only polish Japan's national image, it would also help the world as a whole by promoting human welfare.

KBS leaders were clear about the political motives behind cultural exchange. In a speech on the second anniversary of the Society's creation in April 1936, its pro-American chairman Kabayama, credited understanding of Japan arising from cultural cooperation with the ability to ease international tensions in other areas. Citing one of the main reasons for the foundation of the KBS, Kabayama said, "it is urgent that we make foreign peoples understand our national conditions and culture and plan for cultural cooperation with them in order to resolve our difficulties in the areas of foreign policy, diplomacy, and economics."[20] Kabayama went on to quote Prime Minister Hirota Kōki's statement to the Diet as foreign minister in January 1936. Hirota had asserted: "We are qualified to speak of world peace only when we are truly conscious of our own national responsibility and we understand and respect the positions of other countries. There are many cases in which understanding and respecting the positions of other countries fostered the achievement [of world peace]."[21] Here again was the implication that other countries had to understand and respect Japan's position on the continent.

One of the most frequent criticisms following Japan's withdrawal from the League of Nations was that the League was too European in focus and lacked the understanding of Japan and Asia necessary to make informed decisions. The sense that greater knowledge of Japan might have led to a different decision served as motivation to promote cultural exchange. Diplomat Yanagisawa Ken, whose idea for an "international cultural activities bureau" within the foreign ministry led to the birth of official foreign cultural policy in 1933,[22] scolded his countrymen for their lack of attention to cultural exchange. Regarding the League's decision, Yanagisawa recalled that Japanese at all levels of society had bemoaned other countries' "insufficient understanding" of Japan. But, he added, "if one were to inquire as to the responsibility for the European and American gentlemen's insufficient understanding, I think one would discover that Japan itself – our government and people who neglected foreign cultural works – must take responsibility."[23]

As a permanent member of the League Council, Japan had been recognized as one of the world's major powers. The loss of this high-profile symbol of global status contributed to long-standing anxiety about Japan's international position. Responding to this concern, KBS vice president Tokugawa wrote that cultural exchange between East and West would "guarantee Japan's position in the world and contribute to the advancement of the world's cultural progress."[24] He did not elaborate on the meaning of the phrase "the world's cultural progress," but his use of this vague concept expressed the usual combination of broad, global benefits and Japanese national interests and stature.

The KBS prospectus argued that cultural cooperation would enhance Japan's international position. According to this document, as international relations became increasingly complex and advances in transportation and communications made the world smaller, scholarly and artistic contacts and popular culture exchanges grew in importance. "That being the case, for a country to protect and extend its international position, it must display the quality and value of its native culture side by side with its real strength of wealth and power."[25] The prospectus added the hope that introducing Japanese culture abroad would engender affection, sympathy, and respect for Japan among the peoples of other nations.

Supporters of international cultural exchange also touted its potential domestic benefits. Yanagisawa, the foreign ministry's foremost proponent of cultural foreign policy, lauded the effects cultural exchange would have on the Japanese economy and culture. He suggested that cultural activities would benefit the Japanese economy because greater understanding of Japan's social and labour conditions would lead other countries to limit their use of economic "weapons of attack" against Japan.[26] This was significant given the importance of economic friction in the souring of Japan's relations with Britain and the United States in the 1930s. Yanagisawa further argued that the outward flow of Japanese culture would invigorate domestic cultural activities; it would function as a sort of natural selection process through which the culture's best elements would be preserved and strengthened and the unworthy elements discarded. He even suggested that only when cultural artefacts had been sent abroad and exposed to Western criticism could Japanese know their true value.[27] Yanagisawa's willingness to learn from the West epitomizes the attitude of mutual benefit that characterized the early years of the KBS as well as the cultural anxiety that extended back to the early Meiji period when Westerners such as Ernest Fenollosa found themselves teaching Japanese about the value of their own artistic traditions.

Although Yanagisawa's statement might have suggested lack of confidence in the cultural sensibilities of his countrymen, the new pride in Japanese culture among elites – enhanced by the government's willingness to defy the Western powers in the League – was more prominent. Paralleling this political defiance was the cultural movement to reject the West and return to Asian roots exemplified by Tanizaki Junichirō's 1934 *In'ei raisan* (In Praise of Shadows) and the works of the "Japan romantic school" of writers. This movement called attention to Japan's cultural uniqueness, which bolstered claims that Japan was the natural leader of Asia.[28] Thus, growing cultural pride was another motivation to establish the KBS, with Japanese opinion leaders asserting that their national culture was on par with Western culture.

This cultural self-confidence was evident in early KBS statements arguing that the Japanese nation had concentrated too intently on importing Western culture into Japan while neglecting to export Japanese culture abroad. Takamatsu had stated, regarding the Society's establishment: "Looking back, since the Restoration in Japan, we have been intent on absorbing foreign culture, and although such so-called adopting the good points of others to compensate for one's own shortcomings has led to today's prosperity, activities to introduce our good points abroad have been extremely deficient, and in recent years, we have finally perceived the need for them."[29] The cultural turn to the East revalued native Japanese culture, inspiring the notion that Japan had something worth introducing to the world.

Without rejecting Western culture, Takamatsu claimed that the KBS would help fill this "finally perceived" need. But while the elite made this cultural turn, the Japanese masses did not. The KBS hoped its activities would help raise their national self-confidence. The Society's prospectus proclaimed: "Not only is the promotion of culture necessary to proclaim the country's dignity to the world, but it also should become a force for increasing confidence and pride by arousing the people's self-awareness."[30] The target of KBS activities was not only the peoples of other countries, but the Japanese people themselves. Through its promotion of cultural exchange, the Society aimed to create international understanding and bolster national pride, pursuing a nationalistic goal through international activities.

Champions of international cultural exchange further hoped that introducing Japanese culture to other countries would contribute to "world culture." The KBS Charter stated: "The Society has as its object international cultural exchange, especially the overseas promotion of Japanese and Eastern culture, and aims thereby to contribute to the advancement of world culture and the improvement of human welfare."[31] In this context world culture essentially meant Western culture; although the founders of the KBS claimed to be introducing Japan to the world, the fact that they included "Eastern culture" in their repertoire suggested a Western, rather than an Asian, audience. The KBS maintained its philosophy of international cooperation for mutual benefit, as well as its Western focus, for the early years of its existence. This began to change in 1937 with the escalation of the war in China.

From Cultural Internationalism to Imperialist Internationalism

Shipping out books and films or hosting foreign scholars might not seem like high priorities for a nation at war. But far from being marginalized by the escalation of hostilities, the KBS thrived. After 1937, war nudged the KBS in new directions, but the Society's core mission persisted, and its activities increased. Cultural exchange was simply turned more explicitly towards the cause of expanding Japanese power and empire. This resulted, in part, from a stronger government hand. Essentially rewriting Okakura Tenshin's dictum, "Asia is one," to read "Asia is Japan," the Japanese government set out to reinforce its regional domination through the cultural Japanization of Southeast Asia.[32] Institutional and budgetary changes brought the KBS into this effort. As changes in the foreign policy bureaucracy increased government influence and control over the semi-public organization, its cultural activities became a mechanism of imperialism in the context of mobilization for total war and expansion of empire.

In his study of the KBS, Shibasaki Atsushi identifies five changes in the character of the organization in two periods, the organization's early years (1934–1941) and during the Pacific War (1941–45). Briefly stated, the changes were: 1) in direction, from private initiative (people's diplomacy) to government control; 2) in form, from bilateral or horizontal relations to vertical relations within the Co-Prosperity Sphere; 3) in purpose, from an emphasis on mutual benefit to the imposition of

Japanese culture from above; 4) in content, from cultural exchange for "mutual understanding" to propaganda; and 5) in viewpoint, from the long term to the immediate short term.[33] Shibasaki's analysis captures significant changes in the KBS, but it is important to remember that these changes were gradual and incomplete. The increasing focus on Asia began as early as 1938, while the organization shifted only gradually from a Western audience to a more global scope that included both East and West and then finally to an exclusive attention to Asia. Similarly, the shift from cultural exchange and "mutual understanding" to propaganda is somewhat too sharply drawn. Although the rhetoric of the KBS in its early years highlighted mutual exchange, such activities cannot be separated from the goal of promoting Japan to the rest of the world – in other words, propaganda.

Shibasaki provides a concise and useful summary of the impact of escalating war on the organization: greater government control, a narrowing of focus from the world to Greater East Asia, and a shift from two-way exchange ostensibly for the promotion of mutual understanding to unabashedly unidirectional propaganda. However, an overemphasis on change risks obfuscating important continuities. The KBS never discarded the forms and rhetoric of cultural diplomacy. Changes in the Society's activities can be characterized as a shift from cooperative and peaceful (if nationalistic) "internationalism" to imperialist "internationalism," insidious in its effects on both the domestic and foreign audiences that were its targets. Even in the context of expanding government control and contracting geographical scope, the organization's underlying purpose of providing an alternative avenue for international engagement did not change. To consider these continuities, even while examining changes, highlights the persistence of internationalist ideas in the face of drastically changing circumstances.

The increase in government control stemmed from two factors. First, the organization depended more and more heavily on government funding. The budget of the KBS grew steadily during its early years – more than doubling between 1934 and 1940 and almost tripling by 1944 – the increase coming primarily from the government. The percentage of the budget made up of government subsidies increased dramatically between 1934 and 1939, and remained high until the end of the war. In contrast, private contributions fell to an insignificant level by 1941 and rose only slightly thereafter (Table 2.1). The government's contribution to the KBS increased most significantly between 1938 and 1941, following the start of the China War in July 1937, which informed the

Table 2.1. Sources of Funding of the *Kokusai Bunka Shinkōkai*, 1934–45

Source	1934	1935	1936	1937	1938	1939	1940	1941	1942	1943	1944	1945
	(per cent of budget)											
Government	49	61	60	62	68	84	79	88	82	75	66	71
Private	33	25	16	15	12	5	12	1	8	8	6	10
Total (¥)	405,910	491,781	501,740	522,661	499,100	593,530	887,309	797,341	940,095	1,035,176	1,170,104	1,051,528

Source: Shibasaki, Kindai Nihon to kokusai bunka kōryū, 92, 126, 161.

government's increased interest in "international cultural exchange." Based on budget figures alone, it is clear why government policies had a growing influence on the KBS leadership.

The shift towards government control, however, was not solely based on money. The Cultural Activities Department of the foreign ministry was abolished in December 1940 and the KBS came under the supervision of the Cabinet Information Bureau, established in July 1936, then expanded and reorganized in December 1940 to disseminate propaganda and control speech and thought. By coming under the purview of the Information Bureau's "Foreign Propaganda" section, the KBS became a "subcontractor" to the government.[34] This did not sit well with all KBS officers. In 1940, Aoki, a proponent of pacifism and arms reduction who had previously headed the Tokyo office of the League, resigned his position as KBS general secretary. Although he did not state his reasons, Aoki, according to Takamatsu, had complained that increasing government control was making it difficult to carry out the Society's principle of being a private initiative.[35] In the May 1942 issue of the KBS organ *Kokusai bunka* (International Culture), Information Bureau official Minowa Saburō called state interest in cultural activities part of a "new era in the world." Advocating the creation of a Greater East Asian culture based on Japanese culture, Minowa concluded, "[i]t is impossible to carry out such an important activity, which is difficult and will take a long time, by the power of the government alone, and it goes without saying that the people must put their full strength into it."[36] Even after the shift to Information Bureau supervision, the KBS was headed by private individuals, not government employees. But the relationship between public and private began to be more a case of the government's mobilizing the people than a civil movement with government support.

Although the exigencies of war eventually would turn their organization in unintended directions, KBS leaders at first focused on the silver lining around the dark clouds of war. The start in July 1937 of the China War – or "Incident," as it was called in Japan – increased demand for the organization of foreign cultural activities, and the Society took advantage of the crisis to call for further support. In his annual report for fiscal year 1937/38, Chairman Kabayama pointed out that, for the KBS at least, the China War was good for business. He noted, "[when] the Japan-China Incident broke out … the need for foreign propaganda about our country's culture and national affairs was well recognized, and since then, the Society's activities have been increasingly required."[37] The foreign ministry, noting the need to strengthen foreign cultural activities as a result of the "Incident," sought the Society's assistance to set up an organization for cultural activities in New York.[38] Accordingly, in March 1939, the Japan Institute opened there, with the intention, in the words of its director Maeda Tamon, of "overcoming bad feelings toward Japan due to ignorance" by dispelling "unnecessary misunderstandings and misgivings."[39] Towards this end, the Institute opened a library of English and Japanese books and other materials related to Japan, provided advice to scholars and the interested public, sponsored lectures, and offered language lessons. Although the war with China might have been the impetus for establishing the Institute, its mission of disseminating information did not include information on the war itself. In his opening address, Maeda made it clear that the Institute would provide "information on all subjects ranging from Japanese cookery to industry and art." But, according to a *New York Times* article on the opening of the Institute, he insisted "that controversial subjects, including the Chinese war, were taboo."[40] Maeda, a bureaucrat and leading internationalist, had served for many years as Japan's representative to the International Labour Office in Geneva. But his efforts at promoting friendly relations with the United States were shaped by war.

After the onset of total war with China, the KBS continued its regular activities, with frequent revisions to its content. "Explaining" Japan's position on the war in China became an explicit goal, especially for American audiences. In fiscal year 1937/38, the United States was the foremost recipient of the Society's materials, and two KBS staff members were sent there. At the same time, the Society devoted more resources to activities directed towards China. In 1937, the KBS produced Chinese versions of some of its films for distribution in China, and later produced a new film in Cantonese called *Life Conditions of Overseas Chinese in Japan*. Representatives travelled to North China and Manchuria several times. In 1943, the KBS was involved in both the China-Japan Cultural Association general meeting in Nanjing and the Greater East Asian Writers Conference in Tokyo.

The image of Japanese culture promoted by the KBS changed with the escalation of the war and the expansion of the empire. In October 1940, the editor of the *Kokusai bunka* complained that presentations of Japanese culture had been limited thus far to "making amusement out of our cultural legacy from the past," and that there was little recognition of contemporary Japanese culture. He wanted Japanese to be proud of the Ginza as a contemporary urban street, rather than admiring only remnants of "traditional" Japan. He concluded, "I hope that our foreign cultural activities have a domestic reaction, and a clear concept of Japanese culture is established."[41] By positing the contemporary Ginza as worthy of pride, he placed Tokyo on a par with the modern capitals of the West. The desire to depict Japan as modern also emerged in the materials produced by the Society. In the same year the editorial was written (1940), the KBS produced films about *Industrial Japan* and *Scientific Japan*, a departure from earlier themes such as *Kagamijishi (A Kabuki Dance)*, *Flower Arrangement*, and *Japanese Customs and Costumes*.[42]

The KBS also sought to use the China "Incident" to its advantage by emphasizing the potential for propaganda when proposing new activities. At a meeting in September 1937, two months after the Marco Polo Bridge Incident, the KBS board of directors decided to publish a booklet called "Japan" in English, French, German, Spanish, and Chinese, stating that, "[b]ecause of this Incident, there has been a hearty demand for information about Japan, but there is no appropriate booklet."[43] One such booklet published in English in 1939 contained, in addition to descriptions of Japanese culture, sections explaining the causes of the Manchurian Incident and "Japan's Mission in the Orient," which compared Japan's expansion in Asia to early Western colonialism while assigning Japan special status "as the only enlightened nation in East Asia." The booklet also aimed to ease other sources of friction between Japan and the Western powers, providing justifications for the "deluge of cheap Japanese goods," arguing against tariff walls, and asserting the necessity of Japanese expansion in East Asia. The booklet depicted Japan as a combination of tradition and modernity, pairing photographs of Mount Fuji, the Imperial palace, Buddhist temples, and Shinto shrines with pictures of Tokyo's business districts, factories, and technical schools.[44]

The opening statement of the first issue of *Kokusai bunka*, published in November 1938 – the same month the Japanese government ended forms of cooperation with the League that had continued after withdrawal – argued that the cultural activities of the preceding five years had helped bolster Japan's position in the current crisis. While admitting the impossibility of accurately measuring the effectiveness of cultural exchange, the author nevertheless insisted that, "without the activities in these past few years of the international culture organizations that, prompted by the Manchurian Incident, were all the more strengthened … Japan's international position would be even more difficult."[45] The article went on to point to the effectiveness of using cultural propaganda for political ends. Arguing for continued efforts in cultural exchange, the author wrote, "[f]rom the experience surrounding this Incident, we know that only with propaganda through the introduction of culture itself or of cultural issues is there room to advance international understanding of this kind of crisis."[46] War did not dishearten the internationalists within the KBS; on the contrary, they used it to bolster their championing of cultural exchange as a vehicle for international cooperation.

As the KBS expanded its activities with the escalation of war, its geographical scope contracted. The war in Europe limited the possibility of activities there, while growing concern with Asia – exemplified in Prime Minister Konoe Fumimaro's November 1938 announcement of a "New Order in East Asia" – contributed to an intensified focus on the region. KBS annual reports reflect this shift. Early years showed contact with the United States, Manchuria, China, Australia, the Soviet Union, India, and several countries in Europe and Central and South America. By fiscal year 1940/41, most activities were directed towards countries in East and Southeast Asia. This was accompanied by a significant change in the semantics of KBS statements of purpose. Whereas early annual reports spoke of "the foreign promotion of *Japanese and Eastern culture*," the 1941 report pronounced the organization's efforts towards "the introduction and promotion of Japanese culture"[47]; with the main target of propaganda being other Asian countries, it no longer made sense to talk of introducing "Eastern culture."

KBS chairman Nagai Matsuzō, a foreign ministry bureaucrat involved in the planning of the 1940 Tokyo Olympics, summed up the changes in the KBS's aims in its 1943 annual report. While lamenting the decline in contacts with non-Asian countries due to war, he celebrated Japan's growing cultural involvement in Asia: "Along with progress in this holy war, which aims at the establishment of a New Order in Greater East Asia and its culture, the role of Japanese culture in the East Asian Co-Prosperity Sphere has become increasingly important, and the urgent strengthening of those cultural works has become necessary."[48] By this time, the link between the organization's activities and the war had become standard in the Society's rhetoric. The KBS, founded for the stated purpose of contributing to world peace, was now devoted to the nation's war; nearly the same words and programs intended to promote peace and international cooperation in the early 1930s were now mobilized for imperialism and war.

From 1940, the KBS (under supervision of the Cabinet Information Bureau) began actively to back the "Greater East Asian Co-Prosperity Sphere" through its efforts to create a culture that could bind together the disparate Asian peoples. Managing director Kuroda announced the KBS's new direction in its annual report for fiscal year 1941/42: "Considering the global trends of the development of the China Incident and the establishment of the New Order, we keenly feel that planning the establishment of the East Asian Co-Prosperity Sphere and creating a new culture for it has become an urgent matter."[49] This was a significant change in rhetoric. The Society no longer claimed simply to be building mutual understanding for peace; rather, it was seeking to create a new culture upon which to base the regional identity at the base of Japan's imperialist rhetoric. Nagai discussed the construction of this regional culture in an article published in the February 1942 issue of *Kokusai bunka*: "This unprecedented great enterprise can only be completely achieved if cultural activities advance in a parallel line with the political and economic. Japan, which must be the leader within the Greater East Asian Co-Prosperity Sphere, must at the same time be the builder of a new Greater East Asian culture."[50] In supporting the new scope of KBS activities, Nagai made use of the government's rhetoric depicting Japan as the leader of a new international community in East Asia. The Society took full advantage of the war to promote its own relevance.

Part of the organization's new mission of building a Greater East Asian culture was to aid in establishing its linguistic basis. This goal was based on Japan's colonial experience in Korea and Taiwan, where Japanese language education was central to the efforts of turning colonized peoples into subjects of imperial Japan.[51] One of the KBS's projects in the early 1940s was to publish and distribute materials for teaching Japanese throughout the Co-Prosperity Sphere. By the June 1942 board meeting, the KBS had published a Japanese-French-Annamese (Vietnamese) conversation book and was preparing Japanese-Thai, Japanese-Dutch-Malay, Japanese-English-Malay, Japanese-Burmese, and other conversation books. It is difficult to determine how these books were received, but KBS leaders depicted Southeast Asians as clamouring for Japanese language-learning materials and other Japanese cultural products. In his presentation at the board meeting, Kuroda claimed that, "with the advance of Japanese culture abroad, overseas demands for learning Japanese have suddenly increased, and especially since the outbreak of the Greater East Asian War, Japanese has already played a leading role in the creation of the new order in East Asia as the common language of the East Asian Co-Prosperity Sphere." He insisted that, "as the rapid spread of Japanese has become an immediate necessity, the vital role of this activity has become even more important and national."[52] Kuroda acknowledged the role of war in stimulating foreign interest in the Japanese language but maintained the pretense of peaceful cultural activities within the so-called Co-Prosperity Sphere.

As Japanese military expansion turned towards Southeast Asia, the KBS increasingly focused its activities on the region. In 1941, Kuroda spent three months travelling in French Indochina and Thailand. The Society also sent an exhibition of Japanese art to Southeast Asia to "make known the magnificent and profound Japanese culture and the essence of Japanese spirit that constitutes it."[53] In response to instructions from the Cabinet Information Bureau, the Society established a Committee for Southern Cultural Activities to direct its activities in Southeast Asia, the new focus of Japanese wartime occupation. The committee included representatives from the relevant government offices and organizations concerned with the region, as well as academic researchers. The group met once a month from May to December 1941 and thereafter came under the direct supervision of the Information Bureau. Kuroda claimed that the formation of this group by the KBS "established and strengthened the cultural basis for the Co-Prosperity Sphere."[54] Two years later, Nagai was even more enthusiastic about his organization's role in the Japanese war effort, claiming that, by promoting a Greater East Asian culture, the KBS had "put great effort into contributing to the completion of this holy war."[55] In such ways, the KBS sought to build a cultural basis for imperial expansion.[56]

The KBS produced and disseminated movies, radio broadcasts, and other materials, using the local languages of what they referred to as the southern regions. In fiscal year 1941/42, the organization shipped out translated versions of films, books, and photo collections showing various aspects of life in Japan alongside items such as the film *Naval Japan*, displaying "the dignified appearance of our unchallengeable Navy," which was shown throughout the Co-Prosperity Sphere in eight languages.[57] The following year, the Society produced films showing "the power of contemporary Japan" in various languages of the southern regions.[58] With such films, the KBS introduced not only Japanese culture but images of Japanese power to the countries of East and Southeast Asia. Although conversation books were intended to facilitate cooperation with the Japanese, these images contributed to Japan's domination of the region by suggesting the consequences of a failure to cooperate.

The editor of the *Kokusai bunka* nevertheless asserted that military force alone could not build a meaningful regional community. Hearing "the breath of a new order emerging" from the "pot of confusion" that was the state of world affairs, he argued, "[t]his new order will initially be set up using military strength, and politics and economics will be organized upon that, but culture must also accompany it." Germany provided an apt model: "It is common knowledge that Germany does not forget cultural works along with the political and economic systems that it immediately sets up in its occupied territories."[59] The article also invoked the government's rhetoric of emancipation from European domination to describe Japan's cultural mission. Lamenting the political, economic, and cultural domination of East Asia by the European powers, the writer argued, "[t]he emancipation and independence of the countries of East Asia must necessarily bring an awakening to the ideal of an independent culture of the East Asian people."[60] Japan, he insisted, must be the leader of this cultural emancipation. The call to drive Western culture out of East Asia along with European and American imperialism shows how far the Society had moved from its foundational idea of contributing to a Western-based "world culture." As the world divided into autonomous regions, the proponents of world culture in the KBS followed the prevailing trends.

The rhetoric of emancipation and co-prosperity sometimes hinted at the reality of armed force. Writing in *Kokusai bunka* in 1942, anthropologist and historian Nishimura Shinji, who had recently completed an ethnographical study of Southeast Asia, described the difference between European colonialism in Asia and Japanese "leadership" of a sphere of "co-prosperity" in terms of cultural policies. Because Western colonial powers were interested only in economic exploitation, he argued, they could allow indigenous populations to follow their own cultures. In contrast, Nishimura continued, Japan was working for mutual benefit in a symbiotic relationship, which necessitated deeper concern with local culture. In hinting that native populations might not welcome Japanese culture with open arms, Nishimura argued that "we must plan for common benefit and co-prosperity, even if it is against their will."[61] Recognizing resistance to Japanese leadership among the peoples of Asia, the KBS planned an essay contest on the theme, "Arguing for Greater East Asian Cultural Co-Prosperity" in order to "promote to the world the spirit of our national founding and encourage awakening and cooperation among the peoples of the Greater East Asian Co-Prosperity Sphere."[62]

The KBS linked its activities to aggression and imperialism by supplying a cultural accompaniment to military advance. In discussing its 1940 international essay contest to commemorate the 2,600th anniversary of the accession of Japan's mythical founding emperor Jinmu, the editor of *Kokusai bunka* recognized the overt political nature of the Society's activities: "In recent years, along with changes in the political situation, our international cultural activities perhaps have taken on the colour of foreign political activities; and that is not just a Japanese phenomenon, for there are more extreme cases in other countries, too. While we recognize this as a natural necessity, of course we do not want to forget the importance of these activities as essentially intellectual exchange activities."[63] The author seems to have had qualms about this trend, insisting that international cultural activities must retain some non-political essence – a vain hope in the context of total war. Whatever the intentions of KBS leaders, the realities of wartime, especially government involvement in the Society's planning and activities, prevented them from operating outside the sphere of imperial Japan's national goals. A nationalist subtext was already present in the intellectual exchange activities of the mid-1930s, so the shift that took place from the late 1930s to the early 1940s was, to some extent, merely a matter of degree. The heightened urgency of national goals that accompanied the escalation of war brought them increasingly to the fore of international cultural activities, but the underlying concept of using cultural activities to strengthen Japan's international position remained the same.

In this context, the primary task of the KBS became "spin": to represent Japanese domination to the peoples of "Greater East Asia" as mutually beneficial. In a 1942 *Kokusai bunka* article, Nagai discussed the problem of making the people of Greater East Asia "understand the significance of our holy war." Insisting that they would see the benefits of Japanese intervention if the KBS could "make" them develop their cultures, he concluded that, "in order to make them understand the ideal of the New Order in Greater East Asia, a great effort at enlightenment and propaganda is necessary. It goes without saying that this should be developed on the heels of the military advancement." The activities of the KBS were no longer peaceful international cooperation, but were clearly based on military domination. Suggesting that opposition to Japanese hegemony resulted from lack of understanding, Nagai argued that the leading principle of cultural activities in Greater East Asia must be "to make them grasp the true intention of Japanese

actions," which would be accomplished by "show[ing] them the essence of Japanese culture." The idea that knowledge of Japanese culture
would make Southeast Asian peoples understand and accept the reasons for Japan's actions was not so far removed from the Society's initial rationale. The difference was that, by the early 1940s, Japan was in
a position to force this "understanding" upon its audience. Seeing cultural activities as a central part of Japanese policy in Greater East Asia,
Nagai insisted that "this association feels keenly that its responsibility
to take on one part of the nation's total war is increasingly great."[64] The
KBS's job as a "subcontractor" to the government was to help seduce
the objects of Japan's imperialist desires.

Cultural exchange might not have seemed like a weapon, but total
war meant the mobilization of all elements of society. Minowa, of the
Cabinet Information Bureau, rejected the argument that cultural activities aimed at friendly relations in peacetime had no place in war. On
the contrary, he likened the promotion of culture abroad to military
combat, insisting that "bombarding the enemy countries and their peoples with the essence of our Japanese spirit can perform the function of
a spiritual bullet alongside the armed hostilities."[65] In March 1941, the
lead article of *Kokusai bunka* envisioned cultural exchange as a competition between cultures to determine world culture; it concluded that
Japan could "make a grand entrance into the culture war."[66] A year
later in the same journal, Nishimura borrowed the main trope of imperialist expansion, the idea of *hakkō ichiu*, or "the eight corners of the
world under one roof," to assert that the KBS was making an important contribution to the project. Through cultural contributions to the
Co-Prosperity Sphere, Nishimura claimed, Japan would "finally realize
the great ideal of one capital for the world, the eight corners under one
roof around the whole face of the globe. One may say that establishing a Greater East Asia Co-Prosperity Sphere and creating an Asia for
Asians is one kind of preparatory work."[67] Although *hakkō ichiu* might
suggest an image of the peoples of the world living together in peace,
in the wartime context it connoted the extension of the Japanese Empire
over the entire world.

Conclusion

In August 1945, with the capital in ruins and the KBS's offices taken over
by U.S. Occupation forces, the organization was no longer able to carry
out significant activities. Following a hiatus of a few years, however,

the Society returned to the arena of international cultural activities, structurally unchanged by the transition. Alterations in the organization's charter included little more than a new address. Despite some reshuffling at the top, the post-war leadership included such familiar figures as Prince Takamatsu, Okabe Nagakage, Dan Inō, Maeda Tamon, Kuroda Kiyoshi, Nagai Matsuzō, Anesaki Masaharu, and Tokugawa Yorisada. The Society's early post-war materials highlighted trans-war continuities as well as changes. A 1949 English-language pamphlet introducing the "Organization and Program" of the KBS pointed out that the Society had been established in 1934 and *"has ever since* been actively engaged in multifarious programs to make the world better acquainted with Japanese culture and contribute to amity between nations."[68] Eliding the years of building the cultural Co-Prosperity Sphere, the organization sought to present an image appropriate to the post-war context of democratization.

The pamphlet, however, also highlighted important changes in the organization's mission and operations. Having made "a fresh start with new ideals and goals," the KBS would contribute to "the cultural rehabilitation of Japan."[69] And it would do so without the help of government subsidies. The pamphlet suggested that wartime government support had bestowed "an abundant budget and a large staff" but also "militaristic pressure"; the new independent KBS, though crippled by the loss of financial support, did not long for those days of plenty.[70] Yet when government resumed subsidies in 1953, these were not refused.[71] The KBS continued to operate until 1972, when it was re-organized as the Japan Foundation (*Kokusai kōryū kikin*), a public corporation under the aegis of the Ministry of Foreign Affairs.

In the late 1930s and early 1940s, the imperialist internationalism of the KBS showed how the rhetoric of internationalism could be filled with content of almost any kind. In this sense, the danger of appropriation was present from the Society's inception. Beginning with an effort to disseminate knowledge, turning to the obfuscation of imperialist expansion, and then returning after the war to its more "enlightened" roots, the KBS represented both the risks and promise of internationalism. At the heart of the KBS's internationalism – and at that of many, if not all, examples of internationalist thought and practice – lies a core of nationalism. This does not rule out the possibility of international cooperation for the greater good — no doubt it has served to maintain peace and contribute to human welfare in ways that no state or other group acting alone could. But ideas of internationalism are powerful tools that have been used and abused towards a broad range of ends, not all equally desirable from a global standpoint. If one wants the benefits of internationalism, one must also be wary of its dangers, primarily the ease of appropriating the concept for goals that are the opposite of the internationalist mission.

NOTES

1 Kjell Goldmann, *The Logic of Internationalism: Coercion and Accommodation* (London: Routledge, 1994), 1–2.

2 Micheline R. Ishay, *Internationalism and Its Betrayal* (Minneapolis: University of Minnesota Press, 1995), xxi; Kevin Doak, "Liberal Nationalism in Imperial Japan: The Dilemma of Nationalism and Internationalism," in *Nationalism and Internationalism in Imperial Japan: Autonomy, Asian Brotherhood, or World Citizenship?* edited by Dick Stegewerns (London: Routledge Curzon, 2003), 34.

3 Martin H. Geyer and Johannes Paulmann, eds., *The Mechanics of Internationalism: Culture, Society and Politics from the 1840s the First World War* (Oxford: Oxford University Press, 2001), 12.

4 Ishay, *Internationalism and Its Betrayal*, xxiii.

5 Dick Stegewerns, "The Dilemma of Nationalism and Internationalism in Modern Japan: National Interest, Asian Brotherhood, International Cooperation or World Citizenship?" in *Nationalism and Internationalism*, 4.

6 "Enlightened Nationalism," copy of an article from the *Japan Advertiser* (Japan Foundation Library, KBS Archive, Box E (2), File 21, no. 2), 1.

7 Akira Iriye, *Cultural Internationalism and World Order* (Baltimore: Johns Hopkins University Press, 1997), 51–90.

8 Ibid., 119–23.

9 Aoki Setsuichi, ed., *Zaidan hōjin Kokusai Bunka Shinkōkai setsuritsu keika oyobi Shōwa kyū-nendo jigyō hōkokusho* [hereafter cited as *Setsuritsu keika*] (Tokyo: Kokusai Bunka Shinkōkai, 1935), 13–16.

10 Aoki Setsuichi, ed., *Zaidan hōjin Kokusai Bunka Shinkōkai Shōwa jū-nendo jigyō hōkokusho* [hereafter cited as *Shōwa jū-nendo jigyō*] (Tokyo: Kokusai Bunka Shinkōkai, 1937), 32–4.

11 Aoki Setsuichi, "Quarterly Report," *KBS Quarterly* 2.1 (April-June 1936), 1.

12 Aoki, *Setsuritsu keika*, 5.

13 Aoki, *Setsuritsu keika*, 4-5; and "Who's Who of the Kokusai Bunka Shinkokai," *KBS Quarterly* 1.1 (April–June 1935), 58–60.

14 "Zaidan hōjin Kokusai Bunka Shinkōkai setsuritsu shuisho," *Zaidan hōjin Kokusai Bunka Shinkōkai setsuritsu shuisho, jigyō kōyō oyobi kifu kōi* (Japan Foundation Library, KBS Archives, Box C (1), File 10, #8), 2.

15 In July 1937, a clash between Japanese and Chinese troops escalated into full-scale war. China appealed to the League, which offered in September 1938 to mediate the dispute. The Japanese declined, arguing that the dispute with China was a bilateral one, to be resolved between the two countries. The League Council then threatened to apply sanctions against Japan, and the Japanese government responded by ceasing cooperation with all League committees, the International Labour Office, and the Permanent Court of International Justice. See Japan, Ministry of Foreign Affairs, Diplomatic Records Office [hereafter cited as MOFA-DRO], "Kokusai Renmei shokikan to no kyōryoku shūshi kankei," File no. B.9.1.0.8-2.

16 Japan, MOFA-DRO, "Honpō ni okeru kyōkai oyobi bunka dantai kankei zakken: Kokusai Bunka Shinkōkai kankei" (I.1.10.0.2-17, vol. 2).

17 Mitsui Takaharu, "Kokusai bunka jigyō e no teishō," *Chūō kōron* 55.3 (March 1940), 242.

18 Fujimoto Shūichi, "'Kokusai Bunka Shinkōkai' ni yoru senzen no 3 jigyō ni kan suru kenkyū nōto," *Osaka Keidai ronshū* 45.1 (June 1994), 525–6.

19 Takamatsu Nobuhito, in Aoki, *Setsuritsu keika*, iii.

20 Kabayama Aisuke, in Aoki, *Shōwa jū-nendo jigyō*, 7.

21 Quoted by Kabayama in ibid., 8.

22 Shibasaki Atsushi, *Kindai Nihon to kokusai bunka kōryū: Kokusai Bunka Shinkōkai no sōsetsu to tenkai* (Tokyo: Yūshindō Kōbunsha, 1999), 72.

23 Yanagisawa Ken, "Kokusai bunka jigyō to wa nani zo ya (zoku)," *Gaikō jihō* 706 (May 1, 1934), 41.

24 Tokugawa, in Aoki, *Setsuritsu keika*, iv.

25 "Zaidan hōjin Kokusai Bunka Shinkōkai setsuritsu shuisho," 1.

26 Yanagisawa, "Kokusai bunka jigyō (zoku)," 41.

27 Ibid., 42.

28 Tetsuo Najita and H.D. Harootunian, "Japanese Revolt against the West: Political and Cultural Criticism in the Twentieth Century," in *Cambridge History of Japan*, vol. 6, *The Twentieth Century*, edited by Peter Duus (Cambridge: Cambridge University Press, 1988).

29 Takamatsu, in Aoki, *Setsuritsu keika*, ii. The same idea is found in, for example, the Society's prospectus ("Zaidan hōjin Kokusai Bunka Shinkōkai setsuritsu shuisho," 2) and in its second annual report (Kabayama, in Aoki, *Shōwa jū-nendo jigyō*, 7).

30 "Zaidan hōjin Kokusai Bunka Shinkōkai setsuritsu shuisho," 1.

31 "Kifu kōi," in Aoki, *Setsuritsu keika*, 17.
32 Eri Hotta, *Pan-Asianism and Japan's War 1931–1945*, The Palgrave Macmillan Series in Transnational History (New York: Palgrave Macmillan, 2007) 201.
33 Shibasaki, *Kindai Nihon to kokusai bunka kōryū*, 212–14; changes are summarized in table 8-1, p. 214.
34 Ibid., 214.
35 Ibid., 127.
36 Minowa Saburō, "Kyō no taigai bunka jigyō," *Kokusai bunka* 19 (May 1942), 47.
37 Kabayama Aisuke, *Shōwa jūni-nendo ni okeru Kokusai Bunka Shinkōkai no jigyō* (Tokyo: Kokusai Bunka Shinkōkai, 1938), 1.
38 MOFA-DRO, I.1.10.0.2-17, vol. 2.
39 Quoted in "Good-will institute set up here by Japan," *New York Times*, 29 March 1939, 17.
40 Ibid.
41 "Kantōgen," *Kokusai bunka* 11 (October 1940), 1.
42 *KBS Quarterly* 1.4 (January-March 1936), 38; and *Shōwa jūgo-nendo jigyō gaikyō* (Tokyo: Kokusai Bunka Shinkōkai, 1941), 5.
43 MOFA-DRO, "Honpō ni okeru kyōkai oyobi bunka dantai kankei zakken: Kokusai Bunka Shinkōkai kankei" (I.1.10.0.2-17, vol. 1).
44 Ryūichi Kaji, *Japan: Her Cultural Development* (Tokyo: Kokusai Bunka Shinkōkai, 1939), 49 and passim.
45 "Tai-gai bunka jigyō no eikyūsei," *Kokusai bunka* 1 (November 1938), 2.
46 Ibid., 3.
47 Aoki, *Shōwa jū-nendo jigyō*, 30 (emphasis added); and Kuroda Kiyoshi, in *Shōwa jūroku-nendo jigyō gaikyō* (Tokyo: Kokusai Bunka Shinkōkai, 1942), 4.
48 Nagai Matsuzō, *Shōwa jūhachi-nendo jigyō gaikyō* (Tokyo: Kokusai Bunka Shinkōkai, 1944), 1.
49 Kuroda, *Shōwa jūroku-nendo jigyō gaikyō*, 1–2.
50 Nagai Matsuzō, "Dai Tōa sensō o mukaete," *Kokusai bunka* 18 (February 1942), 2–3.
51 Chou, Wan-yao, "The Kōminka Movement in Taiwan and Korea: Comparisons and Interpretations," in *The Japanese Wartime Empire, 1931–1945*, edited by Peter Duus, Ramon H. Myers, and Mark R. Peattie (Princeton, NJ: Princeton University Press, 1996), 48–55.
52 Kuroda, *Shōwa jūroku-nendo jigyō gaikyō*, 5–6.
53 Ibid., 12.
54 Ibid., 2–3.
55 Nagai, *Shōwa jūhachi-nendo jigyō gaikyō*, 1–2.

56 The KBS was not alone in using culture to promote the expansion of the empire. The military had its own forces devoted to constructing the "cultural edifice of Greater Asia," drafting civilian "men of culture" into service as propagandists. See Ethan Mark, "Appealing to Asia: Nation, Culture and the Problem of Imperial Modernity in Japanese-Occupied Java, 1942–1945," diss., Columbia University (2003), 13, 18.
57 Kuroda, *Shōwa jūroku-nendo jigyō gaikyō*, 7.
58 Nagai Matsuzō, *Shōwa jūnana-nendo jigyō gaikyō* (Tokyo: Kokusai Bunka Shinkōkai, 1943), 8–9.
59 "Kantōgen," Kokusai bunka 10 (August 1940), 1.
60 Ibid.
61 Nishimura Shinji, "Nanpō kyōeiken e no bunka kōsaku no tokushusei," *Kokusai bunka* 18 (February 1942), 11.
62 Nagai, *Shōwa jūnana-nendo jigyō gaikyō*, 14.
63 "Kantōgen," *Kokusai bunka* 15 (August 1941), 1.
64 Nagai, "Dai Tōa sensō o mukaete," 3.
65 Minowa, "Kyō no taigai bunka jigyō," 42.
66 "Kantōgen," *Kokusai bunka* 13 (March 1941), 2–3.
67 Nishimura, "Nanpō kyōeiken e no bunka kōsaku no tokushusei," 11.
68 "Kokusai Bunka Shinkokai: Organization and Program" (Tokyo: Kokusai Bunka Shinkokai, 1949), Japan Foundation Library, KBS Archive, Box C (1), File 13, no. 2, 1 (emphasis added).
69 Ibid., 1–2.
70 Ibid., 3–4.
71 "Zaidan hōjin Kokusai Bunka Shinkōkai" (Tokyo: Kokusai Bunka Shinkōkai, 1954), Japan Foundation Library, KBS Archives, Box A (1), File 3, no. 219.

3 Japanese Pan-Asianism through the Mirror of Pan-Islamism

CEMIL AYDIN

The revival and official endorsement of a pan-Asian vision of regional world order in Japan is one of the most striking aspects of the international history of the 1930s. Pan-Asianism, as a generic term for trends criticizing the intellectual legitimacy of Western hegemony and advocating Asian solidarity to end the Eurocentric world order, has been an important part of Japanese discourse on the West and international order since the 1880s. Aspects of pan-Asianism as a discourse on weak Asia, despite its rich civilizational legacy and achievements, unjustly dominated by the West, has been an important theme in all intellectual currents of modern Japan. Yet, as a political project, pan-Asianism remained an oppositional discourse to mainstream Japanese foreign policy until the 1930s. In fact, pan-Asianism as a vision of alternative world order seemed irrelevant to Japanese foreign policy until the end of the 1920s. Yet, in the 1930s, pan-Asianism gained the status of an officially-sponsored "alternative" vision of world order. This process culminated in the declaration of the Greater East Asia Co-Prosperity Sphere in 1940, a project that relied heavily on the rhetoric of pan-Asian internationalism.

Given that pan-Asianist activists in Japan opposed their country's foreign policy until the 1930s, Tokyo's endorsement of pan-Asianism in its official "return to Asia" raises the question of what changed, either in the nature of pan-Asian thought or in Japan's international relations, to allow the triumph of pan-Asianist rhetoric in Japan's foreign policy in the 1930s.

The story of pan-Asianism in Japan has a global-comparative aspect. The development of pan-Asian thought in East Asia paralleled the formation of similar forms of non-Western internationalisms, such as pan-Islamism and pan-Africanism, in the last quarter of the nineteenth century, when geopolitical thinking became a significant aspect of imperialism driven globalization. Anti-Western critiques in Asia were not peculiar to Japan, as Indian, Chinese, Vietnamese, Iranian, Turkish, and Korean intellectuals also formulated critiques of Western ideas of race, orient, and world order. The relationship between pan-Asian internationalism and the grand strategy of the Japanese Empire was also not unique. In another non-colonized Asian empire, Ottoman Turkey, notions of pan-Islamism developed parallel to pan-Asianism in Japan, and became intertwined with the grand strategy of that empire. In fact, Ottoman Turkey used pan-Islamism in its propaganda in the First World War, long before the Japanese Empire turned to pan-Asianism during the Second World War. Even though the Republic of Turkey had disavowed all claims of pan-Islamic leadership in the Muslim world after the end of the Ottoman Empire, pan-Islamic and pan-Asian discourse on international solidarity continued to be important for the decolonization process and nationalist movements in Asia and Africa. If pan-Asianism was part of global intellectual history, not a particular product of Japanese national politics, and if it had parallels in other societies of West Asia and Africa, what can we learn from a comparison?

Given the parallels between pan-Asianism in the Japanese Empire and pan-Islamism in the Ottoman Empire from the 1880s to the 1910s, a comparison of these two anti-Western visions of world order shows how the Japanese Empire's appropriation of pan-Asian discourse fit into global and regional trends. The comparison further reveals the connection between the two empires' intellectual trends and international policies. Pan-Asianism and pan-Islamism, indeed, need to be seen as important discourses of internationalism, critiquing the Eurocentric imperial world order, and challenging the legitimacy of Western domination in Asia and Africa. Moreover, although this intellectual discourse should be separated from the grand strategy visions of the Ottoman and Japanese elites, it is important to understand when and how this alternative internationalism was appropriated by imperial elites for policy purposes.

The Globality of the Ideas of Civilization and Race

One cannot understand the pan-Asian and pan-Islamic visions of world order without examining the foundational notions of civilizational and racial fault lines that were reinvented and redefined over the second half of the nineteenth century. The genesis of pan-Islamic and pan-Asian visions of world order in the late 1870s and early 1880s was not simply a reaction to European expansion in Asia, which had already been underway since the eighteenth century. Early pan-Asian and pan-Islamic thinkers were modernists, and believed in the benevolence of nineteenth-century globalization, which they hoped would bring progress and prosperity to the whole world. Many intellectuals in the Ottoman Empire, and later in the Japanese Empire, accepted the idea of a universal European civilization raising the level of civilization elsewhere.[1] Formulated in the paradigm of liberal civilizationism, this ideology allowed Ottoman and Japanese elites to challenge the new European international society to be more inclusive. Upon the fulfilment of the required reforms, why should a multi-religious Ottoman Empire ruled by a Muslim dynasty, or a non-Christian Japanese state ruled by a Shinto emperor, not be accepted as equal members of the new system? Ottoman and Japanese elites' appropriation of the notion of a universal civilization also empowered these same elites in domestic politics, as they could present their radical centralizing reforms and imperial agendas over their own populations as civilizing missions.[2]

While assumptions of liberal civilizationism continued, the 1880s witnessed a rupture in Ottoman and Japanese perceptions of Europe, now seen as more imperialistic, aggressive, and racially and religiously exclusive.[3] The "scramble for Africa" and the new imperialism, accompanied by rigid theories of Orientalism and race ideology, established permanent identity-walls between white Christian Europeans on the one hand and "the Muslim world" and the "coloured races" on the other. Muslim responses to the invasions of Tunisia and Egypt in the early 1880s were more alarmed and pan-Islamic than their response to the invasion of Algeria in 1830, about fifty years earlier. While the latter had been considered a singular incident, European expansion and hegemony in the early 1880s was seen as part of a global pattern of uneven and unjust relationships. The West in the 1890s was likewise perceived as a bigger threat by Japan's pro-Western liberal intellectuals, including Fukuzawa Yukichi, than in the 1860s. By the 1890s, Western-educated Japanese intellectuals were more concerned with the international implications of Japan's yellow race identity, despite the fact that Japan was becoming militarily stronger.[4] More important, during the 1890s, Japanese and Ottoman elites began to perceive a non-transcendable racial and civilizational barrier between their own societies and Europe, with a bitter sense of being pushed away by the European centre they were looking to for inspiration. Nevertheless, these non-Western elites gave up neither the ideal of one universal civilization nor the tradition of cooperative diplomacy.

Pan-Islamic and pan-Asian ideas arose among members of the Western educated generation of Meiji Japan and the reform-era Ottoman Empire as a rethinking of the relationship between civilizing processes, the international order, and predominant forms of racial and religious identity. The first pan-Islamic magazine, *al-'Urwat al-Wuthqa*, was published in Paris by Jamal ad-Din Afghani and Muhammad 'Abduh in the early 1880s.[5] Similarly, the first pan-Asianist organization, Kōakai, was established in 1880.[6] The first major book on pan-Asianism, *The Theory of Uniting the Great East*, was written in 1885 by Tarui Tokichi.[7] Since the early 1880s, many in Europe and Asia had been thinking of the potential peril or benefits of Asian and Islamic solidarity, and these ideas gradually entered the vocabulary of writings on international affairs, often paralleling the ideas of pan-Slavism, pan-Germanism, and, later, pan-Europeanism. Yet the governments of the Ottoman and Japanese empires did not endorse such radical political projects. More concerned with fostering friendly relations with the Western powers, they believed their national interests to be better served by dispelling fears of the "yellow peril" or the "Muslim peril" in European public opinion. The ideas of pan-Islamic and pan-Asian solidarity, themselves partly responses to yellow-peril or Muslim-peril discourses in Western public opinion, ultimately would confirm the same peril discourses.

Reformist elites in the Ottoman and Japanese empires, however, shared an interest in challenging the European notion of Oriental inferiority. Ottoman and Japanese intellectuals accepted that they belonged to an Asian, Islamic, or Eastern civilization, but they did not have to concede that theirs was morally inferior and eternally backward. They could concede that Asia, or the Muslim world, was weak and needed revival and progress, but not agree that this weakness was due to racial or religious inferiority. The flexibility of the concepts of Asian, Eastern, and Islamic civilizations – their malleable content in relation to the idealized European civilization – allowed non-Western intellectuals to inject their own visions and subjectivity into these notions of European provenance.

The infuriatingly anti-Muslim speeches of British prime minister William Gladstone were well known in Muslim reformist circles, but Muslim intellectuals rightly viewed Ernest Renan as the most representative name of the new European Orientalism. For Renan, Islam belonged to the inferior "semitic race"; Muslims could never fulfil the standards of civilization so long as they remained Turks, Arabs, or simply believers.[8] Muslim intellectuals not only responded to Renan by publishing refutations of his ideas; they also searched for venues and means to engage in dialogue with European intellectuals.[9] For this purpose, Orientalist congresses in Europe presented opportunities for Muslim intellectuals to address European scholars and to convince them that "the Muslim world" was indeed capable of progress. The Ottoman government sponsored trips by prominent intellectuals such as Ahmed Midhad Efendi,[10] and at other times sent bureaucrats to read semi-official papers.[11] By referring to the past achievements and contemporary legacy of Islamic civilization, Muslim representatives emphasized that Muslims were the "servants of civilization."

While the anti-yellow-race expressions of the German emperor, Kaiser Wilhelm II, showed the political implications of the new Western racism, Japanese intellectuals also struggled with discourses of Christianity's superiority to Buddhism and other Asian religions. Prominent Japanese Buddhist intellectuals, like their counterparts from other parts of Asia, appeared at the Chicago World Parliament of Religions in 1893 to assert the equality of their religions to Christianity.[12] The generation of Westernized Japanese intellectuals in the 1890s, such as Miyake Setsurei and Inoue Enryo, also began to advance powerful anti-Christian notions of world civilizations and progress.[13] This challenging of European imperialism through critiques of Orientalism and race discourse – to affirm the universality of civilization and modernity – characterized the writings of all pan-Islamic and pan-Asian thinkers until the First World War.[14] Their critiques showed that Orientalist notions were omnipresent but not omnipotent; the idea of Eastern and Western civilizations could be redeployed for purposes quite different than the intentions of the original European formulators of the East–West dichotomy. In this non-Western challenge to the contradictions of the ideology of the civilizing mission, the ideas of Asia romantics in Europe and America were appropriated by Asian intellectuals. The pan-Asian ideas of Okakura Tenshin and Rabindranath Tagore cannot be understood without considering the influence of European and American pessimists who condemned Western civilization and searched for a solution to humanity's crisis in the spiritual traditions of Asia.[15]

Parallel to these intellectual efforts to challenge the Eurocentric civilizing mission, pan-Islamic and pan-Asian thinkers began to see turn-of-the-century international relations as a grim state of clashes between civilizations or different races. Observing European colonial activity in "the Muslim world," Ottoman Muslims perceived its "illegitimate" encirclement by the Christian West.[16] While European authors perceived Islamic solidarity as xenophobic anti-Westernism, Muslim writers either denied the existence of a reactionary alliance against the West or noted it was the only way to overcome the unjust rule of the imperial world order. Around the same time, East Asian intellectuals were emphasizing the conflict between "the white and yellow races."[17] Narratives of sinister Western expansion in Asia since the eighteenth century, informed by Hegelian notions of continuous conflict between East and West, hereafter became a pillar of pan-Islamist and pan-Asian discourse. But they all noted that their goal was not to reject all things European.

By the turn of the century, narratives of the East–West encounter and of tensions between the coloured and white races were well established in nationalist imaginations across Asia. The idea of the yellow race's inferiority and "yellow-peril" discourse led pan-Asianists to respond with their own theories of a "white peril" in Asia.[18] One of the most influential pan-Asianist arguments for Japanese-Chinese racial solidarity was written by Prince Konoe Atsumaro upon his return from a lengthy stay in Germany in the 1890s, at the peak of German yellow-peril discourse.[19] Konoe predicted an inevitable racial struggle in East Asia between the white and yellow races, with the Chinese and the Japanese uniting as sworn enemies of the white race. Similarly, as the notion of "the Muslim world" began to imply a racial identity, even the least religious Ottoman intellectuals such as Ahmed Riza felt compelled to write apologetic pieces defending Islam against Orientalist presumptions.[20]

Pan-Asianists and pan-Islamists were not immune to contradictions and internalized racism. Pan-Islamists such as Halil Halid noted that, if European racism and the civilizing mission ideology were limited to the natives of Australia, the Caribbean, and Africa, he would have no objections.[21] He did, however, reject the applicability of the civilizing mission ideology to Muslim, Indian, and Chinese societies, given their past civilizational greatness and continuing legacy of higher moral values. Similarly, Japanese pan-Asianists who insisted on the equality of the yellow and white races or of Asian and Western civilizations saw no difficulty in proclaiming Japan to be the most civilized nation in Asia and other Asian societies to be in need of outside intervention to move from semi- to fully civilized status. Thus, while Ottoman and Japanese elites insisted on their civilizational equality with the West, they developed civilizing missions towards their own regions: the Ottomans claimed a mission to civilize backward Muslim regions, while Japan expressed hopes to civilize East Asia.

The worldwide response to Japan's victory in the Russo-Japanese War of 1905 showed how the idea of the encounter between the white and coloured races, as well as notions of East–West civilizational conflict, had become the globally accepted framework for thinking about international affairs. The Japanese victory was celebrated as the first of an Eastern yellow race nation over a Western white race empire, and was perceived by Turkish, Iranian, Indian, Chinese, and other Asian nationalists as a major challenge to Western hegemony. Despite an Anglo-Japanese alliance, pro-Western Japan became a symbol of Asia's challenge to the imperial world order; with Japanese victory, European discourses on the inferiority of the Asian and yellow races were proven invalid. Reconsideration of the scientific literature on race, to which the racial interpretations of the 1905 Japanese victory contributed immensely, led to the 1911 Universal Races Congress, an event that showed the global impact of the ideas and critiques of non-Western intellectuals.[22] Japan was proving that European-originated civilization and modernity were universal and could be successfully assimilated by Eastern non-white societies.[23]

The Japanese victory confirmed Asian nationalists' hopes that East Asia and "the Muslim World" were not necessarily dead, that they were reawakening to gain their rightful positions in world affairs. Slogans surrounding this "Awakening of the East" inspired constitutional revolutions in Iran (1906), Turkey (1908), and China (1911).[24] By 1914, Ottoman and Japanese intellectuals had developed alternative discourses of civilization in which East and West both had virtues, and believed that a higher level of world civilization would result from their synthesis. Members of the Japanese elite insisted Japan would assume leadership in carrying out this East–West synthesis, thus assuring its equality with the West and leadership in the East.[25]

Lessons of the Ottoman State's Use of Pan-Islamism, 1908–24

Even though pan-Asian and pan-Islamic discourses of solidarity were a reflection of the geopoliticization of globalization, and highly dominant in different intellectual circles all over Asia, these visions of internationalism did not translate directly and necessarily into policy in the Ottoman and Japanese empires, whose elites believed in the utility of cooperating with other empires for the interest of their own. When did pan-Islamic discourses on international affairs begin to shape Ottoman policy? The period between the declaration of a constitution in 1908 and the Ottoman government's entry into the First World War shows the volatility of the idea of an East–West divide. The largely secular and pro-Western Ottoman elite embraced a pan-Islamic vision of world order on the eve of the war partly because it perceived the international crisis of 1912 to 1914 through the lenses of civilizational encounter and conflict. Upon the fulfilment of the 1908 Constitutional Revolution, Young Turk leaders had hoped to turn their state into a "Japan of the Near East" and to secure an alliance with the British Empire, similar to the Anglo-Japanese Alliance of 1902. The Westernized Young Turks were anti-imperialists, but believed in continuing the legacy of cooperative diplomacy with the Western powers. In this moment of optimism following the 1908 constitutional revolution, the Young Turks believed in the possibility of their empire's becoming a full member of European international society, convinced that it could represent the harmony of Eastern and Western civilization. It was only with Italy's 1911 invasion of Ottoman territory in Libya and the 1912 attack by an alliance of Christian Balkan states that Ottoman public opinion began to interpret civilizational differences in conflictual terms. The Western powers' silence about, or even support of, the "unjust" acts of Christian European nations in the Balkan Wars was perceived as another Western injustice against the East, and international affairs once again looked more like a clash of civilizations, a modern Crusade of the West against the Muslim world.[26]

When the Great War started in Europe in 1914, the Ottoman elites and public opinion's perception about the "encirclement of Muslims" by a modern crusade of British, French, and Russian empires became important in their deliberations. Believing that these three crusading empires ultimately would cooperate to end the Ottoman Empire, by then seen as the last surviving Muslim empire, the Ottoman leaders decided to join the war on the side of Germany and mobilize a pan-Islamic revolt against their mutual rivals. The Ottoman leaders even declared a "holy war" against the British, French, and Russians, asking all the colonized Muslims to revolt against these three empires in solidarity with the Ottomans. This pan-Islamic challenge to the European imperial world order was a drastic change from the nineteenth-century Ottoman foreign policy of cooperation with the Western powers. Although the Ottoman insistence on securing a formal alliance with Germany as a precondition for entering the Great War was a continuation of the Ottoman desire to be part of a European system of alliances and diplomacy, popular notions of pan-Islamic solidarity fuelled Ottoman policy makers' visions of exploiting contradictions within the imperial world order, to encourage Muslim disobedience against the British, French, and Russian empires, and, if possible, a global revolt of colonized Muslims against their colonial Christian rulers.

Even though the Ottoman Empire and its German allies lost the war, pan-Islamic internationalism and propaganda left an important legacy for the twentieth-century international order. When the Ottoman Empire entered the war, the British, French, and Russian empires had to make compromises and promise more liberties for their Muslim subjects. The pan-Islamic challenge to the European imperial order ultimately forced the major colonial powers to think about securing a new post-war order with a new set of international organizations and new notions of legitimacy. The emergence of Wilsonian and socialist internationalism towards the end of the war did not end the appeal of pan-Islamic or pan-Asian internationalism either. In fact, pan-Islamic solidarity reached in its peak during the Khilafat Movement between 1920 and 1924, organized by Muslims in India, supported by leading Hindu nationalists such as Gandhi, to support Turkish independence. The Khilafat movement mixed the ideals of Islamic solidarity, anti-colonial nationalism, and Wilsonian notions of legitimacy. While collecting donations for the Turkish war of independence, its leaders petitioned the British government to recognize the right to self-determination of Turkey's Muslim majority. The Turkish national movement ultimately achieved its goals, in part due to the moral and material support of the pan-Islamic movement. Nevertheless, the elite of the new Turkish republic decided to abolish the caliphate and disavow claims to leadership in "the Muslim world," thus indicating their own preference for Wilsonianism. Turkey remained outside the League of Nations for another decade, perceiving it as a means of justifying British and French colonial interests in the region. Yet its decision to abolish the caliphate ended the high moment of post-war *Realpolitik* pan-Islamism.[27] But the abandoning of pan-Islamic discourse did not mean the leaders of the Turkish republic had abandoned the discourse of civilization itself. Instead, they emphasized that Eastern Islamic civilization could not be a real alternative to the West for carrying out modernizing reforms, and that a secular national Turkey could and should be a member of Western civilization.

Even though political activism in the name of Asian or Islamic solidarity had little influence on international politics in the 1920s, a vision
of a revival of Asia and the idea of Eastern and Western civilizations
continued to be shared by the majority of Turkish and Japanese intellectuals, irrespective of their ideological inclinations.[28] The idea of an
encounter and conflict between Eastern and Western civilizations was
upheld by both Westernists and Islamists in Turkish domestic politics. Similar to their Japanese and Chinese counterparts, Turkish intellectuals in the 1920s approached Western modernity through belief in
the existence of an East–West civilizational division. In the 1920s, Turkey's republican intellectuals hoped to "abandon the East" and "join
the West" through cultural Westernization. Japan's liberal intellectuals were more confident about the virtues of Eastern civilization, and
talked more about harmony between the two civilizations rather than
joining one at the expense of the other. Japanese members of the US-
Japan Friendship Association, or those working for the League of Nations, referred to the existence of Eastern and Western civilizations to
facilitate dialogue and cooperation between the two. The "leaving the
East" arguments of the Kemalists in the 1920s were perhaps similar to
the ideas of the May 4th generation in China, but they were far from
hegemonic in the non-Western world. All over Asia, including Japan, a
more liberal vision of the harmony and synthesis of Eastern and Western values, which assumed their binary opposition, was the predominant paradigm in support of the ambivalent yet liberal world order of
the 1920s.

Japan and Pan-Asianism, 1905–31

Pan-Asianism had strong advocates in Japan and began to inspire several organizations and associations in that country, especially in the
aftermath of the Russo-Japanese War in 1905. By this time, Japanese
pan-Asianism had developed a distinct set of ideas on the yellow race–
white race relationship, colonialism in Asia, Western and Eastern civilizations, and Japan's grand strategy or international mission.

The Japanese state's relationship with pan-Asianism was similar to
the Ottoman state's relationship with pan-Islamism: ruling elites were
cautious of any association with an Asian challenge to the West as they
were committed to cooperation with the Western powers and concerned
about Japan's image in Western public opinion. At the same time, the
notion of being an Eastern and yellow-race nation was becoming

entrenched within Japanese identity. One well-known conversation illustrates this division over Asianism within the elite. In September 1907, Gotō Shinpei (1857–1929), president of the South Manchuria Railway Company, described his vision of "Japan's World Policy" to Itō Hirobumi, resident general in Korea. Gotō began by expressed his belief that helping Chinese leaders to create *Tōyōjin no Tōyō* (Asia for Asians) represented the true aim of *Dai Ajia Shugi* (Greater Asianism) and the best means of establishing a real peace in East Asia. Upon hearing this, Itō interrupted Gotō, asked him to explain what he meant by the term *Dai Ajia Shugi,* and cautioned him against carelessness in expressing such an idea, as no benefit could come to Japan from it. Itō also warned that such references to Asianism would cause misunderstanding in the eyes of Westerners, and lead them to associate Japanese power and policies with their prejudiced concept of the yellow peril.[29]

This conversation reveals how segments of top-level Japanese officials in the period following the Russo-Japanese War supported an Asianist orientation in foreign policy. They shared a belief in the cultural association with China and pride that Japan alone had achieved a civilizational synthesis of East and West. They also perceived world events as constituting racial conflict. Influential political figures such as Konoe Atsumaro, Inukai Tsuyoshi, Gotō Shinpei, Ōkuma Shigenobu, and Yamagata Aritomo all expressed Asianist ideals during their political careers.[30] Some of them even met Asian nationalists visiting Japan.[31] On the whole, however, Japanese leaders deliberately tried to avoid appearing friendly to Japan's Asian nationalist admirers.[32] To the contrary, they demonstrated Japan's pro-Western stance by complying, in 1909, with a request from the French Embassy to expel a group of Vietnamese students who had come to Japan, inspired by pan-Asianist ideals, to study the secrets of Japanese progress.[33] It is telling that, in 1910, just when Egyptian nationalists were looking to Japan for inspiration, Prime Minister Ōkuma Shigenobu wrote a preface to a translation of Lord Cromer's *Modern Egypt* emphasizing that the British colonial experience in Egypt could serve as a model for Japan's management of Korea.[34]

As an ally of the British Empire, the Japanese Empire had little to gain from any pan-Asianist revolt during the First World War, which some Indian and Chinese nationalists hoped to achieve. Nonetheless, pan-Asianist intellectuals and groups were active during the war, seeking to emphasize Western subjugation of the coloured races as the main conflict in international affairs and urging Japan to break its alliance with Britain so it could become the leader of Asia in revival. During the Second World War, in cooperation with Asianists in China and India, Japan's pan-Asianists conducted a successful public opinion campaign emphasizing that Japanese national interest would be better served by being the leader of a free Asia than a discriminated member of the all-white superpowers club.[35] At the peace conference following the war, the Japanese government's proposal for a race equality clause in the Versailles Treaty was partly the result of pressure from pan-Asianists, who mobilized behind the proposal, suggesting it would be a litmus test for the sincerity and credibility of the principles underlying the League of Nations. In fact, Asianists perceived the League of Nations as an attempt by Western colonial powers to continue their global hegemony through a new set of institutions. Thus, the pan-Asianists depicted the rejection of the proposed clause as proof of the continuation of white supremacist ideology behind the mask of the League.[36] On the other hand, the Wilsonian idea of national self-determination, in inspiring the Korean national revolt and the May 4th Movement in 1919, revealed the contradictions between Asian nationalism and Japanese pan-Asianism: most Japanese pan-Asianists, in their vision of Asian solidarity, imagined Korea would forever be a part of the Japanese Empire.

Ideas of Asian solidarity survived through the inter-war era, with critiques levelled against both the League of Nations and socialist internationalism. Yet, in the competition among the various internationalist visions, Japanese leaders chose a policy of imperial cooperation, which it identified with the liberal internationalism of the League – although it carried elements of the illiberal internationalism of the pre-war era of imperial cooperation as well. Different pan-Asianist groups continued to campaign for their version of international cooperation with different nationalist movements in Asia and for an alternative mission for Japan in the world, but they clearly lacked influence. For example, an international pan-Asianist gathering in Nagasaki in 1926 was plagued by internal fighting and proved inconsequential.[37] The Japanese Asianist hosts received little sympathy from the government – the meeting had been shifted to Nagasaki partly because the Japanese government had not wanted it in Tokyo. More important, the tension between Japanese imperialism and pan-Asianism became transparent in Nagasaki. Chinese delegates condemned Japanese policies and succeeded in inserting into the final statement a critique of Japan's "Twenty-One Demands" on China. With only a small group of pro-Japanese Koreans present, Korean nationalists noted the absurdity of the conference, while individuals representing India, Afghanistan, and the Philippines were all political exiles in Japan who had little contact with the nationalist movements in their home countries.

Japan's liberal internationalists in the 1920s never viewed the pan-Asiatic movement as a serious rival. Zumoto Motosada, an ardent liberal internationalist, lecturing at a League-affiliated university in Geneva in 1926, responded to Western media attention to the Nagasaki conference by reaffirming Japan's liberal orientation.[38] He looked down on the pan-Asiatic movement in Japan, emphasizing its insignificance for both Japan's foreign policy and international politics:

> How faithfully Japan fulfills this self-imposed mission was shown in connection with the so-called Pan-Asiatic Congress held at Nagasaki at the beginning of August in the present year, about which more or less sensational press dispatches appear to have been printed in Europe and America. During the last twenty years Japan has been visited by a succession of radical leaders and political adventurers from different parts of Asia for the purpose of enlisting Japanese sympathy and assistance in various propaganda against one or another of the European powers. Always finding deaf ears turned to their pleadings, some of these indefatigable plotters recently struck upon the bright idea of realizing their aim under the inoffensive guise of promoting the Asiatic renaissance, and finally succeeded in interesting in their plan a few notoriety mongers of no standing in our public life. The result was the Nagasaki conference in question. It was an event of no consequence whatever, no person of any importance in any country taking part in it. And what is most significant, it was scarcely noticed by the press in Japan.[39]

Despite Zumoto's rejection of the pan-Asian political movement, his liberal internationalism was based on a discourse of civilization similar to the Asianist one – namely, a discourse on East-West relations. While he denied the idea of a race war and clash of civilizations, Zumoto's internationalism recognized the political relevance of civilizational identities. He noted that Japan "imposes upon herself the role of harmonizer between the civilizations of East and West" to aid the cause of international peace within the framework of the League of Nations. He thus proudly described Asia's cultural awakening inspired by the Japanese victory over Russia and then by the Great War in Europe. Zumoto saw liberalism and industrialization in Japan as compatible with the renaissance of Asian culture; he regarded this harmony as a positive contribution to world peace. Alfred Zimmern, deputy director of the League's Institute of Intellectual Cooperation, likened Zumoto to Nitobe in his commitment to intellectual exchange between East and West, and praised Japan's role in this dialogue.[40]

In 1943, seventeen years after the ineffectual 1926 Nagasaki conference had been ridiculed by official and liberal circles in Japan, the Japanese government hosted the Greater East Asia Conference, to which it invited the leaders of the Philippines, Burma, the Provincial Government of India, the Nanking Government of China, Manchukuo, and Thailand. Why and how did this seemingly pan-Asianist political vision become a part of the official Japanese foreign policy agenda? The Manchurian Incident in 1931 and the subsequent diplomatic and foreign policy crisis was a turning point in making pan-Asianism a realist policy option for Japanese leaders.

Rethinking Japan's "Return to Asia" in Comparative Perspective

Pan-Asianists had been active in Japan since the turn of the twentieth century; some continued to work for their cause under the umbrella of patriotic Asianist organizations such as Kokuryūkai and Genyōsha. Marginal in policy-making, patriotic Asianists had often complained about their neglect. However, in the aftermath of the Manchurian Incident of 1931 and Japan's decision to withdraw from the League of Nations in 1932, traditional Asianists found a receptive audience for their ideas among Japanese bureaucrats and army officers.

The story of one Kokuryūkai Asianist, Wakabayashi Han, is telling about this transformation in the early 1930s. Wakabayashi first became interested in Muslims on a visit to India with the Burmese Buddhist monk and anti-colonial nationalist Sayadaw U. Ottama in 1912.[41] This led Wakabayashi to further research on Islam in Asia.[42] According to his own retrospective narrative of the mid-1930s, he worked hard for pan-Asianist causes for two decades, advocating, as a member of a small circle of Islam experts within Kokuryūkai, that Japan develop closer ties with colonized Muslims to gain their support for Japanese leadership of an awakening and independent Asia.[43] The activities of his small group, however, achieved neither results nor government support, and Wakabayashi became pessimistic about its future prospects.[44] Then, in 1932, he was sent to Geneva by Kokuryūkai to observe the League of Nations meeting on the future of the Japanese-sponsored state of Manchukuo, where he witnessed the decision of Japanese diplomats to withdraw subsequent to the League's negative decision. It was only during his long trip back to Japan that Wakabayashi noticed a change of attitude towards Asia among Japanese military officers and had the chance to talk to Lieutenant-Colonel Isogai Rensuke and explain to him the benefits of paying attention to the Muslim world. Upon his return to Japan, Colonel Isogai contacted Wakabayashi and introduced him to army minister Araki Sadao.[45] Wakabayashi's story of what followed is a narrative of triumph, as the Japanese army began to implement a pan-Asianist Islam policy in China and to support the activities of the Kokuryūkai. Japan's withdrawal from the League of Nations thus proved to be the turning point in the government's attitude towards pan-Asianist ideas.

Autobiographical anecdotes of other pan-Asianist activists show similar patterns. The prominent pan-Asianist Ōkawa Shūmei had often clashed with pro-British bureaucrats and politicians. Until 1932, he had tried to influence Japanese foreign policy by establishing radical nationalist organizations, and was even sentenced to prison in 1934 for his involvement in the attempted right-wing coup of 15 May 1932.[46] Upon his release from prison in October 1937, Ōkawa found Japanese foreign policy much more to his liking and volunteered his services for projects inspired by pan-Asianist beliefs. In May 1938, he was reinstated in his position as director of the East Asia Economic Research Bureau in Tokyo. Back in his position of managing one of the largest research institutes in Japan, Ōkawa Shūmei promoted a pan-Asianist agenda in the journal he edited, Shin Ajia (New Asia).[47] In his first editorial, published just a month before the German invasion of Poland, Ōkawa predicted that the outbreak of war in Europe would provide new opportunities for Asian nationalist movements. He also urged the Japanese government to support Asian anti-colonial movements to accelerate their national liberation and create future allies for Japan.[48]

Looking back at the history of Asianism in Japan, 1933 was a turning point and new start for many pan-Asianist projects. Rash Behari Bose, an Indian nationalist exiled in Japan, received funds to start publishing a new English-Japanese language magazine, The New Asia.[49] In editorials on Japanese foreign policy, Bose urged the Japanese government to cooperate with the United States, China, and the Soviet Union to eliminate British colonialism in Asia. For him, Britain was the root of all problems in the region, including Japan's isolation in the international community. As early as 1934, Bose warned that Japan needed to maintain good relations with the United States, as only Britain would benefit from a conflict between them: "Britain is not able to fight Japan singly and therefore waiting for her opportunity, when Japan may be involved in a war with America … An American-Japanese War will weaken these two great powers who are serious rivals of Great Britain. Those Americans and Japanese who are real patriots should do their best to promote American-Japanese friendship." While Rash Behari Bose's journal was read primarily in India, Qurban Ali's *Yani Yapon Muhbiri* (The New Japan Journal), which started publication in the same year, aimed its message at the Muslim world.[50] Although the journal was in Turkish, the cover had a Japanese subtitle describing it as "the only journal that introduces Japan to the Muslim world."

Nineteen thirty-three also witnessed the establishment, by several high-level military and civilian leaders, of *Dai Ajia Kyōkai* (the Greater Asia Association),[51] to promote regional unity in East Asia and solidarity between Asian societies on the world stage; among its prominent members were Konoe Fumimaro, General Matsui Iwane, and General Ishiwara Kanji.[52] The association published the monthly *Dai Ajia Shugi* (Greater Asianism), which became the most important pan-Asianist journal of the period with news and opinion articles covering most of Asia, including its Muslim regions.

Tokyo's support for pan-Asianist projects and its "return to Asia" was recognized by Asian nationalist leaders. Many immediately noted the irony of Japan's claim to be championing Asian liberation while fighting Chinese nationalism. As Japanese policies in China were criticized by leading Asian nationalists, Tokyo's official Asianism had to be based on highly repetitive references to the events and ideas of Asian internationalism in the 1905–14 period. One of the best examples of this is Ōkawa's response to the condemnation of Japanese colonialism under the name of Asian solidarity by leaders of the Indian National Congress. In an open letter to Gandhi and Nehru, Ōkawa recounted his experience of joining Indian nationalists to campaign for India's liberation during the First World War, regardless of Japan's pro-Western policy at the time. For Ōkawa, the history of Indian-Japanese collaboration showed that official pan-Asianism had altruistic roots and reflected a genuine Japanese interest in furthering Asia's decolonization.[53]

It was during this search for Asianism's historical roots that Okakura Tenshin was made an icon of pan-Asian thought, because he wrote about Asian unity and solidarity even before the First World War, when the Japanese government did not follow a policy of Asian solidarity. All of Okakura's works, including a previously unpublished manuscript from his 1901 trip to India called *Awakening of the East*, were published in both English and Japanese between 1938 and 1945.[54] In the same trend of reinventing early Asian internationalism, earlier Asianist books by Ōkawa Shūmei, the British pan-Asianist Paul Richard, and the anti-British Bengali Taraknath Das were reprinted after more than twenty years.[55]

It was the presence of new converts from the socialist and liberal intellectual traditions, however, that succeeded in bringing new energy and vitality to Asianism. In the writings of Miki Kiyoshi, a leading member of the semi-official think tank Shōwa Kenkyūkai (Shōwa Research Association), we see the Asianist discourse of civilization in its most sophisticated form, polished with German philosophy of history. According to Miki, the over-Westernization of world cultures and the Eurocentric character of the social sciences posed a global political problem. Borrowing the inter-war self-critique of European thought, Miki was convinced that Western civilization was in the process of self-destruction. From this, he proceeded to the conclusion that Japan should uphold its civilizational mission to facilitate Asian unity and cooperation and to eliminate Western colonialism. For Miki, Asian cooperation under Japanese leadership served the interests of peace and harmony, as well as of liberation and racial equality.[56] Although Miki's arguments drew on inter-war reflections on modernity and Eurocentrism, they were similar to the ideas of Okakura Tenshin and Ōkawa Shūmei in their basic tenets – namely, belief in the collapse of the Eurocentric world order and the corresponding necessity of offering an alternative based on Asian values and political solidarity.

Other converts to Asianism, such as Sano Manabu, Nabeyama Sadachika, and Akamatsu Katsumaro, also offered their interpretations of pan-Asianist thought.[57] These ex-socialists described a world divided into a proletarian East and a bourgeois West; they believed the fusion of the West, "reorganized by the proletariat," and the East, "awakened through the influence of pan-Asianism," would create a new world order that could finally establish world peace and unity.[58] Their retreat from Comintern socialism was accompanied by a new allegiance to Asian internationalism.

What united the ideology of such diverse groups and figures as the Greater Asia Association, Ōkawa Shūmei, and new converts to Asianism such as Miki Kiyoshi was the discourse of civilization. Japan's "return to Asia" was supported by both ex-liberals and ex-socialists and thus cannot be a simple story of Asianists displacing liberal internationalists. Entangled in a bitter conflict with Chinese nationalism and unable to justify its puppet regime in Manchuria to the world, the Japanese governing elite turned to what their counterparts in Western empires had long been doing: merging the discourse of international solidarity, liberty, and equality with colonial rule. A new interpretation of pan-Asianism was best suited for this purpose, and was supported by a majority of Japanese intellectuals. While wartime Japan became a laboratory for Max Weber's iron cage of bureaucratic rationality, Japanese intellectuals speculated about ideas of "overcoming modernity" and "challenging the Eurocentric world order" through utopias of a new synthesis of East and West.

Conclusion

A comparative world historical approach shows that both pan-Asianism and pan-Islamism were important influences on incipient Turkish and Japanese nationalism, especially in merging civilizational discourses with nationalist critiques of the West. While Ottoman Turkey followed a cautious policy of cooperation with the Western powers, the legitimacy crisis of the Eurocentric imperial order, filtered through its civilizational interpretation, convinced the Ottoman elite to promote pan-Islamism as an alternative vision of world order during the First World War. The defeat of the Ottoman Empire, coupled with new structures of legitimacy in the post-war international order, convinced the Muslim leaders of the Turkish republic to abandon political projects of pan-Islamism in 1924. A counter-discourse of civilization around the redefined notions of East–West or Christian–Muslim civilizational distinction survived, however, and, in its liberal or socialist reinterpretation, became dominant. Although the inter-war era is usually seen as the beginning of global competition between liberal and socialist internationalisms, pan-Islamic and pan-Asian visions of international solidarity continued to be espoused.

As the Ottoman elites had done on the eve of the First World War, in the early 1930s Japan's liberal elites found previous policies of cooperative diplomacy insufficient to defend their national interests in the face of the changing international balance of power. Under the influence of civilizational discourse, they appropriated pan-Asianism as the solution to the crisis of legitimacy partly caused by their own imperialism. But, by then, the international appeal of political pan-Asianism had declined from its 1905–14 heyday; imperialism was in retreat against a

rising tide of nationalism, informed more by Wilsonianism and socialism than by any variant of pan-Asianism.

Thus, Japan's official pan-Asianism of the late 1930s had to be redefined. The complicity of Japan's liberal and socialist intellectuals in the
production of Second World War–era Asianism, similar to the complicity of the Ottoman Empire's liberal Muslim intellectuals in the production of First World War–era pan-Islamism, was denied in the delicate
post-war political atmospheres of both Turkey and Japan. In both cases,
the leaders who decided for war and employed anti-Western visions of
world order preferred to blame the "radical" ideologies of pan-Islamism
or pan-Asianism and their stereotyped advocates. Similarly, both cases
illustrate the need to pay greater attention to the way paradigms of
East–West civilizational differences – products of the late-nineteenth-
century tension between imperialism and globalization – affected the
thinking of intellectuals at key moments of international crisis.

NOTES

1 For a formulation of a universal theory of civilization by the most prominent early Meiji-era intellectual, see Fukuzawa Yukichi, *An Outline of a
   Theory of Civilization*, translated by David A. Dilworth and G. Cameron
   Hurst (Tokyo: Sophia University, 1973). For examples of Ottoman theo-
   rization of the process of civilization, see Namik Kemal, "Medeniyet,"
   Mecmua-i Ulum 5 (1 Safer 1297/14 [January 1880]): 381–3; Münif Paşa, "Mu-
   kayese-i İlm ve Cehl," *Mecmua-i Fünün* 1 (Muharrem 1279 [June 1862]):
   26–7.
2 For aspects of the Ottoman Empire's civilizing mission to its own populations, in the form of reapplying European Orientalism for domestic political purposes, see Ussama Makdisi, "Ottoman Orientalism," *American
   Historical Review* 107, no. 3 (2002): 768–96. For the Japanese version of the
   same process, see Stefan Tanaka, *Japan's Orient: Rendering Past into History*
   (Berkeley: University of California Press, 1993).
3 For the changing global image of the West and the transformation of world
   order during the 1880s, see Hannah Arendt, *The Origins of Totalitarianism*
   (New York: World Publishing, 1962), 123.
4 Matsumoto Sannosuke, "Profile of Asian Minded Man V: Fukuzawa Yukichi," *Developing Economies* 5, no. 1 (1967): 168–9; Albert M. Craig, "Fukuzawa Yukichi: The Philosophical Foundations of Meiji Nationalism," in

Political Development in Modern Japan, edited by Robert E. Ward (Princeton, NJ: Princeton University Press, 1968).

5 Nikkie Keddie, *An Islamic Response to Imperialism* (Berkeley: University of California Press, 1968).

6 Vladimir Tikhonov, "Korea's First Encounters with Pan-Asianism Ideology in the Early 1880s," *Review of Korean Studies* 5, no. 2 (2002): 195–232.

7 Suzuki Tadashi, "Profile of Asian Minded Man IX: Tōkichi Tarui," *Developing Economies* 6, no. 1 (1968): 79–100.

8 For a world historical assessment of Ernest Renan's ideas on the Aryan race, see Vasant Kaiwar, "The Aryan Model of History and the Oriental Renaissance: The Politics of Identity in an Age of Revolutions, Colonialism and Nationalism," in *The Antinomies of Modernity* (Durham, NC: Duke University Press, 2003).

9 Dücane Cündioğlu, "Ernest Renan ve 'Reddiyeler' Bağlamında İslam-Bilim Tartişmalarina Bibliyografik bir Katkı," *Divan* 2 (1996): 1–94.

10 Carter Vaughn Findley, "An Ottoman Occidentalist in Europe: Ahmed Midhat Meets Madame Gulnar, 1889," *American Historical Review* 103, no. 1 (1998): 15–49.

11 Numan Kamil Bey, *Islamiyet ve Devlet-i Aliyye-i Osmaniye Hakkında Doğru bir Söz* (Istanbul: Tahir Bey Matbaasi, 1316 [1898–99]). For a current edition of the text, see Numan Kamil Bey, "Islamiyet ve Devlet-i Aliyye-i Osmaniye Hakkinda Doğru bir Söz: Cenevre'de Müteşrikin Kongresi'nde İrad Olunmuş bir Nutkun Tercümesidir," in *Hifet Risaleleri 1*, edited by Ismail Kara (Istanbul: Klasik Yayınları, 2002). For the French version of the paper presented at the congress, see Numan Kamil Bey, "Vérité sur l'Islamisme et l'Empire Ottoman," présentée au X. Congrès International des Orientalistes à Geneve (Paris: Imprimerie de Charles Noblet et Fils, 1894).

12 James Edward Ketelaar, *Of Heretics and Martyrs in Meiji Japan* (Princeton, NJ: Princeton University Press, 1990), 136–220; and Judith Snodgrass, *Presenting Japanese Buddhism to the West: Orientalism, Occidentalism, and the Columbian Exposition* (Chapel Hill: University of North Carolina Press, 2003).

13 Michael Burtscher, "Facing 'the West' on Philosophical Grounds: A View from the Pavilion of Subjectivity on Meiji Japan," *Comparative Studies of South Asia, Africa and the Middle East* 26, no. 3 (2006): 367–76.

14 Halil Halid, one of the most prolific pan-Islamic thinkers in Europe, consistently wrote in European papers about the issue of Islam and modernity and attended the 14th Orientalist Congress in Algeria in 1905; see S. Tanvir Wasti, "Halil Halid: Anti-Imperialist Muslim Intellectual," *Middle Eastern Studies* 29, no. 3 (1993): 559–79.

15 Stephen N. Hay, *Asian Ideas of East and West: Tagore and His Critics in Japan, China, and India* (Cambridge, MA: Harvard University Press, 1970). This Euro-American influence on pan-Asianism or pan-Islamism did not mean another form of Western influence on the East. Instead, the cross-fertilization of ideas in the global networks that spanned India, Japan, the United States, Europe, and the Middle East – appropriately termed a "global loop" by Richard Jaffe – is a better way of describing this phenomenon since European and American pessimists were influenced by highly articulate anti-colonial intellectuals from Asia. See Richard Jaffe, "Seeking Sakyamuni: Travel and the Reconstruction of Japanese Buddhism," *Journal of Japanese Studies* 30, no. 1 (2004): 65–96.

16 Halil Halid, *The Crescent versus the Cross* (London: Luzac, 1907).

17 Tokutomi Sohō (1863–1957) advocated the term "yellow man's burden," giving voice to an alternative to the idea of "the white man's burden" (based on Rudyard Kipling's famous poem of 1899); see Tokutomi Sohō, "Kōjin no omoni," *Kokumin Shimbun* (January 1906); see also Hirakawa Sukehiro, "Modernizing Japan in Comparative Perspective," *Comparative Studies of Culture* 26 (1987): 29.

18 Yamamuro Shinichi, "Ajia Ninshiki no Kijiku," in *Kindai Nihon no Ajia Ninshiki,* edited by Furuya Tetsuo and Yamamuro Shinichi (Kyoto: Kyoto University Press, 1994): 33–4.

19 Konoe Atsumaro's article, published in *Taiyō* in 1898, was titled "Dōjinshu Dōmei: Shina Mondai Kenkyû no Hitsuyō"; see Marius Jansen, "Konoe Atsumaro," in *The Chinese and the Japanese: Essays in Political and Cultural Interactions,* edited by Akira Iriye (Princeton, NJ: Princeton University Press, 1980), 113.

20 Ahmed Riza, *La faillite morale de la politique occidentale en Orient* (Tunis: Éditions Bouslama, 1979); Ahmed Riza and Ismayl Urbain, *Tolérance de l'islam* (Saint-Ouen, France: Centre Abaad, 1992).

21 Halil Halid, *Hilal ve Salib Münazaasi* (Cairo: Matbaai Hindiye, 1907): 185–8.

22 Robert John Holton, "Cosmopolitanism or Cosmopolitanisms? The Universal Races Congress of 1911," *Global Networks* 2, no. 2 (2002): 153–70. For a recent reassessment of the London Universal Races Congress of 1911, see the special Forum section in *Radical History Review* 92 (spring 2005): 92–132.

23 Cemil Aydın, "A Global Anti-Western Moment? The Russo-Japanese War, Decolonization and Asian Modernity," in *Competing Visions of World Order: Global Moments and Movements, 1880s–1930s,* edited by Sebastian Conrad and Dominic Sachsenmaier (New York: Palgrave Macmillan, 2007).

24 Nader Sohrabi, "Historicizing Revolutions: Constitutional Revolutions in the Ottoman Empire, Iran and Russia, 1905–1908," *American Journal of Sociology* 100, no. 6 (1995): 1383–447.

25 Ōkuma Shigenobu, *Tōzai Bunmei no Chōwa* (Tokyo: Waseda Daigaku Shuppansha, 1990).

26 Mustafa Aksakal, "Defending the Nation: The German-Ottoman Alliance of 1914 and the Ottoman Decision for War" (PhD diss., Princeton University, 2003).

27 For examples of the post–First World War pan-Islamic movement and its ideas, see S.M.H. Kidwai, *The Future of the Muslim Empire: Turkey* (London: Central Islamic Society, 1919); idem, *The Sword against Islam or a Defence of Islam's Standard-Bearers* (London: Central Islamic Society, 1919); and Gail Minault, *The Khilafat Movement: Religious Symbolism and Political Mobilization in India* (New York: Columbia University Press, 1982).

28 For an example of the dominance of this civilizational paradigm, see Hara Takashi, "Harmony between East and West," in *What Japan Thinks*, edited by K.K. Kawakami (New York: Macmillan, 1921).

29 Yamamura Shinichi, "Nihon Gaikō to Ajia Shugi no Kōsaku," *Seiji Gaku Nenpō* (1998), 26–7; taken from Tsurumi Yūsuke, *Gotō Shinpei*, 4 vols. (Tokyo: Keisō Shōbo, 1965–7), 960–1.

30 George Akita and Itō Takashi, "Yamagata Aritomo no 'jinshū kyōsōron," in *Nihon Gaikō no kiki ninshiki* (Tokyo: Yamakawa Shuppansha, 1985).

31 For example, Abdurreşid Ibrahim was able to meet Ōkuma Shigenobu, Itō Hirobumi, and other leading Japanese statesmen who were interested in this Muslim intellectual and pan-Islamist activist with connections to Russian, Ottoman, and Egyptian pan-Islamic circles. For the records of his conversation with Ōkuma in 1909, see Abdurreşid Ibrahim, *Alem-i Islam ve Japonya'da Intişari Islamiyet* (Istanbul, 1927), 386–7. For the roles of Gotō Shinpei and Inukai Tsuyoshi in helping an Indian revolutionary in Tokyo in 1917, see Tapan Mukherjee, *Taraknath Das: Life and Letters of a Revolutionary in Exile* (Calcutta: National Council of Education, Bengal, Jadavpur University, 1998), 109–10. For the attention that Vietnamese nationalist Phan Boi Chau received from Inukai and Ōkuma, see David Marr, *Vietnamese Anti-Colonialism* (Berkeley: University of California Press, 1971), 113.

32 Yamamuro Shinichi, "Nihon Gaikō to Ajia Shugi no Kōsaku," *Nenpō Seijigaku* (Tokyo: Iwanami Shoten, 1998), 26–7; taken from Tsurumi Yūsuke, *Gotō Shinpei*, 4 v. (Tokyo: Keisō Shōbo, 1965–7), 960–1.

33 Marr, *Vietnamese Anti-Colonialism*, 146, 154–5.

34 Miura Tōru, "Nihon no Chutō-Isuramu Kenkyū," *Gekkan Hyakka* 365
    (1993): 18–23. For Ōkuma Shigenobu's comments, see "Preface," in Evelyn
    Baring Cromer, *Saikin Ejiputo*, vol. 1 (Tokyo: Dainippon Bunmei Kyōkai,
    1911), 12–13. For a recent English language assessment of this topic, see
    Miura Tōru, "The Past and Present of Islamic and Middle Eastern Stud-
    ies in Japan: Using the *Bibliography of Islamic and Middle Eastern Studies in
    Japan 1868–1988*," *Annals of Japan Association for Middle East Studies* 17, no. 2
    (2002): 45–60.
35 Taraknath Das, *Is Japan a Menace to Asia?* (Shanghai, 1917); and idem [as
    An Asian Statesman], *The Isolation of Japan in World Politics* (Tokyo: Asiatic
    Association of Japan, 1918).
36 Naoko Shimazu, *Japan, Race and Equality: The Racial Equality Proposal of
    1919* (London: Routledge, 1998).
37 Mizuno Naoki, "Senkyūhyaku Nijū Nendai Nihon, Chōsen, Chūgoku
    ni okeru Ajia Ninshiki no Ichidaimen: Ajia Minzoku Kaigi o Meguru
    Sankoku no Ronchō," in *Kindai Nihon no Ajia Ninshiki*, edited by Furuya
    Tetsuo (Kyōto: Kyōto Daigaku Jinbun Kagaku Kenkyūjo, 1994).
38 Zumoto Motosada, *Japan and the Pan-Asiatic Movement* (Tokyo: Japan
    Times, 1926); the book is based on Motosada's lecture at the Congress of
    the International University in Geneva in 1926.
39 Ibid., 24–5.
40 Ibid., 4.
41 Sayadaw U. Ottama (1879–1939) was an influential figure in Burmese na-
    tionalism. Influenced by both the Indian National Congress and the Japa-
    nese model, Ottama denounced British colonial rule. He was imprisoned
    by the British authorities for a very long time, ultimately dying in prison.
    For Ōkawa's praise of Ottama, see Ōkawa Shūmei, "Ottama Hōshi o
    Omou," in *Ōkawa Shūmei Zenshū* [Collected Works of Ōkawa Shūmei],
    vol. 2, edited by Ōkawa Shūmei Zenshū Kankokai (Tokyo, 1961),
    913–15.
42 Selçuk Esenbel, "Japanese Interest in the Ottoman Empire," in *The Japanese
    and Europe: Images and Perceptions*, edited by Bert Edstrom (Surrey, UK:
    Curzon Press, 2000); El-Mostafa Rezrazi, "Pan-Asianism and the Japanese
    Islam: Hatano Uhō: From Espionage to Pan-Islamist Activity," *Annals of
    Japan Association for Middle East Studies* 12 (1997): 89–112.
43 Tanaka Ippei, a scholar of China and Buddhism, converted to Islam and
    adopted the name Haji Nur Muhammad in 1918 and performed pil-
    grimages to Mecca in 1925 and 1933. Wakabayashi nonetheless describes
    Tanaka Ippei as a fighter for "Sonnū Yūkoku," meaning "Revere the Em-
    peror and Be a Patriot."

44 His brother Wakabayashi Kyūman worked for the same cause, operating undercover as a merchant among Chinese Muslims until he died in Changsha in 1924. For Wakabayashi's reflections on the history of the Kokuryūkai circle of Islam policy advocates, see Wakabayashi Han, *Kaikyō Sekai to Nihon* (Tokyo: Wakabayashi Han, 1937), 1–3.

45 Ibid., 3–7. Araki Sadao (1877–1966) was a leader in the army's Imperial Way faction.

46 On 15 May 1932, Prime Minister Inukai Tsuyoshi was assassinated by a group of radical nationalist army cadets and naval officers. Ōkawa Shūmei was indicted, and found guilty, of providing material assistance to this group. Ōkawa's involvement in Inukai 's assassination is ironic, as pan-Asianists usually viewed Inukai positively and, at the 1926 Nagasaki Pan-Asiatic Conference, honoured him for aiding the cause of Asian people's awakening.

47 The journal was published from August 1939 to the end of the Pacific War.

48 Ōkawa Shūmei, *Shin Ajia* 1, no. 1 (1939): 2–3.

49 The content of *Shin Ajia* included many of Ōkawa Shūmei's arguments, given the close ties that had existed between Ōkawa and Bose since 1915. For example, his contribution to the September-October 1933 issue is very similar to Ōkawa's writings in *Fukkō Ajia no Shomondai* and *Ajia, Yoroppa to Nihon*.

50 *Yani Yapon Muhbiri* often contained didactic articles on the history, economy, and culture of Japan, and news about the Tatar Turkish diaspora living within the boundaries of the Japanese Empire. Since there was a large Tatar Muslim community in Manchuria, the journal included news about Manchukuo, the Manchu dynasty, and developments in China as well.

51 See Richard Storry, *The Double Patriots: A Study of Japanese Nationalism* (Boston: Houghton Mifflin, 1957), 149.

52 In fact, General Ishiwara Kanji's Tōa Renmei Kyōkai (East Asia League Association), founded in 1939, was also based on ideas advocated by Dai Ajia Kyōkai; see Mark Peattie, *Ishiwara Kanji and Japan's Confrontation with the West* (Princeton, NJ: Princeton University Press, 1975), 281–2.

53 Ōkawa Shūmei, "Gandhi wo Tō Shite Indojin ni Atau" and "Nehru o Tō Shite Indojin ni Atau," *Ōkawa Shūmei Zenshū* 2 [1942]: 925–38.

54 For some examples of the flood of publications on Okakura, see Kiyomi Rokurō, *Okakura Tenshin den* (Tokyo: Keizōsha, 1938); idem, *Senkakusha Okakura Tenshin* (Tokyo: Atoriesha, 1942); and Okakura Kakuzō, *Okakura Tenshin Zenshū* (Tokyo: Rikugeisha, 1939). See also Okakura Kakuzō, *Japan's Innate Virility: Selections from Okakura and Nitobe* (Tokyo: Hokuseido Press, 1943).

55 For examples of the publication and republication of books by Das, Paul Richard, and Ōkawa after the China War, see Taraknath Das, *Indo Doku-ritsu Ron* (Tokyo: Hakubunkan, 1944); and [Paul] Risharu, *Tsugu Nihon Koku*, translated by Ōkawa Shūmei (Tokyo: Seinen Shobō, 1941).

56 James Crowley, "Prewar Japanese Nationalism," in *Japan in Crisis: Essays on Taishō Democracy*, edited by Bernard Silberman and H.D. Harootunian (Princeton, NJ: Princeton University Press, 1974), 278–9.

57 Germaine Hoston's study of the writings of ideological conversion of Sano Manabu shows how his interest in Eastern spirituality and intellectual tradition and belief in Japanese exceptionalism fuelled his search for a Japanese context to adopt certain core ideals of Marxism; see Germaine A. Hoston, "Ikkoku Shakai-Shugi: Sano Manabu and the Limits of Marxism as Cultural Criticism," in *Culture and Identity: Japanese Intellectuals during the Interwar Years*, edited by J. Thomas Rimer (Princeton, NJ: Princeton University Press, 1990).

58 George Beckmann, "The Radical Left and the Failure of Communism," in *Dilemmas of Growth in Prewar Japan*, edited by James Morley (Princeton, NJ: Princeton University Press, 1971), 170.

4 Emperor, Family, and Modernity: The Passage of the 1940 National Eugenics Law

SUMIKO OTSUBO

The 1930s was a tumultuous decade in Japanese history, witnessing the steady erosion of electoral party control over the government and the military, brutal suppression of left-wing political groups, military adventurism in Asia, withdrawal from the League of Nations and from international arms control treaties, and domestic terrorism designed to destabilize the party government ... Advocates of reform, from militant terrorists to nativist intellectuals, felt threatened that "external pollution" would contaminate the very essence of indigenous culture and thus legitimized militant action.

– E. Taylor Atkins, *Blue Nippon*

In his analysis of jazz culture in Japan, historian Taylor Atkins summarizes many of the internal and external challenges Japan faced in the tumultuous decade from 1931 to 1941: "Japan versus the West, authentic traditionalism versus inauthentic modernism, group-ism versus individualism and spirituality versus sensuality. These are the polarized discursive categories that shaped Japanese conceptualizations of jazz and set the conditions by which the music was embraced or rejected."[1] In a similar vein, historian Carol Gluck has illuminated the coexistence of the pre-war orthodox ideology – which united modern Japan through such symbols as emperor, loyalty, village, and family state – and a wide range of heterodoxies that had formulations running from conservative to liberal, traditional to modern, and collective to individualistic. In Gluck's view, the orthodoxy rigidified in the 1930s through police enforcement of "spiritual mobilization" for war.[2] Like jazz – identified as quintessentially American – modern science was of Western origin, and both valued "originality" and "ingenuity."[3] But although jazz was deemed a symbol of moral decay and selfish individualism and banned as enemy music after Pearl Harbor, science – despite its foreign origins, power to modernize society, and implicit threat to the integrity of indigenous culture – enjoyed intensified support after the 1931 Manchurian Incident. The appropriation of Western science in the Japanese war effort came with tensions and contradictions.[4]

This chapter examines the debate over Japan's first eugenics statute in the Diet's lower house, where cultural tensions figured more prominently than in the upper house. Eugenics – coined by British scientist Francis Galton in 1883 – is the science of selective breeding to improve human genetic stock, adopted in the following decades by societies with different ideological, political, and economic goals.[5] Japan was one such nation: a sterilization law, enacted as the *Kokumin Yūsei-hō* (National Eugenics Law) in 1940, went into effect the following year. Rather than rejected as a scientific field of foreign origin, it appears that, in Japan, eugenics was officially endorsed.

Because the National Eugenics Law demonstrates Japan's search for an alternative identity – to resituate the nation in Asia and in the world "racially" – a domestic issue such as eugenics legislation matters in any exploration of aspects of Japan's "internationalism" between 1931 and 1941. The wartime regime seems to have extended its control not only over people's choice of music, but also over their sexuality and reproduction. The word for sterilization at the time, *danshu* (the severance of lineage), was an idea that obviously conflicted with the ideology of the Japanese *ie* (patriarchal family) system, which stressed the continuity of family lines and descent from imperial ancestors. The family system thus functioned to unite Japanese through the imagined link of common blood and helped generate a centripetal patriotism in which almost all Japanese rallied around the emperor and the state.

In 1940 Japan commemorated two thousand six hundred years of purportedly unbroken rule by the imperial family dynasty that began with the enthronement of Jinmu, the first emperor and descendant of divine *kami*, in 660 BCE. Many events, including the Olympic Summer Games in Tokyo (cancelled due to Japan's involvement in the conflict with China), were planned to celebrate the occasion.[6] Given the primacy of the nativist, traditionalist,[7] and religious ideology of wartime Japan, the official endorsement in 1940 of a law linked to the Western, modern, and rational science of eugenics is noteworthy.

In examining concepts of nature in Japanese political ideology, historian Julia Thomas challenges the influential rendering of modernity as the opposite of nature "in its celebration of denatured, liberated subjectivity and in its technological control of the physical environment."[8] This view reflects the classic binary relationship between nature (representing tradition) and science (representing modernity). Thomas also reveals a central tenet of Japan's leading intellectuals that "nature is the mark of traditional, conservative, if not right-wing ideals." In their formulation of nature and modernity, Japanese political theorists had to "choose between modernity and nature: nationhood could be founded by transcending nature and pre-modern political forms in alignment with 'the West,' or it could be rooted in references to nature and remain mired in traditional, indeed 'Oriental,' aesthetic, social, and political patterns."[9] Considering the promotion, not suppression, of science, however, the popular and influential dichotomies of "Japan versus the West," "authentic traditionalism versus inauthentic modernism," and "nature and science" did not reflect wartime realities.

As historian of science Hiromi Mizuno has shown, the discussion of science in a 1942 symposium on "Overcoming Modernity" was undoubtedly uneasy. According to Mizuno, the "modernity" of imperial Japan (1868–1945) was characterized by two conflicting desires: the hope to be recognized by the West as a modern, civilized nation, and an aspiration to build a national identity based on the Shinto creation myth, or the emperor-centred family state ideology. This "modernity" was difficult to maintain, as the universality of modern scientific knowledge would make local nationalist logic irrelevant.[10] To understand interwar and wartime "modernity" in Japan, Mizuno proposes a new concept she calls "scientific nationalism," defined as "a kind of nationalism [in which] science and technology are the most urgent and important assets for the integrity, survival, and progress of the nation."[11] The legislative debate on a eugenics law thus highlights the tensions between science and the national myth, and the arguments presented during the course of it help to provide insight into "modernity," science, nationalism, and empire at the end of this crucial decade in Japanese history.

A Brief History of Eugenics in Japan

Although medical experts, scientists, and educators began introducing the Western theory of race improvement into Japan in the late nineteenth century, these ideas did not circulate widely until 1920, when Hiratsuka Raichō, founder of the New Woman Association, began leading a legislative movement inspired by eugenics. Hiratsuka formulated a bill to restrict men infected with venereal diseases from marrying. Hiratsuka stressed the transgenerational aspect of the transmission of such infectious diseases and the urgent need to protect potential mothers to ensure the vitality of the Japanese race. Although the overtly gendered nature of the bill attracted media attention, the movement ultimately failed, but eugenics had now entered mainstream knowledge.[12]

Abortion and birth control activists also appropriated the language of eugenics in the 1920s, a decade when Japan faced numerous challenges, such as economic depression following the war, rapid population growth, passage of the 1924 U.S. immigration law excluding Japanese immigrants, and an international system that limited possibilities for emigration and colonial expansion. Japanese neo-Malthusians – who alarmingly predicted population growth would soon outstrip food supply in a limited land – promoted contraception to stop rising unemployment and falling living standards. Restricting reproduction, they argued, was an alternative to colonial expansion and emigration.

Proponents of birth control also emphasized that limiting births among the poor would improve the population's health.[13] In 1922, the leader of the American birth control movement, Margaret Sanger, was invited to Japan. The government tried to prevent her entry by accusing her of "harbor[ing] dangerous thoughts against national policies."[14] Conservatives opposed birth control out of fear of a deteriorating gene pool (only the middle class, with "desirable" genetic material, could afford it), fear of declining public morality from the separation of procreation and sex, and opposition to women's exercising control over reproduction through voluntary motherhood. These arguments were particularly bothersome for the Diet's upper house, the House of Peers, often considered the guardian of the Japanese patriarchal family system.[15] For conservatives, eugenics associated with birth control was just as unnerving as jazz.

Historian Fujime Yuki has observed that the Japanese birth control movement gained momentum after the unprecedented economic deprivation of the Showa depression (1930–32). At the same time, birth control lost much of its meaning as an alternative social policy with the 1931 Manchurian Incident, since Japanese imperialism created an outlet for excess population while the mass production of "fit" soldiers became an object of policy.[16] In 1930, Japan's leading advocate of eugenics, Nagai Hisomu (1867–1957), created *Minzoku Eisei Gakkai* (Japan Association for Race Hygiene); it became a *kyōkai* (foundation) in 1935. In its inaugural statement, the association criticized the neo-Malthusian birth control movement as a recipe for lowering the quality of the population. Inspired by the 1933 Nazi eugenic sterilization law, the Law for the Prevention of Genetically Diseased Offspring, lower house members Arakawa Gorō (sponsor of Hiratsuka's eugenic marriage restriction bills in the early 1920s) and Yagi Itsurō formulated their own *minzoku yūsei hogo hōan* (racial eugenic protection bills) and submitted them to the Diet in 1934, 1935, 1937, and twice in 1938.[17]

The beginning of full-fledged war with China in July 1937 fuelled official interest in eugenics legislation. The Ministry of Health and Welfare was established in January 1938 with encouragement from the military, which was concerned about the deteriorating physique of recent recruits and the declining birth rate.[18] The new sterilization bill, prepared by bureaucrats, medical experts, and some Diet members, was introduced in the Diet as a government proposal in 1940.[19] By then, eugenic measures, including sterilization and marriage consultation, linked to improving population in quality and quantity were advocated as necessary for victory in the war with China and Japan's survival in the world, and grew into a concern shared by many beyond an esoteric group of medical experts.[20]

Three things distinguished the 1940 bill from earlier ones. First, the government officially sponsored it.[21] Second, its proponents chose to use the new term *kokumin yūsei* (national eugenics) instead of the more familiar *minzoku yūsei* (racial eugenics),[22] although one should note the continuity within this change: both terms emphasized selfless groupism. Third, the 1940 eugenics bill, with its interest in improving population quantity as well as quality, was the first to incorporate pronatalism. In other words, the 1940 plan differed significantly from earlier eugenics bills in language and content that represented the state's commitment to produce a superior race to lead Japan's Asian empire. Japan's ideological, if not biological, search for "racial" identity became a tangible policy in 1940.

The Lower House Debate

On 8 March 1940, during the seventy-fifth session of the Diet, the Yonai Mitsumasa cabinet submitted the eugenics bill to the House of Representatives, and on 12 March it was presented to the lower house by the Minister of Health and Welfare, Yoshida Shigeru.[23] The main part of the bill read as follows:

NATIONAL EUGENICS BILL

ARTICLE 1

The purpose of this law shall be to ensure the improvement of the quality of nation (*kokumin soshitsu*) by means of preventing an increase in the [number of] persons with a predisposition toward malignant hereditary disease and promoting an increase in [the number of] persons who have sound constitutions.

ARTICLE 2

Under this law, "eugenic operations" shall be defined as operations or treatments to be prescribed by order that render reproduction impossible.

ARTICLE 3

When a person suffers from one of the following diseases, and medical experience [suggests] that there is a particularly marked danger that said person's children or descendants will suffer from the same disease, said person may undergo a eugenic operation in accordance with this law. However, these restrictions do not apply if said person is recognized, at the same time, to have a particularly excellent constitution.

    Item 1. Hereditary mental illness
    Item 2. Hereditary mental deficiency
    Item 3. Severe and malignant hereditary personality disorder
    Item 4. Severe and malignant hereditary physical ailment
    Item 5. Severe hereditary deformity

In cases where persons who are married to each other each have or had blood relatives within the fourth degree of consanguinity who suffer, or who suffered, from one of the diseases [listed] in the preceding paragraph, if medical experience [suggests] there is a particularly marked danger that future offspring will suffer from the same disease, [then] the preceding paragraph [applies]. (This includes [people who], even though they are not registered [as married], are married de facto.)

[In cases where] persons have or had children who suffer, or who suffered from one of the diseases [listed] in the first paragraph, if medical experience [suggests] the future offspring will suffer from the same disease, [then] the first paragraph applies.[24]

A unique feature of the bill was its voluntary compliance principle: a person who qualified could file an application for a eugenic operation (Article 4), although it required consent from a spouse (if the person was married or in a de facto marriage), or from a parent (if the person was twenty-five years old or younger). If a candidate was mentally incapacitated, a spouse or parent could apply on his or her behalf (Article 4). If a candidate had a severe and malignant hereditary personality disorder, a designated health professional could file an application on his or her behalf (Article 5). Involuntary sterilization could be imposed without consent of the person or his or her spouse or parent in the name of the public good (Article 6). Applications for eugenic operations, together with medical documents, including a report on heredity, were addressed to local governors (Article 7), who could then authorize an operation after examining the opinion of the local Eugenics Investigation Commission (Article 8). If anyone notified of the governor's decision objected, he or she could make a statement to the Minister of Health and Welfare (Article 9).

Article 14 was notable in that it justified abortion to supplement sterilization for women in the first three months of pregnancy. Article 16 prohibited operations or radiation procedures meant to render reproduction impossible without cause (unless eugenically necessary). Although Article 18 specified penalties for those who performed sterilization and abortion without cause, Article 19 stipulated sanctions for those who disclosed secrets they learnt in the course of performing their duties in eugenic operations.[25]

In his introduction to the debate, health and welfare minister Yoshida emphasized the purpose of the national eugenics bill was to improve the nation's quality. Although the superiority of the Japanese race was apparent by its history, he said, maintaining and improving *kokumin no yūshūsei* (national superiority) was necessary to carry out the great project of building Asia. The transmission of hereditary diseases would cause suffering to patients and their families as well as apprehension about national progress. Yoshida also anticipated an increase in the healthy population as a result of the law's restrictions on unnecessary sterilization and abortion.[26] He thus supported the bill on the grounds of national unity and to prepare for Japan's imperial expansion. Tacitly rejecting the country's follower position in the Western-dominated world, Yoshida articulated, in the language of science-based nationalism, the use of eugenics legislation to support Japan's leadership in Asia.

Muramatsu Hisayoshi, a member of the Rikken Minsei Party who had cosponsored the last racial eugenic protection bill with Yagi in the seventy-fourth Diet session (1938–9), welcomed the government bill. He pointed out, however, that sterilization was unnecessary if the purpose was population growth. He also wondered if knowledge of heredity diseases was advanced enough to judge which diseases were inherited and which could be categorized as severe and malignant. After noting that Japan was a nation built on the *ie* (family) system, he asked who would perform memorial services to the ancestors if a family line were unable to leave an heir. Sterilization thus could destroy the peculiarly Japanese spirit embodied in the family system. Muramatsu also noted that, as research on mental diseases progressed, some of them might become curable. Hence, the irreversibility of sterilization was a problem.[27]

Yoshida responded by claiming that genetics and eugenics would continue to progress, but that the hereditary nature of the diseases included in the bill was well known. On the sensitive topic of the family system, he maintained that those subject to eugenic operations would be limited in number whereas the continuity of the family line could be ensured through the Japanese tradition of adoption.[28] The solution received little attention, which suggested that its support was limited. As for a cure of hereditary illness, Yoshida argued that one might be treated in the future but defective genes nonetheless could be transmitted, and concluded that this was why the eugenics bill was needed.[29]

Upon listening to Yoshida's argument, Sowa Giichi of the Rikken Seiyūkai Party expressed his doubts about the bill. In his opinion, both positive and negative measures were needed to maximize the procreation of the fit and to minimize that of the unfit. He criticized the bill as a misnomer as it addressed only one negative measure, sterilization, rather than dealing with various eugenic measures comprehensively. Sowa found this discrepancy between the bill's name and its actual content highly problematic. The Japanese, he lamented, had always taken pride in reflecting the true content of a document in its name; the contemporary tendency to disregard the importance of "name" showed inconsistencies in national ideology. Sowa then shifted to moral and spiritual arguments by conflating the meaning of *na* (name) into *taigi meibun* (a great moral cause or one's duty to one's lord), as *mei* in *taigi meibun* contains the character representing "name,"[30] an argument that fellow parliamentarians applauded. Sowa wanted a more thorough eugenics program, one that would not go against *Nihon seishin* (the Japanese spirit).

Sowa also criticized the bill from the perspective of Japan as a family state. Since its origins could be traced back to a single source, members of the Japanese nation were all related; he thus opposed the hasty implementation of sterilization, as it would disregard the traditional Japanese respect for life. In the Japanese way of thinking, Sowa continued, children were gifts from family clan deities. If conceived and delivered without being aborted, contrary to the procedure specified by Article 14, even children with hereditary defects could become healthy. Despite being mocked by his colleagues – the moment of truth indicating that representatives were merely *pretending* to believe the myth – Sowa stated unapologetically that there was no denying the chance for children born into a family with malignant hereditary problems to purify themselves because they too were descended from the gods.[31] Sowa then linked sterilization with Judaism and identified (non-spiritual) modern medicine with the Jews. Sowa, in fact, reduced cultural tension between Japan and the West to tension between Japanese and Jews,[32] which opened the way to accept ethnically German medicine. Sowa's identity as a simple traditionalist in the aforementioned nature-modernity dichotomy is thus questionable.

Sowa then went on to lament the lack of spirituality among Japanese physicians, which he attributed to modern medical training that included the dissection of cadavers. Medical students thus did not see bodies as formerly alive human beings, the lords of all creation, and receptacles of the spirit. Sowa also urged the government to take steps to improve medical education by grounding it in spiritually oriented traditional Japanese beliefs. His view was a classic attack on modern materialistic science in the form of sterilization, which he saw as a threat to the integrity of Japanese spirituality, traditions, and family continuity.[33] But his argument was contradictory. While Sowa claimed Western materialism and Japanese spiritualism were "incompatible," he urged incorporating traditional spiritual elements into the existing curriculum.

Yoshida did not simply dismiss his arch-traditionalist colleague. In response to Sowa's concern over the difference between the name and actual content of the bill, Yoshida maintained that the plan represented both negative and positive eugenics; it ensured healthy people would have children by penalizing them for avoiding pregnancies through illegal sterilization or abortion. Improving the race by controlling non-hereditary diseases, he argued, was outside the purview of eugenics. Yoshida also stated that the law alone was insufficient to guarantee the future of the Japanese nation. He did not reject the notion that all Japanese had the same ancestors, which was part of *kokutai*, the fundamental character of the state. Rather than seeing sterilization as something damaging to the web of connections linking ancient ancestors to contemporary Japanese, Yoshida characterized it as a way to mend frayed spots in the web. In this way, the state ideology of the family and sterilization were compatible and would serve the same purpose of reinforcing the blood links of Japanese, past and present. As for Sowa's uneasiness about contemporary physicians untrained in the spiritual aspect of their discipline, Yoshida agreed that reform of medical education was desirable, but did not commit himself to any concrete plans.[34]

Next, Sugiyama Motojirō of the Socialist Party for the Masses took the floor. He opened his remarks in favour of the bill by glorifying Japan and its people, rejoicing that the nation was in year 2,600 of its imperial reign, a feat which could not have been possible without the superiority of the Yamato race. After referring to the war with China, Sugiyama outlined the need to cultivate human resources. Concerns about the quality and quantity of human resources were justified by the declining birth rate, high infant mortality, the growing number of mentally ill patients, and the rising number of young men unqualified for military service. Considering these alarming trends, Sugiyama felt compelled to support the bill. The emperor-centred family state ideology was thus not a monopoly of right-wing ideologues; representatives of the legal left likewise often supported eugenics, nationalism, and imperialism.

Sugiyama referred to the opinion of psychiatrists, according to whom the diseases targeted by the bill were passed on by recessive genes. Since a recessive gene was seen as a physical feature only if both parents had the same problematic gene and passed it on to their child, many carriers had no physical features to detect. Thus, if the state sterilized all feeble-minded persons and hereditary mental disease patients, their numbers would be halved only after fourteen generations. Many experts, including specialists of mental disorders, believed that sterilization was ineffective in ameliorating the general quality of the population.[35] Having emphasized the limits of sterilization alone, Sugiyama proposed measures against tuberculosis, alcoholism, venereal disease, and leprosy, pointing out that the bill did not cover alcoholism, which had been included in the 1933 Nazi sterilization law.[36] Sugiyama's references to psychiatrists' questioning the effectiveness of sterilization shows that the bill was criticized from opposite ends of the traditional-modern spectrum.

A representative with medical training, Tanaka Yōtatsu of the Tōhōkai Party, supported the aim of eliminating unnecessary diseases. Like Sowa, however, Tanaka believed that the law – if mishandled – could cause various tragedies involving the uniquely Japanese family system. He estimated it would take two thousand years to reduce the number of patients by 90 per cent, even if they were to sterilize the two hundred and fifty thousand people currently identified. Noting the costs and time necessary for reducing the number of mental patients through sterilization, Tanaka suggested raising the minimum age of alcohol consumption from twenty to twenty-five, as in the proposed youth alcohol prohibition (YAP) bill. This, he suggested, would be more effective and less expensive than sterilization in achieving their aims, since the most important cause for mental disease was alcoholism.[37] Both Sugiyama and Tanaka were pro-YAP and promoted the bill whenever possible. Minister Yoshida explained that they had removed alcoholism because the hereditary predisposition to alcoholism needed further investigation.[38]

In contrast to the previous speakers, Kitaura Keitarō formulated his questions from a legal perspective. Medical procedures to remove reproductive capabilities permanently would violate the *shintai no jiyū* (bodily freedoms) of *shinmin* (imperial subjects) and thus would be unconstitutional. He noted that official encouragement of eugenically sanctioned abortion grossly contradicted the 1880 Criminal Code, which had made abortion illegal.[39] To make it constitutional, a judge, rather than a local governor, would have to be given the power to authorize eugenic operations in the name of the emperor. Kitaura interpreted the Criminal Code – which penalized pregnant women who induced abortion – as a sign of a civilized nation as it assumed rights for infants and the need to protect fetuses (abortion and infanticide previously had not been considered illegal). He believed only *kamisama* (gods) knew whether offspring of deformed or mental patients would inherit defects. Legalizing sterilization and abortion on the assumption that they were hereditary, he said, was based on limited human knowledge and would signify a return to barbarism.[40] Kitaura thus clearly opposed the bill. He did not agree that sterilization was "modern" or that it could be justified using Enlightenment ideas such as individual rights and liberty. Instead, he characterized sterilization, abortion, and infanticide as pre-modern, uncivilized, and barbaric. Aligning himself with "modern" values, Kitaura criticized eugenics as an appalling tool that would bring back the dark past. But at the same time, he spoke of gods, the emperor, and imperial subjects.

Yoshida objected to the notion that the authorization of eugenic operations by local governors or the health minister was unconstitutional, as these decisions were not primarily legal in nature. He emphasized the fact that the bill was not designed to give unrestricted access to abortion. On the contrary, the law would make it extremely difficult to have an abortion without cause. By clearly defining reasons for exceptions, the law would remain in accordance with the abortion clause of the Criminal Code.[41] The speaker of the lower house then appointed eighteen representatives of the lower house to a committee to discuss the bill.[42]

The Lower House Committee Debate

The committee met for the first time on 13 March 1940 in the first of six meetings before returning the bill to the main floor eight days later. The members elected Yagi as chair.[43] Among the eighteen members, Yagi, Tanaka, Aoki, Nogata Jirō, Nakazaki Toshihide, and Nakazaki's replacement, Watanabe Ken, were physicians.[44] Government committee members included Ministry of Health and Welfare officials Hitotsubashi Sadayoshi (vice-minister), Takano Rokurō (Prevention Bureau Chief, bacteriologist), and Tokonami Tokuji (secretary). Discussion gained momentum at the fifth meeting, where officials from the Ministry of Health and Welfare, the Ministry of Justice, and the Ministry of Education, as well as health and welfare minister Yoshida, were present.[45] Issues concerning the family system, the appropriateness of irreversible sterilization in the context of incomplete knowledge, race improvement measures to control such non-infectious diseases as tuberculosis, venereal disease, and leprosy, the secrecy clause denying public access to sterilization information, and abortion were all examined in detail by the committee.[46]

On 14 March, at the second meeting, traditionalist representative Sowa reiterated his view that discontinuities in family lineage would be a national misfortune. Unlike other countries, Japan was blessed with an unbroken line linking *Tenshisama* (His Imperial Highness) to his subjects, a continuity inseparable from the fundamental national character. Sowa asked how one could judge whether patients were untreatable, noting again the limitations of modern medicine. Modern medicine, even assuming progress, would remain incapable of treating hereditary mental diseases listed in the proposed law because it did not take into account the human spirit.[47] Sowa suggested taking *Kōkan* medicine and religious faith seriously if one wanted to avoid further spiritual erosion; he criticized current education, which dismissed Shinto and Buddhist prayers as superstitious and uncritically privileged Western medicine.[48]

Sowa stated that Japan needed to develop uniquely Japanese academic theories. He believed that health could be attained by praying to *kami* (Shinto deities) and Buddha. He told a story about someone whose eye malady was cured through prayers to *Fudō Myōō*, a Buddhist deity, even though Western medical doctors had deemed the illness incurable. He also attributed the rise of the new religion Tenrikyō to its miraculous healing powers.[49] Sowa argued that Japanese had inherited from their ancestors the common "blood" in their bodies as well as "the way of thinking" in their spirits. According to conventional wisdom, bodies and spirits together constituted individuals; the separation of body and mind was a foreign idea. Traditionally, mental diseases were considered to be physical manifestations that occurred when the spiritual part of humans was corrupted, perverted, and weakened. Sowa thus reduced the national eugenics bill to a Western import, as he believed it failed to reflect the Japanese way of thinking.[50]

In response, Takano contended they had no intention of contradicting the imperial way. He objected, however, to Sowa's assertion that modern medicine was foreign to Japan. Takano argued that the Japanese had internalized German and other European medical knowledge and made it their own. He wanted Sowa and others to understand that they had written the national eugenics bill to benefit *kokka* (the state) and that their efforts were anchored in current Japanese medicine and conditions. Takano thus incorporated modern medicine as part of Japanese nationalism. He also frankly noted that the government was not planning to seek the help of *kami* or Buddha in treating mentally ill patients – that the bill did not incorporate religion.[51]

Sowa then asked Takano if a predisposition to mental disease existed in ancient Japan or whether it came from abroad and subsequent intermarriage.[52] Takano first apologized for his limited knowledge of the history of mental disease in Japan; he acknowledged that the phenomenon of *monokurui* (derangement) had been documented in historical records.[53] He suspected that the number of mental patients was increasing because medicine (including medical documentation and statistics) had progressed and more diseases were being identified and more cases recorded, while social changes associated with rapid industrialization and urbanization were probably conducive to the eruption of mental disorders. Takano stressed he did not doubt the superiority of the Japanese race, which he presumed had comparatively fewer defects caused by genetic mutations. However, mutations occurred in all population groups, even among superior races. The objective of the proposed law was to reduce the number of people with hereditary defects, no matter how small their number.[54]

Diet member Tanaka Yōtatsu then questioned the "Japaneseness" of the statistical data on which the bill was based. He implied the need for statistical data based on studies of the Yamato race to develop a truly national sterilization law.[55]

In the fourth meeting, Yamakawa Yorisaburō inquired about the application procedure for spouses, parents, and other family members when a candidate for a eugenic operation was incapable of applying himself or herself (Article 4).[56] Japan was founded on the principle of *chūkō* (loyalty and filial piety), which separated it from other (Western) countries. Although filial piety was expected from children towards their parents. Yamakawa argued that parents, too, were expected to have *zettai ai* (absolute love) towards children and grandchildren. This love was part of Japanese tradition. Applications by parents for eugenic operations thus would run counter to the country's moral sense, considering the ways of human beings, *kami*, and Buddha.[57]

In response, Yoshida affirmed the importance of love between spouses, and between parents and children, contending that true love encompassed *kanjō* (feeling) and *richi* (intellect).[58] He believed that the intellectual part of love would enable parents to make the difficult but right decision to apply for eugenic operations for their mentally incapable sons and daughters. Thus, parental love did not contradict the nation's family system.[59]

Nakano Torakichi from the First Diet Members Club – known as *Ban Tora* (Barbaric Tiger) for his characteristically loud agitation[60] – observed that the essence of the family system was embodied in the patrilineal imperial succession system described in the second article of the Meiji Constitution. While members of the imperial household maintained the family system, it would be inappropriate for imperial subjects not to emulate the imperial model. If the bill was passed, some imperial subjects would be unable to follow the imperial way, which would erode the fundamental principle of the nation.[61] Health vice-minister Hitotsumatsu declared that the bill was not intended to destroy the family system. Although Hitotsumatsu believed that the blood of the imperial family was indeed superior and inviolable, he did not think the second article of the Constitution and the proposed sterilization law contradicted each other. After Nakano asserted that Hitotsumatsu's double standards for ruler and ruled were deceptive, Hitotsumatsu said he would rather avoid reference to the imperial family – historian Tsuda Sōkichi previously had found the origins of the imperial family as described in Japan's earliest written texts to be a fabrication, and ultra-nationalists in that Diet session had accused him of affronting the dignity of the imperial family, and the memory of such attacks directed at such leading intellectuals as Takikawa Yukitoki, Minobe Tatsukichi, and Kawai Eijirō was still fresh.

In the fifth meeting, Yamakawa Yorisaburō called attention to the arbitrariness of allowing abortion in the first three months of pregnancy. Mobilizing his knowledge of psychology, Shinto, and Buddhism, he concluded that, once conceived, a fetus possessed the spirit and constituted a full-fledged human mind.[62] Like Yamakawa, Tokonami Tokuji felt it difficult to justify abortion regardless of a fetus's age. He added that the eugenics law was designed to tighten restrictions on abortion precisely because the state valued life. Here he argued for the compatibility of science and nature. He also explained that the border between three and four months came from the existing law governing medical practitioners. When midwives brought dead fetuses to the world, they were obliged to report only suspicious cases and those in which the dead fetus was more than four months old.[63]

While health ministry officials were defensive in front of Diet members' comments implying the proposed law would violate uniquely Japanese values and traditions, bureaucrats and representatives sometimes agreed that tradition and eugenics were congruous. In the fourth meeting, lower house member Itō Iwao of the Rikken Seiyūkai Party discussed Japan's tradition of premarital investigations to screen for tuberculosis, leprosy, and mental diseases in the lineage of the prospective bride or bridegroom. If any were detected, marriages were often cancelled, thus limiting procreation of the unfit.[64] Prevention Bureau Chief Takano was pleased to hear of this link between Japanese custom

and eugenics. He noted that the state was considering the establishment of marriage consultation centres throughout Japan to promote eugenic marriages in addition to eugenic sterilization.[65]

Throughout these parliamentary procedures, officials maintained
patience and politeness when handling questions on sensitive subjects
at the heart of ultranationalist ideology. At the same time, they adhered
to the notion that the proposed legislation was nothing more than a
sensible way to control the reproduction of those suffering from medically proven hereditary diseases.[66] On a number of occasions, Diet committee members demanded the government expand the bill's definition
of eugenics to include, in line with most previous eugenics bills, measures against non-hereditary diseases such as tuberculosis and venereal
disease.[67] Representative Tanaka once again expressed the need to add
alcoholism to the diseases listed in the proposed plan because the presumably superior German sterilization law had included it.

Takano, courteous as usual, affirmed the importance of campaigns
against non-hereditary diseases, but held that many of the factors causing alcoholism were environmental; it was therefore unnecessary to address alcoholism in a law designed to control hereditary diseases. He
did acknowledge, however, the possibility of an inherited predisposition to alcoholism and that there was room for further study. Thus,
Takano successfully defended the government's position of excluding
alcoholism – the bill would be based on the scientific theory of inheritance. His defence also highlighted local conditions since, compared to
other countries, Japan had only a small number of malignant alcoholic
patients. If the deliberate omission of alcoholism illustrated an application of science to a peculiar local condition, there were contrasting examples elsewhere.

Leprosy was central in the discussion of race improvement measures concerning non-genetic diseases. In the second meeting, Tanaka
asked what legal justifications existed for sterilizing lepers quarantined
in treatment centres.[68] Tokonami explained that the current Criminal
Code made abortion illegal, but that it did not mention sterilization.
Sterilization could be a crime-incurring act, although such factors as
voluntary application and public well-being might preclude the sterilization of lepers from being seen as a crime. Tokonami also stated that
"eugenic operations" on lepers could not be justified once the national
eugenics bill was enacted, and thus he expressed the need to create a
new legal framework that would allow such operations.[69] Even though
Tokonami used the term "eugenic," his senior colleague Takano immediately rejected this usage. The sterilization of lepers could not be

included in the proposed law because leprosy was non-hereditary. Takano explained that the government was concurrently proposing a bill to revise the Leprosy Prevention Law.[70]

Takano's argument based on strict genetic principles thus gave way when justifying the sterilization of lepers.[71] Apparently, the separate law legalizing sterilization of the genetically healthy and fit contradicted the spirit of strict geneticism and pronatalist eugenics promoted by the Ministry of Health and Welfare. Leprosy traditionally had been known as *Tenkei-byō* (the disease of punishment by heaven),[72] and the number of patients was proof of the backwardness of Japanese medicine and social policy and the unfitness of the Japanese race. In short, leprosy was a national disgrace. The disease had been believed to be hereditary and families with lepers had been discriminated against regardless of individual health. One estimate had fifteen thousand lepers in Japan as opposed to seven or eight thousand in Germany, while Britain reportedly had stamped it out altogether.[73] The contradiction of legalizing the sterilization of patients with infectious leprosy was further attacked by Tanaka, Yamakawa Yorisaburō, and Tsuchiya Seisaburō, a medically trained representative allowed to participate in the discussion by the committee chair.[74]

After five meetings of intense deliberation, the committee met briefly for the last time on 20 March, when Ehara Saburō introduced a revised bill. Major changes included the age limit for spousal or parental consent in Article 4, which now read: "if the said ... child has not reached thirty [originally twenty-five] years of age," thus empowering the patriarchal family system by extending the length of parental control over sons and daughters. Article 14 on abortion was deleted, a major victory for proponents of the emperor and family continuity. A new Article 17 required a person who had undergone a eugenic operation to notify his or her prospective spouse upon request,[75] which ensured a way to find out if a prospective spouse had been legally sterilized, made the sterilization law less threatening to the family system, and addressed concerns about the problematic secrecy principle. These revisions were important compromises to appease opponents of the bill. But eugenic sterilization for mental patients, the core of the proposal, was untouched and remained a threat to the preservation of family state ideology.

Positive comments on the revised bill followed from Yamakawa, Sugiyama, and Nakano. The latter stated that, in the spirit of *shinwa* (affinity), he would abstain from commenting on many of the things he wanted to address. He commended medical bureaucrat Takano

Rokurō's heroic defence of the bill and compared his courage to that of a soldier on the battlefront. He also acknowledged Yagi's persistent efforts on behalf of various eugenic sterilization bills. Nakano was also impressed by the performances of Minister Yoshida and his deputy Hitotsumatsu; his approval was based on *ninjō* (human feelings) and *riron* (theory). Yet he also asked the authorities to deal with the law cautiously.

There were no objections to Ehara's revisions.[76] Nonetheless, the vote was astonishing. Despite intense criticism and reservations expressed by representatives in previous committee deliberations, the committee voted *unanimously* to approve the revisions.[77]

A small, unexpected controversy then arose. After the vote, Sugiyama, who was still in favour of the youth alcohol prohibition bill, made a motion to require the government to create a credible agency to determine whether eugenic operations were necessary for malignant alcoholics. The motion was met by harsh criticism. "Barbaric Tiger" Nakano told Sugiyama not to ruin the congenial atmosphere of the committee by ramming through this amendment to advance his personal agenda.[78] Yamakawa also denounced Sugiyama's motion as a dirty trick. Noticing the quick approval by Hitotsumatsu – who confirmed that Yoshida would be willing to accommodate this amendment – Yamakawa suggested both that Sugiyama's motion had been planted and that questionable negotiations had gone on between the government and lower house members. Hitotsumatsu denied the allegation, while Sugiyama justified his actions. Committee chair Yagi then called for a vote; the amendment was approved, but not unanimously, as tensions between Sugiyama, Nakano, and Yamakawa reflected their stance on the YAP bill.[79]

Following this startling and anticlimactic committee decision, the revised bill made it to the main floor of the lower house the same day. Although the bill was not on the agenda, an emergency motion enabled Muramatsu Hisayoshi to present it along with the committee's amendment. Without any questions or comments, the lower house approved the revised bill.[80] It was then forwarded to the upper house, the supposed guardian of the Japanese patriarchal family system.[81]

Passage of the National Eugenics Law: The House of Peers

Two days later, health and welfare minister Yoshida presented the revised bill to the House of Peers.[82] Dr Takebe Tongo, a sociologist who had published a book on eugenics in 1932, expressed doubts about the law's effectiveness and criticized the underdeveloped nature of the hereditary theories on which it was based. After Yoshida's response, the speaker appointed fifteen peers to a committee to discuss the bill. Four days later, on 26 March, the last day of the seventy-fifth session,[83] the speaker of the upper house suddenly added the national eugenics bill to the agenda and began discussing it.

The upper house committee chair, Viscount Nomura Masuzō, explained that the committee had voted in favour of the bill and summarized its deliberations. He said the bill incorporated elements unparalleled in comparable laws, including the non-compulsory application of the system, which would circumvent possible human rights abuses, and the omission of alcoholism and sexual perversity contained in the German law. He referred to the government's plan to develop pronouncedly Japanese eugenic measures that would be more than rehashes of foreign precedents, based on local health conditions, data, and research.[84] After Nomura's summary of the committee discussion, Takebe again voiced his disapproval, pointing to Japan's traditional respect for *keitō seimei* (the intergenerational transmission of life). Although he drew attention to the discrepancy between the bill and the *keitō seimei* view, this scholarly neologism, which replaced the family system in his analysis, drew limited emotional response from other peers.

In the end, the bill was passed by a majority vote.[85] Despite the upper house's well-known role as the champion of the family system, discussion on the subject, both at the committee and main floor levels, was unexpectedly limited. In the end, unlike the ill-fated racial eugenic protection bills submitted by lower house members in the 1930s, the national eugenics bill received approval from both houses even though many perceived it to compromise family state ideology. It is ironic that, in the two thousand six hundredth year of the imperial family's reign, the Diet would pass a law legitimizing the severance of certain family lines.

Making Sense of Cultural Tensions during the Late 1930s

Why did Japan's lower house give its unanimous approval to the National Eugenics Law in March 1940? What does that say about cultural tensions in Japan in the tumultuous decade of the 1930s, when the empire was trying to find a new role for itself in the world?

The parliamentary discussion on the national eugenics bill raises many questions. What happened to the lower house committee? Why were members arguing over the appropriateness of an amendment motion instead of fighting to protect the national essence embodied in the family system? Why were they able to form a united front for the approval of the revised bill despite deep-seated animosities – a front that fractured over the much less contentious issue of alcoholism? Why did even the obstinate traditionalist Sowa approve the final bill?

The House of Representatives debate seems to answer these questions. Several factors point to the bill's approval being arranged prior to the vote. First, the bill was sponsored by the government and, as such, it had privileged status compared that of earlier private members' bills; for example, the Yagi bill of 1939 had been endorsed by the lower house but was then shelved by the upper house. Given these precedents, it was hardly puzzling but almost predictable that the lower house would sanction the bill. Its *unanimous* support, however, is baffling. Yamakawa had repeatedly proclaimed his staunch opposition,[86] and he, "Barbaric Tiger" Nakano, Sowa, and Tanaka were vocal critics during the parliamentary discussions. When the lower house committee approved the revised bill, Nakano inferred the government had made a deal with the socialist Sugiyama Motojirō. Considering Nakano's unusual emphasis on maintaining a friendly mood and spirit of affinity, it is quite possible that there were prior contacts from bureaucrats to help appease the more entrenched opponents.

Then what prompted "Barbaric Tiger" and his colleagues accept the bill? I suspect government concessions in the revisions presented by Ehara Saburō. The government likely told the reluctant committee members that the bill, however compromised, needed to pass as it was the crown jewel of the projects sponsored by the newly formed Ministry of Health and Welfare. More specifically, the National Eugenics Law would be the *raison d'être* of the ministry's Prevention Bureau.[87] The abrupt introduction of the prepackaged revisions – possibly prepared by the bureaucrats themselves – and lack of discussion in the committee also point to a deal between the bureaucracy and certain members of the Diet.[88] The emergency motion on 20 March that brought the bill back to the main floor of the lower house further supports the view that government backing led to its approval.

It would be a simplification to conclude that the passage of the National Eugenics Law was a triumph of the scientific over the spiritual. Modified to reflect family state ideology, it served as the cornerstone of Japan's new population policy. The plan for the Greater East Asia Co-Prosperity Sphere, which included much of Southeast Asia, was unveiled in August 1940. In January of the following year, the Konoe government announced the *Jinkō Seisaku Kakuritsu Yōkō* (Outline to Establish Population Policies), and made eugenics instrumental in envisioning an alternative international order. The Outline argued that it was the mission of *kōkoku* (the imperial nation) to develop the population of Japan proper in both quantity and quality to help build the Co-Prosperity Sphere, just as it was the duty of the leading race to provide military and labour power for the new *kokubō kokka* (national defence–oriented state). The National Eugenics Law thus upheld a worldview based on family and race, and the dissemination of eugenics ideas through implementation of the law was an important means to improve the population's quality, mentally as well as physically.[89]

Contrary to its ideological significance, the law's impact on Japan's biological reconstruction was extremely limited. Altogether, 538 eugenic operations were performed between 1941 and 1948, while Nazi Germany sterilized nearly four hundred thousand people under its Law for the Prevention of Genetically Diseased Offspring.[90] Perhaps the Japanese family state ideology took the teeth out of the bill.

In sum, the logics supporting the passage of the 1940 National Eugenics Law were seen as a manifestation of Japan's wartime modernity, albeit a conflation of various cultural elements. Despite obvious tensions, the scientific/"modern"/universal and the spiritual/traditional/local were not always mutually exclusive in this legislative attempt to apply science to society. Thus, I argue that the orthodoxy of emperor and family state was essential to the passage of the law. Its supporters overcame eugenics' earlier reputation as premature knowledge, not through progress in research but with traditionalist nationalism. Many doubtful critics would not have voted in its favour had it not been for the sense of urgency arising from the prolonged war with China, imminent conflict with Anglo-America, the deteriorating physique of military recruits, the declining birth rate, the establishment of the Ministry of Health and Welfare, and heightened loyalty towards the emperor. Japan's challenge to the international order was both the context for, and the result of, the passage of the 1940 National Eugenics Law.

Parliamentary deliberations on the eugenics bill constituted an unexpectedly liberal, democratic, (and thereby "modern") process at a time when intellectual freedoms were being restricted. Jazz, too, was about to be banned. Various lawmakers upheld the protection of individuals, including infants and fetuses, from potential abuses, employing such concepts as bodily freedom and human rights. At the same time,

Diet members employed the traditionalist notion of the family system to weaken the repressive nature of the bill – involuntary application and abortion. It is extraordinary that both modern Enlightenment ideas and the traditionalist family system, often associated with authoritarian control, served to help defend the "modern" value of individual liberty. Despite policing and indoctrination, heterodoxies survived in the legislative debate on eugenics well into March 1940. It is ironic that the bill's passage seems to have indicated their death. But it is naive to assume that many Japanese with modern values believed in liberalism; rather, they simply wanted compromise. They accepted eugenics because it justified the national quest to become Asia's leading race, but few believed that eugenics would result in actual biological reconstruction. Their solution was to separate the name from the content by proposing and passing the watered-down law.

Even when emperor and family state orthodoxy gained momentum, a ban on Western science was never advocated in the legislative debate on eugenics. Instead, parliamentarians and bureaucrats promoted a nationalistic vision of eugenics founded on uniquely Japanese patterns. Consider, for example, Japan's smaller proportion of mental patients, sexual perverts, and alcoholics, and greater number of lepers than in the "model" case of Germany. In the legislative debate, participants emphasized local statistical data and local research (traditional and spiritual remedies for mental diseases) within the framework of "modern," universal, scientific research methods. Clearly, there was no easy "either-or choice" between the modern and the traditional, science and nature, or rationalism and spiritualism. On the same note, there was no "either-or choice" between collectivism and individualism or things Western and things Japanese. In order to understand these ambivalences contained in imperial Japan's modernity, Hiromi Mizuno's concept of "scientific nationalism," a strain of nationalism in which science and technology served as highly effective tools for the integrity, survival, and progress of the nation, is useful. However, the "compromised" nature of the passage and application of the National Eugenics Law complicates the picture further as "science" was beneficial in perceived empire building ideologically but not biologically.

NOTES

Earlier versions of this chapter were presented at the University of Minnesota in April 2006, at the History of Science Society Conference, Vancouver, in November 2006, and at the University of California, Los Angeles, in May 2009. I am grateful for comments received at all three. I am also indebted to Masato Kimura, Tosh Minohara, and the anonymous reviewers for their helpful suggestions.

1 E. Taylor Atkins, *Blue Nippon: Authenticating Jazz in Japan* (Durham, NC: Duke University Press, 2001), 119–20. The introductory quote is from page 113.

2 Carol Gluck, *Japan's Modern Myths: Ideology in the Late Meiji Period* (Princeton, NJ: Princeton University Press, 1985), 275–86.

3 See Shigeo Sugiyama, *Nihon no kindai kagakushi* (Tokyo: Asakura Shoten, 1986), 184–6.

4 Regarding the mobilization of science and technology between 1930 and 1945, see Nihon Kagakushi Gakkai, ed., *Nihon kagaku gijutsu-shi taikei*, vol. 4 (Tokyo: Dai-ichi Hōki Shuppan, 1966). Science historian Hitoshige Tetsu considered the 1932 establishment of the Japanese Society for the Promotion of Science (JSPS) epoch-making in modernizing scientific research that could respond to the economic and military needs of the state. See his *Kagaku to rekishi* (Tokyo: Misuzu Shobō, 1965), 147–84, especially 156. Wartime activities of Japanese scientific research organizations, including the JSPS, were a subject of post-war U.S. Occupation investigations. See "Science and Technology in Japan: Scientific and Technological Societies of Japan, Part I," Report 10 (Tokyo: General Headquarters, Supreme Commander for the Allied Powers, Economic and Scientific Section, 1947).

5 See, for example, Frank Dikötter, "Race Culture: Recent Perspectives on the History of Eugenics," *American Historical Review* 103, no. 2 (1998): 467–78.

6 About the cancelled 1940 Olympic Games, see Masaru Hatano, *Tokyo Orinpikku e no harukana michi: Shōchi katsudō no kiseki 1930–1964* (Tokyo: Sōshisha, 2004), especially chap. 2.

7 "Traditionalism" is defined as belief in the importance of traditions and customs. In this chapter, I describe individuals who glorified certain ideas and customs as "traditions" even if they were in fact invented in the modern era. Regarding the concept and examples of invented tradition, see Eric J. Hobsbawm and Terence O. Ranger, eds., *The Invention of Tradition* (Cambridge: Cambridge University Press, 1983); and Stephen Vlastos, ed., *Mirrors of Modernity: Invented Traditions of Modern Japan* (Berkeley: University of California Press, 1998).

8 Julia Adeney Thomas, *Reconfiguring Modernity: Concepts of Nature in Japanese Political Ideology* (Berkeley: University of California Press, 2001), ix.

9 Ibid., ix–x, 2–3, 181–2. See also Kevin M. Doak, "Under the Banner of the New Science: History, Science, and the Problem of Particularity in

Early Twentieth-Century Japan," *Philosophy East and West* 48, no. 2 (1998): 232–56.

10   Hiromi Mizuno, *Science for the Empire: Scientific Nationalism in Modern Japan* (Stanford, CA: Stanford University Press, 2009), 2.

11   Ibid., 12, 180–4.

12   Sumiko Otsubo, "Engendering Eugenics: Feminists and Marriage Restriction Legislation in the 1920s," in *Gendering Modern Japanese History*, edited by Barbara Molony and Kathleen Uno (Cambridge, MA: Harvard University Asia Center, 2005).

13   Fujime Yuki, "Senkanki Nihon no sanji chōsetsu undō to sono shisō," *Rekishi hyōron* 430 (1986): 79–100, especially 88.

14   Ishizaki Shōko, "Seishoku no jiyū to sanji chōsetsu undō: Hiratsuka Raichō to Yamamoto Senji," *Rekishi hyōron* 503 (1992): 92–107, especially 96.

15   Ibid., 97.

16   Fujime, "Senkanki Nihon no sanji chōsetsu undō," 89–90.

17   See these bills in "Minzoku yūsei hogo hō-an," in *Dai rokujūgo-kai Teikoku Gikai Giin Teishutsu Hōritsu-an Daijūgo-gō*, 27 January 1934; "Minzoku yūsei hogo hō-an," in *Dai rokujūnana-kai Teikoku Gikai Giin Teishutsu Hōritsu-an Daiyonjūgo-gō*, 9 February 1935; "Minzoku yūsei hogo hō-an," in *Dai nanajukkai Teikoku Gikai Giin Teishutsu Hōritsu-an Dainijūkyū-gō*, 4 March 1937; "Minzoku yūsei hogo hō-an," in *Dai nanajūsan-kai Teikoku Gikai Giin Teishutsu Hōritsu-an Daisan-gō*, 25 January 1938; and "Minzoku yūsei hogo hō-an," in *Dai nanajūyon-kai Teikoku Gikai Giin Teishutsu Hōritsu-an Daiichi-gō*, 27 December 1938. Yōko Matsubara, "Minzoku yūsei hogo hō-an to Nihon no yūsei-hō no keifu," *Kagakushi kenkyū* 201 (1997): 42–50, especially 46.

18   See "Kōsei-shō no hossoku," in *Nihon kagaku gijutsu-shi taikei*, vol. 25, edited by Nihon Kagakushi Gakkai (Tokyo: Dai-ichi Hōki Shuppan, 1966), 172–9. Yuehtsen Juliette Chung points out that both Chinese and Japanese eugenicists perceived the Sino-Japanese War (1937–45) as a war of population and race; see "Eugenics in the Second Sino-Japanese War and Population Policies," in her *Struggle for National Survival: Eugenics in Sino-Japanese Contexts, 1896–1945* (New York: Routledge, 2002), chap. 5.

19   See "Kokumin yūsei hō-an," in *Dai nanajūgo-kai Teikoku Gikai Seifu Teishutsu Hōritsu-an Daikyūjūgo-gō*, 8 March 1940. Concerning this process, see Kiyoshi Hiroshima, "Gendai Nihon jinkō seisaku-shi shōron (2): Kokumin yūsei-hō ni okeru jinkō no shitsu seisaku to ryō saisaku," *Jinkō mondai kenkyū* 160 (1981): 61–77, especially 62–3. Matsubara Yōko examines the formation of the National Eugenics Law in her "Senji-ki Nihon no danshu seisaku," *Nenpō: Kagaku, gijutsu, shakai* 7 (1998): 87–109.

20 Sumiko Otsubo, "Feminist Maternal Eugenics in Wartime Japan," *US-Japan Women's Journal* (English Supplement) 17 (1999): 39–76. See also Jennifer Robertson, "Japan's First Cyborg? Miss Nippon, Eugenics, and Wartime Technologies of Beauty, Body, and Blood," *Body and Society* 7, no. 1 (2001): 1–34; and idem, "Biopower: Blood, Kinship, and Eugenic Marriage," in *A Companion to the Anthropology of Japan*, edited by Jennifer Robertson (Malden, MA: Blackwell, 2005).

21 These are called *giin rippō* (private members' bills). The marginalization of such bills was reflected in a comment by Yagi in which he discusses his eugenics bill at a lower house committee in 1939. Until then only twelve or thirteen out of several thousands of private bills submitted since the opening of the Diet in 1890 had been passed. See "Dai-nanajūyonkai Teikoku Gikai Shūgiin minzoku hogo hōan iinkai giroku (sokki), dai-nikai," *Teikoku Gikai Shūgiin iinkai giroku*, microfilm reel 31 (1939; Kyoto: Rinsen Shoten, 1990), 368.

22 According to a publication by the Prevention Bureau of the Ministry of Health and Welfare in March 1941, *kokumin yūsei* was a neologism that was in frequent use at the time. The term, combining *minzoku eisei* (race hygiene) and *yūseigaku* (eugenics), referred to a national eugenics. Here, there was no explanation why *minzoku yūsei* was not used. This absence of elaboration seems to suggest that, at least for the people who drafted the bill, *Nihon kokumin* (Japanese nationals) and *Nihon minzoku* (Japanese race) largely overlapped. The terms *minzoku eisei* and *yūseigaku* were not considered adequate. Although *minzoku eisei* was too comprehensive in covering various aspects of hygiene, "eugenics" sounded too individualistic and was not imagined to be an ideology for the nation as a whole. See Koseishō Yobō-kyoku, *Yobō eisei ni kansuru hōki oyobi reiki, fu sankō shiryō* (Tokyo: Koseishō Yobō-kyoku, 1941), 101; reprinted in *Sei to seishoku no jinken mondai shiryō shūsei*, vol. 20, *Yūsei to jinkō seisaku-hen 6 (1940–41 nen)* (Tokyo: Fuji Shuppan, 2001), 117–233, especially 146. For a careful analysis of *kokumin* and *minzoku*, see Kevin M. Doak, "What Is a Nation and Who Belongs? National Narratives and the Ethnic Imagination in Twentieth-Century Japan," *American Historical Review* 102, no. 2 (1997), 283–309.

23 "Dai-nanajūgokai Teikoku Gikai Shūgiin giji sokki-roku, dai-nijūgo-gō," *Teikoku Gikai gijiroku Shūgiin dai-nanajūgokai, 1939–40*, microfilm reel 76 (1940; Tokyo: Yūshōdō, 1984), 575, 577–9.

24 Ibid., 577–9. This translation of the bill is modified from Tiana Norgren's translation of the National Eugenics Law in her *Abortion before Birth Control: The Politics of Reproduction in Postwar Japan* (Princeton, NJ: Princeton

University Press, 2001), 140–5. In addition to making adjustments for revisions made to the original bill, the notable difference is that, while Norgren translates *kokumin soshitsu* as "the national character," I render the term as "the quality of nation."

25   "Dai-nanajūgokai Teikoku Gikai Shūgiin giji sokki-roku, dai-nijūgo-gō," 577–9.

26   Ibid., 579.

27   Ibid., 579–81, especially 581.

28   Concerning adoption practices to ensure family continuity, see Satomi Kurosu and Emiko Ochiai, "Adoption as an Heirship Strategy under Demographic Constraints: A Case from Nineteenth-century Japan," *Journal of Family History* 20, no. 3 (1995): 261–88.

29   "Dai-nanajūgokai Teikoku Gikai Shūgiin giji sokki-roku, dai-nijūgo-gō," 581–3.

30   A similar point was made in the upper house later; see "Dai-nanajūgokai Teikoku Gikai Kizokuin Kokumin yūsei-hō tokubetsu iinkai giji sokkiroku, dai-ni-gō," *Teikoku Gikai Sangiin Iinkai Giroku*, 6.

31   I would like to point out that this usage of "purity" to indicate a "disease-free" condition is typical in the Diet discussion, which was primarily concerned with *kokumin*, or the Japanese nation in Japan proper. The rarity of references to "impurity" caused by cross-ethnic miscegenation within the Greater East Asia Co-Prosperity Sphere was also a notable feature. For another example of purity/impurity, note Yagi Itsurō's formulation: "impurifying blood by inheritance of mental diseases (*ketsueki o nigosareru*)"; see "Dai-nanajūgokai Teikoku Gikai Shūgiin kokumin yūsei hogo hōan iinkai giroku (sokki), dai-yonkai," *Teikoku Gikai Shūgiin iinkai giroku*, microfilm reel 35 (1940; Kyoto: Rinsen Shoten, 1990), 785. In the same committee meeting, Itō Iwao identified the objective of the national eugenics bill as "*Nihon no minzoku no jōka*" (the purification of the Japanese race) and the increase of the healthy population; see 775.

32   "Dai-nanajūgokai Teikoku Gikai Shūgiin giji sokki-roku, dai-nijūgo-gō," 583–4. Despite the military alliance with Germany, Japan had an official policy of protecting Jewish refugees who had escaped to the Japanese concession in Shanghai, in order to maintain the inflow of foreign capital and better relations with the United States. See "Yudaya-jin kyūsai iinkai," in *Shōwa: Niman-nichi no zen kiroku*, vol. 5, *Ichioku no "shin-taisei" Shōwa 13 nen-15 nen* (Tokyo: Kōdansha, 1989), 189. In Jeffrey Herf's list of cultural binaries, while "German" is put together with "soul" and "life" in one category, "Jew" is classified with "mind" and "death" in the opposite category. See the chart in his *Reactionary Modernism: Technocracy, Culture, and Politics in*

Weimar and the Third Reich (Cambridge: Cambridge University Press, 1984), 226–7. Although the nativist desire to produce Japanese knowledge is clearly observable in the Diet proceedings, explicit hostility to foreign science was fairly limited – U.S. scientific data were not dismissed, for example. See Nogata Jirō's remark in "Dai-nanajūgokai Teikoku Gikai Shūgiin kokumin yūsei hogo hōan iinkai giroku (sokki), dai-sankai," *Teikoku Gikai Shūgiin iinkai giroku*, microfilm reel 35 (1940; Kyoto: Rinsen Shoten, 1990), 769; and Sowa Giichi's comment in "Dai-nanajūgokai Teikoku Gikai Shūgiin kokumin yūsei hogo hōan iinkai giroku (sokki), dai-gokai," *Teikoku Gikai Shūgiin iinkai giroku*, microfilm reel 35 (1940; Kyoto: Rinsen Shoten, 1990), 796. Within the general tone of respect for the sophisticated level of German medicine, however, I must point out that, during the fourth committee meeting, medical parliamentarian Tsuchiya Seisaburō criticized sterilization as an example of the German abuse of science to achieve the extermination of the Jews. Considering the timing (March 1940), when there was pressure to align with Germany, as well as the prevailing general esteem of Germany as the centre of medical research, this remark was quite striking. See "Dai-nanajūgokai Teikoku Gikai Shūgiin kokumin yūsei hogo hōan iinkai giroku (sokki), dai-yonkai," 787.

33 "Dai-nanajūgokai Teikoku Gikai Shūgiin giji sokki-roku, dai-nijūgo-gō," 584.
34 Ibid., 584–5.
35 About various objections expressed by psychiatrists at the time, see Matsubara Yōko, "Senji-ka no danshu-hō ronsō: Seishinka-i no Kokumin Yūsei-hō hihan," *Gendai shisō* 26, no. 2 (1998): 286–303.
36 "Dai-nanajūgokai Teikoku Gikai Shūgiin giji sokki-roku, dai-nijūgo-gō," 585–7.
37 Ibid., 588–90.
38 Ibid., 590–1.
39 See Ishizaki Shōko, "Nihon no dataizai no seiritsu," *Rekishi hyōron* 571 (1997): 53–70.
40 "Dai-nanajūgokai Teikoku Gikai Shūgiin giji sokki-roku, dai-nijūgo-gō," 591–3.
41 Ibid., 593.
42 "Dai-nanajūgokai Teikoku Gikai Shūgiin giji sokki-roku, dai-nijūroku-gō," *Teikoku Gikai gijiroku Shūgiin dai-nanajūgokai, 1939–40*, microfilm reel 76 [1940] (Tokyo: Yūshōdō, 1984), 595; and "Dai-nanajūgokai Teikoku Gikai Shūgiin kokumin yūsei hogo hōan iinkai giroku (sokki), dai-nikai," *Teikoku Gikai Shūgiin iinkai giroku*, microfilm reel 35 [1940] (Kyoto: Rinsen Shoten, 1990), 742.

43 Ibid. The committee was made up of Yagi Itsurō, Muramatsu Hisayoshi, Itō Tōichirō, Izumi Kunisaburō (replaced by Ehara Saburō after the second meeting), Nakano Torakichi, Aoki Ryōkan, Shida Giemon, Nakazaki Toshihide (replaced by Watanabe Ken after the fifth meeting), Nogata Jirō, Yamakawa Yorisaburō, Sowa Giichi, Sekō Kōichi, Sugiyama Motojirō, Tanaka Yōtatsu, Miura Torao, Ōta Masataka, Nishida Ikuhei, and Itō Iwao.

44 Biographical information on lower house representatives can be found in Shūgiin Sangiin ed., *Gikai seido hyakunenshi*, vol. 10, *Shūgiin giin meikan* (Tokyo: Ōkura-shō Insatsukyoku, 1989).

45 "Dai-nanajūgokai Teikoku Gikai Shūgiin kokumin yūsei hogo hōan iinkai giroku (sokki), dai-yonkai," 770.

46 See Muramatsu Hisayoshi's summary in "Dai-nanajūgokai Teikoku Gikai Shūgiin giji sokki-roku, dai-sanjū-gō," *Teikoku Gikai gijiroku Shūgiin dai-nanajūgokai, 1939–40*, microfilm reel 76 (1940; Tokyo: Yūshōdō, 1984), 720–1.

47 "Dai-nanajūgokai Teikoku Gikai Shūgiin kokumin yūsei hogo hōan iinkai giroku (sokki), dai-nikai," 745–6.

48 Ibid., 746.

49 Similar examples of religious healing, including that of a new religion, Seichō no ie (the family of growth), were discussed during Representative Nakano Torakichi's question session in the fourth committee meeting. Seichō no ie, characterized by the unity of all religions and the authority of the emperor, was established in 1929 by Taniguchi Masaharu based on Shinto teachings. Like Sowa, Nakano felt that these religious healings made sense because they approached mental diseases not only from a materialist perspective, but also from a spiritual one. See "Dai-nanajūgokai Teikoku Gikai Shūgiin kokumin yūsei hogo hōan iinkai giroku (sokki), dai-yonkai," 784.

50 "Dai-nanajūgokai Teikoku Gikai Shūgiin kokumin yūsei hogo hōan iinkai giroku (sokki), dai-nikai," 746–7. This Japanese medical cosmology was influenced by Chinese medicine; see Ishida Hidemi, *Kokoro to karada: Chūgoku kodai ni okeru shintai no shisō* (Fukuoka: Chūgoku Shoten, 1995), especially chap. 5.

51 "Dai-nanajūgokai Teikoku Gikai Shūgiin kokumin yūsei hogo hōan iinkai giroku (sokki), dai-nikai," 747.

52 Ibid.

53 According to psychiatrist Kaneko Junji, the terms *monokurui, monokurui yamai*, and *monokuruwashi*, which mean mental diseases, are found in such historical documents as *Wamyō ruijushō* (931–7); Tanba Masatada (1021–88), *Shin'ihō*; Tachibana no Tadakane, ed., *Iroha-ji ruishō* (1163–5); Kajiwara

Seizen, *Risai ban'anpō* (1315); and Byōin shinan (1695). See Kaneko Junji,
ed., *Kure Shūzō hakushi no shōgai to sono kōgyō, Nihon seishinbyō gaku shoshi
Edo izen hen, Edo hen* (Tokyo: Nihon Seishinbyō Kyōkai, 1965), 67–140.
54 "Dai-nanajūgokai Teikoku Gikai Shūgiin kokumin yūsei hogo hōan iinkai
giroku (sokki), dai-nikai," 747.
55 Ibid., 749.
56 "Dai-nanajūgokai Teikoku Gikai Shūgiin kokumin yūsei hogo hōan iinkai
giroku (sokki), dai-yonkai," 779.
57 Ibid.
58 In Jeffrey Herf's conceptual opposites, "feeling" is categorized under "culture and technology" together with "blood," "life," "community," "German," and "sacrifice," while "intellect" is categorized under "civilization
and economy" together with "money," "death," "Jew," "America and Russia," and "self-interest"; see his list in his *Reactionary Modernism*, 226–7.
59 "Dai-nanajūgokai Teikoku Gikai Shūgiin kokumin yūsei hogo hōan iinkai
giroku (sokki), dai-yonkai," 779.
60 Katō Junji, *Miseinensha inshu kinshu-hō o tsukutta hito: Nemoto Shō-den* (Nagano: Ginga Shobō, 1995), 185.
61 "Dai-nanajūgokai Teikoku Gikai Shūgiin kokumin yūsei hogo hōan iinkai
giroku (sokki), dai-yonkai," 783.
62 "Dai-nanajūgokai Teikoku Gikai Shūgiin kokumin yūsei hogo hōan iinkai
giroku (sokki), dai-gokai," 796. It is interesting that he referred to monste-
rologist Inoue Enryō's Buddhist study, *Kensei katsuron*, to legitimize his
theory of mind. Inoue's ideas, including monsterology, are discussed extensively in Gerald Figal, *Civilization and Monsters: Spirits of Modernity in
Meiji Japan* (Durham, NC: Duke University Press, 1999).
63 "Dai-nanajūgokai Teikoku Gikai Shūgiin kokumin yūsei hogo hōan iinkai
giroku (sokki), dai-gokai," 796.
64 "Dai-nanajūgokai Teikoku Gikai Shūgiin kokumin yūsei hogo hōan iinkai
giroku (sokki), dai-yonkai," 775. Although Itō claimed that the pre-marital
investigation was "traditional," this was probably a class- and time-spe-
cific tradition.
65 "Dai-nanajūgokai Teikoku Gikai Shūgiin kokumin yūsei hogo hōan iinkai
giroku (sokki), dai-yonkai," 775. Regarding eugenic marriage in Japan, see
Otsubo, "Feminist Maternal Eugenics in Wartime Japan"; and Robertson,
"Biopower."
66 "Dai-nanajūgokai Teikoku Gikai Shūgiin kokumin yūsei hogo hōan iinkai
giroku (sokki), dai-gokai," 789.
67 Improving the environment and disseminating information to ameliorate
race is called "euthenics." Matsubara Yōko defines eugenics as including

euthenics measures and concerns as an expanded, as opposed to restricted, eugenics, which focuses on strictly genetic diseases. See her "Minzoku yūsei hogo hōan to Nihon no yūsei-hō no keifu," *Kagakushi kenkyū* 201 (1997): 42–50.

68 "Dai-nanajūgokai Teikoku Gikai Shūgiin kokumin yūsei hogo hōan iinkai giroku (sokki), dai-nikai," 751.

69 Ibid.

70 Ibid., 752. The seventy-fifth Diet session ended before members finished discussing this leprosy bill. Nevertheless, sterilization of lepers continued after the National Eugenics Law began to be implemented the following year. The eugenic operation was justified as cases with cause; see Fujino Yutaka, *Nihon fashizumu to iryō: Hansen-byō o meguru jisshō-teki kenkyū* (Tokyo: Iwanami Shoten, 1993), 249–50.

71 "Dai-nanajūgokai Teikoku Gikai Shūgiin kokumin yūsei hogo hōan iinkai giroku (sokki), dai-nikai," 752.

72 "Dai-nanajūgokai Teikoku Gikai Shūgiin kokumin yūsei hogo hōan iinkai giroku (sokki), dai-sankai," 769.

73 "Dai-nanajūgokai Teikoku Gikai Kizokuin giji sokkiroku dai-nijūhachi-gō," *Teikoku Gikai Gijiroku Kizokuin Dai-nanajūgokai 1939–1940,* microfilm reel 75 (1940; Tokyo: Yūshōdō, 1984), 742. This is from the speech by Shimomura Hiroshi.

74 Comments by Tanaka and Sugiyama can be found in "Dai-nanajūgokai Teikoku Gikai Shūgiin kokumin yūsei hogo hōan iinkai giroku (sokki), dai-sankai," 768–9. Tsuchiya's view can be found in "Dai-nanajūgokai Teikoku Gikai Shūgiin kokumin yūsei hogo hōan iinkai giroku (sokki), dai-yonkai," 787–8, and "Dai-gokai," 791–2.

75 "Dai-nanajūgokai Teikoku Gikai Shūgiin kokumin yūsei hogo hōan iinkai giroku (sokki), dai-rokkai," *Teikoku Gikai Shūgiin iinkai giroku,* microfilm reel 35 [1940] (Kyoto: Rinsen Shoten, 1990), 799.

76 Ibid., 799–800.

77 Ibid. Of the eighteen committee members, all but Shida Giemon (Rikken Minseitō Party) attended the sixth meeting.

78 About the connection between Nemoto's legislative efforts and eugenics, see Sumiko Otsubo, "Toward a Common Eugenic Goal: Christian Social Reformers and the Medical Authorities in Meiji and Taisho Japan," *Kōnan Daigaku Sōgō Kenkyūjo sōsho* 86 (2006), 43–86.

79 Regarding Nakano's proposal against the bill (submitted to the lower house on 9 February 1939), see "Dai-nanajūgokai Teikoku Gikai Shūgiin giji sokki-roku, dai-jūichi-gō," *Teikoku Gikai gijiroku Shūgiin dai-nanajūgokai, 1939–40,* microfilm reel 76 [1940] (Tokyo: Yūshōdō, 1984),

183; regarding Sugiyama's proposal in favour of it (submitted on 15 February), see "Dai-nanajūgokai Teikoku Gikai Shūgiin giji sokki-roku, dai-jūyon-gō," *Teikoku Gikai gijiroku Shūgiin dai-nanajūgokai, 1939–40*, microfilm reel 76 [1940] (Tokyo: Yūshōdō, 1984), 251; and for Yamakawa's proposal against it (submitted on 21 February), see "Dai-nanajūgokai Teikoku Gikai Shūgiin giji sokki-roku, dai-jūgo-gō," *Teikoku Gikai gijiroku Shūgiin dai-nanajūgokai, 1939–40*, microfilm reel 76 [1940] (Tokyo: Yūshōdō, 1984), 299.

80 "Dai-nanajūgokai Teikoku Gikai Shūgiin giji sokki-roku, dai-sanjūgo-gō," *Teikoku Gikai gijiroku Shūgiin dai-nanajūgokai, 1939–40*, microfilm reel 76 [1940] (Tokyo: Yūshōdō, 1984), 719–21.

81 "Dai-nanajūgokai Teikoku Gikai Kizokuin giji sokkiroku dai-nijūyon-gō," *Teikoku Gikai Gijiroku Kizokuin Dai-nanajūgokai 1939–1940*, microfilm reel 75 [1940] (Tokyo: Yūshōdō, 1984), 327.

82 Ibid.

83 Hidehisa Ōyama, "Teikoku gikai no un'ei to kaigiroku o megutte," *Refarensu* (May 2005), 32–50, especially 48.

84 The committee discussion on this point can be found in "Dai-nanajūgokai Teikoku Gikai Kizokuin Kokumin yūsei-hō tokubetsu iinkai giji sokkiroku, dai-ni-gō," 11–12, and "Dai-nanajūgokai Teikoku Gikai Kizokuin Kokumin yūsei-hō tokubetsu iinkai giji sokkiroku, dai-san-gō," *Teikoku Gikai Sangiin Iinkai Giroku*, 1–5.

85 "Dai-nanajūgokai Teikoku Gikai Kizokuin giji sokkiroku dai-nijūhachi-gō," 424–31.

86 Regarding Yamakawa's opinions, see "Dai-nanajūyonkai Teikoku Gikai Shūgiin giji sokki-roku, dai-nijūroku-gō," *Teikoku Gikai gijiroku Shūgiin dai-nanajūyonkai, 1938–39* (17 March 1939), 609–10. For a summary of the 1939 Yagi plan, see Matsubara, "Minzoku yūsei hogo hōan to Nihon no yūsei-hō no keifu," 44.

87 Yoshida Shigeru stated that, in general, eugenics policies, including those beyond the proposed bill, encompassed every facet of the Ministry of Health and Welfare's affairs; see "Dai-nanajūgokai Teikoku Gikai Kizokuin Kokumin yūsei-hō tokubetsu iinkai giji sokkiroku, dai-san-gō," 1. Issues related to the implementation of the National Eugenics Law were the most important responsibilities of the Prevention Bureau; see Koseishō Yobō-kyoku, *Yobō eisei ni kansuru hōki oyobi reiki*, 381.

88 Contrary to the abrupt introduction of the revisions in 1940, the lower house committee had discussed revising the racial eugenics protection bill point by point in its fourth meeting the previous year; see "Dai-nanajūyonkai Teikoku Gikai Shūgiin minzoku hogo hōan iinkai giroku

(sokki), dai-yonkai," *Teikoku Gikai Shūgiin iinkai giroku*, microfilm reel 31 [1939] (Kyoto: Rinsen Shoten, 1990), 379–82.

89 "Jinkō seisaku kakuritsu yōkō," in *Sei to seishoku no jinken mondai shiryō shūsei*, vol. 20, 114–16.

90 Yutaka Fujino, *Nihon fashizumu to yūsei shisō* (Kyoto: Kamogawa Shuppan, 1998), 368; and Robert N. Proctor, *Racial Hygiene: Medicine under the Nazis* (Cambridge, MA: Harvard University Press, 1988), 108.

PART TWO

The Empire and Imperial Concerns

5 Strengthening and Expanding Japan through Social Work in Colonial Taiwan

EVAN DAWLEY

In 1940, while the Second Sino-Japanese War dragged on, a Japanese official within the Taiwan Government-General published a 1,200 page tome on the history of social work in Taiwan. The weighty volume culminated in a section describing how Japan altered the nature and method of these undertakings after it had liberated and reformed (*kairei*) the island. A vice-minister of the Imperial Household, Baron Shirane Matsusuke juxtaposed social work with the war in China and the establishment of a *shin chitsujo* (new order) throughout East Asia. In his introduction to the volume, he wrote that the system of social work in Taiwan had been developed to strengthen the Japanese Empire and to prepare for imperial expansion across Asia.[1] Japan's leaders saw social work as a tool for internal assimilation and the incorporation and transformation of new regions into Japanese territory.

Since the mid-nineteenth century, the international system had been characterized by the predominance of Western nation-states in diplomacy, trade, intellectual developments, and cultural production. For decades, Britain, France, the United States, and others had exerted primary control over global events through their colonial and mercantile empires, and even as they turned away from the rhetoric of empire after the First World War, these nations retained the balance of power. After the Meiji Restoration, Japan's leaders decided to join this system, forging Japan into a modern nation-state with its own regional empire. Around the turn of the twentieth century, Japan became the first nation located entirely within Asia to enter the upper ranks of the global hierarchy. However, as suggested by the naval agreements at Washington (1922) and London (1930), as well as by the exclusion of Japanese immigrants by legislation in the United States (1924), Japan was a junior partner.[2]

The sort of thinking displayed by Baron Shirane epitomized Japan's two-phase challenge to local societies and the international system in the 1930s.[3] Early in the decade, policies in Taiwan suggested an emphasis on strengthening the empire from within through greater state involvement in managing society and in assimilating non-Japanese subjects. The challenge reached a new phase in 1937, when it shifted from a primary focus on internal strengthening and reform to external expansion. Now Japan sought to establish a new world order with itself in the top rank, the unquestioned leader in Asia. In Taiwan, as well as in Korea (see Jun Uchida's chapter in this volume), wartime developments in Japan's colonies were an integral part of the larger challenge to the international system. Both stages represented variations on internationalism, as Japan made use of common modern techniques in achieving its goals, but the latter's focus on overthrowing the existing order marked a shift. Social work was a key part of the expanding state control that defined both phases of Japan's challenge.[4]

The Setting

The geographic focus of this chapter is the port of Jilong (Keelung, or Kiirun during the colonial period), a small city on the northern coast of Taiwan. Although both the Dutch and Spanish attempted to establish colonial outposts there in the seventeenth century and the Qing Dynasty incorporated Taiwan into its territory in 1684, Jilong remained thinly settled and rarely used for trade until the late nineteenth century. Nearby deposits of coal and its proximity to tea- and camphor-producing regions in the northern part of the island prompted Jilong's opening as a Chinese treaty port in 1863, but this had little impact on the settlement.

It was only after Japan gained sovereignty over Taiwan in the settlement of the First Sino-Japanese War (1894–5) that Jilong's fortunes began to change. To rule over and develop its first colony, Japan needed a port to bring people and materials to the island and to ship out commodities such as sugar and rice. Jilong had the best natural harbour in northern Taiwan and faced the Japanese home islands, while late Qing efforts at modernization had provided it with a rail link to the nearby capital of Taibei. These factors made Jilong the obvious choice, and within a decade it was the island's most important port, a modern city complete with plumbing, electricity, and telephone lines. The population increased from under ten thousand to more than one hundred thousand, roughly 25 to 30 per cent of whom were Japanese settlers. This dramatic physical and demographic transformation meant that Jilong was a locus for just the sorts of social ills that social work aimed to cure, and is a perfect place to examine how social work was connected to Japanese empire building and expansion in the 1930s.

Social Work in Global Perspective

What is social work? Where did it come from? How, and why, did it arrive and develop in colonial Taiwan? The answers to these questions are important to understand how social work contributed to the internal and external expansion of the Japanese Empire.

Social work emerged out of prior traditions of social welfare in the United States and Europe in the late nineteenth and early twentieth centuries. In a recent book on social work in the United States, Daniel Walkowitz argues that the term described a more scientific and professional way of giving aid to the needy. The first social workers were mostly middle-class white women who performed social survey research and administered aid to predominantly lower-class African-Americans and southern European migrants. By the 1920s the most common social worker was the case-worker who dealt with clients on an individual basis. From the beginning, social work had transformative impulses in that it aimed to alter its subjects' lifestyles, and it was scientific in the sense that it relied upon careful, often clinical, observation of social conditions and detailed planning for resolving problems. Funding for social work came either from private donations or, particularly after 1920, from public sources, although the state refrained from legally managing the practice until the middle of the twentieth century.[5]

During the Meiji Era, Japanese looked to Europe and the United States for many of their models. Social work was no exception. The emphasis on social surveys and the scientific outlook that differentiated *shakai jigyō* (social work) from more traditional *shakai kyūsai* or *shakai fukushi* (social welfare) were adopted from abroad, though characteristics that reflected Japan's historical legacy remained. As described by Sheldon Garon, social welfare during the Tokugawa period had developed a hierarchy of assistance in which the state gave aid to people who could not be helped by family members or their neighbours. Although some large-scale aid programs existed in cities, projects that pushed thrift, self-reliance, and mutual assistance – such as one developed by rural reformer Ninomiya Sontoku in the early nineteenth century – were more common. These basic traits persisted into the Meiji Era and beyond as the state did everything it could to maximize managerial control and minimize expenses, relying primarily on local actors and moral suasion rather than on direct economic aid. According to Garon, "Japanese style welfare was to be administratively simple, strongly didactic, relatively immune from taxpayers' opposition to public assistance, and embedded in the traditional relationship between the benevolent ruler and his subject."[6] Although these native traditions persisted, Japan adapted them to modern international standards.

Modern social work developed in Japan during the 1910s, when the state increased its funding and the approach became more scientific in its use of surveys and regularization of assistance. Male volunteers continued to do most of the work, in contrast to the United States, where it was a predominantly female profession.[7] The form of social work Japan exported to the colonies stressed state oversight along with reliance on private institutions and mostly non-professional social workers to develop local solutions. The tacit formula was moral assistance whenever possible and material assistance when necessary. Japanese bureaucrats did most of the planning, but at the local level both Japanese and Taiwanese designed and implemented programs.

Traditions of social welfare existed in Taiwan during the pre-colonial period; colonial-era sources emphasize that mostly ad hoc institutions were organized on the basis of *hankan hanmin* (half-official, half-private) initiatives. These institutions dealt with a wide range of issues, including aid to infants, children, and the aged, and provided for public burial grounds and defence against bandits. In addition, a number of organizations cared for vagrants and aided travellers who became sick or died while in Taiwan.[8] Despite the dismissive tone of colonial-era observers, the practice of social welfare in Qing Taiwan was not unlike that which existed in early Meiji Japan. This similarity might help to explain why indigenous residents of Taiwan[9] became active participants in the institutionalization of social work in the 1920s and 1930s. Regardless of this similarity, Japanese made social work an important part of their empire-building project to transform Taiwan and the Taiwanese in the 1930s.

The Early Colonial Period

From the first decade of Japanese rule in Taiwan, colonial officials included social welfare projects and legislation in their plans to reform and control Taiwanese society. The most important figure in establishing the early structure of state-initiated welfare was Gotō Shinpei, who became head of the Civil Administration in 1898 under Governor-General Kodama Gentarō. Gotō arrived in Taiwan with plans to transform the island into a model colony. He had previously studied social policy in Germany, and in the early 1890s had led a movement to reform Japan's 1874 *Jukkyū kisoku* (Relief Regulations) to increase state aid, especially to the working poor. Although that effort had failed, he was able to implement similar measures in Taiwan. In 1899 he imported the existing Relief Regulations from the home islands and issued them in modified form as the *Taiwan kyōmin kyūjo kisoku* (Taiwan Poor Relief Code). Alterations included an expanded age range, standardization of the amount of aid given, and the funding of aid through taxes and levies rather than through donations alone.[10]

At the same time, Gotō and Kodama reopened a number of pre-colonial health care institutions to address disease and related obstacles to colonization.[11] They began with a large *jikei in* (clinic) in Taibei and then re-established six other clinics, one in each of the colony's prefectures. Thereafter, the state re-authorized a number of other social welfare institutions around the island and began promoting the founding of new institutions through public and private initiatives. In the following months and years, the Government-General issued laws to regularize disaster relief, assistance to travellers, aid to veterans, and youth reformatories.[12] Beginning in 1901, the Government-General used imperial donations to establish *onshi zaidan* (imperial benevolence foundations) to provide financial support to local and island-wide institutions.[13]

Together, these laws and institutions established both a framework for social welfare and a pattern for state involvement that would prevail in the later colonial period. Prior to 1920, social work did not exist in Taiwan or on a large scale in Japan; even so, these early acts and institutions marked a major shift towards the regular provision of assistance. As the hand of the state was relatively light and the nature of these welfare projects beneficial, there was little resistance among Taiwanese to this particular instance of colonial reform and control. These early successes in social welfare thus paved the way for the creation and growth of a full-blown system of social work in the 1920s and 1930s.

The Social Work System

Although the Government-General created the basic framework for an extensive and intensive system of modern social work in the 1920s, it was not until the following decade that it began to threaten Taiwanese social and cultural patterns. The importation of social work followed closely on the heels of developments in Japan, where economic and social changes brought on by the war in Europe had led to the reformation of social welfare and the flourishing of new social work institutions as well as new bureaucratic structures to oversee, guide, and coordinate their activities.[14]

In 1921 Governor-General Den Kenjirō issued an edict for the promotion of social work to address emerging social problems in Taiwan. He called for a survey of social conditions and a major reform of the existing practice of social welfare. More important, he mandated the establishment of new institutions to offer medical assistance, provide aid and education for children, reform existing markets, help people find jobs, construct or provide inexpensive or even free lodging, encourage the observance of official holidays, and establish public baths and pawnshops. Den had in mind a centralized hierarchy similar to the bureaucracy already in existence in the colony.[15] In implementation, however, the new system relied on the efforts of local organizations and companies to relieve the burden on the state.[16] In practice, and to an extent in conception, the early system of social work was a partnership between the state and private initiatives.

Later in the decade, private social workers joined bureaucrats to create two umbrella institutions to improve and coordinate operations throughout the island. First came *Shakai jigyō taikai* (the Social Work Conference, SWC), founded in 1928, which almost immediately established *Shakai jigyō kyōkai* (the Social Work Association, SWA) in commemoration of the second anniversary of the Showa emperor's assumption of the throne. Both the SWC and SWA facilitated the spread of information and provided leadership for conducting research and surveys on social conditions throughout Taiwan.[17] Almost from its inception, the SWA began to publish the monthly journal *Shakai jigyō no tomo*, which connected social workers around the colony and increased the reach and impact of the system.[18] Both umbrella organizations and the journal had close ties to the state, but most of their members, contributors, and readers were private citizens, both Japanese and Taiwanese. Thus, social work was not simply imposed from the top; it also owed much to the grass-roots actors who performed most of the surveys and provided most of the assistance.

The main types of social work carried out in Taiwan were medical assistance, economic assistance, cultural reform, and social control. Although medical care was crucial and one of the main aspects of Japan's attempts to modernize Taiwan,[19] the other three are more relevant here, as they clearly show how the system became tied to the expansionist impulses of Japanese imperialism.[20] For reasons explored at greater length below, the manner in which economic assistance and cultural reform were carried out best displayed the sort of transformation of local society that Baron Shirane associated with social work. At the same time, it was the social control activities that served as the bridge between social work and Japan's imperial expansion in the late 1930s.

Institutionalizing Social Work in Jilong

Jilong is an ideal place to look at the development of social work in Taiwan, as it was a centre for many of the problems these programs were designed to cure: unemployment, housing shortages, poor health, poverty, transience, and persistent backward customs.[21] Locals attached importance to social work's success in Jilong because the city was seen as a model for development.[22] In addition, Jilong's Taiwanese and Japanese elites shared a strong organizational culture and a sense of dedication to their city, predisposing them to become involved in the institutional machinery of the social work system and to help their fellow residents.[23] As a result, the system became more entrenched in Jilong than in most other parts of Taiwan.

The system took shape in Jilong through both public and private effort. According to the municipal government, the Taiwan Government-General, the Taibei Prefecture authorities, and the Taiwan SWA all provided a framework and encouragement for the social work system, but in practice did little more.[24] Local initiative and leadership, government co-optation of existing organizations, and the formation of new institutions by local authorities came to define the institutional network and praxis of social work. The municipal government got involved as early as 1921, when it built a public health clinic and the first of its public housing projects, primarily for Japanese residents. Two years later the regional authorities established a system of local *hōmen iin* (welfare commissioners), while the city opened a number of publicly run pawnshops to protect people from the usurious rates charged by existing ones. Then, in the latter half of the 1920s and early 1930s, there was a proliferation of public and private social work institutions, with at least two dozen institutions either established or incorporated into the growing system.[25] These included five institutions to provide housing of one form or another, four to give medical assistance, four to give economic assistance, seven to perform multiple functions (everything from counselling to cultural reform), and four others.[26] Although many of these institutions overlapped in function, there was no shortage of work to be done, especially in the 1930s.

Several high-profile cases illustrate the two-stage challenge of these policies – to local society as part of internal strengthening, and to the international system as part of imperial expansion. These cases include the creation of new social civilization policies and institutions in the early 1930s; the state's takeover of an important Taiwanese-founded social work institution, the *Haku'ai dan* (Jilong Fraternity Group, JFG); and the system of local welfare commissioners.

Social Civilization

The first major development in social work in the 1930s was linked to the project of assimilation through *shakai kyōka* (social civilization), a complex term that Sheldon Garon translates as "moral suasion," and that Patricia Tsurumi renders as "acculturation."[27] As Garon shows, moral suasion was a key component of state-initiated programs to mobilize, reform, and manage Japanese society, especially during the inter-war period.[28] In Taiwan, the connotation was more transformative, as the Japanese felt they were raising the cultural level of the Taiwanese by bringing them modern civilization. This involved a sense of moral superiority akin to the spirit, if not the letter, of "acculturation," which Tsurumi frames broadly to include civilizing, evangelizing impulses. To stress the culturally hierarchical use of the term in Taiwan, however, the more literal translation of "social civilization" seems more appropriate. In any event, the linkage between it and social work represented the intensification of both a prior impulse towards assimilation within Japanese colonialism, and of state involvement in managing local society.

The colonial government had long issued policies designed to assimilate Taiwanese to Japanese social and cultural norms. The education system that Kodama Gentarō and Gotō Shinpei created in 1898 was designed to promote gradual assimilation. Taiwanese students received instruction in Japanese language and ethics as well as in hygiene and practical knowledge over six or seven years of primary education. It was a two-tier system, with Japanese and Taiwanese students attending separate and unequal schools for most of the colonial period. Even when the divisions were relaxed in the 1920s, very few Taiwanese children attended the formerly Japanese schools. According to Patricia Tsurumi, "[e]ducation was seen as an instrument of fundamental social, political, economic, and cultural change; it was to transform a segment of traditional China into an integral part of modern Japan."[29]

The first movement towards rapid assimilation came in the mid-1910s from a group of Taiwanese elites who found allies among Japanese reformers – most notably Itagaki Taisuke – in the home islands. They sought full political and legal equality for Taiwanese through a program of education and cultural reform, but were quickly defeated by opponents in the colonial government.[30] Several years later, in 1922, the colonial government appeared to change direction when Governor-General Den Kenjirō issued an edict banning discrimination in education in order to accelerate assimilation. The state, at least on paper, had the machinery to carry this out, as it had recently co-opted a network of privately established *Dōfūkai* (customs assimilation associations, CAAs) whose primary objective was the cultural transformation of the Taiwanese. One of the largest and oldest of these groups was located in Jilong.[31]

Until the early 1930s, assimilation proceeded slowly, as there was resistance from both Taiwanese and Japanese, officials and private citizens. One of the clearest measures of this was the rate of Japanese language acquisition: by 1932, after more than thirty-five years of colonial rule, a mere 20 per cent of Taiwanese in Jilong claimed Japanese proficiency,[32] despite mandatory classes in schools and numerous other opportunities for language study. Traditions such as marriages based on a system of bride prices, which the colonial authorities had identified as backwards and targeted for eradication decades earlier, remained prevalent in Jilong into the early 1930s.[33] So far, efforts at assimilation were an abject failure.

Concerned with this lack of success, in 1931 the colonial government launched a drive for social civilization that entailed replacing all the CAAs with "social civilization associations."[34] Jilong was idiosyncratic in that its local CAA remained in existence under the leadership of Taiwanese elites; even so, it soon established a social civilization division. Local officials established a network of Japanese-led institutions because the civilizing mission required Japanese leadership. The umbrella organization for these groups was the *Shakai kyōka rengōkai* (Jilong Social Civilization Union, SCU), which aimed at "the achievement of a national society" through its coordinating role. It tried to instil in city residents an emperor-centred vision of the nation (*kokutai kannen*),[35] further the teaching of Japanese, and reform local customs. A small committee of nine Japanese ran the SCU. The city mayor and a leading Japanese resident (a businessman and scholar named Ishizaka Sōsaku) were chair and vice-chair, respectively, but other residents did much of the real work through a number of affiliated organizations. Schools, youth groups, and Japanese-language training centres ran most of these organizations, while Japanese religious institutions, the Women's Association, and the Jilong CAA all managed a few groups. The SCU divided Jilong into thirteen different *kyōka ku* (civilization wards) and six *buraku* (settlements). The latter were located around the city's periphery; the former were distributed throughout the city centre.[36]

Invariably Japanese-led local *chōnaikai* (neighbourhood committees) managed the downtown civilization wards regardless of their ethnic composition; the less-populous peripheral zones were purely Taiwanese-led. To institute policies and coordinate activities throughout the city, the SCU also appointed a group of fifty-six *kyōka iin* (civilization commissioners), the majority male Japanese, although prominent local Taiwanese businessmen, doctors, and educators held about a quarter of the positions; only two were women. Similarly, Japanese residents ran almost all the affiliated organizations.[37] In short, the social civilization project redirected social work towards a Japanese-led effort to reform Taiwanese society and culture thoroughly in the early 1930s.

The transformative nature of social civilization came in part from its close connection to the practice of *shakai kyōiku* (social education), which had three main components: 1) to spread the spirit of *kokumin seishin* (national citizenship) and strengthen *kokumin teki jikaku* (national consciousness); 2) to train people as good citizens with a sense of *jichi teki kannen* (self-reliance); and 3) to develop practical knowledge and remove the non-essentials from life.[38] Similar projects were underway in the home islands by the early 1930s, but in the colony the focus was on the indigenous residents. The Japanese framers of social work policy instituted large-scale efforts to teach Japanese language and transform religious and other traditions, and to complete swiftly the process of modernizing and Japanizing the Taiwanese.

Given both the importance Japanese placed on language instruction and its dismal progress, the initial focus of social civilization was on teaching Japanese. In 1934 colonial officials and local residents launched a major push to establish more programs for Japanese instruction in Jilong. Plans called for ten regular language training centres to be added to the eight that existed in 1934, including those run by existing semi-private institutions. In addition, two more basic *kan'i* (training centres) were to be built for a total of three. Japanese administrators were to replace the Taiwanese who had been running many of the existing centres. The plan envisioned more than tripling the number of Taiwanese with Japanese-language proficiency by the early 1940s, to around 70 per cent of the population.[39]

Achieving this level of language proficiency was part of the larger goal of forging a homogeneous population of imperial subjects. Although there was always ambivalence about this among Japanese, seen in the persistence of gradualism in assimilation policy the social civilization programs represented an intensification of existing strategies ultimately to eradicate a separate Taiwanese culture. Social civilization expressed a form of internationalism by embodying Japan's application of modern methods of social work. At the same time, the new institutions displayed a greater effort on the part of the colonial state to manage society. These shifts were components of the broader internal strengthening of the Japanese Empire that took place prior to the outbreak of war in 1937.

The Jilong Fraternity Group

The JFG was among those privately established institutions that only gradually became incorporated into the social work system. It was founded in 1920 by local Taiwanese mining magnate Yan Yunnian and two other important Taiwanese businessmen, Gu Xianrong and Lin Tai-wei, after a tremendous typhoon swept the north of the island the previous year, leaving devastation in its wake, particularly in Jilong. Most of the labourers drawn to the city by the opportunities of the post-war economic boom had been living south of the harbour in hastily erected huts and were now homeless. The JFG's primary goal was thus to provide inexpensive housing to Jilong's labourers and other poor residents.

The JFG project centred around the construction of a large modern brick building in the southern part of Jilong, next to one of the city's largest public markets. The top two floors were reserved for rental accommodation while the ground floor contained space for shops. In many ways, it resembled large settlement houses in the United States, such as the well-known Hull House in Chicago, which offered training programs and other services for its residents.[40] During the 1930s, in particular, the JFG provided job placement and training, medical care, and classes in hygiene and other subjects.[41] Although a few Japanese resided there over the years, it was primarily for Taiwanese. The combination of residential, social, and occupational functions meant it influenced all aspects of its residents' lives.

Despite generous funding from the three founders – in the vicinity of a staggering 350,000 yen – the organization quickly ran into financial trouble. The early 1920s downturn in Taiwan's economy forced the donors to reduce their contributions, and in the end they delivered only about a third of what they had originally promised. By this time the JFG had taken out a large loan for the construction of the main building, which it was unable to repay even though it continued to receive private donations and grants of imperial assistance.[42] Although the early debts would come to haunt the organization, it quickly came to stand at the forefront of social work in Jilong, particularly through its efforts to ease the housing shortage.

The JFG's prominence was largely due to its involvement in *keizai hogo jigyō* (economic protection work) in support of one of social work's highest goals: to retrieve people from, and prevent them from falling into, poverty.[43] The primary aspects of economic welfare included poverty relief, inexpensive housing, and finding jobs for the unemployed. The state encouraged private groups, corporations, and banks to provide the logistical and financial bases for economic welfare projects,[44] which were thought crucial in minimizing the potential for social instability and political unrest. Especially during the early 1930s, agitation for local self-government and a colonial legislative assembly left colonial authorities concerned that discontent was rising, while the dislocations and rising unemployment brought on by the global Depression only exacerbated these fears.

A Buddhist leader and social worker in Jilong proposed a harmonious, circular model of society to explain the connection between economic problems and social unrest. In explaining the origins of social ills, he wrote that, "[w]hen the society which I inhabit is out of balance, this will cause social ills to arise." But how did a society get out of balance? Borrowing a scientific metaphor, he explained that people were the cells of the social body: much as a tumour in one cell or group of cells could damage the health of the entire body, so, too, could the difficulties of one individual or a small group hinder the progress of a whole society.[45] Thus, the economic difficulties of a small number of people could disrupt an entire community, which in turn would give rise to more social ills. Therefore it was crucial to solve individual economic problems before they could damage society at large.

Officials and residents in Jilong were particularly concerned with vagrants and excess workers, who might come under the influence of dangerous political forces. One Japanese resident related the story of an acquaintance who came to Taiwan in the early 1930s in search of manual labour after losing his job in Japan, but without success. Although he sympathized with his friend, the author saw three dangers lurking in his friend's continued unemployment: crime, mental illness possibly leading to suicide, and, worst of all, attraction to *musan undō* (social or proletarian movements).[46] In such a way, homeless and jobless people could endanger the entire colonial project and thus the internal security of the Japanese Empire.

As the island's major port city, Jilong was exposed to large population flows – between 1929 and 1931, almost twenty-five thousand migrants arrived in search of work,[47] exacerbating the city's chronic housing shortage. Through the colonial period, the JFG remained the largest and among the least expensive options for the city's workers; at peak capacity, the main structure housed up to a thousand people, for a few yen a month each. The JFG also owned a number of single-family dwellings that it leased for less than ten yen a month, but even before the Depression there had been no vacancies in the twenty existing units.[48]

The JFG received praise from social workers around the island for the range of services it provided.[49] By the early 1930s, these included public baths open to the entire neighbourhood, midwifery care, a sanitation union, a pawnshop, a purchasing cooperative, a health clinic, a work program, and an employment agency.[50] As a full-service institution, the JFG loomed large in the practise of social work in colonial Jilong, especially for its mostly Taiwanese residents.

The JFG's early financial difficulties never eased, however, and eventually led to the Jilong city government's taking over the institution. As early as the late 1920s, Yan Guonian (the younger brother of Yan Yunnian, who several years earlier had taken over management of the JFG), proposed that the city purchase the organization. As the government had its own fiscal limitations, the issue was delayed for several years. Then, in 1935, a deal was concluded whereby the Jilong city government assumed control of the main building and other properties and took on the JFG's outstanding debt of 170,000 yen.[51] This placed the state in control of one of Jilong's most important institutions and gave it greater influence over the lives of a large number of city residents.

The timing of this takeover after years of reluctance had to do with the expansion of state efforts at assimilation through social civilization. Shortly after the city took control, the shift became apparent in two initiatives launched by a joint association of municipal officials and inhabitants of the main building. The new management set up a Japanese-language training centre for children and a Japanese-language nursery school that focused on, among other things, raising the national spirit of its Taiwanese pupils.[52] Even the JFG's public baths received a new objective: "To plant the tradition of bathing in the Taiwanese."[53] Jilong had other institutions for social civilization, but the city government needed the JFG to access a segment of society that previously had been beyond reach. By taking over an institution created and run by Taiwanese, Japanese colonial authorities tried to use social work as a means to expand their control and influence.[54]

The Local Welfare Commissioners

In contrast to the home-grown JFG, the system of local welfare commissioners[55] was an import from the Japanese home islands. The system originated in Okayama Prefecture in 1917 as a mechanism to survey and deliver aid to the needy. The following year, the bureaucrat who began the project moved to Osaka, where he set up the first formal network of unpaid commissioners, each responsible for gathering information and distributing aid in their districts.[56] After the unrest of the 1918 Rice Riots, the system spread to other cities, in part because its strong local presence was deemed useful to promote public order. It also fit well with the guiding principle of social welfare in Japan: to discourage reliance on governmental financial assistance.[57]

The commissioner system spread swiftly to Taiwan, where it became the centrepiece of much of the social work activity in the colony. After the first programs were established in Taibei and Jilong in 1923, it spread to the other major cities of the island, and then over the next decade to the smaller cities and towns. Within a few years, commissioners were handling thousands of cases involving the registration of local residents, medical care, aid to children in need, counselling and dispute mediation, financial assistance, and a range of others. By the end of 1937, the commissioners had handled almost 1.3 million cases throughout the island.[58] Taiwan's population at this time was just under three million, many of whom were out of the reach of the commissioner system.

Although commissioners in each municipality worked quite independently, two practices linked their efforts. One was the *Hōmen iin tai-kai* (Local Welfare Commissioners Conference), which met every year starting in 1929 to share knowledge and coordinate activities around the island. The other, which began around the same time, involved sending groups of both Japanese and Taiwanese on annual trips to inspect social work institutions and practices in the home islands. Upon their return, the commissioners would report their findings in *Shakai jigyō no tomo*. The conference was geared towards intra-island coordination and enhanced state control, but the annual trip served to emphasize social work as a Japanese creation, something sent out from the metropole to effect change in the colony.

The organizers of the commissioner system divided Jilong into five districts, each with three commissioners to oversee operations. Included in this initial group were local luminaries such as Yan Guonian and Ishizaka Sōsaku, who used their status in the community to help establish the system. Two more districts were added by 1931, and by the early 1930s there were twenty-five regular commissioners throughout the city supported by a roughly equivalent number of staff and advisors. This gave Jilong the highest concentration of commissioners per district, as well as the largest support staff, of any city in northern Taiwan.[59]

The commissioners represented a cross-section of Jilong's elite, except for the key fact that almost all were men. In addition to such central figures as Ishizaka Sōsaku and Yan Guonian, several other first- and second-tier elites served as commissioners and/or advisors. In 1940 the twenty-five commissioners included fourteen Japanese and eleven Taiwanese. For the most part, Japanese commissioners worked with Japanese settlers and Taiwanese commissioners with Taiwanese residents, although the Japanese had a much larger presence within the Taiwanese community than vice versa. By the late colonial period, almost all commissioners came from the professional classes: merchants, company officers, shipping agents, contractors, business owners, doctors, school principals, and a few bureaucrats.[60] Although they lacked the professional training in social work that characterized their counterparts in the United States, their established positions in society helped them function as bridges between the state and its subjects.

What Jilong's commissioners might have lacked in training, they made up for in dedication. As Table 5.1 shows, in the early 1930s they

Table 5.1. Cases Handled by Local Welfare Commissioners, North Taiwan Cities, 1930–40

| Type of Case | 1930 | 1931 | 1932 | 1933 | 1934 | 1940 | | | |
	Jilong					Jilong	Taibei	Luodong	Yilan
Counselling	511	972	682	865	681	66,029	34,607	4,985	7,637
Child Aid	23	7	154	22	145	950	2,539	200	151
Medical	1,311	1,564	4,234	5,260	4,234	92,951	74,383	113,761	44,061
Mediation	254	605	1,070	1,093	1,061	16,628	17,822	132	1,265
Donations	2,588	1,333	2,185	1,558	2,185	10,797	17,015	204	353
Registration	355	443	442	532	442	20,214	48,203	6,321	7,916
Other	170	254	947	1,229	947	16,413	16,762	287	2,923
Total	5,212	5,178	9,714	10,559	9,704	223,982	211,331	125,900	64,306

Sources: Kiirun shi yaku sho, *Kiirun shakai jigyō yōran*, ed. Kin-gendai shiryō kankōkai, in *Shokuminchi shakai jigyō kankei shiryō-shū: Taiwan hen 45 Taiwan shakai jigyō sōran: chijō shakai jigyō 7* (Jilong: Kiirun shi yaku sho, 1935–2001), 278–9; for the 1940 figures, see Taihoku shū hōmen iin rengōkai, *Shakai jigyō gaiyō Shōwa jūgo nendo*, ed. Kin-gendai shiryō kankōkai, in *Shokuminchi shakai jigyō kankei shiryōshū: Taiwan hen 39 Taiwan shakai jigyō sōran: chijō shakai jigyō* (Taihoku: Taihoku shūyaku sho, 1941–2001), 48–9. The system arrived in Yilan in 1927 and in Luodong in 1932, small cities on the east coast.

handled between five and ten thousand cases annually, the great majority of them involving medical, financial, or counselling assistance. By 1940 they had processed more cases than any other city in northern Taiwan, including Taibei.[61] Jilong certainly had a plethora of social ills to cure, but it is also likely that the commissioners there had a higher profile than elsewhere. The relatively high concentration of commissioners and staff per district coupled with Jilong's compact size meant that more people were aware of their presence. This enhanced the system's ability to achieve its goals.

Some of the objectives were entirely within the realm of assistance, as seen in the large number of cases for counselling, medical aid, and donations, but others were better suited for transformation and enhancing state control. Beginning in 1934, the Jilong commissioners began raising and distributing donations to the city's poor during annual *dōjō shūkan* (sympathy weeks).[62] In the late 1930s, however, the commissioners increasingly turned to customs reform and social control. This was the period of the *Kōminka undō* (Kōminka Movement), which began in Taiwan in 1936 and thereafter spread to Japan's other colonies.[63] Its goal was to transform all colonial subjects into good citizens of the Japanese Empire, which, at least rhetorically, meant a thorough and rapid assimilation of Japanese social and cultural norms. It was also the period of wartime mobilization, which required a much higher level of social control than had previously been attained. The local welfare commissioners were well suited to the needs of both transformation and mobilization.

Regarding customs reform, the commissioners put forth their greatest efforts in the *Jibyō seiri undō* (Temple Regulation Movement), launched in 1937. This was a two-stage effort to amalgamate and close Taiwanese religious institutions and replace them with their Japanese counterparts, most notably Shinto shrines but also Japanese Buddhist temples. Local welfare commissioners participated in this radical effort to remake Taiwan, and in similar projects such as an attempt to stop the burning of ghost money to honour the spirits.[64] Social workers viewed the reform of religious institutions and practices as a central part of the larger project of social civilization in Taiwan,[65] and commissioners made use of their local presence to enact major reforms in Taiwanese society.

The commissioner system changed after the outbreak of war with China, as Japan's leaders placed greater emphasis on the social control aspects of social work. In one sense, this shift in focus contained within it the same internationalism that had first led Japan to adopt modern social work standards. Within the framework of wartime mobilization, however, officials in Taiwan redirected the system to support the war on the home front. On the one hand, they reoriented the system so that, instead of concentrating on local solutions to local problems, social work was now directed towards meeting supposedly empire-wide war objectives.[66] On the other hand, predominantly Taiwanese organizations such as the JFG received less attention, with greater emphasis now on the Japanese-dominated local welfare commissioners. The commissioners became the nucleus of wartime social work.

As Japanese forces expanded the scope of the so-called China Incident, the danger to Taiwan's security strengthened the commissioners' position. The southward spread of the conflict forced many Japanese and Taiwanese to flee the Chinese mainland, while many in the colony were drafted – at first only Japanese, but later many Taiwanese as well. The commissioners were instructed to increase their efforts to provide care for the refugees, aid the families of draftees, and put the island on a wartime footing.[67] The welfare commissioners were well placed to deal with the lowest levels of society and attempted to mobilize the masses to aid Japan's imperial expansion.

From 1937 on, the commissioners' work revolved around the war. Medical assistance, charitable donations, counselling, and other tasks all received new urgency; social ills now had to be cured quickly and cheaply so that resources would not be diverted from the all-important war effort. Commissioners also acquired new tasks that furthered social control. New regulations empowered local commissioners to register military families in their districts and to determine appropriate levels of aid under the recently passed *Gunji fujo hō* (Military Assistance Law). Since refugees from the mainland, numbering more than five thousand in Taibei Prefecture alone, fell outside this new law, the commissioners lobbied to extend the existing *Kyūgo hō* (Aid Law) of 1929 to provide for their support.

Despite these financial provisions, the commissioners maintained their primary focus on moral and spiritual assistance rather than material aid. To minimize state expenditures, social workers encouraged people to be *jiritsu jikatsu* (self-reliant), and helped individuals and families to develop plans for self-support. Commissioners also united neighbourhoods and even entire cities through mutual-assistance activities during the increasingly difficult wartime conditions. All these tasks were performed in the name of conserving state resources for the war effort.

The commissioners also directed greater efforts towards social control. At the start of the war, local commissioners launched a survey of their districts to gather information on needy families, updating data on existing *hogo kaado* (special assistance cards) to track the local population. They also established several centres in and around Jilong to hold beggars after their removal from town and city streets. Local committees played a much greater role in coordinating social work activities – although they did not take control of other social work institutions, they kept track of each group's activities and finances.[68] Local welfare commissioners thus became overseers of the entire system of social work in Taiwan.

The enhanced role of the commissioners was tied to Japanese expansion on two levels. First, many in Taiwan saw it as an attempt to make the colony even more like the metropole. Greater uniformity within the Japanese Empire presumably would solidify the effort to extend Japan's territory. Second, the commissioners' devotion to wartime mobilization made their work a direct part of the larger project of Japanese expansion. Welfare commissioners thus contributed to both the intensification of Japanese rule over colonial Taiwan and the spread of Japanese military forces in the construction of a new order in East Asia.

Conclusion

Social work might not be the most obvious topic for an exploration of the ways in which Japan challenged the international system in the 1930s. It is a profoundly inward-looking practice, one that employs local actors to solve primarily local problems. Japanese social work, however, also had an international dimension. It emerged as a scientific approach to welfare, first in Europe and the United States, and then spread to Japan and out to its colonies. Practitioners in colonial Taiwan looked to international conferences to define their field.[69] This was benign internationalism, and Japanese efforts to spread the practice in itself would not have caused international disruptions.

Japan's colonial authorities, however, brought social work to Taiwan expressly to disrupt, change, and transform. Although some of their reforms were positive – improving medical care, finding jobs, providing low-cost housing, and counselling those in need – the links between social work and social civilization on the one hand, and social control on the other, meant that the new system posed a serious threat to Taiwanese social and cultural traditions. The system largely depended on the incorporation of Taiwanese and their institutions, but the transformational goals of social work in the 1930s made it part of the internal strengthening of the Japanese Empire. The state involvement and the aim of assimilation that characterized the first stage of Japan's challenge only intensified between 1931 and 1936.

Stage two began with Japan's shift to a wartime footing after full-scale war erupted with China in 1937. Soon after the conflict began, local welfare commissioners led the way in redirecting the entire social work system towards mobilization for the war effort. Social work still contained elements of social civilization for the Taiwanese, and its practise meant that there was real continuity with the earlier internationalism. All elements of the system were reframed, however, in terms of mobilization of the home front, and the emphasis shifted from assistance to control as the state exerted an increasingly heavy hand in the management of local society. In the age of total war, organizing local society, helping people to help themselves, and keeping track of local residents all supported the spread of Japanese military forces throughout continental and maritime Asia. Thus, the quintessentially local practice of social work became a crucial, if understated, part of Japan's efforts to destroy the existing international system and create a new order in Asia with itself at the helm.

NOTES

I would like to thank the contributors to this volume for their helpful suggestions for revising this essay into its current form, as well as Professors William Kirby, Andrew Gordon, Akira Iriye, and Alan and Katy Dawley, as well as numerous colleagues, for their extensive comments on previous versions of the present work.

1 Kinebuchi Yoshifusa, "Introduction," in *Taiwan shakai jigyō shi* (Taibei: Seishin shōji kabushiki kaisha, 1940), 11. Primary funding of the research for this chapter came from a Fulbright IIE Fellowship. The ideas it contains are mine alone, and do not reflect the positions or policies of the United States Department of State.

2 Another sign was the rejection of Japan's proposed amendment to the Treaty of Versailles for racial equality.

3 Although I use the terms Japan and Japanese throughout this chapter, I do not wish to suggest that these words represent unified, monolithic entities. Instead, I usually discuss a particular aspect of Japan, its colonial face, and a subset of Japanese, those who lived and worked in Taiwan. In the context of Taiwan, however, definite divisions existed between Japan/Taiwan and Japanese/Taiwanese, so my use of the terms is to a large extent guided by these divisions.

4 As the goal of this chapter is to show how Japanese viewed and made use of social work, the Taiwanese voice is intentionally left out. In reality, Taiwan was neither a blank slate upon which Japan wrote its designs nor a setting in which it pursued its goals without resistance. However, Taiwanese efforts to resist and manipulate social work for their own purposes are beyond the scope of this work.

5 Daniel J. Walkowitz, *Working with Class: Social Workers and the Politics of Middle-Class Identity* (Chapel Hill: University of North Carolina Press, 1999), prologue and chap. 1.

6 Sheldon Garon, *Molding Japanese Minds: The State in Everyday Life* (Princeton, NJ: Princeton University Press, 1997), 49.

7 Ibid., chap. 2.

8 This description is drawn from several different accounts, including: Kinebuchi, *Taiwan shakai jigyō shi*, 1129; Taiwan sōtokufu, "Taiwan shakai jigyō yōran 1," in *Shokuminchi shakai jigyō kankei shiryōshū: Taiwan hen 1: Taiwan shakai jigyō sōran*, edited by Kin-gendai shiryō kankōkai, *Senzen senchūki Ajia kenkyū shiryō 2* (Tokyo: Kin-gendai shiryō kankōkai, 1926 [2001]), 47; Taihoku chō sōmu ka, *Taihoku chō shi 1*, vol. 202, *Zhongguo fangzhi congshu: Taiwan diqu* (Taibei: Taihoku chō sōmu ka, 1919 [1985]), 591–3.

9 During the colonial era, indigenous residents were divided into two main groups, *hontōjin* (islanders), descended from Chinese settlers, and *banjin* (aborigines), who, following Qing Dynasty practice, were subdivided between *seiban* ("raw aborigines") and *jukuban* ("cooked aborigines"). The "raw aborigines" lived in the more mountainous, less populated regions of the island, while the "cooked" lived in the plains regions and had a history of intermingling with Chinese settlers. In this chapter, I am concerned only with the islanders, as there were no aborigines left in Jilong by 1895, and I refer to them alternately as both islanders and Taiwanese.

10 Imai Kōji, "Nihon tōji shita Taiwan ni okeru shakai jigyō no tenkai: fukushi no kindaika o motarashita Nihon tōji kōhanki no shakai jigyō," *Gendai Taiwan kenkyū* 25 (2003). The latter of these modifications was instituted when the regulations were revised in 1903.

11 These institutions had been briefly shut down as part of a larger strategy to undercut resistance to Japanese rule by removing many of the institutions that previously had knit society together, including temples and other community-based organizations; see ibid., 24.

12 Ibid.; Kinebuchi, *Taiwan shakai jigyō shi*, 1120, 1129; Taiwan sōtokufu, "Taiwan shakai jigyō yōran 1," 48. The last of these makes no mention of the fact that Qing-era institutions were initially shut down.

13 Kinebuchi, *Taiwan shakai jigyō shi*, 1120, 1138–9. There were four of these relief associations; three bore the reign names of the Meiji, Taisho, and Showa emperors, and the fourth, the Taiwan Relief Association, was founded to commemorate the visit of the soon-to-be Showa Emperor to Taiwan in 1923.

14 This particular post-war boom is discussed in Garon, *Molding Japanese Minds*, 49ff.

15 At first, the Home Affairs Bureau delegated authority for social work to local government offices. In 1924, when the colonial bureaucracy was reorganized, local social work officers and the existing offices for *Gakumu ka* (education), *Henshū ka* (censorship), and *Shaji ka* (shrine management) were combined within the new *Bunkyō ka* (Office for Education and Culture) in the Home Affairs Bureau. As a result, control over social work activities shifted from local offices to the centre. Two years later, this office was elevated to the status of a bureau, and within it a new *Shakai ka* (Office for Social Affairs) was set up to oversee all social work offices at the prefecture, county, city, town, and village levels. See Kinebuchi, *Taiwan shakai jigyō shi*, 1134–5.

16 Ibid., 1130–3; these pages contain a reprint of the original edict.

17 Ibid., 1136–8. Kinebuchi helped to found and run the Taiwan Social Work Association. Coordination became increasingly important as the number of institutions rose from 748 in 1926 to around 1,300 a decade later; see ibid., 1137, for the first figure, and Taiwan sōtokufu, "Taiwan shakai jigyō yōran 5," 34, for the latter.

18 This journal, which ran from 1928 to 1943, also provides a crucial record of the activities of social workers in colonial Taiwan. The name was derived from the journal of the Japan Social Work Association, *Shakai jigyō*; thus, the Taiwan journal was literally the companion to the one in the home islands.

19 And also to modernize itself, as suggested by Sumiko Otsubo, in this volume.

20 One other reason I do not focus upon medicine here is that Ming-cheng Miriam Lo has already explored the impact of modern medicine on

Taiwan, specifically in terms of developing a new class of Taiwanese elites who received medical training; see Ming-cheng Miriam Lo, *Doctors within Borders: Profession, Ethnicity, and Modernity in Colonial Taiwan* (Berkeley: University of California Press, 2002).

21 Both Kiirun shi yaku sho, "Kiirun shakai jigyō yōran," in *Shokuminchi shakai jigyō kankei shiryōshū: Taiwan hen 45 Taiwan shakai jigyō sōran: chijō shakai jigyō 7*, edited by Kin-gendai shiryō kankōkai, *Senzen senchūki Ajia kenkyū shiryō 2* (Tokyo: Kin-gendai shiryō kankōkai, [1935] 2001), 268; and Jian Wanhuo, *Jilong zhi* (Jilong: Jilong tushu chuban xiehui, 1931), 174, emphasize that, as the entryway to Taiwan and a rising city (*shinkō toshi*), Jilong contained a particularly serious set of social ills.

22 Cai Qingyun, "Kiirun shi seikatsu kaizen no gaikō to tōmen no jigyō," *Shakai jigyō no tomo* 96 (November 1936), 26.

23 The organizational activities of local elites, as well as certain aspects of their dedication to developing Jilong, is discussed at length in my "Constructing Taiwanese Ethnicity: Identities in a City on the Border of China and Japan" (PhD diss., Harvard University, 2006), chap. 3.

24 Kiirun shi yaku sho, "Kiirun shakai jigyō yōran," 268.

25 Ibid., 263–4, 268–9; Taihoku shū yaku sho, *Taihoku shi Taihoku shū yōran 2*, edited by Chengwen chubanshe youxian gongsi, vol. 204, *Zhongguo fangzhi congshu: Taiwan diqu* (Taibei: Taihoku shū yaku sho, [1925] 1985), 75; and Nakajima Shinichirō, *Kiirun shi annai* (Jilong: Kiirun shi yakusho, 1930), 88. The first source, initially published in 1935, lists 11 public and 13 private social work organizations, but omits several groups. Even so, while the total in Jilong was far less than the 58 in the capital of Taibei, proportional to population Jilong had a higher concentration, since Taibei's population was more than triple Jilong's.

26 Kiirun shi yaku sho, "Kiirun shakai jigyō yōran," 1–2. The four in the "other" category included the public pawnshops, public beaches, a credit union, and a counselling centre.

27 Garon, *Molding Japanese Minds*, 7; and E. Patricia Tsurumi, *Japanese Colonial Education in Taiwan, 1895–1945*, Harvard East Asian Series 88 (Cambridge, MA: Harvard University Press, 1977), 146.

28 Garon, *Molding Japanese Minds*, chaps. 2–4. Some of the key campaigns Garon describes involved cracking down on the so-called new religions, regulating prostitution, and expanding the role of women in managing life within the home. The involvement of women was central to these campaigns, a tactic that does not seem to have carried over to Taiwan.

29 The foregoing is a condensed version of developments described in Tsurumi, especially chaps. 2–5; quote on 2.

30 This is discussed in Tsurumi, *Japanese Colonial Education in Taiwan*, 66–9; and Harry J. Lamley, "The Taiwan Literati and Early Japanese Rule, 1895–1915: A Study of their Reactions to the Japanese" (PhD diss., University of Washington, 1964), 450–7.

31 For more on the customs assimilation associations, especially the one in Jilong, see Dawley, "Constructing Taiwanese Ethnicity," chap. 3; see also Wang Shih-ch'ing, "Huangminhua yundong qian de Taiwan shehui shenghuo gaishan yundong: yi Haishan qu wei li, 1914–1937," *Si yu yan* 29, no. 4 (1990): 5–63.

32 Kiirun shi kyōka rengōkai, *Kiirun shi shakai kyōiku kyōka shisetsu gaikyō* (Jilong: Kiirun shi kyōka rengōkai, 1936), 16–17. To an extent, the low numbers derived from the fact that a large percentage of Jilong's Taiwanese residents were migrants from the countryside and had received little if any Japanese training prior to entering the city. Nonetheless, in theory every child raised there should have been taught Japanese at school since the early 1900s, which amounted to more than the percentage found in 1932. This does not include the many adults who learned Japanese.

33 Cai Qingyun, "Hontōjin no hei kin seido no heigai wa wakaki danjo o shiro e yūdō," *Shakai jigyō no tomo* 37 (December 1931), 56–9.

34 Wang, "Huangminhua yundong qian de Taiwan," 11–13.

35 *Kokutai kannen* is a difficult term to express in English. The term *kokutai* is generally rendered as "national polity," and is essentially equated with the imperial institution. Thus, a more literal translation could be "national polity idea," which is a bit vague. In the context of the SCU, the goal was to teach people reverence for the emperor as the leader and embodiment of the Japanese nation.

36 The foregoing is taken from Kiirun shi yaku sho, *Kiirun shi shakai kyōiku gaiyō*; quote on 78.

37 Ibid., 88–93.

38 Kiirun shi yaku sho, *Kiirun shi shakai kyōiku gaiyō*, 2–4. The term translated here as "self-reliance" is *jichi*, which can also mean "self-government." In the present context, the state clearly did not mean to promote the political participation of its subjects but rather wanted to train them to be less in need of state assistance, hence the rendering as self-reliance.

39 Kiirun shi kyōka rengōkai, *Kiirun shi shakai kyōiku kyōka shisetsu gaikyō* (Jilong: Kiirun shi kyōka rengōkai, 1936), 16.

40 For more information on Hull House, where Jane Addams helped to pioneer the field of social work, see Jane Addams, *Twenty Years at Hull House with Autobiographical Notes* (Urbana: University of Illinois Press, 1990).

41 The foundation and early history of the JFG is detailed in Irie Kyōfū, *Kiirun fūdo ki* (Taibei: Eriguchi shōkai insatsu kōjō, 1933), 180–6; and Nagahama Minoru, *Gan Kokunen kun shoden* (Taibei: Taiwan nichinichi shinpō sha, 1937), 47.

42 In 1929 and 1930, the JFG received special grants of 1,390 yen from the Taisho Relief Association and 1,470 yen from the Taiwan SWA to build new offices and conduct renovations; see Katsuya Kentarō, "Kiirun haku'ai dan," *Shakai jigyō no tomo* 19 (May 1930), 76.

43 Kinebuchi, *Taiwan shakai jigyō shi*, 1184–5.

44 Taiwan sōtokufu, "Taiwan shakai jigyō yōran 1," 52–3.

45 Akeyama Sei'en, "Shakai jigyō to sono seishin," *Shakai jigyō no tomo* 4 (March 1929), 87–8.

46 Katsuya Kentarō, "Kiirun kō runpen sōkan ōrai chō," *Shakai jigyō no tomo* 37 (December 1931), 65–76.

47 Taiwan sōtokufu kanbō tokei ka, *Taiwan Genjū kokō tōkei* (Taibei: various publishers, 1905–31), for 1929–31. This huge influx was mostly offset by out-migration, but even so there was a net increase of some 5,000 people.

48 Taihoku shū hōmen iin rengō kai, "Shakai jigyō gaiyō showa jūichinen," in *Shokuminchi shakai jigyō kankei shiryōshū: Taiwan hen 39 Taiwan shakai jigyō sōran: chijō shakai jigyō*, edited by Kin-gendai shiryō kankōkai, *Senzen senchūki Ajia kenkyū shiryō 2* (Tokyo: Kin-gendai shiryō kankōkai, [1936] 2001), 50–1.

49 In 1935 Taiwan's annual Social Work Conference was held in Taibei, during which a group of 65 delegates visited Jilong for a tour of the social work institutions there. The author of a report on this visit said that the JFG was one of the most famous institutions in all of Taiwan. See "Daisanhan kiirun shisatsu ni ka harite," *Shakai jigyō no tomo* 85 (December 1935), 90–2.

50 Taiwan sōtokufu, *Taiwan sōtokufu kōbun ruisan* (Nantou, Taiwan), 10748.8, 1938, 12, 28–32; Taihoku shū hōmen iin rengō kai, "Shakai jigyō gaiyō Showa jūgo nendo," 150.

51 Taiwan sōtokufu, 10682.2, 1935.8.1, 14–16; and 10748.8, 1938, 2. For a sense of how long it took the city to take control, see "Taiwan nichinichi shinpō" (Taibei: Taiwan nichinichi shinpō sha), "Jilong shishunian xuan'an bo'ai tuan yuanman jiejue," 1935.8.29, 8.

52 Taiwan sōtokufu, 10682.2, 1935.8.1, 20–1.

53 Ibid., 10682.2, 1935.8.1, 15.

54 Taiwanese had the means to moderate the new social civilization projects. Since the vast majority of residents were Taiwanese, they could influence the daily operations of the association overseeing the management of the institution's many services.

55 "Local welfare commissioners" is a translation of the Japanese *hōmen iin* that I have borrowed from David Ambaras, "Social Knowledge, Cultural Capital, and the New Middle Class in Japan, 1895–1912," *Journal of Japanese Studies* 24, no. 1 (1998) 1–34. Sheldon Garon translates the term more directly as "district commissioner" (see *Molding Japanese Minds*, 52); as I feel this does not convey what the commissioners did, I prefer Ambaras's more descriptive translation.

56 Kinebuchi, *Taiwan shakai jigyō shi*, 1124; and Garon, *Molding Japanese Minds*, 52–8. Kinebuchi suggests that the Osaka system relied upon a German model.

57 Garon, *Molding Japanese Minds*, 52; and Namae Takashi, "Hōmen jigyō," *Shakai jigyō no tomo* 26 (January 1931), 86. Namae discusses the impact of the Rice Riots on the growth of the system.

58 Kinebuchi, *Taiwan shakai jigyō shi*, 1223–5; Taiwan sōtokufu, "Taiwan shakai jigyō yōran 1," 247; Taiwan sōtokufu, *Taihoku shi Taihoku shū yōran 3*, edited by Chengwen chubanshe youxian gongsi, vol. 204, *Zhongguo fangzhi congshu: Taiwan diqu* (Taibei: Taihoku shū yaku sho, [1927] 1985), 84–5.

59 Taihoku shū, "Shakai jigyō gaiyō Shōwa sannen," in *Shokuminchi shakai jigyō kankei shiryōshū: Taiwan hen 39 Taiwan shakai jigyō sōran: chijō shakai jigyō*, edited by Kin-gendai shiryō kankōkai, *Senzen senchūki Ajia kenkyū shiryō 2* (Tokyo: Kin-gendai shiryō kankōkai, [1928] 2001), 32–3; Taihoku shū hōmen iin rengō kai, "Shakai jigyō gaiyō Showa jūichinen," 16; Kiirun shi yaku sho, "Kiirun shakai jigyō yōran," 278. According to the second source, in 1936 Taibei had 97 commissioners, each responsible for 677 households, compared with one commissioner for every 800 households in Jilong. If the rest of the staff is included, the ratio shifts favourably towards Jilong, with each person working with 389 households compared with 591 in Taibei. This was still far from the 1:200 ratio originally set up in Osaka.

60 Taihoku shū, *Hōmen iin meihaku: fu hōmen iin sho kitei* (Taibei: Taihoku shū, 1941), 13–17.

61 Taihoku shū hōmen iin rengō kai, "Shakai jigyō gaiyō Showa jūgo nendo," 48–9; I was unable to locate figures for the southern part of the island.

62 Kiirun shi yaku sho, "Kiirun shakai jigyō yōran," 9–12. Each year there were two of these weeks, one at the end of the solar year for Japanese residents and one at the end of the lunar year for Taiwanese. Local welfare commissioners in the home islands began to hold nation-wide sympathy weeks in 1936; the practice went island-wide in Taiwan in 1937. See "Sentō hōmen iin dōjō shūkan kaisai yōmō," *Shakai jigyō no tomo* 108 (November 1937), 73.

63 Kōminka is often translated somewhat ambiguously as "imperialization"; see, for example, Leo T.S. Ching, *Becoming "Japanese": Colonial Taiwan and*

the Politics of Identity Formation (Berkeley: University of California Press, 2001), especially chap. 3. I feel that this rendering does not quite carry the full meaning of the original, which more literally, and accurately, would be "transformation into the emperor's people." In essence this meant Japanization because, given the family model of the relationship between the emperor and his subjects, the true "emperor's people" were the Japanese. However, the term assimilation (*dōka*) also meant Japanization, albeit through more gradual means than were employed during the Kōminka Movement. Although I do not agree with Ching that assimilation and imperialization were fundamentally different, I believe there was enough difference in methods and pace to warrant separating the terms. Since the most accurate English rendering of *kōminka* is cumbersome, I leave the term in the original.

64 "Dai jū kai Taihoku shū hōmen iin sōkai yōmō," *Shakai jigyō no tomo* 108 (November 1937), 79. This paper money was not actual currency, but a symbolic donation to the deity or spirit to which one wished to pay homage or ask for assistance. It was, and remains, a widespread practice in Taiwan.

65 Okabe Kaidō, "Shūkyō to nichijyō no kinmi o taiken shite Bukkyō shin taisei no kakuritsu o sakebu," *Shakai jigyō no tomo* 145 (December 1939), 42–6.

66 The declining importance of local issues is seen in the tables of contents of *Shakai jigyō no tomo*. From August 1937 until the journal closed in 1943, the vast majority of articles were about home-front defence and support for military forces in action as well as general issues of health and hygiene, while local issues appeared rarely.

67 "Shina jihen to hōmen iin no katsudō," *Shakai jigyō no tomo* 106 (September 1937), 1.

68 The foregoing pages are compiled from a number of different sources. See Taiwan sōtokufu, 10873.13, 1940.1.1, and the following articles from *Shakai jigyō no tomo*: "Nichi-shi jihen to hōmen iin no katsudō," 106 (September 1937), 1; Suzuki, 108 (November 1937), 12–15; "Sentō hōmen iin dōjō shūkan kaisai yōmō," 108 (November 1937), 73–4; "Hōmen kanshi hi settei no shushi narabini hōhō," 108 (November 1937), 74; "Dai jūkai Taihoku shū hōmen iin sōkai yōmō," 108 (November 1937), 75–9; and "Taihoku shū hōmen iin sōkai yōmō," 121 (December 1938), 67–9.

69 Specifically, they cited a definition that came out of the International Social Work Conference held in Paris in 1929; see Namae, "Hōmen jigyō," 86.

6 Between Collaboration and Conflict: State and Society in Wartime Korea

JUN UCHIDA

The concept "colonial totalitarianism,"[1] as Gregory Henderson once described the Japanese Empire in Korea, might strike one as redundant. Colonialism by its nature is characterized by excess – authoritarian governance, a penchant for control, and reliance on coercion. To be sure, the empire was never static. Although essentially a military regime backed by vast a bureaucracy and police, the colonial authority in Korea refashioned itself as "enlightened" cultural rule after the March First Movement of 1919, and further evolved into a corporatist state linked to multiple levels of society following the Manchurian Incident of 1931. Nonetheless, in contrast to most European colonial regimes that gradually moved towards an indirect form of rule, the "excessive attention"[2] of colonial power in Korea never lessened, and even increased after 1931. For most of its existence, colonial Korea remained yoked to the administrative will and scrutinizing gaze of the governor-general, or "an empire within the empire."

The excesses of colonialism were most apparent following the outbreak of the Sino-Japanese War in 1937. In the years leading up to the Pacific War, fascism, colonialism, and pan-Asianism – the key "isms" that propelled Japan's total war – coalesced into the policy of *naisen ittai* (unity of Japan and Korea) in Korea under the new governor-general, Minami Jirō (1936–42). Just as the Japanese Empire began to over-stretch itself into Southeast Asia and beyond, it began to over-imagine itself as a multi-ethnic community of Asian races bound by supranational ties to the emperor. A "have-not nation," Japan's challenge was to forge a new globe-spanning order centred in East Asia that would supplant Anglo-American hegemony. Central to this new pan-Asianist vision was the *kōkoku shinminka* or *kōminka* (imperialization) of Koreans, literally meaning "transforming [them] into subjects of the emperor." To be sure, the colonial state had always been committed to the assimilation of Koreans, however vaguely understood or defined. But in its drive to enforce homogeneity on colonizer and colonized, the wartime policy of *naisen ittai* had few parallels in the empire[3] or, arguably, in twentieth-century colonialism at large.

Existing studies on wartime Korea have focused on policy-making and policy imposition from above.[4] But a look into the local apparatus for enforcing the *naisen ittai* policy reveals that it was undergirded by a dense net of civic and semi-official institutions that operated under the auspices of the Government-General and the Chōsen Army (the Japanese army stationed in Korea). While resembling the mass organizations that mushroomed in wartime Japan, the Korean institutions were more centralized and more widely mobilized for ensuring cooperation with state policies. Long subject to the governor-general's autocratic style of rule, the colony, one may posit, provided a structure more amenable to mass mobilization, offering lessons that could be transplanted back to the metropole.

Using a number of previously unused sources, this chapter aims to provide a broad sketch of how the colonial regime of *naisen ittai* sought to mobilize Korean society and systematize official-civilian collaboration under total war. While noting some parallels with developments on the home islands, it also seeks to illustrate how the local dynamics of wartime mobilization in the colony were complicated by such intersecting factors as gender, class, region, and ethnicity.

Grassroots Initiatives

In response to the outbreak of the Sino-Japanese conflict in July 1937, the movement for unifying the wills of state and society behind Japan's new continental empire first emerged in Korea among a circle of prominent civilians in Seoul. They coalesced to form the Chōsen Gunji Kōen Renmei (Chōsen Military Assistance League, hereafter Chōsen League), which became central to drumming up public support for Japan's imperial army stationed in Korea. With its headquarters in Seoul, it quickly built a network of branch leagues at provincial, municipal, district, and island levels.[5] The Seoul Military Assistance League, chaired by Mayor Saeki Akira, encompassed the entire range of leading civic and semi-official organizations: the Imperial Soldiers' Assistance Association, the Local Reservists Association, the Patriotic Women's Association, and the Greater Japan National Defense Women's Association; neighbour-hood heads' associations, social work organizations, religious groups, assimilationist and "pro-Japanese" organizations; newspaper agencies; and the Seoul Chamber of Commerce and other commercial and occu-pational associations.[6] Apart from the military and patriotic organiza-tions headquartered in Japan, most of these institutions were formed and controlled by local civilian elites, Japanese and Korean, who had been cooperating with the authorities since the 1920s. The formation of the Chōsen League served to further institutionalize this collaboration between the upper strata of colonial society and the colonial state.

The Chōsen League supported Japan's continental expansion in a variety of ways that echoed the grassroots movements in the metro-pole. One of its main activities was fundraising for the Japanese impe-rial army. Within a year of its birth, the league had collected 923,800 yen[7] – an amount so much higher than that raised in Japan relative to population that it "astonished" metropolitan observers.[8] Another mis-sion of the league was to pay *imon* (consolation) visits to families of conscripted or deceased soldiers and financially support them as a way of compensating for the lack of state aid provided by the *Gunji Fujo hō* (Military Aid Law).[9]

The league's representatives also visited troops at the front. In Octo-ber 1937, the Chōsen League dispatched its first *imon* mission led by the Chōsen Army's Major-General Abe Yoshio. It was composed of eight civilian delegates, including Cho Pyŏng-sang of the Kyŏnggi Provin-cial Assembly and Japanese members of other provincial assemblies. For seventeen days they toured cities in northern China to visit troops dispatched from Korea, and donated 8,850 yen as *imon* money.[10] A sec-ond *imon* mission, led by Major-General Maeda Noboru, visited some 34,500 soldiers during the New Year season, with two *rōkyokushi* (*nani-wabushi* reciters) and a pair of comedians from Osaka in tow.[11] To enter-tain troops was an important part of another mission led by Yoshigami Naosaburō, who brought an entourage of comedians, *rōkyoku* players, and dancers to comfort Korean military volunteers recruited into the imperial army from 1938 on.[12] After they returned to Korea, members of these missions reported moving encounters with soldiers, including touching stories of commanding officers "moved to tears of joy" at see-ing their soldiers roar with laughter.[13]

To draw more people into its activities, the Chōsen League mobi-lized its regional branches to hold lectures and film screenings, and used pamphlets and radio broadcasts to spread the concept of military assistance among the Korean public.[14] In July 1938, the league sponsored Tokyo Sumo Wrestling in Seoul, the proceeds of which were used for its military support activities.[15] The Chōsen League's participating organizations also helped spread the *imon* campaign. The local Japanese press, including the *Keijō Nippō* and the *Chōsen Kōron*, launched their own *imon* drives for Korean troops and organized annual *imon* visits to border guards stationed in northern Korea. The Korean Headquarters of the Patriotic Women's Association, run by Japanese and Korean wives of high-ranking colonial bureaucrats and aristocratic elites, assisted Chōsen League leaders while conducting their own *imon* campaigns. During the first year of the league's operation, members of the Patriotic Women's Association helped manufacture 20,000 *imon* bags for the league to donate to Korean troops stationed in north China.[16]

As in the imperial metropole, women were central participants in the grassroots patriotic movement. While male leaders planned activities, women often engaged in more concrete and laborious tasks such as preparing *imon* bags and sewing *senninbari* ("thousand-stitch" belts). Members of local women's groups stood on street corners to collect donations, ostracize extravagance, and alert people to the national emergency. Recognizing the utility of such hardworking women, the Imperial Soldiers Assistance Association of Kyŏnggi Province appointed part-time female employees to visit and care for soldiers' families in Seoul, In'chŏn, Kaesŏng, and Suwŏn.[17] Special female officers were appointed in local community councils as well. The role of women continued to increase as the colonial state moved to micro-manage people's daily lives for shoring up Japan's effort to wage all-out war.

The National Spiritual Mobilization Campaign

Civilian-led *imon* drives were further centralized under the rubric of the state-sponsored *Kokumin Seishin Sōdōin Undō* (National, or "People's," Spiritual Mobilization Campaign), launched in response to Prime Minister Konoe's December 1938 declaration of the "New Order in East Asia." The Korean League for National Spiritual Mobilization was created as the campaign's executive organ, with Vice Governor-General Ōno Rokuichirō as its chair. Its board of directors, made up of prominent civilians, colonial bureaucrats, and army officers, was headed by the colonial education bureau chief Shiobara Tokisaburō, Governor-General Minami's right-hand man. Known as "the peninsula's Hitler," Shiobara supervised the administration of the spiritual campaign in its first years of operation.[18] In addition to integrating sixty-one civic organizations into its membership, the Korean League for National Spiritual Mobilization built its chain of command by creating local executive organs at all administrative levels, as well as in schools, corporations, banks, large factories, and stores. Even Korean *kisaeng* (female entertainers) were organized.

At the very bottom of this hierarchy, a network of patriotic neighbourhood associations (*aikokuhan*, in Japanese; *aegukpan*, in Korean), counterparts to Japan's *tonarigumi* and composed of about ten households per unit, was created to bring all families, Korean as well as Japanese, under centralized state control.[19] Underlying this empire-wide network of neighbourhood associations was the logic of total war, which held that not only soldiers at the front but also citizens must actively share the burden of war through "defence of the home front."[20] In Korea, provincial leagues were instructed to complete their networks of patriotic neighbourhood associations by February 1939. The majority of Korean families soon belonged to one kind of patriotic neighbourhood association or another, affiliated to local organs of the spiritual campaign or those established for various occupations. The institutional web of neighbourhood associations quite literally became a family tree that spread into all provinces, districts, cities, and villages, and across the entire social fabric. This tree grew faster in Korea than it did in Japan – where the state struggled to goad its urban residents into organizing community institutions[21] – indicating how the colony, already inured to extensive state control, was easier to refashion into a system for total war mobilization.

As in Japan, Korea's patriotic neighbourhood associations typically were headed by local men of influence: the well-established leadership class of merchants, manufacturers, landlords, officeholders, educators, and professionals. According to Shiobara, spiritual mobilization was designed to overcome the limits of colonial schools and programs that aimed at Korean social engineering.[22] One such program implemented in 1932, the Rural Revitalization Campaign (*nōson shinkō undō*), sought to create a new leadership class of young owner-cultivators to replace the old landlords and to raise agricultural productivity while restoring harmony in rural areas torn by tenant disputes. Like the spiritual mobilization campaign, the rural revitalization campaign targeted individual families. By 1938, however, the aim of establishing a detailed revitalization plan for each household had been realized only among 17 per cent of farming families.[23] Moreover, as less than a third of school-aged Korean children were enrolled in school in 1937, the importance of the new spiritual campaign for mobilizing the majority of uneducated Koreans was considerable.[24]

The ideology of national spiritual mobilization reflected the imperatives of total war as well as Governor-General Minami's personal zeal to assimilate Koreans as imperial subjects, a zeal that far surpassed that of his predecessors. The colonial authorities explained the unfolding war as a combination of military, economic, and ideological warfare. Each was a vital component of total war, but, as Minami explained, people's "spiritual strength" would be the ultimate determinant.[25] Japan under total war, like other major participants in the Second World War, carried out a policy of "enforced homogeneity" "to unite all the people under the slogan of a common destiny as citizens of a single national community and to intervene against the momentum toward social exclusion and conflict."[26] This policy arguably found its most forceful expression in Korea and Taiwan, where social divisions were not only economic but also ethnic in nature. The mobilization of colonial subjects entailed a more coercive program of eradicating both dissent and difference, through the imposition of the emperor cult, Shinto worship, the Japanese language, and even Japanese names. Wartime mass mobilization became virtually synonymous with the imperialization of Koreans within the national spiritual campaign.

The imperialization of Koreans, in turn, was considered pivotal for the creation of the "New Order in East Asia," which required Japan to overcome the West while transcending its own bounded nationalism. Colonial Korea, one can argue, became the crucible of Japan's new internationalism, its effort to remake *kokutai* (the emperor-centred polity) into a supranational order. As a local Japanese ideologue explained, "[t]he completion of *naisen ittai* in the peninsula signified the highest and the last stage of the completion of *yūkika* [organic unity] within the East Asian bloc"; without completing *naisen ittai*, the East Asian Community would be an empty and ossified structure.[27] In this deceptively simple vision, Koreans would join Japanese in constructing and leading the new East Asian community by becoming members of the Yamato *minzoku* (ethnic group) – that is, by voluntarily renouncing their separate national identity. While calling for the unity of the sovereign nations of Japan, China, and Manchukuo (and later of the Southeast Asian nations under the Greater East Asia Co-Prosperity Sphere), Japan's "New Order in East Asia" pursued a colonial project of racial fusion diametrically opposed to its alleged respect for national autonomy.[28] This contradictory dynamic, long at the heart of colonial policies in Korea, captures Japan's wartime, and ultimately doomed, effort to reconcile racial expansionism with its new Asian-centred internationalism.

The policy platform of the Korean League, laid out in September 1938, shows how the wartime mobilization and imperialization of Koreans constituted the core of the national spiritual campaign: the raising of the spirit of the imperial state, the completion of *naisen ittai*, the renovation of life, cooperation with wartime economic policy, patriotic service through labour and business, support on the home front, and the prevention of communism and espionage. The twenty-one *jissen yōmoku* (practical objectives) for implementing this platform included imperial rituals such as worshipping at Shinto shrines, bowing towards the Imperial Palace, and respecting and hoisting the Japanese flag; daily life concerns such as the use of Japanese, thrift and savings, the reduction of consumption, the conservation of resources, and physical labour; and military support activities such as sending off and welcoming soldiers and supporting families of the bereaved.[29] Among the bewildering list of objectives, the campaign soon instructed local spiritual mobilizers to focus on "bowing towards the Imperial Palace" and "labour and savings" as the two most important duties.[30]

Local agents, rather than relying on radio or newspapers with limited reach among ordinary Koreans, ceaselessly organized speeches, lectures, and informal discussion meetings.[31] Following the metropolitan example, *kamishibai* (paper theatres) were used for inculcating Korean children in *naisen ittai* ideals.[32] Koreans were goaded – in the case of Christians, harassed – into bowing towards Shinto shrines and the emperor in Tokyo on all public occasions and, in a practice enforced only in Korea, reciting "the Oath as Subjects of the Imperial Nation":[33]

1 We are the subjects of the imperial nation; we will repay His Majesty as well as the country with loyalty and sincerity.
2 We the subjects of the imperial nation shall trust, love, and help one another so that we can strengthen our unity.
3 We the subjects of the imperial nation shall endure hardship, train ourselves, and cultivate strength so that we can exalt the Imperial Way.

In the course of the war, emperor-centred rituals became a routine of daily life, binding metropolitan Japanese and colonial peoples together as an "imagined community" of the emperor's subjects. From

September 1937, Patriotic Day was observed by schoolteachers and students, and later by all other residents, who were required to hoist the *hinomaru* flag, worship at local Shinto shrines, bow towards the Imperial Palace in Tokyo, recite the Imperial Oath, and perform public labour service.[34] Patriotic Day later became Public Service Day for Asia, to be observed on the first of every month in response to an August 1939 Japanese cabinet decision. In February 1942, it was again renamed, as Imperial Edict Day, to be observed by metropolitan and colonial populations on the eighth of each month to commemorate Japan's declaration of war against the United States on 8 December 1941. On this day, all residents in Korea, as members of local patriotic neighbourhood associations, were instructed to hold "early morning assembly" to observe a set of imperial rituals and to promote thorough understanding of the campaign's objectives.[35] This practice had not yet been implemented in Japan, where young people reportedly spent the day window shopping or strolling through parks instead.[36] Here was another example of how the colony set the trend ahead of the metropole.[37]

Provincial spiritual mobilization leagues promoted the imperialization of Korean residents as local agents of the Government-General's policy. From 1938, South Chŏlla Province's town and village spiritual mobilization leagues offered simple Japanese-language workshops to Koreans ages fifteen to thirty. The plan was to teach 400,000 Koreans at a thousand different locations over a period of eight years.[38] The provincial government also instructed local administrators to choose at least one candidate from each town and village for each round of recruitment for Korean military volunteers. The selected candidates were further screened by the provincial authorities who then recommended a list of finalists to the army.[39]

Controlling Everyday Life

As imperial rituals increasingly permeated public life in the colony, so the private lives of ordinary residents also became the object of state control.[40] The idea of the "home front" behind the organization of patriotic neighbourhood associations linked everyday life, including mundane details of food, clothing, and shelter, directly to the progress and outcome of the war. In October 1938, the spiritual mobilization campaign established detailed "guidelines for emergency national life improvement" regulating people's dress, diet, shelter, rituals and ceremonies, and social life.[41] Instead of wearing traditional white dress,

Korean males were encouraged to wear coloured clothing, which was deemed more economical and suited to labour, as it required less frequent washing, lasted longer, and thus conserved fabric. In daily diet, simple and nutritious meals as well as the custom of serving tea to visitors were promoted. Houses were to be kept clean and Korean-style houses were to meet new construction standards. Banquets were restricted to the hours before 11 pm while the exchange of wine cups was banned altogether. While Japanese imperial rituals were imposed on Korean families, Korean traditional rituals, especially weddings and funerals, were simplified and curtailed in accordance with the *Girei Junsoku* (Regulations on Rituals) issued in 1934.[42]

Spiritual mobilizers relied on women to implement these guidelines, especially educated Koreans known as *sin yŏsŏng* (new women), including Kim Hwallan of Ehwa Woman's College and Son Chŏnggyu of Kyŏnggi Higher Women's School. These Korean female educators formed their own organization, the Chosŏn Yŏsŏng Munje Yŏn'guhoe (Korean Women's Problems Research Association) to promote the improvement of Korean family life,[43] and worked closely with local Japanese female leaders such as Tsuda Setsuko of the Ryokki Renmei (Green Flag League).[44] Middle-class Korean and Japanese women frequently went on lecture tours to the provinces to urge residents to practise frugality, avoid waste, curtail consumption, and refrain from conducting elaborate ceremonies and traditional rituals. The Chongno Police Department in Seoul enlisted the aid of Korean female teachers and leaders of Christian women's organizations to hold women's-only rallies of local housewives and students from women's schools.[45]

Women were active, vocal, and independent agents when discussing issues concerning daily life. In late 1939, Son Chŏnggyu, Tsuda Setsuko, and Cho Kihong held a roundtable discussion on how to make Korean family life, "fraught with contradictions and irrational complexities," "more suitable for imperial subjects" and to cultivate greater self-awareness among Korean women.[46] While fostering spiritual assimilation through the Imperial Oath and other rituals, Tsuda argued, "we must also promote *naisen ittai* by correctly organizing people's material life pertaining to clothing, food, and shelter,"[47] a task she believed "lies in the hands of women."[48] The female leaders discussed how to improve urban family life by carefully planning meals and using fewer condiments, keeping the home clean and hygienic, and conducting less elaborate ceremonies. For poorer rural residents, they proposed a mixed-grain diet instead of white rice, and cooking rice only once a day to conserve fuel. While they encouraged Koreans to wear coloured clothing in lieu of traditional white dress, they also recommended Japanese women wear the *ch'ima* (Korean skirt), emphasizing its convenience and superiority to the *kimono* for housework and labour.[49] Korean dress was so ideal that Tsuda herself wore it in the summer and occasionally in the winter as well.[50] For these female leaders, *naisen ittai* policy was less about the simple Japanization of Korean life than about the promotion of the Japanese lifestyle infused with traditional Korean wisdom.

Limits of the Campaign

The efforts of its organizers notwithstanding, the campaign did not proceed as smoothly as hoped. When Governor-General Minami went on an inspection tour around the country in June 1939, he noted with disappointment the pervasive lack of self-awareness among members of patriotic neighbourhood associations and the failure of some provincial federations to form neighbourhood associations as instructed.[51] Lack of enthusiasm among the urban upper class was also widely reported. Maeda Noboru, head of the Seoul Defence Corps (Keijō Bōgodan), complained that whether it was shoring up support for the imperial army or conducting air-raid drills, it was always the middle, and not the upper, classes who were earnest.[52] Moreover, awareness of the current state of affairs was much greater in the countryside than in the cities, where people seemed "indifferent" to patriotic calls for rallying behind the empire.[53]

In addition to class and regional discrepancies, ethnic differences in patterns of campaign attendance were frequently observed. Japanese settlers often accused Koreans of lacking enthusiasm, complaining that bureaucrats and intelligentsia, especially, were lacklustre in supporting the state and mobilizing society.[54] On the other hand, settlers were far from perfect. Against the common Japanese accusation of Korean non-cooperation, Pak Tu-yŏng pointed to gender imbalance in Japanese participation, claiming that it was mostly women who took part, while all Koreans in rural areas – men and women, elderly and children – joined in sending off soldiers.[55] As a police report noted, some Koreans were more militant than settlers in expressing their support for war. One Korean businessman in Seoul chided Japanese attitudes as "lukewarm" and called for more coercive measures to deal with anti-war elements, as in Nazi Germany.[56]

Tension between settlers and Koreans also complicated the work of patriotic neighbourhood associations in mixed neighbourhoods. On the one hand, Korean neighbourhood heads might offend settlers by admonishing them to be more mindful of *naisen ittai* ideals and to abandon their sense of superiority.[57] On the other hand, Japanese neighbourhood heads had trouble dealing with wealthy Korean families who rarely attended community meetings and often sent their housemaids.[58]

Aside from these subtle gestures of elite disobedience, there was overt resistance among Christians who refused to bow to Shinto shines even though pressured by police to comply.[59] Those who failed to do so were persecuted on charges of harbouring *hikokumin shisō* (unpatriotic thought). In May 1938, when some Presbyterians in Sin-ŭiju refused to worship at shrines, their most "bigoted" leaders were taken into police custody.[60] Coercion and the surge of patriotic events ultimately compelled Christian leaders to pledge publicly their support for the spiritual campaign in fall 1938.[61]

Consolidating the Campaign

In April 1939 the National Spiritual Mobilization Committee, headed by Vice Governor-General Ōno Rokuichirō, was set up within the Korean Government-General to fortify the spiritual mobilization campaign.[62] Coordination with the Chōsen Army was strengthened by appointing military and *kenpeitai* police officers as advisors to its executive committee.[63] Instead of entrusting its operation to local officials and leaders of civic groups, Government-General bureau chiefs became directly involved in the management of the Korean Federation for National Spiritual Mobilization. The Government-General and the national spiritual campaign, in effect, became "two sides of the same coin."[64]

The institutional consolidation of the campaign paralleled the intensification of official efforts at imperializing Koreans. The Korean Education Rescript had been revised in 1938 to unify the school system for Japanese and Koreans and to expand Japanese-language study. The Korean language became optional in primary schools[65] and disappeared from the curriculum altogether in 1941.[66] The notorious name-changing campaign (*sōshi kaimei*, or "creating surname, changing name"[67]), enacted in November 1939 and implemented in February 1940, transplanted the Japanese *ie* (family) system to Korea and "allowed" Koreans to create Japanese-style family names and change their given names to match their new family names.[68] The promotion of intermarriage between Japanese and Koreans, only vaguely touted since the 1920s, also became part of the official agenda and the spiritual campaign's "plan of activities" from 1940.[69]

Governor-General Minami continued to emphasize the uniqueness of Korea's spiritual campaign, stressing the special importance of promoting Shinto worship, respect for the Japanese flag, singing of the national anthem, physical labour service, and rural revitalization, all of which were geared towards the "ultimate aim of the realization of *naisen ittai*."[70] A civilian ideologue of *naisen ittai* and leader of Ryokki Renmei, Tsuda Katashi, even suggested that Korea was leading the empire-wide spiritual mobilization campaign on behalf of Japan, whose failure to comprehend the meaning of *naisen ittai* made the colony lecture to the imperial metropole instead.[71]

As a means of ensuring mass participation, provincial governors, government employees, mayors, and district magistrates were instructed to inspect local patriotic neighbourhood associations during their trips to the provinces. Provincial authorities also poured their energy into training future leaders for the spiritual campaign. The most notable development was the creation in 1939 of *suishintai* (promoting corps),[72] mainly composed of Korean graduates of the official youth leaders' training centre and individuals who had completed their duty as military volunteers or had served as members of the Kō-A Kinrō Hōkoku Chōsen Butai (Korean Corps for Patriotic Youth Labour Service for Asia).[73] *Suishintai* members were dispatched to the villages to engage in volunteer activities and spread colonial propaganda, and to hold workshops on consolidating the work of local spiritual mobilization leagues and patriotic neighbourhood associations. From June 1939 the campaign's bulletin, *Sōdōin* (Total Mobilization), and from 1940 the Korean-language magazine *Saebyŏk* were distributed to local patriotic neighbourhood heads to promote understanding of their duties.[74] Other measures to diffuse popular awareness of the campaign included distributing federation badges for members,[75] recording the campaign's promotional songs,[76] manufacturing the campaign's flag,[77] and using films, posters, pamphlets, and later even *manga*[78] for propaganda.[79]

Nonetheless, all these measures, in Shiobara's view, were superficial glosses of genuine mobilization, which he believed hinged upon institutional consolidation.[80] For mobilizing the masses in rural areas, the campaign used its vast organizational network to cope with drought,[81] an issue that directly affected Koreans' livelihood. Its efficacy was demonstrated in the drought of 1939, which reduced the rice harvest in the

central and southern provinces by 10 million *koku*. One of the most affected provinces, South Chŏlla, had a total of 33,454 patriotic neighbourhood associations with 614,260 members.[82] Touring the province,
one *Keijō Nippō* reporter observed that every intersection had a sign
reading "Rising together, overcoming drought," while local villagers
devoted themselves to daily farm labour "under the patriotic neighbourhood association flag fluttering in the autumn wind."[83] Local spiritual mobilization leagues also aided the provincial government's relief
effort by collecting money for victims and mobilizing labour for land
reclamation, erosion control, and other construction works.[84]

Spiritual mobilizers in South Ch'ungch'ŏng Province likewise held
a mass rally for overcoming drought in fall 1939.[85] The success of local
neighbourhood associations in coping with the drought was publicized
the following year in official reports and by the local media. Masuda
Michiyoshi, director of the South Kyŏngsang Provincial League of Spiritual Mobilization, proudly stated that prevailing against a drought of
such magnitude owed to Korea's more successful spiritual mobilization compared to the metropole. He quoted as proof a recent *Bungei
Shunjū* opinion poll showing the Japanese public's disapproval of the
metropolitan spiritual mobilization campaign, a "failure" acknowledged by Tokyo officials themselves.[86]

Local police officers held *jikyoku zadankai* (current affairs discussion
meetings) to complement the spiritual campaign's still-imperfect organization at the lowest levels and to solicit the cooperation of farmers
with state economic policies.[87] Between August and November 1939,
42,844 such meetings were held and attended by more than two million
people in the southern provinces.[88] These discussions, sometimes accompanied by the use of photos, pictures, and paper theatre, aimed to
foster a spirit of self-reliance among rural residents and to guide them
to cope with drought and other issues related to daily living. They also
served as forums for villagers to address and discuss daily concerns. In
turn, local officials used them to sound out people's views on wartime
policies such as the required delivery of rice and grain and the unpopular tightening of economic controls.[89]

A much thornier task was to gain the active participation of city
dwellers. In contrast to peasants, well-informed urbanites were difficult
to mobilize. A Korean company employee in Seoul criticized the inef-
fectiveness of the campaign, pointing to how people's sentiments were
"regressing" to that before the Sino-Japanese Conflict, with the "national excitement" witnessed at the time of that incident nowhere to be

seen.[90] Another resident who served on the Seoul City Assembly complained that local patriotic neighbourhood associations "merely collected fees to feed their staff," and opposed the idea of reinforcing their authority, as they were "a nuisance to citizens."[91] As official and police reports noted, the educated upper classes were the most sceptical. Son Chŏnggyu bemoaned the passivity and apathy of educated Korean women, who rarely attended lectures and meetings.[92] Kim Hwallan similarly lamented that fellow urban females lacked awareness of the current state of affairs; instead, they had become more extravagant.[93]

There were also disagreements over how to mobilize the population and how best to carry out the campaign. Pessimistic about using the Korean intelligentsia, a Korean director of the spiritual campaign, Yi Sŭng-u, argued that the task of mobilizing the masses ultimately depended on colonial officials, especially the police.[94] On the other hand, the Japanese editor of *Chōsen Kōron* argued that spiritual mobilization should be carried out in a more "relaxed" manner by eliminating designs and colours that evoked "an oppressive feeling."[95] Others doubted Minami's excessive devotion to the diffusion of the Japanese "national spirit." Shakuo Shunjō of the *Chōsen oyobi Manshū* argued that the governor-general should focus on the expansion of production and the development of industry in Korea.[96]

The journalist's wish was granted the following year. In response to the inauguration of the Imperial Rule Assistance Movement in Japan, Korea's spiritual mobilization campaign was restructured in October 1940 as the Kokumin Sōryoku Undō (National Total Strength Campaign).[97] Apart from a reshuffle of leadership, the total strength campaign broadly inherited the objectives of the spiritual campaign,[98] but now "the expansion of productivity" was the main objective. The shift in emphasis to material production nonetheless left the spiritual component of the campaign intact[99] by stressing the expansion of production as a means of reinforcing spiritual mobilization as well as of coping with drought.[100]

The organizational structure of the total strength campaign differed from its predecessor in two important ways. First, the management of the campaign was more directly integrated into the colonial administration. Its executive organ, the Korean Federation for National Total Strength, was now headed by the governor-general and its administrative bureaus placed directly under the colonial bureau chiefs according to their areas of expertise.[101] Second, all existing lower-level organizations and campaigns pertaining to spiritual mobilization and moral suasion were absorbed into town and village organs of the total strength campaign and their patriotic neighbourhood associations.[102] As a result, the "spiritual mobilization" and "rural revitalization" campaigns were unified in the total strength campaign, and patriotic neighbourhood associations became the basic units for carrying out the entire range of colonial policies at the local level.[103]

In turn, patriotic neighbourhood associations came to function more fully as grassroots organs of imperialization. The city of Taegu launched an effort to raise one Korean military volunteer from each town league of the total strength campaign.[104] In Seoul, the city's total strength league used the school summer break to offer Japanese-language workshops for local residents, who apparently responded with "great enthusiasm," and achieved "great results."[105] By mid-1941, a Kyŏnggi police report noted, wedding ceremonies had become less elaborate; the traditional custom of requiring the groom to host an elaborate banquet after the ceremony had almost been done away with, while some Korean couples now wedded at Shinto shrines.[106] In South Ch'ungch'ŏng Province, patriotic neighbourhood associations produced statistics displaying members' ability to recite the Imperial Oath.[107] Throughout the peninsula, local patriotic neighbourhood associations encouraged families to adopt Japanese names in support of the name-changing campaign.[108]

As Japan's military ambitions extended into Southeast Asia, patriotic neighbourhood associations also turned increasingly into instruments of war. When food rationing began in the cities in 1940, rations were distributed through town leagues of the total strength campaign, thereby making it mandatory for residents to join a local league.[109] One village (*myŏn*) head evidently refused to give rations to local residents unless they could recite the Imperial Oath in Japanese.[110] In some rural areas, local patriotic neighbourhood associations served as administrative organs for requisitioning grains or storing emergency food supplies.

Local administrators used patriotic neighbourhood associations to implement the labour draft, which began in 1939,[111] and to support the new system of Korean conscription implemented in 1944.[112] Patriotic neighbourhood associations also played an instrumental role in promoting savings – one of the important sources of wartime finance. They encouraged local residents to have postal savings and postal life insurance, entrust their assets to banks and financial unions, and buy government bonds, savings bonds, and *hōkoku* (patriotic service bonds) to raise the estimated 100 million yen needed for military expenses each year.[113] Thanks to the efforts of local neighbourhood heads, these savings exceeded targets each year between 1938 and 1943.[114]

Available documentation suggests that, by the outbreak of the Pacific War in 1941, the spiritual and total strength campaigns had achieved some success in mobilizing local residents for war, even in fostering Korean patriotism for the Japanese Empire. In Kyŏnggi Province, according to one police report, Korean-run neighbourhood associations began collecting waste materials and donating ironware and brass products. Korean women in particular became more keenly aware of the home front: they now "competed with one another to participate and devote themselves seriously in air-raid drills they had previously tended to avoid."[115] More dramatically, another publication noted how Koreans of all ages and occupations – including members of women's groups, textile factory workers, labourers, miners, *kisaeng*, Confucian scholars, railway workers, primary school children, and the elderly – were avidly making donations to the army from their modest daily earnings.[116]

The total strength campaign also ran into obstacles, however. Not only were both Korean and Japanese residents turned off by its orchestration from above;[117] many did not comprehend the campaign's vaguely phrased aims and long-winded objectives.[118] Even as late as 1943, some town leagues and patriotic neighbourhood associations in Kyŏnggi Province reportedly failed to understand and communicate the will of the authorities to local residents.[119] The message of frugality also seems to have been lost among urban residents. In Seoul, a police officer noted, local residents came to treat each neighbourhood meeting as "a kind of party [*matsuri*]": they adorned their children with beautiful clothes and prepared food and drinks, while the host purchased unnecessary drawers and book shelves or upgraded *zabuton* [cushions], gestures which "made light of the total strength campaign's aim."[120]

War weariness set in as the colonial state made increasing demands on Korean labour and sacrifice. Social and economic grievances occasionally erupted into open confrontation with local authorities. According to a Kyŏnggi report of 1940, the policy of restricting lending froze the money supply, causing farmers to demand prompt cash payments for rice requisitioned by authorities. Some villagers even threw stones and resorted to other acts of violence towards local officials.[121] The total strength campaign sought to circumvent this trend of war weariness, but with limited success. The deepening of the control economy caused a surge in prices and a shortage of daily necessities, especially of the textile canequim, rubber shoes, petroleum for lamps, and tobacco. The growth of rationing also restricted the distribution of daily necessities to officially designated purveyors, putting many merchants, especially rice millers, out of business. Faced with hardship and various restrictions on their daily lives, many Koreans began to desire a quick end to the conflict.[122]

Declining morale was also noted in the cities. A local Japanese merchant in Seoul observed that, in comparison to Japan, residents in Korea did not cooperate with the state, as witnessed by the continued prosperity of the pleasure quarters.[123] Indeed, only few restaurants, cafes, and brothels were forced to close or change their business as a result of the *seikatsu shintaisei* (New Life Order).[124] Although their earnings dropped, many of these businesses continued through wartime.[125] Ironically, as one police report noted, it was the officials who did not abide by the restrictions and held the longest banquets. The consumption of luxury goods also continued unabated, and moviegoers, most of them Korean, flocked to the theatres.

Although people actively sought pleasure, they seemed far less excited about expending energy on patriotic activities. Residents grumbled about unnecessary discipline imposed by neighbourhood meetings, such as taking off their jackets in cold weather; others wanted the payment of fees for meetings abolished, as in Japan.[126] Another sign of increasing popular discontent was the fluctuating (and declining) number of visitors to Chōsen Shrine – in Kyonggi Province, visitors numbered 128,336 in February 1941, compared with 201,518 the previous month and 175,283 the previous February.[127]

Lack of cooperation among the educated upper classes also did not disappear, as neighbourhood heads continued to complain of their absence from meetings and communal activities.[128] A Korean city assemblyman in Seoul argued that the focus of the campaign should be redirected to the Korean intelligentsia and upper-class youths who exhibited "critical" and "contemptuous" attitudes.[129] To address this, prominent Korean elites such as Yun Ch'iho, Ch'oe Rin, Cho Pyŏngsang, and Han Sang-nyong formed a variety of patriotic organizations and called upon regional leaders to join in. Their moves were met with little enthusiasm and much scepticism.[130]

A gulf in awareness continued to divide country from city. One informed Korean resident in Seoul lamented that, while young and old in rural areas devoted themselves to their duties, young men in the cities "lived idly." Elites would drive their cars to the countryside to buy land, or build houses in the mountains as places of refuge, unnecessarily stirring anxiety among local villagers.[131]

Contrary to the official emphasis on shared duties as imperial sub-jects, some Koreans began to demand rights as Japanese citizens by appropriating the rhetoric of *naisen ittai*. As an official report noted, or-dinary Koreans "confuse *naisen ittai* with *naisen byōdō* [equality]" while "at every meeting" a growing number of wage earners demanded the right to additional *kahō* (allowance), as the Japanese received.[132] Internal affairs bureau chief Yamamoto at the North Chungchong Provincial As-sembly cautioned against the Korean tendency to "confuse *naisen ittai* and hasten it only in form," and dismissed the issue of ethnic discrimi-nation as "peripheral" to the goal of creating true imperial subjects.[133]

As these examples illustrate, even in the midst of total war, the co-lonial state had only limited control over people's everyday lives and thoughts. The colonizer's will could even be subverted with demands for more rights in return for support of war. Meanwhile, the imperi-alization campaign, hastily accelerated in the course of war, did not progress as fast as the Japanese had hoped. Even in 1941, barely 20 per cent of Koreans spoke Japanese[134] while intermarriage between Japa-nese and Koreans, another gauge of *naisen ittai*, continued to make up a tiny fraction of the total number of marriages.[135]

Although the imperialization of Koreans progressed slowly, de-mands on their labour and sacrifice did not. In the 1940s, the Japanese government began forcibly to transfer thousands of Koreans to Japan to work in dangerous mines and factories or to construct airfields, and Korean women were "recruited" to serve Imperial Army soldiers as "comfort women." Partly in response to signs of non-compliance and lack of discipline among local residents, punishment for violating the *Kokka Sōdōin Hō* (State General Mobilization Law) also became much harsher in the last years of the war.[136] Presbyterian missionaries who refused to bow to Shinto shrines now faced jail or virtual expulsion from the peninsula.[137] In their effort to solicit "voluntary" mass coop-eration, the Japanese rulers to the end did not lessen their dependence on coercion.

Conclusion

The spiritual mobilization campaign represented a colonial experiment of unprecedented scope and ambition. It built an all-encompassing framework for mobilizing each and every family towards the ultimate goal of transforming all Koreans into Japanese in "form, mind, blood, and flesh."[138] The wartime policy of imperialization also produced Korean advocates of *naisen ittai*[139] and a new generation of Koreans thoroughly Japanized in appearance, language, and thought. By the beginning of the Pacific War in 1941, virtually all families had to cooperate with the state through local patriotic neighbourhood associations. Any attempt to isolate "collaborators" thus might be a futile exercise – it is hard to identify those who turned their backs on the Korean *minjok* (nation) when the entire population was forced to bow towards the emperor.

Totalizing in its intent to mobilize and transform the Korean population, the wartime colonial regime nonetheless produced tensions and contradictions that prevented the Japanese from meeting their lofty ambition. There were class, regional, and racial discrepancies in people's attendance within the spiritual mobilization campaign, and although its institutional framework was more or less complete by 1941, it is difficult to gauge the extent to which local residents internalized the campaign's messages and slogans, which often amounted to vague, moralistic hectoring from above. Although many Koreans participated alongside Japanese residents in activities in support of the war, some with enthusiasm, available documents and police records suggest that, even in Kyŏnggi Province, the location of the bureaucratic capital of Seoul, the authorities struggled to the end to spread awareness and mobilize local residents for war.

These findings, much as they tell us of the transformative design of the colonial regime, warn us against the danger of taking its power for granted. The Japanese rulers built an elaborate institutional apparatus for collaboration between state and society, but the use of coercion was indispensable for sustaining this structure. Beneath the guise of totalitarian control, a delicate balance between persuasion and coercion always existed – a balance that increasingly shifted towards the latter in the course of war.

NOTES

I owe special thanks to Tosh Minohara and Masato Kimura for including me in this collaborative project and to all the participants of the conference, "Tumultuous Decade: Japan's Challenge to the International System, 1931–41," at the University of California, Berkeley, for their comments on the earlier version of this chapter.

1 Gregory Henderson, *Korea: Politics of the Vortex* (Cambridge, MA: Harvard University Press, 1968).

2 Hyman Kublin's term, used in Chulwoo Lee, "Modernity, Legality, and Power in Korea under Japanese Rule," in *Colonial Modernity in Korea*, edited by Gi-Wook Shin and Michael Robinson (Cambridge, MA: Harvard University Asia Center, 1999), 37, 39.

3 In Taiwan, the Japanese colonial government carried out the same accelerated program of assimilation known as *kōkoku shinminka* or *kōminka* (imperialization). But, as Wan-yao Chou has pointed out, the imperialization policy was in many respects carried out more harshly and comprehensively in Korea than in Taiwan. For a comparison of the imperialization policy in the two colonies, see Chou, "The Kōminka Movement in Taiwan and Korea: Comparisons and Interpretations," in *The Japanese Wartime Empire, 1931–1945*, edited by Peter Duus et al. (Princeton, NJ: Princeton University Press, 1996), 40–68.

4 The representative works include Miyata Setsuko's pioneering study, *Chōsen minshū to 'kōminka' seisaku* (Tokyo: Miraisha, 1985) and Ch'oe Yuri's *Ilche malgi singminji chibae chŏngch'aek yŏngu* (Seoul: Kukhak Charyowŏn, 1997).

5 Chōsen Gunji Kōen Renmei, *Gunji Kōen Renmei jigyō yōran* (Keijō [Seoul]: Chōsen Gunji Kōen Renmei, 1939), 3.

6 Honshi kisha, "Keijō Gunji Kōen Renmei wa nani o shiteiruka?" *Chōsen oyobi Manshū* (August 1938), 66–7.

7 Ōtake Jūrō, "Chōsen ni okeru gunji engo jigyō no gaikyō," *Dōhōai* 16, no. 11 (November 1938): 24.

8 "Aikoku Chōsen o kataru zadankai," *Keijō Nippō*, 19 August 1938.

9 Chōsen Gunji Kōen Renmei, *Gunji Kōen Renmei jigyō yōran*, 6.

10 Ibid., 13–14.

11 Ibid., 14–15.

12 Yugami Naojirō, "Dai-issen no imon yori kaerite," *Sōdōin* 1, no. 6 (November 1939): 52–7. This system permitted four hundred able-bodied Korean males ages seventeen and above to serve in the Japanese army. In response to the popularity of the program, the number of recruits was raised every year; Miyata Setsuko, "Sōshi kaimei no jidai," in Miyata Setsuko, Kim Yŏng-dal, and Yang T'ae-ho, eds., *Sōshi Kaimei* (Tokyo: Akashi Shoten, 1992), 23, 48–51.

13 Chōsen Gunji Kōen Renmei, *Gunji Kōen Renmei jigyō yōran*, 18–19.

14 For a detailed explanation of the federation's activities, see Chōsen Gunji Kōen Renmei, *Gunji Kōen Renmei jigyō yōran*, 6–26.

15 Honshi kisha, "Keijō Gunji Kōen Renmei wa nani o shiteiruka?" *Chōsen oyobi Manshū* (August 1938), 67.

16 Chōsen Gunji Kōen Renmei, *Gunji Kōen Renmei jigyō yōran*, 21.

17 Honshi kisha, "Keijō Gunji Kōen Renmei wa nani o shiteiruka?" 67.
18 The colonial Education Bureau's Social Education Section was the main bureaucratic organ in charge of the national spiritual mobilization campaign at its inception.
19 See the diagram entitled "Kokumin Seishin Sōdōin Undō soshiki" in Morita Yoshio, ed., *Chōsen ni okeru kokumin sōryoku undōshi* (Keijō [Seoul]: Kokumin Sōryoku Chōsen Renmei, 1945), 31.
20 Takahashi Hamakichi, "Katei to kokumin seishin sōdōin undō," *Sōdōin* 1, no. 1 (June 1939): 26–7.
21 Thomas R.H. Havens, *Valley of Darkness: The Japanese People and World War Two* (New York: W.W. Norton, 1978), 40–1.
22 Shiobara Tokisaburō, "Kokumin seishin sōdōin ni tsuite," *Sōdōin* 1, no. 3 (August 1939): 16.
23 Anzako Yuka, "Chōsen ni okeru sensō dōin seisaku no tenkai: 'kokumin undō' no soshikika o chūshin ni," *Kokusai Kankeigaku Kenkyū* (Tsudajuku Daigaku) 21 bessatsu (March 1995): 4.
24 Shiobara's comments in ibid., 3.
25 Minami Jirō, "Renmei shidōin ni nozomu," *Sōdōin* 1, no. 1 (June 1939): 5; Kada Naoji, "Jūgo keizaisen to kokumin seishin sōdōin," ibid., 20; Ōno Rokuichirō, "Seihai ha tsunagatte seishinryoku ni ari," *Sōdōin* 1, no. 2 (July 1939): 7–8.
26 Yamanouchi Yasushi, "Total-War and System Integration: A Methodological Introduction," in *Total War and "Modernization,"* edited by Yamanouchi Yasushi, J. Victor Koschmann, and Narita Ryūichi (Ithaca, NY: Cornell University, East Asia Program, 1998), 3. Yamanouchi hypothesizes that the total-war system accelerated the process of social reorganization, which entailed "a shift from a class to a system society." Although his hypothesis is limited to the domestic context of Japan, one might surmise that a parallel process of social reorganization took place in the colonies, especially Korea under the policy of *naisen ittai*.
27 Tsuda Katashi, *Naisen ittai ron no kihon rinen* (Keijō [Seoul]: Ryokki Renmei, 1939), 82, 84.
28 For an interrogation of the concept of sovereignty, see Prasenjit Duara, *Sovereignty and Authenticity: Manchukuo and the East Asian Modern* (Lanham, MD: Rowman and Littlefield, 2003).
29 Chōsen Sōtokufu, *Chōsen ni okeru kokumin seishin sōdōin* (Keijō [Seoul]: Chōsen Sōtokufu, 1940), 34–36; "Kokumin Seishin Sōdōin Chōsen Renmei kōryō, jissen yōmoku," *Sōdōin* 1, no. 1 (June 1939): 38–40.
30 Chōsen Sōtokufu, *Chōsen ni okeru kokumin seishin sōdōin*, 48.

31 These lectures and discussion meetings focused mostly on the role of
the Korean Federation for National Spiritual Mobilization and patriotic
neighbourhood associations. In addition, there were many lectures on the
"Japanese spirit," attended by the federation's executives, educators, and
scholars, and high-ranking colonial officials. For instance, in August 1939,
Minoda Muneki, a right-wing chauvinist well known for his attack on
Minobe Tatsukichi's emperor-as-organ theory, was invited to speak. See
Sōdōin 1, no. 4 (September 1939): 30–4.
32 *Chōsen Kōron* (May 1938), 66.
33 Taiwanese were never obliged to take the Imperial Oath, showing that
the Japanese had less difficulty in securing their loyalty. Chou, "Kōminka
Movement in Taiwan and Korea," 43.
34 Chōsen Sōtokufu, *Chōsen ni okeru kokumin seishin sōdōin*, 33.
35 Ibid., 49; and Kokumin Sōryoku Chōsen Renmei, ed., *Kokumin sōryoku
undō yōran* (Keijō [Seoul]: Kokumin Sōryoku Chōsen Renmei, 1943), 33.
36 Havens, *Valley of Darkness*, 17.
37 The colonial internal affairs bureau chief Ōtake also stated with confidence
that "Korea has always taken the initiative ahead of Japan in the national
spiritual campaign"; *Keijō Nippō*, 5 August 1939.
38 "Hijōji kokumin no sasshin: Kokumin Seishin Sōdōin Zenra Nandō Renmei no katsuyaku," *Chōsen Kōron* (November 1939), 94–5.
39 Ibid., 95.
40 In previous decades, the colonial government had been concerned primarily with nurturing pro-Japanese collaborators while countering Korean nationalists. As organized nationalist movements all but disappeared in the
repressive climate after 1937, the colonial authorities turned to micro-man-
aging the everyday life of the masses.
41 Chōsen Sōtokufu, *Chōsen ni okeru kokumin seishin sōdōin*, 36–39; "Seikatsu
sasshin no kyōka," *Sōdōin* 1, no. 3 (August 1939): 18.
42 *Chōsen shakai jigyō* 12, no. 12 (December 1934): 9–17. The new regulations
simplified wedding ceremonies and receptions, and reduced betrothal
gifts from the family of the groom to the family of the bride. They also
made mourning dress less ornamental and shortened the period of mourning, while abolishing the custom of "formal wailing" for condolences. An-
cestor worship was limited to two generations instead of four as had been
done in the past, while the number of Korean festivals was drastically
reduced.
43 Cho Kihong, "Seikatsu kaizen ni tsuite," *Sōdōin* 1, no. 3 (August 1939):
24. The association's proposal concerning Korean female dress became

directly incorporated into the above guidelines; Chōsen Sōtokufu, *Chōsen ni okeru kokumin seishin sōdōin*, 37.

44 For a detailed study of the Green Flag League, see Takasaki Sōji, "Ryokki Renmei to 'kōminka' undō," in *Kikan sanzenri* 31 (fall 1982).

45 Keijō Shōro Keisatsu Shochō, Keijō Shōro Keisatsu Shochō to Keijō Chihō Hōin Kenjisei, police report, "(Jikyoku kōenkai) shūkai torishimari jōkyō hōkoku, tsūhō," no. 5813-1 (30 June 1938), 4–5, *Shisō ni Kansuru Jōhō* 9, Han'guk Yŏksa Chŏngbo Tonghap Sisŭtem [Korean History Data Integration System; hereafter cited as HYCTS], Kuksa P'yŏnch'an Wiwŏnhoe, Kyŏnggi-do Kwach'ŏnsi, South Korea.

46 Son Chŏng-kyu et al., *Gendai Chōsen no seikatsu to sono kaizen* (Kyō no Chōsen Mondai Kōza 5) (Keijō [Seoul]: Ryokki Renmei, 1939), 1–4.

47 Ibid., 2.

48 Ibid., 3.

49 Ibid., 23.

50 Chōsen Shakai Jigyō Kyōkai, *Dōhōai* 14, no. 4 (April 1936): 30.

51 Anzako, "Chōsen ni okeru sensō dōin seisaku no tenkai," 12.

52 Maeda Noboru, "Kyokoku icchi no shinseishin," *Chōsen Kōron* (August 1937), 29–30.

53 "Aikoku Chōsen o kataru zadankai," *Keijō Nippō*, 19 August 1938.

54 Shakuo Tōhō, "Jiron: Minami sōtoku no naisen ittai ron," *Chōsen oyobi Manshū* 379 (June 1939): 6.

55 "Aikoku Chōsen o kataru zadankai (7)," *Keijō Nippō*, 24 August 1938.

56 Keikidō Keisatsu Buchō to Keimu Kyokuchō, police report, "Jikyoku ni taisuru bumin no gendō ni kansuru ken," nos. 413–23 (27 March 1941), *Shisō ni Kansuru Jōhō* 13, 1, Keijō funai bō kaisha, Ri Ichi Ei [Yi Il-yŏng], HYCTS.

57 Keikidō Keisatsu Buchō to Keimu Kyokuchō and Keijō Chihō Hōin Kenjisei, police report, "Jinsen furiin no shitsugen mondai ni kansuru ken," no. 1810 (24 July 1939), *Shisō ni Kansuru Jōhōtoji* 4, HYCTS.

58 Iijima Mitsutaka, letter to author, 2 August 2003, 25.

59 For instance, the Presbyterian leaders in Ch'ŏngju were given "friendly admonitions" by the police authorities and reportedly "awakened" to their mission as imperial subjects to worship at shrines, hoist a Japanese flag, and bow toward the Imperial Palace; "Warera mo kōkoku shinmin: jinja sanpai wa jukkai ni somukazu," *Keijō Nippō*, 1 April 1938.

60 "Jinja sanpai kyohi no kyōto o danko kensoku," *Chōsen Shinbun*, 18 May 1938.

61 "Jinja sanpai mondai ga sanpunkan de kaiketsu," *Chōsen Shinbun*, 12 September 1938.

62 At the governors' conference in the same month, Minami also expressed his determination to implement his "Five-Point Political Platform," which consisted of *kokutai meichō* (the clarification of national polity), *Sen-Man ichinyo* (unity between Korea and Manchuria), *kyōgaku sasshin* (the promotion of learning), *nōkō heishin* (the parallel development of agriculture and industry), and *shosei sasshin* (the renovation of general governance).

63 In December 1938 Minami had already invited General Kawashima Yoshiyuki, former Chōsen Army commander and the army minister at the time of the 26 February Incident, to head the Korean Federation of National Spiritual Mobilization.

64 "Renmei ihō," *Sōdōin* 1, no. 1 (1939): 37; "Renmei ihō," *Sōdōin* 1, no. 2 (1939): 39. In August the federation further expanded its leadership by incorporating more prominent civilians; "Ashinami soroete sōkyōryoku e," *Keijō Nippo*, 5 March 1939.

65 As a result of the revision, the separation between "those who use Japanese regularly" and "those who do not use Japanese regularly" – the basis for dividing Japanese and Koreans in school education since the Education Rescript of 1922 – was abolished and school names were unified (the term "normal school," applied to Korean schools, was replaced by the same generic terms used for Japanese schools, such as "primary school," "middle school," and "high school"); Shiobara Tokisaburō, "Chōsen Kyōikurei no kaisei ni tsuite," Chōsen Sōtokufu, *Chōsen* 275 (April 1938): 9–12; *Keijō Nippō*, 2 July 1937.

66 Kim Puja, *Shokuminchiki Chōsen no kyōiku to gendā: shūgaku fushūgaku o meguru kenryoku kankei* (Yokohama: Seori Shobō, 2005), 41.

67 *Sōshi* referred to the setting up of an *ie* (family) and adopting a Japanese-style family name in accordance with it, while *kaimei* meant that one could also change his or her given name to match the new family name; Yang T'ae-ho, "'sōshi kaimei' no shisōteki haikei," in *Sōshi Kaimei*, 126.

68 Revisions to the *Chōsen Minji rei* (Korean Civil Law) concerning inheritance (issued November 1939; in effect February 1940) allowed the creation of Japanese-style family names (*uji*) and the adoption as an heir the husband of one's daughter (*muko yōshi engumi*); see "Waga koyū no kazokusei ishoku Chōsen no shinzoku sōzoku kaisei," *Tokyo Nichinichi Shinbun*, 25 June 1939; "Naigaichi ittaika no shinzoku sōzokuhō kakuritsu," *Chōsen Kōron* (July 1939), 7.

69 Morita, *Chōsen in okeru kokumin sōryoku undōshi*, 102. Other measures for the "completion of *naisen ittai*" included the diffusion of the Japanese language, the propaganda and diffusion of the system of military volunteers,

the promotion of the system of adopting Japanese family names, and the fusion of Japanese and Korean manners and customs (101–2).

70 Minami Jirō, "Renmei honrai no shimei: giron yorimo jikkō e," *Sōdōin* 1, no. 2 (July 1939): 59–60.

71 Tsuda, *Naisen ittai ron no kihon rinen*, 73.

72 *Sōdōin* 1, no. 5 (October 1939): 64–5.

73 The system of Patriotic Youth Labour Service for Asia was created in the name of building the New East Asian Order. In the summer of 1939, ten thousand Japanese youth were mobilized to engage in volunteer labour service in Manchuria, north China, and Mongolia for three months, while Korea also organized its own corps of 144 men (ten young men were selected from each province) who did labour service in the Kantō area in Japan for two months. Takagi Masamitsu, "Kōa Seinen Kinrō Hōkokutai ni sanka shite," *Sōdōin* 1, no. 6 (November 1939): 58, 62.

74 *Sōdōin* 1, no. 1 (June 1939): 3; *Sōdōin* 1, no. 6 (November 1939): 88–91; Anzako, "Chōsen ni okeru sensō dōin seisaku no tenkai," 15. As of mid-October 1939, a total of 14,350 copies of the *Sōdōin* had been distributed to all provinces in Korea as well as in Manchuria. Later, 350,000 copies of *Saebyŏk* were distributed.

75 *Sōdōin* 1, no. 2 (July 1939): 5.

76 *Sōdōin* 1, no. 3 (August 1939): 30–4; *Sōdōin* 1, no. 5 (October 1939): 65, 78–9. Out of 1,787 applications to the contest, a song composed by a local Japanese primary school teacher was selected as the federation's theme song. The judges included famous Japanese writers such as Hirakawa Seifū, Kume Masao, and Kikuchi Kan.

77 *Sōdōin* 1, no. 3 (August 1939): 35–7.

78 Morita, *Chōsen ni okeru kokumin sōryoku undōshi*, 56–8.

79 Provincial organs of the campaign also devised their own guidelines and strategies for consolidating the activities of local patriotic neighbourhood associations. For the example of the North Ch'ungch'ŏng provincial league, see *Sōdōin* 1, no. 4 (September 1939): 35–6.

80 Shiobara Tokisaburō, "Kokumin seishin sōdōin ni tsuite," *Sōdōin* 1, no. 3 (August 1939): 15–6.

81 "Renmei no sōgai taisaku," *Sōdōin* 1, no. 4 (September 1939): 8–9; and "Sōgai taisaku to rōgin teppu jigyō ni tsuite," *Sōdōin* 1, no. 5 (October 1939): 54–5.

82 "Hijōji kokumin no sasshin: Kokumin Seishin Sōdōin Zenra Nandō Renmei no katsuyaku," *Chōsen Kōron* (November 1939), 97.

83 Matsuda Sadahisa, "Kangai o kokufuku suru aikokuhan no katsuyaku o miru," *Sōdōin* 1, no. 7 (December 1939): 63–4.

84 "Hijōji kokumin no sasshin," *Chōsen Kōron* (November 1939), 95–6.

85 *Sōdōin* 1, no. 7 (December 1939), 87–8.

86 Ibid.

87 Matsuda Toshihiko, "Sōryokuki no shokuminchi Chōsen ni okeru keisatsu gyōsei: keisatsukan ni yoru 'jikyoku zadankai' o jiku ni," *Nihonshi Kenkyū* 452 (April 2000): 204–10.

88 Chōsen Sōtokufu Keimukyoku Hoanka, *Jūgo o mamoru jikyoku zadankai* (Keijō [Seoul], May 1940), 12.

89 As Matsuda Toshihiko notes, these signs of discontent might not have been expressions of anti-Japanese hostility per se so much as general socio-economic grievances aired by citizens under war; Matsuda, "Sōryokuki no shokuminchi Chōsen," 213–16.

90 Keikidō Keisatsu Buchō to Keimu Kyokuchō, police report, "Jikyoku ni taisuru bumin no gendō ni kansuru ken," nos. 413–23 (27 March 1941), 1, "Keijō funai bōkaishain Yi Ichi Ei," *Shisō ni Kansuru Jōhō* 13, HYCTS.

91 Ichi kisha, "Dōkai to fukai o nozoite," *Chōsen oyobi Manshū* 389 (April 1940), 82.

92 Son Chŏnggyu, "Hijōjikyoku to hantō no josei," *Sōdōin* 1, no. 2 (July 1939): 29–30.

93 Kim Hwallan, "Jikyoku to tokai josei," *Sōdōin* 1, no. 1 (June 1939): 28–31.

94 Yi Sŭng-u, "Chō renmei ni hakusha jikkō sasetai teian ichini," *Sōdōin* 1, no. 2 (July 1939): 17–18.

95 He pointed out that progressive metropolitan writers in Japan had already called for abolishing Public Service for Asia Day and changing it to a day of entertainment, to separate people from their workplaces where they were made to feel ready to defend the home front at all times; "Seidō ni hitokoto," *Chōsen Kōron* (August 1940), 1.

96 Shakuo Tōhō, "Jiron," *Chōsen oyobi Manshū* (May 1939), 5.

97 Morita, *Chōsen ni okeru kokumin sōryoku undōshi*, 42–4. At the same time, the Government-General carefully noted that Korea's New Order movement was "not a political movement."

98 The objectives were now reorganized into three main categories: the "unification of thought" through "the elevation of the Japanese spirit" and "the completion of *naisen ittai*"; *kokumin sōkunren* (national total training) through "occupational service" and the "establishment of a new life system"; and "the expansion of productivity" through "the promotion of wartime economy" and "increased production"; see Nishiyama Riki, "Chōsen no shintaisei," *Chōsen oyobi Manshū* (November 1940), 18.

99 "Honkakuteki sōryoku undō o tenkai," *Chōsen Kōron* (May 1941), 33, 35. By this time the idea of shared ancestry of Japanese and Koreans had also

become widespread in the colony. Okuyama Senzō, an executive of the Korean Federation for National Total Strength, characteristically argued that Japan and Korea had been one since the age of gods: "a myriad of Korean people had already emigrated to Japan and mixed with the Japanese people to form the great Yamato race. The blood of the Korean people flowed in the vein of our ancestors in the largest quantity"; Okuyama Senzō, "Shintaisei to naisen ittai," *Chōsen oyobi Manshū* (January 1941), 23.

100 "Naisen ittai gugen to seikaku ni chūsū o oku," *Chōsen Shinbun*, 15 March 1940.

101 Nishiyama, "Chōsen no shintaisei," 18–19.

102 Although the central administrative organ was restructured accordingly, local administrative federations as well as the patriotic neighbourhood associations essentially remained unchanged. The board of directors, councillors, and advisors remained more or less the same as before (a combination of high-ranking bureaucrats, military officers, and prominent civilians). Town leagues of the *chō renmei* (total strength campaign) were organized on the basis of the districts of *chōkai* (community councils) while *chō sōdai* (neighbourhood heads) became the chairs of town leagues; see "Kokumin Sōryoku Chōsen Renmei yakuin meibo," Kokumin Sōryoku Chōsen Renmei, *Kokumin sōryoku undō yōran*, 89–114. In addition, occupational leagues of the total strength campaign were formed in the areas of commerce and industry, mining, marine products, and education. Patriotic neighbourhood associations within occupational leagues were also renamed *shihōtai* (service/volunteer corps) and treated separately from the patriotic neighbourhood associations within local administrative leagues of the total strength campaign; Morita, *Chōsen ni okeru kokumin sōryoku undōshi*, 71–3.

103 Nishiyama, "Chōsen no shintaisei," 19. This solved the incipient friction between patriotic neighbourhood associations of the spiritual campaign and rural revitalization councils that came to operate simultaneously in rural villages. After the Rural Revitalization Campaign was integrated into the National Total Strength Campaign as *buraku seisan kakujū keikaku* (plan for the expansion of rural production) in October 1940, the role of *buraku renmei* (village leagues) and *kuchō* (district chiefs) who oversaw them increased dramatically.

104 Anzako, "Chōsen ni okeru sensō dōin seisaku no tenkai," 11.

105 Keikidō Keisatsu Buchō to Keimu Kyokuchō et al., police report, "Jikyokuka no minjō ni kansuru ken," no. 2426 (29 August 1941).

106 Keikidō Keisatsu Buchō to Keimu Kyokuchō, et al., police report, "Jikyoku ka no minjō ni kansuru ken," no. 1743 (30 June 1941), n.p., *Shisō ni Kansuru Jōhō* 13, HYCTS.

107 As Anzako points out, given the slow diffusion of Japanese among Koreans, the recitation of the oath served as a kind of litmus test for Koreans to confirm their obedience or "absence of hostility" to Japan; Anzako,
"Chōsen ni okeru sensō dōin seisaku no tenkai," 14.
108 Morita, *Chōsen ni okeru kokumin sōryoku undōshi*, 102.
109 Anzako, "Chōsen ni okeru sensō dōin seisaku no tenkai," 11. In South
Kyŏngsang Province, for instance, the rationing of rubber shoes, cotton cloth, and fertilizer, as well as the production and delivery of grains,
fertilizer, hemp, cotton, and straw sacks were all conducted through patriotic neighbourhood associations; see Nakagawa Kamezō, "Keinan no
renmei to aikokuhan (1)," *Chōsen Kōron* (May 1941), 27–8.
110 Anzako, "Chōsen ni okeru sensō dōin seisaku no tenkai," 14.
111 The Korean Federation for National Total Strength also helped the Government-General carry out its policy of forced labour and a system of
teishintai (female service corps) by publishing a pamphlet that provided
a detailed explanation of the new system of *kokumin chōyō* (national conscription); see Tawara Minoru, Kokumin Sōryoku Chōsen Renmei, eds.,
Kokumin chōyō no kaisetsu (Keijō [Seoul], 1944).
112 In preparation for conscription, for instance, local neighbourhood associations helped the state promote people's understanding of the new system and assisted the local authorities in sorting local household registers;
Anzako, "Chōsen ni okeru sensō dōin seisaku no tenkai," 14.
113 *Sōdōin* 1, no. 1 (June 1939): 17; Shiobara Tokisaburō, "Keizaisen no suikō
wa seikatsu o tōshite," *Sōdōin* 1, no. 7 (December 1939): 5–6.
114 Anzako, "Chōsen ni okeru sensō dōin seisaku no tenkai," 14.
115 Ibid.
116 Hayashi Katsuhisa, *Hantō no jūgojin* (Keijō [Seoul]: Chōsen Gunji Kōen
Renmei, 1940), 143–239.
117 Morita, *Chōsen ni okeru kokumin sōryoku undōshi*, 63–4; *Chōsen Kōron* (May
1939), 35.
118 In Kyonggi Province, the organizational network for the campaign was
completed in mid-October 1941, but rural villagers did not completely
understand its aims. The diffusion of its aims and practical objectives (*jissen yōkō*) as well as the training of patriotic neighbourhood associations
thus became priorities. Keikidō Keisatsu Buchō to Keimu Kyokuchō, police report, "Saikin dōnai no minjō ni kansuru ken," no. 3201–3 (24 December 1940), *Shisō ni Kansuru Jōhō* 13, HYCTS.
119 Anzako, "Chōsen ni okeru sensō dōin seisaku no tenkai," 11.
120 In Seoul, patriotic neighbourhood associations held their mandatory
monthly assemblies in different locations under a rotating system;

Keikidō Keisatsu Buchō to Keimu Kyokuchō, et al., police report, "Ji-kyoku ka no minjō ni kansuru ken," no. 2426 (29 August 1941), n.p., HYCTS.

121 Keikidō Keisatsu Buchō to Keimu Kyokuchō, police report, "Saikin ni okeru dōnai no minjō ni kansuru ken," no. 3201–2 (19 December 1940), n.p., HYCTS.

122 Questions asked by Korean participants at *jikyoku zadankai* (current affairs discussion meetings) similarly showed their growing desire for the end of war; see Matsuda, "Sōryokuki no shokuminchi Chōsen ni okeru keisatsu gyōsei," 213–16.

123 Keikidō Keisatsu Buchō to Keimu Kyokuchō et al., police report, "Jikyoku ni taisuru bumin no gendō ni kansuru ken," no. 413–17 (14 March 1941), 1, "Keijō-fu Moto-machi, imonogyō, Kuromatsu Matahichi," *Shisō ni Kansuru Jōhō* 13, HYCTS.

124 Keikidō Keisatsu Buchō to Keimu Kyokuchō et al., police report, "Ko-kumin sōryoku undō ni tomonau minjō ni kansuru ken," no. 141–3 (25 March 1941), *Shisō ni Kansuru Jōhō* 14, HYCTS.

125 According to an official report, these establishments desired longer business hours and complained about official regulations. Many failed to obey the prescribed business hours and the ban on serving alcohol during the day. Keikidō Keisatsu Buchō to Keimu Kyokuchō et al., po-lice report, "Jikyokuka no minjō ni kansuru ken," no. 1743 (30 June 1941), n.p., HYCTS.

126 Ibid.

127 Keikidō Keisatsu Buchō to Keimu Kyokuchō et al., police report, "Ko-kumin sōryoku undō ni tomonau minjō ni kansuru ken," no. 141–3 (25 March 1941), n.p., HYCTS. The number again plummeted from 265,723 in April to 188,125 in May; Keikidō Keisatsu Buchō to Keimu Kyokuchō et al., police report, "Jikyokuka no minjō ni kansuru ken," no. 1743. In Au-gust the decline was particularly prominent among visitors from the edu-cated classes; Keikidō Keisatsu Buchō to Keimu Kyokuchō et al., police report, "Jikyokuka no minjō ni kansuru ken," no. 2426 (29 August 1941), n.p., HYCTS.

128 Keikidō Keisatsu Buchō to Keimu Kyokuchō et al., police report, "Jikyo-kuka no minjō ni kansuru ken," no. 1743, 6; "Kokumin sōryoku undō ni taisuru bumin no gendō," n.p., HYCTS.

129 Keikidō Keisatsu Buchō to Keimu Kyokuchō et al., police report, "Jikyo-kuka no minjō ni kansuru ken," no. 2426.

130 Keikidō Keisatsu Buchō to Keimu Kyokuchō et al., police report, "Kō-A Hōkokudan setsuritsu junbikai kaisai ni kansuru ken," no. 372 (25 August

1941), *Shisō ni Kansuru Jōhō* 13, HYCTS; and "Chōsen Rinji Hōkokudan no dōsei ni kansuru ken," no. 2569–6 (8 October 1941), *Shisō ni Kansuru Jōhō,* 14, HYCTS.

131 Keikidō Keisatsu Buchō to Keimu Kyokuchō et al., police report, "Jikyoku ni taisuru bumin no gendō ni kansuru ken," no. 413–24 (28 March 1941), 2, "Keijō funai kyojū, Senjin yūshikisha," HYCTS.

132 Keikidō Keisatsu Buchō to Keimu Kyokuchō et al., police report, "Kokumin sōryoku undō ni tomonau minjō ni kansuru ken," no. 141–3 (25 March 1941), n.p., HYCTS. An additional overseas allowance was given to Japanese corporate and bureaucratic employees (usually 50–60 per cent of the regular salary). It was viewed as a symbol of ethnic discrimination against Koreans and a contradiction of the principle of *naisen ittai*; X.Y.Z., "Chōsenjin chūryū katei no seikeihyō," *Chōsen oyobi Manshū* (January 1938), 83.

133 "Chūhokudōkai dai muikame: naisen ittai o hakichigae keishiki nomi o isoguna," *Chōsen Shinbun*, 20 March 1940.

134 Ibid., 14.

135 The rate of intermarriage did increase over time, with a sudden climb from 476 in 1937 to 760 in 1938, but it did not rise dramatically thereafter; Tange Ikutarō, ed., *Chōsen ni okeru jinkō ni kansuru shotōkei* (Keijō [Seoul]: Chōsen Kōsei Kyōkai, 1943), 50–1. It was also symbolized by the failure of *naisen kekkon* between members of the Yi royal family and the Japanese imperial and aristocratic families in the 1930s, patterned after the politically arranged marriage between Yi Wang-ŭn and Nashinomotomiya Masako in 1920; see Suzuki Yūko, *Jūgun ianfu, naisen kekkon: sei no shinryaku, sengo sekinin o kangaeru* (Tokyo: Miraisha, 1992), 88–93.

136 Keikidō Keisatsu Buchō to Keimu Kyokuchō et al., police report, "Jikyoku ni taisuru bumin no gendō ni kansuru ken," no. 413–23 (27 March 1941), 3, "Keijōfu Fukoku gomu kōjōshu, An Pyŏng-wŏn," HYCTS.

137 By the summer of 1939, it became virtually impossible in P'yŏngyang (a traditional bastion of Christianity) to continue or open divinity schools to train clergymen and missionaries without agreeing to worship at shrines. This was due to the new licence requirement imposed by the provincial authorities; the very survival of these schools came to hinge on their agreement to shrine worship. "Jinja sanpai ni hantai no ganmei bokushi o haigeki," *Chōsen Shinbun*, 22 December 1939. While mission schools were forced to worship at shrines or face closure and a few defiant ministers were jailed, Roman Catholics apparently took this opportunity to expand their influence in the region. "Jinja sanpai ka haikō ka," *Keijō Nippō*, 25 August 1939.

138 Minami Jirō, "Renmei honrai no shimei: giron yorimo jikkō e," *Sōdōin* 1, no. 2 (July 1939): 57–8.
139 The best-known Korean ideologue of *naisen ittai* was Hyŏn Yŏng-sŏp, author of *Chōsenjin no susumu beki michi* [The way the Koreans must proceed] (Keijō [Seoul]: Ryokki Renmei, 1940), in which he urged Koreans to master the Japanese language, abandon the Korean vernacular, and become completely Japanese.

7   The Thought War: Public Diplomacy by Japan's Immigrants in the United States

YUKA FUJIOKA

The thought war is a war without arms ... Now that the China Incident has entered a new phase, the thought war will be increasingly important. The power of propaganda in this war must be demonstrated by us with more vigor than before. To begin with every member of the public is a fighter in this thought war which takes place everyday ... I strongly urge that everyone, even those who are not in the battlefields, should actively serve as fighters in this thought war.

– Yokomizo Kōki, Cabinet Information Department, 1938[1]

From the conclusion of the Pacific War to this day, Japan has received scant support from Japanese Americans on major issues in US-Japan relations, as was particularly poignant during the trade friction of the 1980s. This lack of support is in stark contrast to that of other major immigrant ethnic groups in the United States that maintain a strong bond with the country of their ancestors and lobby Congress in support of it.[2]

But Japanese Americans were not always so aloof. During the pre–Second World War period, the Japanese government enjoyed a "special relationship" with immigrants in the United States.[3] Although unthinkable today, the pre-war mainstream Japanese immigrant community (*nikkei*) not only sympathized with, but actively supported Japan in times of political difficulty.[4]

The 1930s in particular witnessed a period of intense support among *nikkei* for Japan's increasingly militaristic foreign policy.[5] Some of their activities even alarmed Tokyo. Concerned by the possibility of antagonizing the American public, the *Gaimushō* (foreign ministry) even went so far as to issue a statement cautioning them to refrain from overtly provocative pro-Japanese activity.[6] This was the period when Japan was trying to reverse its diplomatic isolation following the Manchurian Incident of 1931, its subsequent withdrawal from the League of Nations, and the commencement of the Sino-Japanese War in 1937. Japan was also attempting to convince the world of the legitimacy of its foreign policy, an area where Japan lagged the Great Powers.[7]

Realizing that adroit Chinese public diplomacy was a contributing factor to Japan's international isolation, the leaders in Tokyo understood the need to bolster efforts in public diplomacy to improve the prevailing international sentiment against Japan.[8] This was the *Gaimushō*'s primary objective when it decided to use Japanese immigrants in the United States as part of its overall strategy.[9]

Despite the numerous studies examine the history of Japanese Americans, the 1930s has long been regarded as an "unexplored period,"[10] made challenging for historians by the lack of historiographical materials. Japanese immigrants who were interned beginning in spring 1942 were permitted to take only what they could carry. Their suitcases thus quickly filled with necessities,[11] and documents such as business records, diaries, letters, books, and periodicals were left behind. A few *issei* (first-generation immigrants)[12] were able to hold on to such material (either in storage or in someone else's care), but much became fragmented, dispersed, or damaged over time.[13] After the attack on Pearl Harbor, many *issei* discarded personal documents that indicated their allegiance to Japan, especially information that could reveal their support for Japanese militarism in the 1930s.[14] In addition, the official records of the Japanese Association of America (JAA) – the main organ of Japanese immigrants with strong ties to the Japanese government – are still unavailable today. Some were promptly confiscated by the Federal Bureau of Investigation (FBI) once war commenced with Japan; having received no request for their return by *issei* leaders who could officially represent the JAA, the FBI destroyed them in 1996.[15] Other records were stored in several places in Japanese Town in San Francisco during the war, but their whereabouts are unknown.[16] Still other JAA records might have been destroyed in secrecy by *issei* fearing that they might be used as evidence of their loyalty to Japan.[17]

The post-war silence of Japanese immigrants has been another obstacle for historians researching this period. Decades after the war, many *issei* still declined to be interviewed about their pre-war activities. Many did not permit their personal records and documents to be made public for fear of reigniting another anti-Japanese movement similar to the one they had experienced in the period prior to the war.[18] With their passing, another source of information on the 1930s was permanently lost.

Ironically, the movement to obtain an apology and reparations from Washington also contributed to the silence.[19] With American public opinion gradually coming to support redress for the unlawful internment of Japanese Americans, it was imperative to avoid anything that could taint or derail that objective. Revealing their "un-American" activities in the 1930s, even for the sake of academic knowledge, was thus unthinkable.[20] With this as a backdrop – and by using hitherto untapped Japanese diplomatic records – in this chapter I describe and analyse Japan's public diplomacy towards the United States in the 1930s, and reveal the role of Japanese immigrants in the context of Japan's imperial expansionism.[21]

Japan's Public Diplomacy in the United States: Overture to the 1930s

Despite the existence of anti-Japanese sentiment on the Pacific Coast, early US-Japanese relations were on the whole amicable. Japan's 1905 victory in the Russo-Japanese War, however, changed US attitudes towards Japan and the Japanese. For the first time, Americans began to perceive Japan as a potential rival and a future threat across the Pacific.[22]

This shift in US views manifested itself in various ways. Exclusionary measures targeting Japanese immigrants on the Pacific Coast were at times accompanied by mob violence.[23] The most acute anti-Japanese incident occurred in San Francisco in 1906, when the school board passed a resolution proposing the segregation of children of "Mongolian" – that is, Japanese – descent from the city's public schools.[24] This coincided with debate over the likelihood of a future war between the two countries that began to appear in the jingoist press.[25]

The intensification of the anti-Japanese movement on the Pacific Coast prompted the Japanese government to renew its efforts in public diplomacy.[26] In the past, Tokyo had cultivated harmonious relations with Washington at the expense of its immigrants, whom it viewed as inferior subjects of imperial Japan.[27] With the rise of the anti-Japanese movement, Tokyo saw it was a matter of national interest to have an effective public diplomacy strategy in the United States.[28] The addition of public diplomacy to its arsenal was a turning point for Japanese foreign policy.[29]

Japan's emergence as a major power following the Russo-Japanese War likewise prompted a re-evaluation of priorities. Tokyo previously had considered public opinion in the United States and Europe to be of more or less equal importance; public diplomacy was hence referred to as *taiōbei senden* (US-European-targeted propaganda). Gradually, however, Japan began to see the United States as the more important target, which led to the renaming of its operations as *taibei senden* (US-targeted propaganda).[30]

In April 1914 the *Gaimushō* established a *senden kyoku* (publicity bureau) to disseminate Tokyo's views to the American press, through the Pacific Press Bureau in San Francisco and the East and West Press Bureau in New York. It also established a *keihatsu undōbu* (campaign for education bureau) to manage public relations (PR) activities.[31] Operating secretly under the direction of the Japanese embassy in Washington, these bureaus represented Japan's first significant effort to target American public opinion.[32]

Despite the unprecedented investment of human and financial resources,[33] Japan's early public diplomacy suffered a tremendous blow with the passage of the 1924 Immigration Act banning Japanese immigration to the United States.[34] Viewed from Japan, the passing of the act showed that its previous efforts to influence American public opinion had failed dismally.[35] For Japanese immigrants, the act was a shocking event, an outright rejection by America. It also led many to believe that they could no longer depend on Tokyo to look after their well-being. Since *issei* were now classified as "aliens ineligible for citizenship" in the United States, they remained subjects of imperial Japan (*nihonteikoku shinmin*).[36] Despite this, they received virtually no protection from Tokyo.

Of course, the passage of the 1924 act did not stem from the failure of Japanese public diplomacy alone; it resulted from numerous causes that included international, economic, and racial factors. Japan's foreign policy, exemplified by the infamous Twenty-One Demands upon China in 1915 and its self-serving diplomacy at the Paris Peace Conference in 1919, had invited international suspicion and criticism. Effective Chinese propaganda against Japan in the United States did little for Japan's image among Americans.[37] Within US society, the economic success of Japanese immigrants increasingly had come to be perceived as a threat. Under the circumstances, Japanese efforts to influence American public opinion could not have prevented the act's passage.[38]

Nonetheless, in the 1930s, the need to influence American opinion became urgent once again, this time as a result of the Manchurian Incident of July 1931. Influential Americans were alarmed by the actions of the Japanese Army, which were clearly infringing on the Open Door.[39] Japanese aggression in China proper, exemplified by the Shanghai Incident – and again accompanied by astute Chinese public diplomacy[40] – went far to undo whatever recent improvements there had been to Japan's image.[41] By the beginning of the Sino-Japanese War in 1937, Japan was badly in need of an effective policy to gain international understanding and to prevent further isolation.

This was a Herculean task, however, as the Japanese military resisted government pressure to halt its drive into China.[42] To manage relations with Washington, the only remaining option for Japan was to have its position understood by the American public. As US policy was seen as easily swayed by public opinion, it was believed that effective public diplomacy would help improve relations.[43] Tokyo thus decided to make use of Japanese immigrants in the United States, mostly *issei*, as foot soldiers in its campaign called *tai beijin shidō naishi keihatsu* (education campaign for Americans).

Tokyo also saw the potential value of *nisei* immigrants in its campaign.[44] Many *nisei*, however, who were born in the United States and were American citizens, were unsympathetic to the Japanese cause or, if young, were indifferent to Japan,[45] and hence they first had to be "enlightened." Thus, Japanese immigrants in the United States were both the agents and targets of Japanese public diplomacy.

In sum, in its public diplomacy in the 1930s, Japan tried to counter the fallout from its foreign policies in China to prevent the further deterioration of relations. At the same time, it sought to expand the empire's sphere of influence abroad and to assert the superiority of Japanese ethnicity and culture to the world. From Tokyo's perspective, Japanese immigrants in the United States were ideal candidates for this endeavour.[46]

The *Gaimusho*'s Public Diplomacy Strategy, pre-1937

Under the banner of *shidō to keihatsu* (campaign of education), the Information Division[47] of the *Gaimushō* led the public diplomacy effort in the United States. Strategies were developed to influence two targets: Americans and Japanese immigrants.

Requests for increased funding from Japanese consulates to foreign minister Hirota Kōki in 1935[48] reveal the consulates' strategies on the eve of the Sino-Japanese War. The public diplomacy campaign was conducted on two fronts. Conventional strategies included maintaining closer contacts with the American press, nurturing personal relations with influential Americans, participating in events sponsored by local chambers of commerce and industry, inviting prominent Americans to tour Japan, organizing public lectures, screening promotional films, and distributing promotional pamphlets and leaflets.[49] Indirect strategies, where the involvement of the Japanese government would be less apparent, included employing third parties and/or private individuals as spokespersons for the Japanese cause. The main strategies targeting Americans included employing the JAA;[50] recruiting non-government personnel; promoting social work; promoting pro-Japanese views within Japan-related associations led by Americans; and promoting Japan and Japanese culture through American scholars.

The *Gaimushō* saw the JAA as the most appropriate entity to be entrusted with its PR and intelligence activities. The indirect method followed the *Gaimushō*'s philosophy on public diplomacy: "rokotsunaru senden wa mushiro yūgainari" (overt publicity is detrimental).[51] The *Gaimushō* first needed to re-empower the JAA by providing it with adequate operating funds. The JAA's importance had declined since the passage of the 1924 act, as exclusion had eliminated its central function[52] of providing passports and other documents to Japanese immigrants.[53] The *Gaimushō* felt that subsidizing the JAA would "add prestige to its leadership over various other Japanese associations"[54] while making the organization more faithful to Tokyo. Funds also might help to prevent future anti-Japanese movements from arising.[55] As the *Gaimushō* partially attributed the rise of anti-Japanese movements to the lack of social contact between Japanese and Americans, funds were also apportioned to host events that would allow contacts to develop.

For public diplomacy not to be perceived as government propaganda, the consulates needed private individuals to do their work. Prominent Japanese immigrants in their respective communities were thus secretly placed on the payroll as *shokutaku* (adjunct employees). The consulate in Los Angeles hired Professor Ken Nakazawa of the University of Southern California (USC) to participate in public dialogues to further the American public's understanding of Japan. In essence, Nakazawa was an unofficial spokesman of the Japanese government – in 1934 alone he gave nearly 150 public speeches.[56]

Similarly, the consulate in San Francisco hired Professor Yamato Ichi-hashi of Stanford University, while the consulate in Seattle hired two prominent Japanese immigrant lawyers, Mr Arai and Mr Masuda, to maintain close ties with members of the California state legislature in Sacramento.[57] Consulates in New York, Chicago, New Orleans, and Portland, Oregon, also paid prominent Japanese immigrants for the same purpose.

By funding Japanese immigrants' involvement in social work, the *Gaimushō* aimed to portray *issei* as a great asset to American society. The understanding was that this would be an "extremely significant measure"[58] for improving Japan's image among Americans.

The *Gaimushō* also provided secret subsidies to associations such as *Nichibei kyōkai* and *Nihon kyōkai* whose core memberships consisted of Americans. By supporting these chronically underfunded associations, the *Gaimushō* aimed to foster pro-Japanese sentiment among their members and to motivate them to fight any future anti-Japanese measures. The *Gaimushō* judged that, by providing guidance and motivation, these American associations – in coordination with Japanese immigrant organizations – could become valuable assets in public diplomacy.

Although it was recognized that promoting Japan within academia would not have an immediate impact, the *Gaimushō* felt it could serve Japan's long-term interests. To prevent further isolation, Japan had ac-celerated its overseas cultural activities after withdrawing from the League of Nations in 1933.[59] In Los Angeles, the *Gaimushō* funded the *Nihon bunka kenkyū kyōkai* (Japan Cultural Research Association), an as-sociation established by Americans to further studies of Japanese cul-ture. These funds were used for individual research projects as well as to establish the Japanese studies department and Japan library at Cla-remont University.

In a similar fashion, the *Gaimushō* launched a scholarship program at both USC and Claremont for graduate students studying Japanese culture. Through these scholarships, future American scholars would be trained to pursue advanced studies in Japan, a cost-effective way to sow the seeds for future amity. As the *Gaimushō* did not want the schol-arships to be perceived as part of its campaign, they were administered through the *Kokusai bunka shinkōkai* (Society for International Cultural Relations).[60]

The *Gaimushō* meanwhile pursued a policy of appealing to Japanese immigrants. The plan to guide and enlighten overseas Japanese was explained in May 1935 as follows: "The state of development of the

Japanese immigrant community has a direct and profound effect on diplomatic and commercial relations between the Empire and the community's country of residence. As their influence has no small impact on the future of our nation's destiny, guidance, enlightenment and support for them definitely cannot be neglected."[61]

Nisei were the primary targets of this campaign, the success of which was considered vital for the long-term future of the Japanese Empire.[62] Although *nisei* were mostly American citizens, they remained overseas subjects of imperial Japan.[63] They were perceived as potentially powerful unofficial spokespersons for Japan given their English-language ability, which many of their *issei* parents lacked. Moreover, *nisei* were regarded as valuable human resources for the Japanese Empire's overseas expansion policy, as Tokyo felt that if the *nisei's* social, economic, and political status in America were improved, Japan's global prestige would rise as well.[64]

To unleash their potential, the *Gaimushō* first had to provide *nisei* with comprehensive "education" on Japan, especially on the subject of eugenics. Born and raised in the United States, many *nisei* had escaped the influence of the *kyōiku chokugo* (Imperial Rescript on Education). Re-education was thus indispensable for *nisei* to understand their roots, to take pride in their membership of the *yamato minzoku* (Japanese race), and to overcome feelings of inferiority caused by their parents' second-class status in American society.[65] All this had to be accomplished in an inconspicuous way. Although US citizens, *nisei* were seen by many Americans as Japanese and their loyalty was suspect. Thus, the *Gaimushō* carried out its campaign with utmost care.[66] *Nisei* students were encouraged to learn about Japan through the donation of books (including current affairs publications) to libraries at the University of California, Stanford University, and other private colleges. The aim was to provide future leaders of the *nisei* community and Americans interested in Japanese studies easy access to resources.[67]

As well, since many *nisei* students eventually would engage in public diplomacy in the United States or work for Japanese organizations, the *Gaimushō* encouraged them to study in Japan. Following the Manchurian Incident, this was part of wider educational policy. Many language schools for *nisei* were opened in Japan in the 1930s,[68] and their graduates were given opportunities to work for Japanese government associations. Many graduates of *Heishikan*, a training school for *nisei* founded in Tokyo in 1939 and funded mainly by the *Gaimushō*, were employed by *Dōmei*, the *Nihon Times*, the radio room at the *Gaimushō*, and the South Manchuria Railway Company;[69] other graduates found positions in Japanese consulates.[70]

The *Gaimushō* also offered scholarships to *nisei* who excelled in their academic studies to attend elite universities in the United States. This was also a means to encourage them to move from California, where prejudice against Japanese immigrants made it difficult for them to attain higher social status. Japan's prestige in America would rise by diversifying the geographic distribution of its immigrants as well as by raising the social status of the next generation.

As well, the *Gaimushō* established subsidized *kokugo gakkō* (Japanese-language schools) to improve learning opportunities for *nisei*. Such schools were run mostly by parents, local Japanese associations, and religious organizations. As most were facing financial difficulties, the *Gaimushō* could step in with generous subsidies to consolidate smaller schools and to provide more systematic instruction. Subsidies were also used to hire more teachers and to improve the quality of education.

Another strategy was to encourage the use of *kokutei kyōkasho* (official textbooks) in the Japanese-language schools. The aim was to nurture *yamato minzoku seishin* (the spirit of the Japanese people), promote national dignity, and teach the official view of Japan's "advance" into China. By the mid-1930s, the number of schools that had adopted the state-sanctioned textbooks, rather than *nihongo dokuhon*, an alternative series of textbooks compiled by Japanese immigrant communities, had increased dramatically.[71]

The *Gaimushō* was also of the opinion that *nisei* required help in overcoming their inferiority complex towards whites – a *nisei* who was not proud would make a poor defender of Japan. Towards this end, the *Gaimushō* expanded the spiritual and academic functions of the *Nikkei shimin kyōkai* (Japanese American Citizens League, JACL), where students were subsequently taught the superiority of the Japanese race and culture. The *Gaimushō* chose the JACL because it was the largest and most prominent *nisei* organization, and it became the recipient of regular, secret subsidies.[72] Some payments were made in the form of prize money to winners of essay contests, to cover expenses for educational trips to Japan.[73] The *Gaimushō* also provided financial support to the *Japanese American Courier*, an English-language weekly published in Seattle by prominent *nisei* Sakamoto Yoshinori that carried Japanese government press releases, in the hope that such assistance would enhance the government's ability to disseminate pro-Japan news.

It should be noted that Japan's attempts to "educate" and use *nisei* in its public diplomacy coincided with the needs and wishes of *nisei* themselves, who were relegated to subordinate positions in every aspect of American life.[74] According to Ichioka, "politically, they were identified with Japan as foreigners; economically, they faced severe job discrimination; socially, they were barred from certain neighborhoods, public facilities, and social institutions; and racially, they were considered inferior, unassimilable, and undesirable."[75]

In the 1930s, most *nisei* were confined to the Japanese immigrant community. Although many excelled in school, occupational discrimination together with the Depression had forced them to find employment either within the Japanese ethnic community or, to a lesser degree, in branch offices of Japanese firms.[76] The majority of college-educated *nisei* could find only menial jobs.[77] There was thus every incentive for them to learn Japanese: it improved their employment opportunities and prospects for climbing the social ladder.

Among the other factors stimulating *nisei* interest in Japan[78] were several pieces of anti-Japanese legislation that had preceded the 1924 act. These laws made *nisei* feel their prospects in the United States were limited, and prompted some individuals and their parents to turn towards Japan. The laws further created within the Japanese immigrant community the idea that *nisei* could play a role as *kakehashi*, as bridging the United States and Japan. This, of course, required them to be knowledgeable about Japan. Thus, many *nisei* in the 1930s, aided by the depreciation of the yen, went to Japan to study Japanese language and culture on their own initiative or that of their parents; an average of 1,500 *nisei* enrolled in Tokyo language schools, high schools, and universities each year.[79] Their disillusionment with American society often led to a sense of affinity with their ancestral homeland. Some *nisei* eventually became the staunchest defenders of Japan's military actions in China.[80]

The *Gaimushō*'s Public Diplomacy Strategy, post-1937

With the beginning of the Sino-Japanese War in 1937, the *Gaimushō* intensified its public diplomacy efforts. It also modified and clarified its goals. Prior to 1937, the so-called *nihonjin mondai* (Japanese problem) had been high on the agenda. After 1937, the *Gaimushō*'s priorities shifted towards defending Japan's actions in China and countering Chinese propaganda in the United States.[81] The strategy basically remained unchanged, with the *Gaimushō* relying on indirect tactics to keep its involvement more subtle in the eyes of the American public.[82] Kawai Tatsuo, chief of the *Gaimushō*'s information division, reported that, "[s]ince public diplomacy in the US is the most important tool in dealing with the China Incident, we must devote our greatest effort to it. Thus, immediately after the incident, our embassy and consulates in the US began planning a strategy and concluded that private organizations, such as the Japanese Chambers of Commerce and Japanese Associations in various states, should actively engage in actual public diplomacy on all fronts."[83]

The campaign's intensity grew considerably after 1937. The consulates increased their financial support of Japanese associations while consul generals held *jikyoku taisaku iinkai* (emergency committee) meetings every week in San Francisco at the *Gaimushō*'s public diplomacy headquarters for the western states. One way the *Gaimushō* sought to influence American public opinion on Japan's war in China was by distributing material to US newspapers, magazines, academic journals, and radio stations.[84] To avoid its being seen as a government initiative, the consulates delegated the work to emergency committees consisting mainly of Japanese immigrant organizations. The committees sent proposals for editorials and feature stories, promotional photos, and pro-Japan interviews by American politicians. In addition, the consulates had pro-Japan articles originally written by Japanese authors published under pseudonyms.

As well, efforts to reach out to journalists, public school authorities, academics, travellers, and business groups – people who were not high public officials but who nevertheless could influence public opinion – were intensified. Again, the consulates delegated this work to the emergency committees. The committees also produced literature justifying Japan's actions in China to send to Japanese-language schools, public schools, universities, libraries, newspapers, influential organizations, and individuals.

In addition to the consuls' own public-speaking engagements, the consulates hired Japanese immigrants (including *nisei* leaders),[85] Japanese dignitaries visiting the United States, and influential American sympathizers to deliver pro-Japan speeches. The consulates had them publicly explain Japan's position on China and later published the speeches. The consulates also invited influential Americans and Japanese immigrants to Japan, Manchuria, and China with the aim of having them write articles supportive of Japanese policy. In addition, the consulates arranged for pro-Japan radio addresses by private citizens such as prominent Americans and Japanese immigrant leaders, including *nisei*.[86] In November 1937, the consulate in Los Angeles had the local emergency committee approach a radio station (KFWB) about broadcasting speeches in defence of Japan by "private" individuals.[87]

The consulates further intensified their public diplomacy efforts to influence *nisei* through education.[88] They increased their financial support of organizations such as the JACL, whose leaders were mobilized to explain the "legitimacy" of Japan's actions in China to other *nisei* and young white Americans. The consulates also increased subsidies to Japanese-language schools, where *issei* educators taught Tokyo's interpretation of the war to *nisei* students, and instructed them to write letters of appreciation to Japanese soldiers.[89] Themes such as "How I as a *nisei* can justify Japan's case in China" were typical in essay contests.

Although much of the public diplomacy was planned by the consulates and implemented under their strict supervision, some strategies were conceived and carried out by Japanese immigrants on their own initiative. By late 1937, *issei* leaders in every Japanese immigrant community had voluntarily established *jikyoku taisaku iinkai* and were competing to raise funds. These committees collected *imonkin* (war relief funds) and basic supplies to send to Japan. They also sent to Japanese soldiers in China *imonbukuro* (comfort kits), which included medication, literature, assorted dry goods, and *senninbari*.[90] Some *issei* raised *kokubō kenkin* (national defence funds) for the Japanese military by calling door-to-door within their communities.

In 1937 and 1938 the emergency committees in southern California donated funds for the purchase of military aircraft, including a liaison aircraft for the army and a fighter bomber for the navy.[91] The committees also held patriotic meetings to commemorate Japanese victories and national holidays, including the anniversary of the Marco Polo Bridge Incident on 7 July, the fall of Canton and Hankow and the Meiji emperor's birthday in November, and the *kigensetsu* on 11 February.[92] The committees sought to show support for Japan by commemorating events that they had never before observed.

Immediately after the outbreak of the Sino-Japanese War, many Japanese immigrant communities sent their *issei* leaders to the Chinese front as *imonshi*, or special emissaries. They delivered relief funds and supplies to the Japanese military, consoled sick and wounded soldiers, and attended special ceremonies. *Imonshi* was an important public diplomacy strategy. Upon their return to the United States, *issei* leaders gave public eyewitness accounts of the war to fellow Japanese immigrants.

Issei were not the only envoys sent to Japan. Immigrant leaders saw ignorance as a chief source of past anti-Japanese movements in the United States, and communities sent their *nisei* youngsters to Japan on *kengakudan* (study tours) to prepare them to defend Japan before the American public.[93] The focus of these study tours changed, however, from promoting harmonious relations between the United States and Japan to defending Japan's actions in China; they began to include side trips to Korea and Manchuria after 1931 and to north China after 1937.

In addition to the emergency committees, Japanese immigrants in the United States formed various other organizations to exalt patriotism and to support Japan's war effort. By 1941, more than three hundred such organizations existed;[94] they included *Heimushakai*, a patriotic body composed of men of draft age organized in August 1937; *Nihon aikoku fujinkai rafushibu* (Women's Patriotic Society of Japan, Los Angeles Branch), formed in April 1938 to encourage Japanese immigrant women to be thrifty and promote *aikoku chokin* (patriotic saving) at home; and a Los Angeles branch of *Nippon kaigun kyōkai* (Japanese Navy Association), established in November 1938 with the encouragement of high-ranking Japanese naval officials with the goal of strengthening of the Imperial Japanese Navy and ensuring Japan's strength as a maritime power.

All associations enthusiastically participated in fundraising — *Heimushakai* even used strong-arm tactics to collect donations. The Los Angeles branch of *Nippon kaigun kyōkai* not only collected contributions; its "research" section studied domestic and foreign navies and other matters relating to maritime affairs. Its activities resulted in the arrest and internment of all its members on 7 December 1941 for allegedly supplying information to the Japanese navy.[95] The list of "dangerous enemy aliens" included such prominent *issei* leaders as the president and vice presidents of the Central Japanese Association; some *issei* thus supported Japan to the extent of risking their own well-being.[96]

Conclusion

Japanese immigrants' support for Japan's war effort cannot be explained without examining the international and domestic environment in which they lived. First and foremost, their support was more than just a matter of obligation and loyalty. Rejection by American society drove many *issei* to look to Japan for support and protection in the 1930s.[97]

Legally defined as "aliens ineligible for citizenship," *issei* were denied the right of naturalization and barred from owning land and property in western states where many of them resided. Politically, immigrants were unable to participate in American society; economically, they faced a lack of suitable jobs; socially, they were barred from certain public and private facilities; and racially, they were considered inferior, inassimilable, and undesirable. The 1924 Immigration Act was the final blow that convinced many *issei* that their rejection was absolute. This prompted them to forsake America and to look towards Japan, not only for moral support, but also for a sense of belonging. This was what motivated them to support Japan's war.

Recognition by the Japanese government was another motive. During the anti-Japanese movement of the early twentieth century, Japanese diplomats had valued maintaining amicable US-Japanese relations over immigrants' welfare. Among immigrants, however, this fuelled a sense of abandonment, a feeling encapsulated in the term *kimin* (abandoned citizens), while officials' contempt only aggravated the community's sense of rejection. The Japanese elite generally looked down on Japanese immigrants, calling them *kakyū rōdōsha* (low-class workers) and *katō imin* (inferior immigrants). Some Japanese diplomats even claimed the immigrants themselves were to blame for the anti-Japanese movement. Thus, Japan's hour of need, when it came, was an opportunity for immigrants to demonstrate the significance of their presence in the United States and to remove the stereotype of "inferior subjects of imperial Japan."[98] Japanese immigrants' support of Japan's war effort in the 1930s reflected their underlying desire for acceptance by Tokyo.

Pragmatic self-interest also informed *issei* willingness to participate in Tokyo's public diplomacy campaign.[99] For *issei*, who were always identified with Japan in American society, relations between the two countries directly affected their lives: deterioration threatened their status in the United States, while improvement in Japan's international position held the promise of improved social status.[100] War between Japan and the United States thus had to be avoided at all costs.

For the average *issei*, opinion on the Sino-Japanese War was shaped by information manipulated by the Japanese authorities and distributed by the Japanese immigrant press, which relied heavily on the biased *Dōmei* for coverage of the war.[101] *Issei* believed what they were doing was right – after all, they were Japanese not only by citizenship but also by heart. Their enthusiasm in supporting Japan's war effort was natural. They felt a great sense of pride in their mother country's growing prowess on the international stage.[102]

Japan kept close tabs on its nationals abroad to advance its agenda.[103] The government treated Japanese immigrants in the United States according to fluctuating "national interest" – sometimes with contempt, at other times acknowledging their importance. In the 1920s, the *Gaimushō* tried to fuel immigrants' pride with the hope of using them to expand Japan's sphere of influence abroad. As diplomat Arai Kinta noted in a speech entitled *Kaigai hatten suruniwa* (to prosper overseas) to a Japanese immigrant audience in Hawaii in 1924, "[g]radually, the world changed into one in which we can no longer wage wars, and we can no longer use force to exalt national dignity and to expand our territory, though it was Japan's biggest strength from ancient times. Thus, to exalt the national pride and to expand our land property, there is no better way than to rely on immigrants."[104]

Japan's strategy for public diplomacy and imperial expansionism through mobilizing its immigrants reached its apex in November 1940 when the government invited 1,673 Japanese immigrants from abroad to the First Conference of Overseas Japanese in Tokyo.[105] The *Gaimushō* and the Ministry of Overseas Affairs cosponsored the event, which aimed to strengthen Japan's image abroad by formalizing relations with overseas immigrants and by introducing them to Japan. Among the official delegates from North and South America, Southeast Asia, and Manchuria were sixty-two from the United States, selected by the Japanese consulates, accompanied by more than four hundred *issei* visitors. Tokyo particularly welcomed the *issei* delegates from the United States, who were placed at the head of a grand procession and presented awards by foreign minister Matsuoka Yōsuke, whom many *issei* held in high esteem.[106] Holding the event in conjunction with the commemoration of the 2,600th anniversary of Japan's birth further boosted the delegates' morale and nationalism.

But in the end, the *Gaimushō*'s commitment notwithstanding, public diplomacy failed to produce the desired outcome – Japan was unable to convince American public opinion to support its cause. Why? For one, indirect and often clandestine tactics were less appropriate in the United States, where direct appeals were more often effective.[107] More fundamentally, Japan's failure revealed the limits of public diplomacy. However skilfully campaigns might have been implemented, defending Japan's increasingly militaristic foreign policy was simply impossible. Although public diplomacy can be useful to promote one's policies, it can rarely paper over significant geopolitical tensions.

NOTES

I would like to thank Matsushita International Foundation and Suntory Foundation for their financial support in conducting this research.

1 Aired by the Tokyo Central Broadcast Station, 8 February 1938; see Yo-komizo Koki, *"Shisōsen ni oite,"* in *Shisōsen tenrankai kirokuzukan,* Naikaku jōhōbu, December 1938, reprinted in *Naikaku jōhōbu jōhōsenden kenkyū shiryō,* vol. 8, edited by Tsuganesawa Toshihiro and Sato Takumi (Tokyo: Kashiwa Shobo, 1994). Unless otherwise noted, all translations are my own.

2 In recent years, some Japanese American leaders have reconnected with Japan, as can be observed by the initiatives of the US-Japan Council. This new development is dealt in a forthcoming monograph by the author.

3 Yuji Ichioka, "Japanese Associations and the Japanese Government: A Special Relationship, 1909-1926," *Pacific Historical Review* 46, no. 3 (1977): 436. This article reveals the bureaucratic functions delegated to the Japanese associations as the basis of the special relationship between the Japanese government and immigrants in the United States.

4 Japanese immigrants had given material and moral support to Japan in earlier conflicts, including the Sino-Japanese War of 1894–95, the Russo-Japanese War of 1904–05, and the First World War; see Yuji Ichioka, "Japanese Immigrant Nationalism: The Issei and the Sino-Japanese War, 1937–1941," *California History* 69, no. 3 (1990): 274.

5 *Nikkei* refers to Japanese who have emigrated.

6 Ichioka, "Japanese Immigrant Nationalism," 263–4.

7 *Naikaku jōhōbu jōhō senden kenkyū shiryō,* vol. 8, 401. Atsuta Miruko, Nitchū senso shoki niokeru taigai senden katsudō," *Hōgaku Seijigaku Ronkyū* 42 (September 1999): 133–4.

8 For studies on Chinese public diplomacy, see, for example, Matsumura Masayoshi, "Manshūjihen niokeru chūgokuno pabuliku dipulomashī," *Teikyō Kokusai Bunka* 6 (1993).

9 There are various definitions of public diplomacy. See Leonard W. Doob, *Propaganda: Its Psychology and Technique* (New York: Henry Holt, 1935); Sidney Rogerson, *Propaganda in the Next War* (London: Geoffrey Bles, 1938); *Chōsa hōkokusho: Igirisuniokeru pabulikku dipulomashī* (Tokyo: Japan Foundation, 1994); Matsumura Masayoshi, *Shinban kokusai kōryūshi: kingendaini-honno kōhōbunkagaikō to minkankōryū* (Tokyo: Chijinkan, 2002), 9–15; and idem, "Manshūjihen niokeru chūgokuno pabulikku dipulomashī," *Teikyō Kokusai Bunka* 6 (1993): 98. Public diplomacy, as used in this chapter, is public relations/propaganda activities by a country to develop favourable

views of its foreign policies among the general public abroad through informing, influencing, and convincing them, and possibly to change other countries' foreign policies so that they are more advantageous to the country engaging in such diplomacy.

10 Sakata Yasuo, "Sengo gojyūnen to nikkei amerikajinshi kenkyū: katararenai 1930 nendai," *Iminkenkyū Nenpō* 1 (March 1995): 3; and Ichioka, "Japanese Immigrant Nationalism," 260.

11 As a result of Japan's attack on Pearl Harbor, Executive Order 9066 forced Japanese immigrants on the West Coast to relocate from their homes to internment camps.

12 *Issei* refers to first-generation Japanese immigrants; leaders of Japanese immigrant communities at the time were *issei*.

13 Yasuo Sakata, comp., *Fading Footsteps of the Issei: An Annotated Check List of the Manuscript Holdings of the Japanese American Research Project Collection* (Los Angeles: Asian American Studies Center and Center for Japanese Studies, University of California, Los Angeles, and the Japanese American National Museum, 1994), 5–6.

14 Sakata, "Sengo gojyūnento nikkei amerikajinshi kenkyū," 16.

15 That the FBI destroyed the pertinent records on 11 March 1996 was confirmed on 16 July 2008 by a response by the US Department of Justice to the author's Freedom of Information-Privacy Acts request (Request No.: 1115286-000).

16 As of 3 March 1943, attorney Raymond D. Williamson (Room 804, Hearst Building, Third and Market Streets) was given power-of-attorney to store any articles not disposable, including records and documents. Files were stored in the warehouse of Lynch and Sons, 2164 Market Street, under warehouse receipt contract number 2066; in the basement of a house at 1759 Sutter Street; and at the Japanese Young Men's Christian Association. See Record Group 131, San Francisco Field Office Investigative Files 1943-55, Box 3, National Archives and Records Administration, College Park, MD. The author has visited these three places, but there is no trace of the pre-war buildings.

17 *Fading Footsteps of the Issei*, 8.

18 Ibid., 17–18.

19 The redress movement came to fruition when President Ronald Reagan signed HR 442 into law in August 1988. It acknowledged that the incarceration of more than 110,000 individuals of Japanese descent was unjust, and offered an apology and redress payments of $20,000 to each person incarcerated.

20 Existent works addressing Japanese immigrants in the 1930s include Forrest E. La Violette, "The American-born Japanese and the World Crisis,"

Canadian Journal of Economics and Political Science 7, no. 4 (1941): 517–27;
Bob Kumamoto, "The Search for Spies: American Counterintelligence and
the Japanese American Community, 1931–1942," *Amerasia Journal* 6, no.
2 (1979): 45–75; John J. Stephan, *Hawaii under the Rising Sun: Japan's Plans
For Conquest after Pearl Harbor* (Honolulu: Hawaii University Press, 1984);
Roger Daniels, "Japanese America, 1930–1941: An Ethnic Community in
the Great Depression," *Journal of the West* 24, no. 4 (1985): 35–49; Brian Masaru Hayashi, *For the Sake of Our Japanese Brethren: Assimilation, Nationalism, and Protestantism among the Japanese of Los Angeles, 1895–1942* (Palo
Alto, CA: Stanford University Press, 1995); Sakaguchi Mitsuhiro, *Nihonjin amerika iminshi* (Tokyo: Fuji Shuppan, 2001); Yoshida Ryo, *A History of
Transnational Education (Ekkyo Kyoiku) of the Japanese Immigrants in the U.S.,
1877–1945* (Tokyo, Nihon Tosho Center, 2005); Minamikawa Fumisato,
"Imin nationalizumu to esunishitī: 1930 nendaisueno zaibeinikkeiimin niokeru minzoku," in *Nation no kiseki: 20 seiki o kangaeru*, edited by Yamawaki
Naoji et al. (Tokyo: Shinseisha, 2001); Brian Masaru Hayashi, *Democratizing
the Enemy: The Japanese American Internment* (Princeton, NJ: Princeton University Press, 2004); Eiichiro Azuma, *Between Two Empires: Race, History,
and Transnationalism in Japanese America* (Oxford: Oxford University Press,
2005); and Gordon H. Chang and Eiichiro Azuma, eds., *Before Internment:
Essays in Prewar Japanese American History* (Palo Alto, CA: Stanford University Press, 2006).

21 This chapter focuses on the *Gaimushō*'s public diplomacy. Japan did not
have a unified public diplomacy strategy, as the army, navy, and the
Gaimushō operated independently. For the conflict between ministries regarding public diplomacy/propaganda strategy, see Atsuta, "Nitchūsensō
shokiniokeru taigaisendenkatsudō," 135–8.

22 La Violette, "American-born Japanese," 519; Matsumura, *Shinban kokusai
kōryūshi*, 150.

23 Matsumura, *Shinban kokusai kōryūshi*, 161.

24 For a detailed study of the 1906 exclusion of Japanese children from public schools in San Francisco as the starting point of the Japanese exclusion movement (*hainichi undō*), see Minohara Toshihiro, *Kariforuniashu no
hainichiundō to nichibei kankei* (Tokyo: Yuhikaku, 2006), chap. 1.

25 For example, books were published depicting war waged by Japan against
the United States. The *San Francisco Chronicle* launched its anti-Japanese
editorial series in February 1905.

26 For instance, in a cable sent on 9 May 1913 to Chinda Sutemi, Japanese
Ambassador in Washington, foreign minister Makino Nobuaki pointed
out the urgent need for Japan to use American public opinion to manage

anti-Japanese attitudes in the United States. Makino recognized that, as part of its future diplomacy in the United States, Japan needed to enforce institutionalized propaganda. Makino asked Chinda for his opinion; the latter recommended propaganda strategies in a 16 June 1913 cable. For a detailed study of the beginning of Japan's institutionalized public diplomacy efforts in the United States, see Matsumura Masayoshi, "Shippaino kōhōgaikō: taishōkinihon no iminhaisekio meguru taibei keihatsuundō," *Teikyō Kokusai Bunka* 3 (1990): 17–20; and Takahashi Katsuhiro, "Taishōninen (1913) kaliforuniashū hainichitochihō to nihonno taibeikeihatsuundō," *Kokugakuin Hōkenronsen* 17 (1990): 89–127.

27 How Japanese pre-war elites looked down on immigrants can be observed in various primary sources; see, for example, *Nihon gaikō bunsho: taibei iminmondai keikagaiyō* (Tokyo: Ministry of Foreign Affairs, 1972), 224–41. At the same time, immigrants were seen as representatives of Japan and their treatment by American society was the matter of national dignity to the Japanese government. See Aruga Sadao, "Hainichimondai to nichibeikankei: hanihara shokan o chūshinni," in *Senkankino nihongaikō*, edited by Iriye Akira and Aruga Sadao (Tokyo: Tokyo University Press, 1984), 70–5.

28 For example, on 10 November 1907, Hanihara Masanao, Japanese consul general in San Francisco, reported to foreign minister Komura Jutarō via Takahira Kogorō, the Japanese ambassador to the United States: "The exclusion of low-class Japanese immigrants is no longer a regional problem in the US. It has already become a matter to be dealt with by the central government, and it possesses the danger of affecting Japan-US relations"; for the Japanese-language original, see *Nihon gaikō bunsho*, 236.

29 Matsumura, *Shinban kokusai kōryūshi*, 166–7.

30 Otani Tadashi, *Kindai nihonno senden* (Tokyo: Kenbun shuppan, 1994), 344.

31 For detailed studies on the establishment and activities of *senden kyoku* and *keihatsu undōbu*, see Takahashi, "Taishōninen," 93–101; and Matsumura, "Shippaino kōhōgaikō," 17–47.

32 The Japanese government founded the Oriental Information Agency in New York in 1909 to prevent further aggravation of American views of Japan after the Russo-Japanese War. This was Japan's first publicity organization established overseas, but it did not go as far as distributing Japan-related information to the US media. For a detailed study on the agency, see Takahashi Katsuhiro, "Nichirosensōgo niokeru nihonno taibeiyoronkōsaku-New York tōyōtsūhōsha o megutte," *Kokushigaku* 188 (March 2006): 35–67.

33 Between 1913 and 1919 at least US$450,000 was spent for public diplomacy in the United States; see Takahashi, "Taishōninen (1913)," 95.

34 The act passed in May 1924.

35 For studies on why Japan's public diplomacy failed to prevent the passage of the Immigration Act of 1924, see Takahashi, "Taishōninen (1913)," 127; Matsumura, "Shippaino kōhōgaikō," 53; and idem, *Shinban kokusai kōryūshi*, 176.

36 Before the enactment of the 1924 Immigration Act, *issei* were already denied the chance to naturalize or to own or lease land by the Alien Land Law, even under the names of their US-born children who had US citizenship. Thus, while most of their young children had dual nationality, *issei*, who were the mainstay of the Japanese immigrant community, remained Japanese nationals. See Sakaguchi, *Nihonjin amerika iminshi*, 273–96; and Minohara Toshihiro, *Hainichiiminhō to nichibeikankei* (Tokyo: Iwanami Shoten, 2002), 30–56.

37 For further detail on the efficacy of Chinese propaganda at the time of the Paris Peace Conference, see, for example, Matsumura, *Shinban kokusai kōryūshi*, 231–5.

38 The Japanese government closed its press bureaus in San Francisco and New York in 1921, as American media had come to regard this source of information as propaganda; see Matsumura, "Shippaino kōhōgaikō," 52.

39 In December 1932 Wakasugi Kaname, Japan's consul general in San Francisco, reported to the foreign ministry in Tokyo Dr Harvey Guy's observation that American intellectuals had serious antipathy towards Japan and deep suspicion over its international credibility following the Manchurian Incident; see *Nihon gaikō bunsho*, 1164.

40 The efficacy of Chinese propaganda in the United States after the Manchurian Incident was recognized by the Japanese government. The *Gaimushō's* information department listed the countering of Chinese propaganda against Japan as one of its ten goals (*senden keihatsu konpon yōkō*) after the outbreak of the Sino-Japanese War in July 1937. See Foreign Ministry Information Department, *Shōwa jyūninendo shitsumuhōkoku*, 2–3 December 1937, in the Diplomatic Records Office, Ministry of Foreign Affairs, Tokyo [hereafter cited as DRO]. For another example, see Cabinet Information Bureau, *Jyōhōkyoku no soshiki to kinō*, 1 April 1941, 3, reprinted in Ariyama Teruo and Nishiyama Takesuke, eds., *Kindainihon mediashi shiryō shūsei dainiki: jyōhōkyoku kankeishiryō daiikkan* (Tokyo: Kashiwashobō, 2000), 4019.

41 In March 1932 Wakasugi reported to the *Gaimushō* that the Manchurian and Shanghai Incidents had damaged US views of Japan, which had been improving to the point that revision of the 1924 Immigration Act had seemed possible; see *Nihon gaikō bunsho*, 1143–62.

42 Forrest E. La Violette, "The American-born Japanese and the World Cri-
    sis," *Canadian Journal of Economics and Political Science* 7, no. 4 (1941): 521.

43 Cabinet Information Bureau, *Jyōhōkyoku no soshiki to kinō*, 4019.

44 Kumei Teruko, "Nihon seifu to Nisei ekkyō kyōiku: heishikan o jire-
    itoshite," in *A History of Transnational Education (Ekkyo Kyoiku) of the Japa-
    nese Immigrants in the U.S., 1877–1945*, edited by Yoshida Ryo (Tokyo:
    Nihon Tosho Center, 2005), 257.

45 Not all *nisei* were raised in the United States. Some, known as *kibei*, were
    sent to Japan for education and later returned. These individuals generally
    had more affinity towards Japan than did other *nisei* immigrants who had
    been brought up and lived all their lives in the United States.

46 For statements by Japanese government officials to use Japanese immi-
    grants in the United States to expand Japan's sphere of influence, see, for
    example, telegram no. 174, from Tomii Shu, Consul General of San Fran-
    cisco, to Hirota Koki, Foreign Minister, 30 May 1934, DRO: J-1-2-0-J7.

47 Spurred by Japan's setback at the Paris Peace Conference, the *Gaimushō* es-
    tablished the *Jōhōbu* on 1 April 1920 as a division for public diplomacy; for
    more details, see Matsumura, *Shinban kokusai kōryūshi*, 229–40.

48 For example, see telegram no. 182, from Hori Kōichi, Consul General of
    Los Angeles, to Hirota, 7 June 1935; telegram no. 174, from Tomii to Hi-
    rota, 30 May 1935; telegram no. 188, from Uchiyama Kiyoshi, Consul
    of Seattle, 15 May 1935; telegram no. 121, from Tsurumi Ken, Consul of
    Portland, to Hirota, 23 May 1935; telegram no. 117, from Nakauchi Kenji,
    Deputy Consul of Chicago, to Hirota, 11 May 1935; telegram no. 209, from
    Sawada Renzō, Consul General of New York, to Hirota, 11 June 1935; tele-
    gram no. 188, from Tamura Sadaharu, Consul General of Honolulu, to Hi-
    rota, 16 June 1935, DRO: J-1-2-0-J7.

49 For various direct public diplomacy strategies used by the Japanese con-
    sulates, see, for example, telegram no. 121, from Tsurumi to Hirota, 13
    May 1935, DRO: J-1-2-0-J7.

50 The central organ founded in 1908 by Japanese immigrants, with strong
    connections to the Japanese government.

51 Telegram no. unknown, from Tomii to Hirota, 30 May 1935, DRO:
    J1-2-0-J7.

52 Since 1909 the Japanese government had been delegating certain bureau-
    cratic functions to Japanese associations, which provided them substantial
    income. It became a means for the government to gain greater control over
    immigrants and the basis of the special relationship. For a detailed study
    on the relationship between Japanese associations and the Japanese gov-
    ernment, see Ichioka, "Japanese Associations," 409–37.

53 For a more detailed account of the decline of Japanese associations, see Daniels, "Japanese America, 1930–1941," 40.

54 Telegram no. 182, from Hori to Hirota, 7 June 1935, DRO: J-1-2-0-J7.

55 US views of Japan, which had improved considerably after the enactment of the 1924 Immigration Act, deteriorated again as anti-Japanese legislation was submitted in California and Washington; see telegram no. 188, from Uchiyama to Hirota, 15 May 1935, DRO: J-1-2-0-J7.

56 Telegram no. 182, from Hori to Hirota, 7 June 1935, DRO: J-1-2-0-J7.

57 Telegram no. 188, from Uchiyama to Hirota, 15 May 1935, DRO: J-1-2-0-J7.

58 Telegram no. 182, from Hori to Hirota, 7 June 1935, DRO: J-1-2-0-J7. For the amounts provided to social works by Japanese immigrants, see, for example, *Zaigai yūryōshakaijigyōdantai nitaisuru gokachōkinshirabe*, DRO: J-1-2-0-J7-5.

59 Telegram no. 182, from Hori to Hirota, 7 June 1935, DRO: J-1-2-0-J7.

60 Founded on 11 April 1934, this was the first Japanese organization dedicated to cultural exchange; see Matsumura, *Shinban kokusai kōryūshi*, 271–5.

61 Foreign Ministry America Bureau, *Zaigaihōjin shidōkeihatsu teiyō*, May 1935, DRO, 1.

62 Azuma Eiichiro, "Nisei no nihon ryūgaku no hikari to kage: nikkei amerikajin no ekkyō kyōiku no rinen to mujyun," in *History of Transnational Education*, 227–30.

63 Kumei, "Nihon seifu to Nisei ekkyō kyōiku," 252.

64 Azuma, "Nisei no nihon ryūgaku no hikari to kage," 227–9.

65 There are many primary sources on the inferiority complex *nisei* were suffering, which was described by Japanese government officials and Japanese immigrants themselves; for diplomatic records, see, for example, telegram no. 121, from Tsurumi to Hirota, 13 May 1935, DRO: J-1-2-0-J7.

66 Telegram no. 174, from Tomii to Hirota, 30 May 1935, DRO: J-1-2-0-J7. The *Gaimushō*'s tactic of providing an "education" to *nisei* in an inconspicuous way continued during the post-1937 period; see telegram no. 156, from Sato Toshihito, Consul General of San Francisco, to Foreign Minister Arita Hachiro, 20 June 1940, DRO: J-1-2-0-J7-5.

67 Telegram no. 174, from Tomii to Hirota, 30 May 1935; telegram no. 51, from Tomii to Hirota, 15 June 1935, DRO: J-1-2-0-J7.

68 Azuma, "Nisei no nihon ryūgaku no hikari to kage," 227–44.

69 *Honshōshokuin yōsei kankei zakken*, DRO: M2-4-2-3.

70 Female *nisei* were also drafted to engage in propaganda activities during the war; see Kamisaka Fuyuko, *Tokyo Rose: Senji bōryakuhōsō no hana* (Tokyo: Chuōkōronsha, 1995).

71 Sakaguchi, *Nihonjin amerika iminshi*, 195–7.

72 For example, Uchiyama funded the JACL in his jurisdiction via the *nisei*-run *Japanese American Courier*; see telegram no. 188, from Uchiyama to Hirota, 15 May 1935, DRO: J-1-2-0-J7.
73 *Gaimushō* Information Division, *Shōwa 13 nendo shitsumu hōkoku*, December 1938, DRO, 177.
74 For the discriminatory circumstances in which *nisei* lived, see Yuji Ichioka, "Kokugo Gakko: The Debate over the Role of Japanese-Language Schools," 76; idem, "A Study in Dualism: James Yoshinori Sakamoto and the Japanese American Courier, 1928–1942," 118; idem, "The Meaning of Loyalty: The Case of Kazumaro Buddy Uno," 161, all in *Before Internment*.
75 Ichioka, "A Study in Dualism," 118.
76 The extreme difficulty *nisei* had in finding employment is stated in many diplomatic records and secondary sources. For diplomatic records, see, for example, telegram no. 182, from Hori to Hirota, 7 June 1935, DRO: J-1-2-0-J7. See also Daniels, "Japanese America, 1930–1941," 43–7.
77 Yamamoto Eriko, "*Kengakudan to ekkyō kyōiku*," in *History of Transnational Education*, 177.
78 On the growing enthusiasm among Japanese immigrants to study Japanese, see, for example, Kojima Masaru, "*Nihon no imin kyōiku ron*," in *History of Transnational Education*, 209.
79 Azuma, "Nisei no nihon ryūgaku," 221.
80 The *nisei*, of course, were not monolithic. There was major disagreement between those who professed loyalty to the United States by cooperating with the government in the war against Japan (for example, by providing intelligence) and those who professed loyalty to the United States by facilitating bilateral relations (through educating Americans about Japan, acting as a bridge of understanding between the two countries). There was a further generational rift between *nisei* and *issei*. For a detailed study on the latter, see Yuji Ichioka, "*Dai Nisei Mondai*: Changing Japanese Immigrant Conceptions of the Second-Generation Problem, 1902–1941," in *Before Internment*.
81 Foreign Ministry Information Department, *Shōwa jyūsannendo shitsumu hōkoku*, December 1938, DRO, 4.
82 The use of indirect tactics by Japanese consulates can be observed, for example, in the following report: "As a countermeasure, more frequent and thorough publicity campaigns of enlightenment that meet this situation must be our first priority … By contacting leaders of the Japanese immigrant communities, we are steadfastly carrying our mission to correct the views on the China Incident held by Americans"; telegram no. 330, from Ōta to Hirota, 6 November 1937, DRO: A-1-1-0-30-2.

83 Ibid., 162.
84 For further detailed public diplomacy strategies, see *Shōwa jyūsannendo shitsumu hōkoku*, December 1938, DRO, 137–91.
85 Telegram no. 330, from Ōta to Hirota, 6 November 1937, DRO: A-1-1-0-30-2. Miyakawa Tetsuo, a Japanese immigrant hired by the Japanese consulate in New York, delivered 46 speeches in 1938; see *Shōwa jyūsannendo shitsumu hōkoku*, December 1938, DRO, 137–91.
86 Telegram no. 355, from Ōta to Hirota, 13 December 1937, DRO: A-1-1-0-30-2.
87 Two Japanese immigrants (Nakazawa Ken and Sugawara Kay, a *nisei* leader and winner of the essay contest by *Rafu shinpō*, a Japanese immigrant newspaper in Los Angeles) and two Americans (Helen King, a contributor to the *Los Angeles Times* and Nathan Bentz, chairman of the Japan-US Association in Santa Barbara) delivered the radio addresses.
88 For the *Gaimushō's* renewed financial support to Japanese immigrants, see telegram no. unknown, from Satō to Arita, 12 June 1940, and Yūki to Arita, idem, DRO: J-1-2-0-J7-5.
89 Ichioka, *"Dai Nisei Mondai,"* 36–9.
90 Sakaguchi, *Nihonjin amerika iminshi*, 31–2. *Senninbari* is a handmade talisman with a thousand red stitches knitted by a thousand female Japanese immigrants to wish for the soldiers' unfailing success in war.
91 *Shōwa jyūsannen gogatsu zenbei ryōjikaigi gijiroku*, DRO: M-2-3-0-1-1.
92 *Kigensetsu* refers to the day the first Japanese emperor ascended the imperial throne. Although mythical, it denotes the unbroken imperial line.
93 Regarding the beginning and the transformation of the study tours, see Yuji Ichioka, "Kengakudan: The Origin of *Nisei* Study Tours of Japan," in *Before Internment*.
94 By 1941, over 300 Japanese immigrant organizations existed in the United States to raise Japanese consciousness and to provide social alternatives for those frustrated with the US society that displaced them; see the list of major organizations in Kumamoto, "The Search for Spies," 62.
95 Yuji Ichioka, "National Security on the Eve of Pearl Harbor: The 1941 Tachibana Espionage Case and Implicated Issei Leaders," in *Before Internment*.
96 There was a generational gap between *issei* and *nisei* in their stance towards Japan's militarism in China. In fact, some *nisei* tried to prove their loyalty to the US government by helping the FBI compile lists of *issei* leaders who actively supported Japan, which led to their round-up on and after 7 December 1941.
97 *Fading Footsteps of the Issei*, 12.

98 Ichioka, "Kengakudan," 61.

99 Minamikawa, "Imin nationalizumu," 183–202.

100 Yoshida Ryo, "Nihonjin imin no ekkyo kyoikushi ni mukete," in *History of Transnational Education*, 9.

101 Daniels, "Japanese America, 1930–1941," 41.

102 The pride of the *issei* is epitomized in the 1941 official report of their visit to Imperial Army and Navy units in Tokyo: "It is the motherland that the offspring of the Japanese race have never forgotten even while asleep. In recent years, the image of our mother country has grown greatly before us with her advancement. The source of the advancement is our imperial military. Overseas brethren long for the ancestral land and appreciate the imperial military that empowers it"; Kaigaidōhōchuōkai, *Kigen nisenropyakunen hōshuku kaigaidōhō tōkyōtaikai hōkokusho*, May 1941, 20.

103 La Violette, "American-born Japanese," 519.

104 Arai Kinta, *"Kaigai hatten suruniwa,"* October 1924, DRO.

105 For details of the First Conference of Overseas Japanese, see Kaigaidōhōchuōkai, *Kigen nisenropyakunen hōshuku*; and Nihontakushoku-kyokai, *Koki nisenropyakunen zaigaidōhōdaihyō o mukaete,* March 1941. For a study that treats the conference as a crucial Japanese imperial expansion policy, see Eiichiro Azuma, "Pioneers of Overseas Japanese Development: Japanese American History and the Making of Expansionist Orthodoxy in Imperial Japan," *Journal of Asian Studies* 67, no. 4 (2008): 1187–226.

106 As a youth, Matsuoka emigrated to the United States and eventually earned a degree from the University of Oregon. From this background, he rose to become foreign minister. He was thus an admired and heroic figure within the Japanese immigrant community.

107 Bruno Lasker and Agnes Roman, *Propaganda from China and Japan: A Case Study in Propaganda Analysis* (New York: American Council, Institute of Pacific Relations, 1938), 117.

PART THREE

High Diplomacy and the Statesmen

8 Meiji Diplomacy in the Early 1930s: Uchida Kōsai, Manchuria, and Post-withdrawal Foreign Policy

RUSTIN GATES

On 25 August 1932 Japanese foreign minister Uchida Kōsai (Yasuya) declared to the Imperial Diet that Japan would recognize the new state of Manchukuo, even if it meant reducing the country to "scorched earth." Uchida followed this blustery statement seven months later with his notice to withdraw Japan from the League of Nations. As contemporary observers noted, Japan's days of cooperative diplomacy were over, replaced by Uchida's brand of *jishu gaikō* (autonomous diplomacy), which would continue until Japan's defeat in the Pacific War.

Although strongly worded, Uchida's statement might not have raised the world's eyebrows had it not come from a man known in the 1920s as a multilateralist. As foreign minister in three successive cabinets from 1918 to 1923 (those of Hara Takashi, Takahashi Korekiyo, and Katō Tomosaburō), Uchida came to be associated with the Paris Peace Conference, the Washington Conference, and the Kellogg-Briand (No War) Pact of 1928. The internationalist Uchida of the 1920s was foil to the militarist Uchida of the 1930s.

The common view of Uchida is that he "went over" to the military after the Manchurian Incident (18 September 1931). Ian Nish writes that by 1932 Uchida had become a hard liner and an accomplice of the military; Japanese scholar Ikei Masaru explains Uchida's about-face by highlighting his affinity for Asia and his lack of backbone against army pressure.[1] In this chapter, however, I present Uchida as a practitioner of diplomacy of the Meiji era (1868–1912); to understand Uchida after the Manchurian Incident, it becomes necessary to use the lens of Meiji imperialism, not that of 1920s "Taisho democracy."

As foreign minister in 1932–33, Uchida possessed two articles of faith: that the establishment of Manchukuo was the *only* way to resolve the problem of deteriorating Japanese interests in Manchuria, and that co-operative relations with the Anglo-American powers were of value. The two beliefs developed first-hand during Uchida's earlier experiences as foreign minister, and although they appeared to be at odds, he remained committed to both.

Uchida's defence of Japan's Manchuria policy – to the extent of withdrawing from the League of Nations – did not lead him to abandon efforts to maintain positive relations with the West, particularly Britain and the United States. Rather, he sought to keep relations intact by repositioning Japanese foreign policy from the multilateralist framework of the League to one of bilateral relations between Japan and each power. Uchida's foreign policy in the early 1930s was thus consistent with that of his mentors, Mutsu Munemitsu and Komura Jutarō, as well as with imperialist diplomacy of twenty-five years earlier.[2] Although his adoption of military means in the 1930s gives the impression of an inexplicable foreign policy shift, Uchida's motivations and rationale remained constant throughout his final tenure. Within the realm of Japanese foreign policy, the Manchurian crisis (1931–33) can be seen as the last gasp of Meiji imperialism, rather than the first volley of Shōwa militarism.

Uchida Prior to the Manchurian Incident

Uchida entered the foreign ministry after graduating from Tokyo Imperial University in 1887. His career advanced rapidly. After secretary posts to Washington and London, Uchida became minister to Peking (Beijing) in 1901, a post he held for five years before serving as ambassador to Austria and then to the United States. In 1911 Uchida was called back from Washington to serve as foreign minister in Saionji Kinmochi's second cabinet (1911–12).

After a stint as ambassador to Russia in 1917, Uchida again took over as head of the foreign ministry in 1918, this time serving with Prime Minister Hara Takashi. Uchida held the post for the next five years through two successive cabinets (those of Takahashi and Katō) before retiring to private life in 1924. Foreign Minister Shidehara Kijurō then called him out of retirement in 1931 to become president of the South Manchuria Railway (SMR). It is from this position that Uchida returned to the foreign ministry to serve his third tenure as minister in June 1932.

The basis of Uchida's diplomacy falls squarely within what is known as *Kasumigaseki seitō gaikō* (Kasumigaseki diplomacy), Kasumigaseki being the area in Tokyo where the ministry is located. According to the historian Uchiyama Masakuma, Kasumigaseki diplomacy consisted of policies that remained constant over changes in era and the international environment.[3] Its two main tenets were gaining the respect and trust of the Western powers through cooperation, and joining them as an imperialist power in East Asia. Thus, Japan full heartedly cooperated with the West to revise the unequal Ansei treaties while pursuing aggressive policies against China and Korea. Throughout the Meiji, Taishō, and early Shōwa periods (through Uchida's tenure in 1932–33), the foundation of Kasumigaseki diplomacy remained international cooperation – first focused on the Western powers generally, then centred on Britain after the Anglo-Japanese Alliance (1902), then on Britain and the United States in the 1920s, and finally on bilateral relations with the Anglo-Americans and Chinese following the Manchurian Incident.

The origins of Kasumigaseki diplomacy, however, were rooted in the Meiji era. Uchida was mentored by two Meiji-era practitioners, Mutsu Munemitsu (1844–97) and Komura Jutarō (1855–1911). Mutsu headed the foreign ministry from 1892 to 1896; Komura served twice as foreign minister (1901–06 and 1908–11). Both pursued friendly, cooperative relations with Britain and the United States while initiating and furthering Japan's imperial endeavours. It was Mutsu who revised the unequal treaties and guided Japanese foreign policy during the Sino-Japanese War, resulting in the creation of Japan's first colony, Taiwan. Likewise, Komura continued to push Japanese expansion by challenging Russia for control over the Korean peninsula – a move that yielded the transfer of the SMR and the Kwantung Leased Territory. Considered the masters of Meiji-era (that is, Kasumigaseki) diplomacy, Mutsu and Komura were two of the prime architects of Japanese imperialism.[4]

Uchida's policies during his earlier stints as foreign minister resembled those of his mentors. He favoured cooperative relations with the West, particularly Britain and the United States; cementing Japan's foothold in Manchuria; and peacefully expanding Japanese economic and political interests in China. Like many of his predecessors, Uchida played a strong hand in Asia (especially in Manchuria) while continuing to be deferential to the Anglo-Americans. Unlike other Japanese leaders, however, Uchida did not support intervention on the continent. He opposed a Japanese expedition during the Chinese civil war, and resigned his post as ambassador to Russia to protest the Siberian Intervention (1917).

Uchida's opposition suggested a pragmatic, realistic approach to international relations in East Asia: as a junior power, Japan was not in a position to engender foreign hostility through impetuous grabs for power. Still, when Japan was directly threatened and could claim just cause, as in the wars against Qing China and Russia, Uchida was willing to resort to force to ensure the island nation's survival. The tenets of Uchida's diplomacy – pragmatism, realism, opportunism, imperialism, and cooperation – clearly mimicked those of his mentors. Uchida was an attentive student while a junior and middle-level diplomat under Mutsu and Komura, and although the latter did not live to see the Taishō and Shōwa eras, Uchida faithfully kept their legacies alive through his policies.

Foreign Minister Uchida in the Saitō Makoto Cabinet

The generation of diplomats with whom Uchida entered the foreign ministry in the late 1880s had mostly passed away by the time he returned to Kasumigaseki in 1932. In the intervening nine years, the ministry had fractured into those who adhered to Kasumigaseki diplomacy and those who believed Japan should follow a more independent policy in Asia. The latter group, known collectively as the reform bureaucrats, was itself split into factions, such as the Asia faction headed by Vice Foreign Minister Arita Hachirō and the Axis faction headed by Information Bureau chief Shiratori Toshio.[5] Uchida was not directly associated with any of these groups, which were largely composed of younger men who had entered the foreign ministry nearly twenty years after him.

Without a faction to call his own, Uchida knew he could be hindered by intra-ministry divisions. Prior to his installation, Uchida issued a friendly warning to ministry bureau chiefs: "You've pulled me [into this position], so you'll have to cooperate with me or we won't be able to reach any agreements."[6] From the outset Uchida felt Japan needed a united ministry to survive the "crisis." The League of Nations' commission to review the Manchurian Incident, headed by Britain's Lord Lytton, arrived in Japan on 29 February 1932, and Uchida had to face the commission for a second time on 12 and 14 July lacking a united front.[7] His first meeting with the commission had been two months earlier in Manchuria, when he was president of the SMR, and his position on Manchukuo had not changed since. What had changed, however, was that Manchukuo had declared its independence in March 1932, a fact which could not be denied by either the League or the Chinese. Therefore, Uchida argued, the only outstanding matter was Japan's recognition of Manchukuo, which was at the top of the government's priority list.

Uchida believed that recognition was the only permanent solution to the Manchuria problem. Despite Uchida's fervent beliefs, Lytton and other members of the commission remained convinced that recognition contravened the Nine Power Treaty of 1922 (in which Japan and the other powers had agreed not to infringe upon Chinese sovereignty), the League Covenant, and the No War Pact of 1928 (which Uchida himself signed). Recognition, they warned, "would put Japan in a bad moral position." Uchida rebutted that the Nine Power Treaty had not been violated since Manchukuo was not a signatory and, as such, was beyond the realm of the treaty. Moreover, since Japan had acted in self-defence, there was no infringement of the No War Pact.

The difference in opinion between Uchida and the commission rested on the nature of the Manchurian Incident and the creation of Manchukuo. Uchida maintained that Japan had acted in self-defence and that Manchukuo was an indigenous, fully legitimate expression of independence. Accordingly, Japan had neither violated treaties nor required the League's intervention. The dispute was a local issue to be taken up by China and Japan (and Manchukuo) through direct negotiations. The League, he continued, while an important international institution, was still developing and not yet in a position to intervene in international relations. This latter argument was gaining support in Japan, where it had not gone unnoticed that many important European issues in the 1920s had been resolved outside the League, including the Corfu Incident and the Locarno Treaties (1925).[8] Just as the European powers had done with their regional issues in the 1920s, the Japanese and Chinese, Uchida claimed, could resolve this regional problem on their own.

Lytton and the commission, on the other hand, viewed the Incident as Japan's own doing and concluded that the creation of Manchukuo would have been impossible without Japanese assistance. In short, Japan had not acted in self-defence, but had blatantly violated Chinese sovereignty by establishing the puppet state of Manchukuo. League participation, Lytton insisted, was necessary because Japan and China were members, China had formally appealed to Geneva, and the commission itself was the result of Tokyo's proposal to the League. Uchida disagreed, stating that the commission originated out of the policy of his predecessor, which he did not support.

With the two sides so directly at odds, the meetings were heated. Uchida was defiant and obstinate during his two interviews by the commission.[9] Tired of being peppered by pointed statements and questions from commission members, Uchida made his impatience clear at the end of the second interview: "China has been playing with Japan for too long and has ignored historic facts and treaty obligations. The endurance of the Japanese people had come to an end." This statement concluded Uchida's discussions with the League commission.

Uchida's hostile attitude might have been unexpected by the commission, but not his position. Uchida had steadfastly maintained Japanese support for and recognition of Manchukuo since the Manchurian Incident. His goal was not to defy the League but to solve Japan's long-standing problems in Manchuria permanently. Nearly all Japanese leaders, including Uchida, agreed that Japan needed to maintain its policy of international cooperation.

The "Scorched Earth" Declaration

Uchida is infamous in Japanese history for his "scorched earth" declaration. The fiery image it conjures is no doubt the main reason historians consider him a militarist foreign minister. Upon closer examination, however, Uchida's "scorched earth" declaration neither signified support for Japanese military aggression nor portended Japanese defeat in a major war. Rather, Uchida's overdramatic choice of words was perhaps meant to express his determination to solve the Manchuria problem once and for all by recognizing Manchukuo.

At the 63rd session of the Imperial Diet on 25 August 1932, Foreign Minister Uchida outlined Japan's policy towards Manchukuo. Although the speech marked Uchida's first comprehensive policy statement since he assumed his post, his points were familiar: Japan would recognize Manchukuo as soon as possible; Japan had not violated any international treaties; and Japan would work to convince the world of the justness of Japanese actions.[10] Since the Diet had passed a resolution for Japanese recognition of Manchukuo unanimously two months earlier, Uchida was essentially preaching to the choir.

One choir member, however, was not convinced. Diet member Mori Kaku, a vocal member of the conservative *Seiyūkai* party, doubted whether Japan was prepared to face the international consequences. Unilateral recognition, Mori counselled, would declare to the world the autonomy of Japanese foreign policy. It certainly would harm

US-Japanese relations and might even require Japan to withdraw from the League of Nations. Mori asked Uchida: how complete are Japan's preparations for recognition? how will Japan deal with the international repercussions? how will recognition affect Japan's international financial position? and is Japan ready to address a potential international crisis?[11]

Uchida replied to Mori's first question that preparations were ongoing and that recognition would be accorded upon completion; unfortunately, he was not at liberty to divulge the nature or content of those preparations. Uchida then addressed the remaining three questions by rehashing arguments from his earlier speech: work remained to convince the world of the justness of Japan's Manchuria policy, but he believed his efforts ultimately would assuage international scepticism. Furthermore, he emphasized his resolve to recognize Manchukuo. Uchida stated that he and the Japanese people "would not give up one inch, even if the country [Japan] is turned into scorched earth."[12] Radical nationalist Nakano Seigō then commented that Uchida need not worry about the United States and the possibility of scorched earth since the issue was not serious enough to warrant such a response. Uchida agreed that an adverse US reaction was unlikely, acknowledging his expression was only meant to show his resolve.[13] Japan was committed to solving the Manchurian crisis unilaterally, on its own terms, because it was a purely domestic – and not an international – problem.

Clearly, the bark of the "scorched earth" declaration overstated its bite. Recognition of Manchukuo was a popular cabinet policy supported by Prime Minister Saitō Makoto. In an editorial on Uchida's speech, the *Tōkyō Asahi Shimbun* noted that the Diet had passed a resolution calling for recognition two months earlier.[14] *New York Times* reporter Hugh Byas praised the speech, considering it the most lucid statement on Manchuria from the Japanese government to date; he believed it would be well received in the West as a clear explanation of Japanese actions.[15]

Uchida's speech did not surprise his diplomatic counterparts. British ambassador Sir Francis Lindley found Uchida's statement unremarkable, and made no substantive comments on it in his cable to London. Back at the Foreign Office in London, one official commented, "all the old positions are maintained in full force. But there is nothing new in it."[16] Even the ultra-critical Americans were unmoved, and commented that they had heard it all before.[17]

The wording of Uchida's resolution, however, succeeded in signalling to his audience – both domestic and international – that Japan would not waffle on the question of recognizing Manchukuo. Vice Foreign Minister Arita viewed Uchida's "scorched earth" declaration as a strong show of opposition to elements in the military bent on a clash with the Soviet Union. According to Arita, Uchida knew Mori favoured recognition, and was not questioning the basis of the policy, but rather its timing. Mori favoured continental expansion into Siberia, and feared recognition would render the situation in Manchukuo too static and binding for a future northern assault; thus, Japan should postpone recognition and instead occupy Siberia from its bases in Manchuria.[18] Arita realized that Uchida had used strong language to undermine such a course of action.

The tragic irony is that Japan truly would become "scorched earth" at the hands of the Americans in the Pacific War, although this fate was not set in motion by Uchida's 1932 declaration. His Manchuria policy ultimately would push him into a non-conciliatory corner in Geneva, but Uchida and many in the government continued to believe that recognition and cooperation with the League were compatible.

Meiji Foreign Policy in the Early Shōwa Era

On 27 August 1932, two days after Uchida's speech to the Diet, the cabinet devised a new foreign policy entitled "Proposed Policy to Deal with the Current Situation from the Point of View of International Relations" (*kokusai kankei yori mitaru jikyoku shori hōshin an*).[19] This policy, spearheaded by Uchida and the war and navy ministers, is commonly perceived as the beginning of Japan's "independent" diplomacy. A closer analysis reveals, however, that this policy was not the first move towards independence but a statement advocating the practice of diplomacy developed in the Meiji era.

Other than the use of strong language to warn that Japan might be forced to leave the League should it "threaten the future of our national destiny," the proposal on the League's intervention in Manchukuo contained the basic features of traditional Meiji-era diplomacy. The proposal merely reiterated that the Saitō cabinet would seek to pursue an earlier decision by the Inukai Tsuyoshi cabinet making clear the government's intention to withdraw Japan's delegates should the League issue a resolution that constrained Japanese action. The Manchuria policy was based not only on the hitherto decidedly non-independent foreign policy of the

Inukai cabinet, but also on the policy of maintaining a free hand in the region that dated back to the conclusion of the Russo-Japanese War. Indeed, Uchida had been striving to achieve some form of "independent" policy in Manchuria for more than twenty-five years.

The proposal's recommendations hearkened back to earlier Japanese foreign policy towards China proper and the Western powers. The China policy was to be detached from the Manchuria policy, a tenet followed by Japanese governments in practice if not in name since the Portsmouth Peace Treaty (1905). The only exception to this had been during Shidehara's first tenure as foreign minister (1924–27). Japan would also cooperate with the powers in China to maintain peace and an "open door," another policy that could be traced back to the turn of the century. Finally, Japan would promote friendly bilateral relations with the powers; Uchida and the cabinet were cognizant that the powers held individual views separate from their respective positions in the League.[20] The emphasis on bilateral relations of pre–First World War Japanese diplomacy, which gave way to multilateralism in the 1920s, was thus resuscitated by Uchida and the Japanese government in the early 1930s.

Far from signalling a "go-it-alone" international policy, this "new" plan, for the most part, reiterated the traditional goals of Japanese diplomacy developed in the Meiji era. Cooperative relations with the powers (especially Britain and the United States), economic imperialism in China, and a dominant position in Manchuria were features that marked nearly every proposal guiding Japanese relations, from Komura's tenure as foreign minister through Uchida's in the 1910s, 1920s, and now 1930s, as well as nearly every foreign minister's in between.

Japan's Withdrawal from the League

As announced, Japan officially recognized Manchukuo on 15 September 1932, soon after Uchida's speech to the Diet. Recognition came in the face of the Lytton Commission's repeated requests not to do so before it had published its report and in disregard of British ambassador Lindley's warning that, if it acted in this manner, "Japan would find herself isolated in a hostile world."[21] If an aspect of Japanese diplomacy could be called independent, it was surely Japan's unilateral recognition of Manchukuo.

The Lytton Commission's report appeared in early October 1932, and taken up in the League council in November and December. The

Japanese leadership required a skilled linguist and negotiator to head its delegation in Geneva to debate the report's findings, and this person was found in former diplomat Matsuoka Yōsuke, who in May had negotiated the conclusion of the Shanghai Incident. Matsuoka was reluctant to take the assignment, but agreed after former prime minister Saionji personally assured him that Japan would not leave the League. As with all but the most extreme elements, Matsuoka, along with Saitō and Uchida, did not advocate withdrawal because they believed some sort of compromise in Geneva was possible.

As Matsuoka's activities in Geneva are well documented, a brief sketch will suffice for this chapter.[22] Arriving in November, Matsuoka began to court delegates of the major powers thought to be sympathetic to Japan. Matsuoka played both good and bad cop, simultaneously searching for grounds for compromise while maintaining the justness of Japanese actions in Manchuria. He and the other Japanese delegates were open to a British proposal to create a conciliation commission that would include the Committee of Nineteen, Japan, China, and two non-members of the League, the United States and the Soviet Union;[23] by inviting the Soviets, Matsuoka hoped to play their imperialistic interests against the increasingly hostile smaller powers.[24]

Uchida, however, was adamantly against including non-members in a League committee. His position was based on a practical and realistic assessment of US sentiment against Japan; Secretary of State Henry L. Stimson had declared in January 1932 that the United States would not recognize any situation brought about by means contrary to the No War Pact of 1928 – that is, Manchukuo.[25] Uchida believed US presence on the committee would only increase the number of hostile delegates and thus hurt Japan's chances for conciliation. Uchida was not alone in holding this view – most high-level ministry officials in Tokyo concurred, as did two moderate Japanese diplomats in Geneva, Tōgō Shigenori and Sugimura Yōtarō, who counselled Matsuoka against including the United States.[26] Although Uchida's intransigence concerning the conciliation commission is often cited as the cause of Japan's withdrawal from the League, he neither acted alone in refuting the proposal nor felt that the failure of the commission would lead to Japan's departure from Geneva.[27]

With the conciliation commission proposal dead in the water, in January 1933 Sugimura and his British counterpart Secretary-General Eric Drummond developed a compromise plan supported by Matsuoka. The plan allowed for a League resolution based on the Lytton Report and its settlement recommendations, but with the provision that any suggested settlement must be adapted to the new situation in the Far East. Moreover, the president of the League would be required to agree not to comment on either the restoration of the *status quo ante* or the recognition of Manchukuo in an explanatory statement on the resolution.[28] Following cabinet consultation, Uchida rejected the plan as it did not repeal the section of the resolution that excluded the maintenance and recognition of Manchukuo as an acceptable solution. He communicated this to British ambassador Lindley on 1 February 1933, in a memorandum in which he went on to say that "[n]o Japanese Government could go further in the way of conciliation and retain office."[29] If the League resolution included language that condemned the existence of Manchukuo and/or Japanese recognition of it, Japan would have no choice but to leave the League;[30] Uchida would not be forced to compromise on what he believed to be the only realistic long-term solution to the Manchurian problem.

Despite this, Uchida was not bent on withdrawal. One day earlier, in a cable to Geneva, Uchida had stated that the government would make its final decision only after careful consideration of the resolution adopted by the League.[31] The wording of the resolution was crucial for Japan: if it was critical of or condemned Japanese recognition of Manchukuo, Japan would be forced to withdraw, but a resolution that offered only vague references to the new state and Japanese policy would provide Japan sufficient wiggle room to remain a member. As late as mid-February, Uchida and even hardliner War Minister Araki Sadao still expected some sort of appeasement or compromise from the major powers.[32] In Geneva, Matsuoka remained frustrated by Uchida's rejection of the compromise formula and on 16 February cabled Tokyo that there was no other option left on the table but to withdraw. The effect was profound. Hopes for a compromise vanished, and the Japanese leadership, Uchida included, now swayed towards withdrawal.[33]

In hindsight, the hope for a compromise was an exercise in self-delusion. The mood in Geneva had taken a decisive turn against Japan after it occupied the Chinese city of Shanhaikuan on New Year's Day 1933. Japan's position was further damaged when Uchida consistently refused to compromise if the League did not retract its condemnations. After a cabinet decision on 21 February, Uchida sent instructions to Matsuoka stating that the delegation might need to walk out should the body adopt the Council of Nineteen's report, but that this would not necessarily lead to Japan's withdrawal from the League.[34] On 24

February, Matsuoka cast the lone vote against the resolution, made a brief but brilliant speech, then resolutely led the Japanese delegation out of the assembly.

Uchida's Post-withdrawal Foreign Policy

Uchida's conception of Japan's post-withdrawal foreign policy was not radically different from that during his earlier tenures as foreign minister: Japan would pursue cooperative relations with the Anglo-American powers in China and elsewhere, affirm the territorial integrity of China proper, and staunchly defend its position in Manchuria. As the problem of Japan's recognition of Manchukuo had been taken off the table, Japan could now focus on bilateral relations unrelated to Manchuria outside the League, thus continuing its international relations without modification. Uchida affirmed this strategy in a March 1933 statement to the Privy Council: "Japan's policy of international harmony is the same as it was formerly. The clash of opinion with the League at this time is concerned only with Manchuria."[35]

According to the historian Inoue Toshikazu, Uchida and the foreign ministry "placed Japan's withdrawal from the League in the context of international cooperation."[36] Unable to reach a satisfactory resolution in Geneva because of anti-Japanese pressure from the small powers, Japan opted to shift its international relations outside the League. Through the traditional, Meiji-era approach to diplomacy, Tokyo was able to avoid isolation and maintain cooperative relations after withdrawal, right up to the Sino-Japanese War of 1937.

As can be seen, Uchida's diplomacy supports the notion that Japan earnestly strove to avoid isolation and expand its relations with the world. Although Japan's international relations were now mostly bilateral, the underlying theme of cooperation still remained.[37] The "independent" strand in Uchida's diplomacy manifested itself only in his policy towards Manchuria, not in his policies aimed at China or the powers or in Japan's ongoing participation in international conferences.

China Proper

At the core of Uchida's China policy was the separation of Manchuria from China. Manchuria (now Manchukuo) was Japan's "lifeline," so crucial to the nation's security that Uchida countenanced military action in defence of Japanese interests. China, in Uchida's estimation, had never been more important. During his earlier tenures as foreign minister, he had supported economic penetration of China and respect for Japanese interests on the mainland, but had stopped short of interfering with Chinese sovereignty. Unlike Tanaka Giichi, but like Shidehara, Uchida never sanctioned Japanese military intervention in China. He had refused the demands of military hardliners in 1911 to join the fray in the Chinese Revolution, and later, as Hara Takashi's foreign minister, had opposed dispatching troops to Chinese cities to suppress boycotts and anti-Japanese activity. In the wake of the Manchurian Incident, Uchida consistently maintained that Japan had no territorial ambitions in China proper.[38] Now, in the early 1930s, with the Manchurian problem more or less out of the way, Uchida persisted in his policy of non-intervention by demanding Japanese forces not move south of the Great Wall. He also promoted greater economic relations with China.

As outlined in the cabinet policy of 27 August 1932, Japan viewed China as a market for trade and industry. To capitalize on this market, Japan realized the need for peace in China, Chinese respect for Japanese interests, and the maintenance of the Open Door. A unified and stable China that respected the rule of law and followed a consistent foreign policy was essential to the protection of Japanese economic interests. As the head of China's Republican government, Chiang Kaishek was best placed to satisfy these requirements; Uchida thus did not regard Chiang as a foe.[39] Just as Uchida had hoped to include the Republican government in the SMR railway negotiations, so he sought to resolve the Manchurian Incident through direct negotiations with Chiang. Although this became impossible in early 1933 due to Japan's campaign to seize the Chinese province of Jehol (Rehe), Uchida remained a proponent of dealing directly with Chiang's government.[40] Under his watch, Japan would keep the Open Door in place through its relations with the powers.

The Powers

BRITAIN

Britain was arguably the most sympathetic to Japan's position in the League. Unlike the United States, Britain had never considered economic sanctions against Japan and consistently supported compromise to keep Japan in Geneva. Thus, Uchida was confident that British goodwill would continue even after Japan's withdrawal. The key, he felt, was to reach an accord over Anglo-Japanese cooperation in China.

Uchida's "firm" policy on Manchuria required Japan to placate the British in other parts of China.[41] Japan would pursue cooperative and friendly relations with Britain by duly respecting British interests in Shanghai, Canton, the Yangtze region, and southern China. As James Crowley has accurately argued, Uchida sought a *modus vivendi* with the British government based on Japan's respect for its interests in China and Britain's acceptance of the Japanese-engineered situation in Manchuria.[42] Uchida once again stressed the importance of Japanese interests in Manchuria and China, making it clear that his "independent" diplomacy stopped at the Great Wall. In this way, cooperative relations with Britain were crucial to Uchida's diplomacy, just as they had been in the 1910s and 1920s.

The value Uchida placed on British goodwill went far beyond that of other officials in the Japanese government, to the extent that Uchida was chastised for being too conciliatory. In the spring and summer of 1933, economic matters came to dominate Anglo-Japanese relations. Japan's December 1931 decision to leave the gold standard and float the yen had resulted in a greatly depreciated yen relative to sterling, allowing Japanese exporters to flood South and Southeast Asian markets with low-priced cotton goods.[43] Protests from Indian and British cotton mill owners spurred the Indian government to raise import duties on non-British cotton goods and then, when this had no effect on Japanese exports, to abrogate the India-Japan Commercial Treaty of 1904. Announced in April 1933, abrogation was to take effect six months later. This announcement, coupled with the Indian government's decision in June to increase the tariff on non-British cotton goods to 75 per cent, shocked mill owners in Osaka, who retaliated by boycotting Indian raw cotton. A cotton war had begun.[44]

To head off this cotton war and to conclude a new treaty, an India-Japan conference was planned to be held in Simla, India, during September and October 1933. With the Japanese press chastising Britain for pursuing policies (via the Indian government) to protect Lancashire cotton mills and Osaka exporters warning of impending Anglo-Japanese hostilities,[45] Uchida attempted to ease animosities and foster a mutually beneficial compromise. In August, he and the foreign ministry devised a proposal to lower Japanese tariffs on Indian pig iron and rice and to guarantee purchase of Indian cotton. In return, London would promise not to modify any agreements reached between Japan and India at the Simla conference. The agriculture and commerce ministries in Tokyo immediately attacked Uchida's "weak-kneed" plan, denouncing the offering of compromises so early in the negotiations.[46] "Hardline" Uchida had now become "weak-kneed," a slight more commonly associated with Uchida's predecessor Shidehara.

This episode further reveals that Uchida's "independent" or "hardline" diplomacy was limited to Manchuria; towards Britain Uchida rooted his policy in cooperative relations, where compromise was still preferable to confrontation. As with his China policy, Uchida's friendly and cooperative approach to Anglo-Japanese trade issues aimed to obtain British understanding of and sympathy for Manchukuo.[47]

THE UNITED STATES

In contrast to the relatively friendly British, the Americans were among the most vocal critics of Japanese actions in Manchuria. Stimson's doctrine of non-recognition was a clear statement that Washington would not condone Japan's Manchurian policy. Considering the United States was a major power in the Pacific, Japan was forced to create a working arrangement with Washington for post-withdrawal East Asia.

As Inoue has argued, Japan returned to its most orthodox of foreign policies – cooperative diplomacy with the United States.[48] Thus, when Franklin D. Roosevelt invited Japan and the other participants of an upcoming London Economic Conference to Washington in May 1933 for preliminary discussions, Uchida and the foreign ministry jumped at the chance to improve relations between the two countries. The discussions in Washington would allow Japan to alleviate American anxieties over Japanese intentions on the Asian mainland. To carry out this mission, Uchida chose former foreign minister Ishii Kikujirō, a consummate statesman who shared many of Uchida's policy goals and who was not a militant hardliner. He even enjoyed relative popularity in the United States, having served as ambassador to Washington in 1918–19. Uchida and the rest of the foreign ministry held high hopes for Ishii's trip.

Uchida issued instructions to Ishii before his departure on 2 May 1933.[49] Ishii was to make clear to Roosevelt that Japan had no ambition to occupy or control China politically and desired only economic relations along with Chinese stability. Further, Ishii should impress upon the Americans that Japan would not send troops south of the Great Wall and would, as Uchida had already stated publicly, respect and support the Open Door principle in Manchukuo. Ishii's mission appeared to be successful. Following his conversations with Roosevelt, Tokyo believed it had obtained Washington's tacit approval of its Manchuria policy.[50]

US–Japanese relations, which had appeared on the brink of doom several months earlier under the threat of US-led economic sanctions, improved noticeably by late spring 1933. A British diplomatic dispatch to London noted in late May that "there have been a number of signs recently of the growth of better feelings in this country towards the United States."[51] US ambassador Grew expressed a similar sentiment in his diary entry of 8 June 1933, when he wrote of the "notable improvement in American–Japanese relations."[52] Despite this, Grew remained sceptical of Japan's current foreign policy, noting in a cable to Washington that it appeared Japan had only one firm policy – control over Manchuria – and that its policies were otherwise opportunistic. Others in the State Department, however, disagreed; they added comments to the cable stating that, while admitting recognition of Manchukuo was of paramount interest to Japan, Tokyo was generally exhibiting good behaviour in an attempt to rehabilitate itself internationally.[53]

THE SOVIET UNION AND FRANCE

Japanese relations with the Soviet Union in 1933 centred on two main issues – the non-aggression pact and the sale of the Chinese Eastern Railway (CER) to Manchukuo. The Soviets proposed the pact, which was coolly received by the Inukai cabinet, in late December 1931. According to the historian Kitaoka Shinichi, Uchida initially supported the pact as a way to stabilize Japanese-Soviet relations in the wake of the Manchurian Incident. Later, after falling under the influence of strongly anti-Soviet War Minister Araki, he opposed it.[54] Uchida's biographer, however, offers a different perspective, noting that Uchida refused to take sides in the debate over the pact that raged in the foreign ministry. The biographer goes on to explain that Uchida believed earlier treaties between Japan and the Soviet Union, as well as the No War Pact, already provided for non-aggression.

Kitaoka's claim of War Minister Araki's influence on Uchida is supported by entries in Harada Kumao's diary. On several occasions Finance Minister Takahashi Korekiyo recounted to Harada conversations with Uchida where the foreign minister made comments such as "the Army does not agree [with the pact]" and "the Army was concerned [with the pact] because it might more easily allow the spread of communist propaganda."[55] That Uchida himself was pragmatic towards communism – he had told British ambassador Lindley that the communist movement in Japan was a nuisance but not a danger, and that the future of communism in general was far from certain[56] – suggests that Araki did influence Uchida's stance on the non-aggression pact. Yet the pact was clearly of secondary significance for Uchida; obtaining Soviet recognition of Manchukuo was far more important for his foreign policy.

One way to obtain this recognition was to accept the Soviet offer to sell the Chinese Eastern Railway. Russia had built the CER in the late nineteenth century as an extension of the Trans-Siberian railroad that cut across northern Manchuria and terminated in Vladivostok. With the creation of Manchukuo and stagnant economic development in the Russian Far East, the value of the CER to the Soviets was declining rapidly. Unwilling to challenge the Japanese over this issue, Moscow sought to eliminate a potential flashpoint of imperial rivalry by selling the CER to Japan or Manchukuo. In May 1933, the Soviet ambassador to Tokyo, Konstantin Yurenev, met with Uchida to discuss the sale. Uchida agreed with the proposal but suggested that, since the railway was in Manchukuo territory, the Soviets should offer it to Manchukuo, while Japan could act as a mediator at a conference in Tokyo. By shifting the buyer of the railway from Japan to Manchukuo, Uchida was effectively securing de facto Soviet recognition of the new state. Uchida personally convened the first Manchukuo-USSR conference, held at the foreign ministry in Tokyo on 28 June 1933. Negotiations lasted for another eighteen months, concluding in March 1935, long after Uchida had resigned as foreign minister.[57] The sale of the CER brought Japan (and Uchida) a step closer to the goal of securing Manchukuo's international recognition.

Japan also sought to improve relations with France in the wake of the Manchurian Incident. Uchida expressed his willingness to reach an *entente* with France in a cable to Nagaoka Harukazu, ambassador to Paris, on 26 August 1932. Noting France's relatively friendly attitude towards Japan since the Manchurian Incident, Uchida asked Nagaoka to begin talks on an *entente* based on Franco-Japanese cooperation in the Far East.[58] Japan further sought closer ties to France by securing French financing for development projects in Manchukuo. Stronger financial relations, Uchida and Saitō hoped, would lead to closer political relations.[59]

Facing hostility in the League from the smaller powers and then potential isolation following withdrawal, Japan worked to steady itself by reaching out to fellow imperial powers – France, the USSR, the United States, and Britain. Some were receptive, others sceptical, but in the end

Japan was able to avoid international isolation by establishing a framework of bilateral relations.

International Institutions and Conferences

Despite outward appearance, Japan's post-withdrawal behaviour was still multilateralist on several fronts. Japan continued to participate in non-political League activities and organizations and in international conferences. Japanese delegates and representatives were sent to the Permanent Court of International Justice, the International Labour Organization, and a variety of League committees, including those addressing the protection of women and children, opium, and health. Although Japan did not send representatives to the League Council, it participated in other League organs and continued to pay dues until its withdrawal became official in 1938.

To what extent was Japan willing to cooperate for the sake of the greater international good? Contemporary observer Joseph Grew argued that, whereas most nations approached international conferences from a position of enlightened self-interest – knowing some concessions would be necessary for the good of the whole – Japan's attitude was one of nationalist defiance. Japan would concede nothing and its interests were not enlightened.[60] But Grew's judgment was too harsh, as Uchida's willingness to make concessions to the British in trade negotiations with India reveals.

Rather, Uchida's goal in the spring and summer of 1933 was to continue his long-held policy of international cooperation. Through bilateral relations in the political sphere and participation in multilateral conferences in economic, labour, and other spheres, Uchida demonstrated his commitment to preserving Japan's ties to the rest of the world – even if Japanese foreign policy appeared to be "autonomous." Uchida upheld Japan's diplomatic tradition of international cooperation, one which predated the creation of the League and continued after Japan's withdrawal. Japan could not escape Grew's charge that it was pursing its own interests, but in this it was no guiltier than most other nations in the political and economic climate of the early 1930s.[61]

Ending a Career: Uchida's Resignation

By the summer of 1933, the stress of guiding Japanese foreign policy through a period of "crisis" had begun to take its toll on the almost-sixty-eight-year-old Uchida, to the point where he mentioned to Harada Kumao, "I am afraid I don't know what's what anymore."[62] Waning confidence in his abilities, political censure, and the stress of mediating competing domestic interests contributed to Uchida's doubt and the breakdown of his health. In the cabinet and the Diet, Finance Minister Takahashi and Ashida Hitoshi criticized Uchida's policies for following the priorities of War Minister Araki and the army. Others, including Privy Council member Kaneko Kentaro, had other reasons to be critical. In February 1933, Kaneko reprimanded Uchida for not fully explaining Japan's foreign policies; six months later, Kaneko, in a discussion with Saitō, assaulted Uchida's personal character with "malicious" words.[63] As if the attacks on his policies and character were not enough, Uchida found himself caught between the demands of the military and the moderate views of most of the civilian leadership. As US ambassador Grew wrote in his diary, "He [Uchida] has had hard sledding with the various internal forces in the Government pulling him in different directions."[64]

At the end of August 1933, Uchida retreated to his villa in Hakone to nurse his ailing health and to gain respite from the acrimony of Tokyo politics. Before leaving, Uchida noted that he was becoming hard of hearing and was unsure if he could continue in the cabinet.[65] The extent of his poor health went beyond his deafness. According to some of his colleagues, Uchida had been active and healthy when he became foreign minister, but the position had taken its toll; at times his hands would shake and words would not leave his mouth.[66] Count Kabayama Aisuke informed Grew that Uchida was a "physical wreck and on the verge of nervous prostration."[67]

Uchida returned to the capital in early September and informed Premier Saitō of his intention to resign. As a reason he gave his deteriorating health and mounting frustrations: "The foreign minister in any country always gets the short end of the stick. My generation is growing older and my health is doing badly. I continue to work only by thinking that I am holding down the fort until a younger foreign minister is ready."[68] That younger minister, Uchida's personal recommendation, was Hirota Kōki, most recently ambassador to the Soviet Union, a well-respected statesman with extensive experience in the West and in China, although he had the reputation of being an ultranationalist.[69]

Some were happy to see Uchida resign because of his perceived closeness to the military. Grew thought Uchida shared the military's chauvinism,[70] a view shared by Governor-General of Korea Ugaki

Kazushige, who believed Uchida was greatly influenced by the military's shortsightedness.[71] Thus before taking office, Hirota requested a guarantee from Saitō that he alone would be responsible for directing foreign policy, a clear sign that he thought the independence of the foreign minister had been compromised.[72] Historian Sakai Tetsuya has argued that the Japanese public saw Hirota as a welcome change from Uchida, whom they associated with a general sense of "crisis." According to Sakai, Hirota's appointment moderated the sense of crisis, thus weakening the army's influence upon foreign policy.[73]

Although the army indeed had Uchida's ear, its influence has been overstated. Uchida's insistence on securing Japanese interests in Manchuria aligned the army's (particularly Araki and his supporters') interests with the foreign minister's, not the other way around. Uchida's China policy differed from the army's. Their common ground was Manchuria, the dominant issue during Uchida's last tenure as foreign minister: both he and the army supported the creation of Manchukuo and recognition of the new state. But while some in the army viewed Japan's control of Manchuria (through its Manchukuo puppet) as a means to an end, Uchida clearly considered Manchukuo as an end in itself. Protection of Japanese interests in Manchuria, which Uchida had worked towards for more than two decades, informed his support of the army's plans – not some vision of wars in China or Russia. Uchida's diplomacy began and ended in Manchuria.

Conclusion

Hirota's appointment is often seen as marking the beginning of a more conciliatory Japanese approach to the powers, which eventually hardened in 1935. In fact, Hirota initially followed the trail that Uchida blazed, something Uchida no doubt expected when he chose him as successor. Yet there were significant differences between Uchida and the foreign ministers who followed him, most notably Hirota (1933–36, 1937–38), Arita Hachirō (1936–37, 1938–39, 1940), and Matsuoka (1940–41). This group, which led Japanese diplomacy during the Sino-Japanese War and into the Pacific War, belonged to a new generation of imperialists who sought to replace the old order of Western imperialism in Asia with one dominated by Japan. Cooperation was secondary to establishing Japan's paramount position throughout the entire region including China, Southeast Asia, and the Pacific. When these new imperialists did seek cooperative relations with the West, they turned away from the Anglo-American nations and towards the upstart powers of Nazi Germany and the Soviet Union. Uchida, on the other hand, remained an old imperialist, more akin to Meiji-era statesmen than those of early Shōwa. By understanding Uchida as a Meiji imperialist, we can understand his reactions to and policies for Japanese activities in Manchuria in the early 1930s.

From the standpoint of diplomacy, Uchida approached the Manchurian Incident as Komura had approached the Portsmouth Peace Conference after the Russo-Japanese War.[74] The policies of both men incorporated opportunism and the desire to extend and secure the Japanese Empire, while recognizing the importance of cooperation with the powers. Behind Uchida's insistence that Manchukuo was the only means to solve the Manchurian problem were his twenty-five years of efforts to protect Japanese interests in the region. Uchida believed that, just as a Japanese-dominated Korea was critical to the security of Japan in 1904, so too was Manchuria crucial to Japan's larger empire in 1931. With a mindset similar to Komura's, Uchida attempted in the early 1930s to secure the empire, not to pave the way for Japanese domination of China. He did so by establishing and recognizing Manchukuo with one hand, while with the other pursuing Japan's traditional diplomacy of cooperation with the powers and peaceful economic relations in China. In contrast, foreign ministers who came after Uchida – Hirota, Arita, and Matsuoka – were increasingly hostile towards Britain and the United States, moved Japan closer to Nazi Germany, and openly supported Japanese aggression in China.

After inheriting the diplomatic legacy of the Meiji statesmen via Uchida's foreign policies of the early 1930s, a new generation of imperialists guided Japanese foreign policy to its logical conclusion. During the Meiji era, independent diplomacy had been impossible because of Japan's weakness relative to the other powers; in the 1930s, Tokyo could follow a less conciliatory foreign policy because Japan's power in the region was no longer countered easily by Britain or the United States. The new generation thus fulfilled the ultimate goal of the Meiji men – an independent Japan unconstrained by power differentials with the West – and it was the foreign ministers from this generation who challenged the international order in East Asia in the late 1930s. The challenge was neither set in place by Uchida nor predetermined by the Manchurian crisis of 1931–33.

Uchida's case presents evidence that the Manchurian crisis was not the first domino to fall on the road to Pearl Harbor. Far from the beginning of Japanese aggression on the mainland, the crisis represented the end – the last domino – of Japanese efforts to protect its interests in the region.[75] When Uchida stepped down as foreign minister, he left Manchuria – Manchukuo – as a land poised for rapid industrial development, a place where Japanese rights were secured. Threats to Japanese businesses, including his erstwhile employer the SMR, had been largely eliminated. His main goals had been accomplished; he saw no need for further extension of military activity or Japanese domination outside Manchuria.

In the international arena, Japan more or less came through unscathed. After the creation of Manchukuo and Japan's withdrawal from the League, no group of powers intervened, as they had in 1895; nor were economic sanctions imposed. Japan was not isolated. In 1933, Japan was still attending international conferences and had not yet repudiated international arms-limitation agreements.

Many scholars regard the early 1930s as a new era in Japanese foreign policy led by a new generation of leaders who initiated Japan's wars of aggression in China and the Pacific. Uchida, however, was most decidedly of the old generation, and his experience suggests that, at least as late as 1933, the new leadership had not yet set Japan on a path that intractably led to war.[76] Instead, an older generation was attempting to harmonize Japanese actions in Manchuria with the diplomatic principles of Meiji imperialism.

NOTES

Research for this chapter was made possible, in part, by funding from the Matsushita International Foundation. The author would like to thank the members of the Harvard Kenkyūkai, as well as Andrew Gordon, Akira Iriye, and Dani Botsman for commenting on earlier versions of this chapter.

1 Ian Nish, *Japanese Foreign Policy, 1869–1942: Kasumigaseki to Miyakezaka* (London: Routledge & Kegan Paul, 1977); Ikei Masaru, "Uchida Yasuya: Shōdo gaikō e no kiseki," *Kokusai seiji* 56 (1976): 1–21.

2 For an overview of Komura's diplomacy, see Minohara Toshihiro, "Nichirosensō to rekkyō eno taitō," *Kokusai Mondai* 546 (September 2005), 7–22; and idem, "The 'Rat Minister': Komura Jutarō and U.S.-Japan Relations," in *World War Zero: The Russo-Japanese War in a Global Perspective*, vol. 2, edited by David Wolff et al. (Leiden: Brill, 2007).

3 Uchiyama Masakuma, *Gendai Nihon Gaikōshi ron* (Tokyo: Keiō Tsūshin, 1971), 5.

4 This chapter uses the terms "Meiji-era diplomacy" and "Meiji imperialism" as rough synonyms for each other and for "Kasumigaseki diplomacy."

5 This is a simplistic sketch of factions within the foreign ministry. For further detail, see Shiozaki Hiroaki, "Gaimushō kakushin no genjō daha ninshiki to seisaku," in *Nenpō: Kindai Nihon kenkyū 7: Nihon gaikō no kiki ninshiki* (Tokyo: Yamakawa Shuppansha, 1985); Usui Katsumi, *Chūgoku wo meguru kindai Nihon no gaikō* (Tokyo: Chikuma Shobō, 1983); and Barbara Brooks, *Japan's Imperial Diplomacy* (Honolulu: University of Hawaii Press, 2000).

6 Uchida Yasuya Denki Hensan Iinkai, ed., *Uchida Yasuya* (Tokyo: Kajima Kenkyūjyō Shuppandai, 1968), 348.

7 Grew to Stimson, 25 July 1932; record of the interviews found in State Department Records, Records Group 59 [Hereafter cited as RG59]: 793.94-Commission/307.

8 Thomas Burkman, "Nationalist Actors in the Internationalist Theatre: Nitobe Inazō and Ishii Kikujirō and the League of Nations," in *Nationalism and Internationalism in Imperial Japan: Autonomy, Asian Brotherhood, or World Citizenship?* edited by Dick Stegewerns (London: Routledge Curzon, 2003), 95.

9 Morishima Yasuhiko, ed., *Shōwa no dōran to Morishima Gorō no shōgai* (Fukuoka: Asahi Shobō, 1985), 60.

10 Uchida's speech can be found in *Uchida Yasuya*, 350–6; *Teikoku Gikai gijiroku: Dai 63 kai* (Tokyo: Naikaku Kanpōkyoku, 1932), 13–14; RG59: 894.00/430; and *New York Times*, 25 August 1932.

11 *Mori Kaku* (Tokyo: Mori Kaku Denki Hensankai, 1940), 821–31; *Uchida Yasuya*, 357–8; *Teikoku Gikai gijiroku*, 16–18; and *Documents on British Foreign Policy, 1919–1939*, 2nd series, vol. 10 (London: Her Majesty's Stationery Office, 1969), 719–20.

12 *Teikoku Gikai gijiroku*, 18; *Uchida Yasuya*, 359.

13 *Teikoku Gikai gijiroku*, 37, 41; *Uchida Yasuya*, 359–60.

14 *Tōkyō Asahi Shimbun*, 26 August 1933.

15 *Trans-Pacific*, 1 September 1932, 15.

16 *Documents on British Foreign Policy, 1919–1939*, 2nd series, vol. 10, 717.

17 Acting Secretary of State Castle and Ambassador Grew commented to that effect; RG59: 894.00/432 and 894.00-P.R./57.

18 Arita Hachiro, *Bakahachi to hito wa iu: Gaikokan no kaisō* (Tokyo: Kōwado, 1959), 63–4.

19 *Nihon Gaikō nenpyō narabi ni shuyō monjo,* vol. 2 (Tokyo: Gaimushō, 1967), 206–10; Sadako Ogata, *Defiance in Manchuria: The Making of Japanese Foreign Policy, 1931–1932* (Berkeley: University of California Press, 1964), 161–2. For a lengthier discussion of the policy, see Ogata, *Defiance in Manchuria,* 160–70. Here and in another article, Ogata argues that the policy was clearly new in that it was based on "independent" diplomacy and laid the basis for Japan's eventual withdrawal from the League. Ogata Sadako, "Gaikō to yoron – Renmei dattai wo meguru ikkōsatsu," *Kokusai seiji* 41 (April 1970): 40–55.

20 *Nihon Gaikō nenpyō narabi ni shuyō monjo,* vol. 2, 207–8.

21 *Documents on British Foreign Policy, 1919–1939,* 2nd series, vol. 10, 581.

22 In English, see David Lu, *The Agony of Choice: Matsuoka Yōsuke and the Rise and Fall of the Japanese Empire, 1880–1946* (Lanham, MD: Lexington, 2002); and Ian Nish, *Japan's Struggle with Internationalism* (London: K. Paul International, 1993). In Japanese, see Usui Katsumi, *Manshūkoku to Kokusai Renmei* (Tokyo: Yoshikawa, 1995).

23 The Committee of Nineteen was established by the assembly after the Manchurian Incident and included the assembly president, twelve council members, and six assembly members; Lu, *Agony of Choice,* 87.

24 Matsuoka believed that Uchida had sanctioned this plan of attack prior to his departure for Geneva; ibid., 81.

25 For an explanation of the doctrine, see Henry L. Stimson, *The Far Eastern Crisis* (New York: Council on Foreign Relations, 1936).

26 Inoue Toshikazu, *Kiki no naka no kyōchō gaikō* (Tokyo: Yamakawa, 1994), 34–7.

27 For arguments against Uchida, see, Lu, *Agony of Choice,* 92; and Usui, *Manshūkoku to Kokusai Renmei,* 140–69.

28 Tatsuji Takeuchi, *War and Diplomacy in the Japanese Empire* (Garden City, NY: Doubleday, Doran, 1935), 408.

29 *Documents on British Foreign Policy, 1919–1939,* 2nd series, vol. 11 (London: Her Majesty's Stationery Office, 1970), 292.

30 Ibid.

31 Inoue, *Kiki no naka,* 41–2.

32 Ibid., 44.

33 Ibid., 49.

34 Uchiyama Masakuma, "Manshū Jihen to Kokusai renmei dattai," *Kokusai seiji* 43 (1970): 168–9.

35 Harada Kumao, *Saionji-kyō to seikyoku,* vol. 3 (Tokyo: Iwanami Shoten, 1951), 38.

36 Inoue, *Kiki no naka,* 50.

37 For more on the argument that bilateral relations replaced multilateral relations, see Sakai Tetsuya, *"Eibei kyōchō" to "nicchū teikei,"* in *Nenpō: Kindai nihon kenkyū 11, Kyōchō seisaku no genkai* (Tokyo: Yamakawa Shuppansha, 1989), 27; and Kitaoka Shinichi, "Rikugun habatsu tairitsu (1931–35) no saikentō: taigai, kokubō seisaku wo chūshin to shite," in *Nenpō: Kindai nihon kenkyū* (Tokyo: Yamakawa Shuppansha, 1979), 72.

38 This was not merely rhetoric. When considering Uchida's earlier policies and stance, his statement seems to be grounded firmly in his own convictions. British ambassador Lindley believed Uchida's claim and reported to that effect to his government. *Documents on British Foreign Policy, 1919–1939,* 2nd series, vol. 20 (London: Her Majesty's Stationery Office, 1984), 71.

39 Sakai, *"Eibei kyōchō" to "nicchū teikei,"* 29.

40 Some in the military criticized Uchida's approach because they saw Chiang's supposed moderate stance toward Japan as insincere, ibid., 40–1.

41 James Crowley, *Japan's Quest for Autonomy: National Security and Foreign Policy, 1930–1938* (Princeton, NJ: Princeton University Press, 1966), 191.

42 Ibid.

43 Osamu Ishii, *Cotton-Textile Diplomacy: Japan, Great Britain, and the United States, 1930–1936* (New York: Arno Press, 1981), 104.

44 For a more detailed discussion, see ibid., 98–114.

45 Ibid., 108–12.

46 *Trans-Pacific,* 10 August 1933, 9.

47 Historian Kagotani Naoto argues that the foreign ministry continued this approach in trade conferences with European powers in 1933–34; *Ajia Kokusai tsūshō chitsujo to kindai Nihon* (Nagoya: Nagoya University Press, 2000).

48 Inoue Toshikazu, "Kokusai renmei dattaigo no Nihon gaikō: taibei kyōchō no mosaku: 1933 nen," *Hitotsubashi ronsō* 43, no. 2 (1985): 210.

49 These instructions can be found in *Uchida Yasuya,* 365–6; Inoue, "Kokusai renmei dattaigo no Nihon gaikō," 213; and *Documents Diplomatiques Français, 1932–39,* 1st series, vol. 3 (Paris: Imprimerie nationale, 1964), 423–4.

50 Inoue, "Kokusai renmei dattaigo no Nihon gaikō," 214.

51 British Foreign Office 371/17158 Japan: 1933, Snow to Orde, 25 May 1933.

52 Joseph Grew, *Ten Years in Japan* (London: Hammond, 1944), 90–1.

53 Grew to Hull, 9 August 1933, RG59: 794.00/57, Box 4494.

54 Kitaoka, 75–6.

55 Harada, *Saionji-kyō to seikyoku,* vol. 2, 418, 429.

56 *Documents on British Foreign Policy, 1919–1939,* 2nd series, vol. 11, 7.

57 The information for this paragraph is from *Uchida Yasuya,* 366–9.

58 *Nihon Gaikō Bunsho – Manshū Jihen*, vol. 2, part 2 (Tokyo: Gaimushō, 1979), 387–8.

59 Kitaoka, 72–3.

60 For this opinion, see Grew to Hull, 3 May 1933, State Department 500.C 001/808, RG 59, Box 2475; and Grew to Hull, 9 August 1933, State Department 794.00/57, RG 59, Box 4494.

61 For example, the United States as much as any other power deserves the blame for the failure of the London Economic Conference.

62 Harada, *Saionji-kyō to seikyoku*, vol. 3, 126.

63 For the first episode, see *Trans-Pacific*, 16 February 1933; for the second, see Harada, *Saionji-kyō to seikyoku*, vol. 3, 126–7.

64 Joseph Grew Diary, 14 September 1933, Houghton Library, Harvard University.

65 Harada, *Saionji-kyō to seikyoku*, vol. 3, 126.

66 *Uchida Yasuya denki sōkō*, vol. 14.

67 Joseph Grew Diary, 14 September 1933.

68 *Uchida Yasuya*, 387.

69 This is according to the *Times*, 14 September 1933.

70 Joseph Grew Diary, 3 April 1933.

71 Ugaki Kazushige, *Ugaki Kazushige Nikki* (Tokyo: Misuzu Shobo, 1970), 853–6.

72 *Hirota Kōki* (Tokyo: Hirota Kōki denki kankōkai, 1966), 107.

73 Sakai, *"Eibei kyōchō" to "nicchū teikei,"* 50.

74 For further details of Komura and the peace conference, see Minohara Toshihiro, "Potsumasu kōwakaigi to Komura gaikō," *Kobe Annals of Law and Politics* 22 (2006): 59–95.

75 For a similar argument, which stresses that we should view the Manchurian crisis as a unique, singular event, see Sandra Wilson, *The Manchurian Crisis and Japanese Society, 1931–33* (New York: Routledge, 2002), 221.

76 One such scholar is Sadako Ogata; see Ogata, *Defiance in Manchuria*, 180–1.

9   Japan's Diplomatic Gamble for Autonomy: Rethinking Matsuoka Yōsuke's Diplomacy

SATOSHI HATTORI

The diplomacy that began with the Manchurian Incident and the "scorched earth diplomacy" of Foreign Minister Uchida Kōsai (Yasuya) reached its zenith with the outbreak of the Sino-Japanese War in 1937. Although the war did not inevitably follow the Manchurian Incident, the economic and political conditions it created fuelled the outbreak of the Pacific War.

The Pacific War came about because Japan failed to settle its war with China. From the end of 1938, the leaders of the Imperial Japanese Army (IJA), confronted by their inability to force China's capitulation, decided on an alliance with Germany to bolster Japan's strategic position. This was opposed by both the Imperial Japanese Navy (IJN) and the Ministry of Foreign Affairs (*Gaimushō*). This conflict within Japanese policy-making circles was partially resolved by the Russo-German Nonaggression Pact of August 1939, as it counterbalanced Japan's existing alliance with Germany – namely, the anti-Comintern Pact.

Nevertheless, Germany's military superiority and the likelihood of its dominance in Europe – which looked increasingly certain in the summer of 1940 – increased Japanese enthusiasm for an alliance with that country. Japanese policy-makers (particularly those in the IJA) thought it would help bring a resolution to the Sino-Japanese War. It is in this light that Tokyo decided to conclude the Axis alliance.

The Tripartite Pact immediately aggravated Japan's relations with Britain and the United States, and it was the subsequent deterioration of relations with these two nations that eventually led to the Pacific War. To understand Japan's path to the Pacific War, it is thus imperative to examine the central figure responsible for the conclusion of the Tripartite Pact. This individual was none other than Foreign Minister

Matsuoka Yōsuke. It was Matsuoka who broadened the bilateral conflict of the Sino-Japanese War into a general East Asian War and, in doing so, ultimately brought about the destruction of Japan. Yet it was not Matsuoka's intention to precipitate a general war. He was well aware of international realities, and sought to avoid conflict with the all-powerful United States. With this in mind, this chapter examines the nature and objectives of Matsuoka's diplomacy.

The Three Factions of the *Gaimushō*

The *Gaimushō* in the 1930s was divided into three main factions.[1] One consisted of traditionalists who emphasized cooperation with the United States and Britain. Led by Shidehara Kijurō (1872–1951), this group was dominant in the *Gaimushō* from the time of its creation through to the end of the 1920s, but its influence waned rapidly after the Manchurian Incident.

A second faction consisted of pan-Asian reformists led by a younger generation of diplomats, including Hirota Kōki (1878–1948), Arita Hachirō (1884–1965), and Shigemitsu Mamoru (1887–1957). The faction came to the fore after the Manchurian Incident and formed the core group within the *Gaimushō* throughout the 1930s; its influence on foreign policy can be seen by the length of these three men's tenure as foreign minister.[2] The faction's primary goal was to create a new order in East Asia, an autarkic economic bloc under Japanese leadership. They regarded the existing international order with disdain, distrust, and hostility; they nevertheless hoped to achieve this new order through diplomacy, and were keen to avoid outright conflict with the Anglo-American powers. In this respect they were quite moderate in comparison with the third faction.

Known as *kakushin-ha* (renovationists), this third faction was composed of the remainder of the diplomats in the *Gaimushō*. The key figure was Shiratori Toshio (1887–1949), a charismatic leader supported by the *Gaimushō*'s rank and file. The faction's position was similar to that of the pan-Asianist group, but its members were more radical in that they called for an end to Western influence in East Asia. The *kakushin-ha*'s policy goals virtually assured collision with Britain and the United States, but unlike members of the pan-Asianist faction, the renovationists (to an extent) welcomed conflict and worked to precipitate it. They envisioned an anti–Anglo-American front consisting of Japan, Germany, Italy, and the Soviet Union – the so-called Four Power Alliance.

It is important to note that pro-communist elements were absent from the *Gaimushō* and that the *kakushin-ha* based their policies on the centrality of *kōdō gaikō*, the imperial system and the emperor. As this was their guiding principle, they were staunch anti-communists. But geopolitical commonsense dictated allying with Germany, Italy, and – however distasteful – the Soviet Union, although association with the latter was never seen as anything more than a temporary marriage of convenience.

Shiratori's leadership and influence on the *kakushin-ha* was enormous. Within the *Gaimushō* he was virtually a cult personality, influencing many with his radical thinking. Divergence of opinion among the *kakushin-ha* was slight: all shared the common basic idea of Japan's position in East Asia, while events following the Manchurian Incident helped further expand the group's appeal.

Because of their radicalism, the *kakushin-ha* were viewed with suspicion by both the traditionalist and the pan-Asianist factions. As members of the latter were more senior and occupied key posts in the ministry, the influence of the *kakushin-ha* was held in check, though this did not prevent them from attempting to influence policy.[3]

Matsuoka as Diplomat and Politician

Matsuoka became foreign minister in July 1940. Although his ideas were often quite similar to those of the *kakushin-ha*, he was never a member. Matsuoka, more moderate and more of a realist, was careful to distinguish himself from Shiratori. Matsuoka had his own circle of admirers and supporters inside and outside the *Gaimushō*. This became apparent after his appointment as foreign minister, when the *kakushin-ha* split in two: Shiratori's more radical majority and a smaller, more moderate group backing Matsuoka. Although the two groups shared many ideas, they often collided over foreign policy.[4]

The main difference between the groups was their stance towards the United States. Although both wanted a Japan-dominated regional order and an anti–Anglo-America coalition towards this end, they differed markedly over means. Certain it would result in the end of the Japanese Empire, Matsuoka was adamant that Japanese policy not precipitate a war with the United States. Shiratori, on the other hand, believed war with the United States was not only necessary but inevitable to realize Japan's new order.[5] Whereas Matsuoka's approach was informed by a sound understanding of international realities, Shiratori's was not.

Let us turn to Matsuoka the politician. After spending his youth in the United States, he graduated from the University of Oregon in 1901, and began his career as a professional diplomat in 1904 after returning to Japan. Following his time in the foreign ministry, he served as an executive officer of the South Manchuria Railway (SMR).[6] In 1930 he successfully ran for the House of Representatives as a *Seiyūkai* party candidate. Unable to form his own power base within the party, he relied upon public opinion to garner support. Matsuoka was not a traditional party politician; indeed, he regarded political parties as harmful to the democratic process, especially in the arena of diplomacy.

In 1933 Matsuoka organized a movement calling for the dissolution of political parties.[7] Although he professed loyalty to the emperor, he was a supporter of fascism and viewed Hitler's Germany as an ideal regime, one capable of formulating and implementing policy without concerning itself with the vicissitudes of naive and irresponsible public opinion.

Upon his return from Geneva in 1933, where he announced Japan's withdrawal from the League of Nations, he promptly resigned his seat in the House and resumed his campaign against political parties. Although he managed to attract popular support, he was unable to decisively influence Japanese politics. Realizing the futility of his actions, he abandoned his campaign and returned to the SMR as its president in 1935. The masses were never more than a tool to realize his personal ambitions.[8]

Matsuoka remained in the political hinterlands until Prime Minister Konoe Fumimaro called him to join the cabinet as foreign minister in July 1940. Konoe regarded Matsuoka as the perfect choice for foreign minister as he would no doubt realize the *nanshin seisaku* (southward advance policy). Matsuoka previously had harboured an ambition of joining the cabinet, but had abandoned the hope when his campaign to dissolve the political parties fizzled. Here was a new opportunity he had not foreseen. With his ambition reignited, Matsuoka came to entertain visions of assuming the premiership once he had secured Japan's diplomatic objectives.

Matsuoka's revisionist foreign policy ideas and tendency to play to the masses came to the fore in his new position. Since leading the Japanese delegation out of the League of Nations in 1933, he had enjoyed enormous popularity as a figure representing the common people. The public had high expectations of Matsuoka as foreign minister, and he tried to live up to these by pulling off complex and conspicuous diplomatic coups. Understanding Matsuoka's diplomatic goals, however, has been hindered by a lack of relevant Japanese sources. Many of the records dealing with his tenure as foreign minister were destroyed before Japan's defeat in August 1945. It has generally been believed that Matsuoka's ultimate objective was to negotiate an agreement with the United States that would lead to the conclusion of the Sino-Japanese War. This would explain Matsuoka's strategy to expand the Tripartite Pact to include the Soviet Union[9] – to pressure Washington to conclude negotiations on terms favourable to Japan. This commonly accepted interpretation, however, suffers from lack of archival evidence. It is also plagued by contradictions that undermine an accurate understanding of Matsuoka's diplomacy.[10] In light of the discovery of new archival material, a re-evaluation of Matsuoka's diplomacy is overdue.

The Southward Advance Policy: Matsuoka's Diplomatic Objective

Careful examination of Matsuoka's speeches, policy decisions, and other Japanese documents from 1940 reveal no plans to include the Soviet Union in the Tripartite Pact. Moreover, contrary to what is traditionally believed, Tokyo's political objective at the time was not to end the Sino-Japanese War. Rather, economic incentives dictated that Japan expand its sphere of influence over Southeast Asia by taking advantage of German domination in Europe.[11]

The commonly accepted explanation for Matsuoka's diplomacy cannot reconcile these two goals. In this light, the MAGIC intercepts – Japanese diplomatic transmissions intercepted and decoded by the US Army and Navy – become an invaluable resource for re-evaluating Matsuoka's diplomacy. Although doubt has been cast on their accuracy (due to mistranslations), I have compared them with surviving original Japanese telegrams deposited in the Diplomatic Records Office in Tokyo.[12] In doing so, I was able to verify the authenticity of the MAGIC documents and to conclude that the intercepts were deciphered and translated fairly accurately. This allows us to use the MAGIC documents as a substitute for the lost Japanese originals.

It must be pointed out, however, that the appointment of Matsuoka as foreign minister in the summer of 1940 coincided with other factors pushing Japan towards building an autarkic bloc in East Asia. In early 1940, Washington notified Tokyo of its decision to abrogate the 1911 Treaty of Commerce and Navigation. This was a severe blow, as Japan depended on the United States for about 80 per cent of its strategic goods and materials, and, contrary to original Japanese plans, the war in China had only increased dependence on US imports.[13] Beginning in the fall of 1939, Japan tried to reduce dependence on US strategic materials by strengthening economic ties with Southeast Asia.[14]

While Tokyo was making this transition, war broke out in Europe. The capitulation of France and the Netherlands following Germany's lightning advance and Italy's decision to enter the war on the side of Germany meant Britain was isolated. It was an opportune moment for Japan to expand the "New Order in East Asia" into Southeast Asia. Japan correctly believed that British and French military and economic assistance – through Burma and French Indochina – was sustaining Chinese resistance. If Britain were forced to surrender, such assistance would cease and the Sino-Japanese War could be won.[15]

Tokyo and the IJA decided to take advantage of the moment and seize outright the European colonies in Southeast Asia. Since it was understood that the "New Order in East Asia" would be an imperfect autarkic bloc, the conclusion was quickly reached that self-sufficiency could be increased only if the resource-rich European colonies were incorporated into the new order.[16] The ultimate goal was to acquire a voice in the disposition of the colonies in the ensuing peace conference expected to take place after the war. Believing it would be modelled along the lines of the Paris Peace Conference of 1919, Japan's leaders sought to strengthen their position at the bargaining table by offering military support to Germany, which they were sure was on the verge of defeating Britain. Military cooperation was to be in the form of a Japanese invasion of Southeast Asia (excluding the Philippines), effectively removing the Western powers from the region. The most important strategic goal was to capture British Malaya and Singapore. As Japan's natural resources were nearing exhaustion, the invasion needed to take place precisely when Germany would provide the *coup de grâce* to Britain. Specifically, this meant that Japan's advance into Southeast Asia needed to coincide with Germany's invasion of the British Isles. It was widely thought that German landing operations would come in September 1940. Thus, an alliance with Germany had to be concluded prior to this for Japan to secure the fruits of war.[17]

Although favoured by general public opinion and Japanese political parties, the main advocate of this plan was the IJA. The IJA had supported the southward advance policy since early June 1940 and helped to create the second Konoe Fumimaro cabinet (formed 22 July 1940) to implement it. As foreign minister in this cabinet, Matsuoka promptly proceeded with the southward advance policy, a daring plan he was both temperamentally and ideologically suited to realize.

The First Stage: The Conclusion of the Tripartite Pact

Matsuoka's diplomacy can be separated into four distinct stages, beginning with his appointment as foreign minister and ending with his resignation. The first phase lasted from the instalment of the Konoe cabinet in July 1940 until the conclusion of Tripartite Pact in September.

The southward advance policy presented four challenges. First, entry into the European war necessitated escape from the quagmire of the Sino-Japanese War. Towards this end, Japan forced the French colonial government – isolated after France's defeat in June – to close the supply route from French Indochina to Chongqing. To appease Japan, Britain in July likewise decided to close the supply route from Burma for three months.[18] Chiang Kai-shek's government in Chongqing was thus no longer able to obtain war supplies. This allowed the IJA to make peace overtures, known as the *Kiri-kōsaku*, towards the Chiang government and by June an accord was very close to being reached.[19] Matsuoka was counting on IJA success to end the war.

The second challenge concerned Japanese-Soviet relations. For the southward advance to succeed, restoration of relations with the Soviets was vital – as important as ending the war with China. Relations had been fragile since the Nomonhan Incident of 1939;[20] now, in an attempt to stabilize them, Tokyo concluded a non-aggression pact with Moscow. It has been commonly understood that Matsuoka entered negotiations on the understanding that the Soviet Union eventually would join the Tripartite Pact, with Germany acting as intermediary.[21] But despite their non-aggression pact, German-Soviet relations had not improved. The Soviets invaded Finland in November 1939, and in the peace treaty of March 1940 forced that country to cede a huge swathe of territory. Soviet expansionism thus posed a threat to German interests. German fears were heightened when the Soviet Union threatened Romania into ceding part of its territory, followed by further efforts at expansion in the region in July 1940. Matsuoka understood the realities of German-Soviet relations and correctly judged that admitting the Soviet Union into the Tripartite Pact was impossible.[22] At the same time, he did not give up on improving Japanese-Soviet relations with German assistance. He surmised that icy relations between Germany and the Soviet Union would be an incentive for the Soviets to conclude a non-aggression pact with Japan.

The third challenge concerned restructuring relations with Southeast Asia. Although Matsuoka explained his policy of establishing the Great East Asia Co-Prosperity Sphere on 1 August, he did not disclose his intention of advancing into Southeast Asia;[23] in his mind, there was no question that Britain and the Netherlands were the enemies. He resumed economic negotiations with the Netherlands East Indies, begun by the previous cabinet, sending Kobayashi Ichizō, Minister of Commerce and Industry, as chief of mission; details of a new conference were concluded in early September.[24] Matsuoka then concluded an agreement with Charles Arsène-Henry, the Vichy French ambassador in Tokyo, on 30 August in which Japan and French Indochina mutually conferred most-favoured-nation status and agreed on early September negotiations to discuss the stationing of Japanese troops.[25]

Matsuoka also devoted himself to negotiating the Tripartite Pact with Germany – his fourth and largest diplomatic challenge. Negotiations began on 9 September between Matsuoka and German representative Heinrich Stahmer.[26] The most important issue was whether Germany, which now controlled most of western Europe, would accept an alliance with Japan. Realizing Germany most feared the United States' entry into the war, Matsuoka proposed the pact as a military alliance against both London and Washington, explaining to Stahmer that Japanese naval power would deter US entry. The IJN, which wanted to avoid any possibility of war with the United States, was opposed to such an alliance, and even Matsuoka himself had doubts. He nevertheless proceeded to conclude the Tripartite Pact before Germany brought the European war to a close without Japan. Were this to happen, Japan's southward advance would become untenable.

As a safeguard, Matsuoka insisted that the Japanese government alone would decide on opening hostilities with Britain and the United States. With this clause in place, Japan and Germany concluded the pact on 27 September. Meanwhile, negotiations between Japan and French Indochina's military authorities ended in Hanoi with an agreement that Japanese troops would be placed in northern French Indochina from 23 September.[27]

The Second Stage: The Beginning of US-Japanese Negotiations

The speculative nature of the southward advance policy soon began to manifest itself. The Japanese government and military officials had predicted Germany would invade Britain in September 1940 and that the European war would end shortly thereafter. This was why Matsuoka had pressed his policy with such urgency. The German invasion, however, did not take place as envisioned. From this point, the southward advance policy began to go awry. With nothing occurring in September, Matsuoka calculated the next opportunity for an invasion of the British Isles would not come until the following spring due to adverse weather in the English Channel. With his original timetable off schedule, Matsuoka could only continue to address his other challenges.

Ending the Sino-Japanese War was the first. The IJA aimed to achieve this through the *Kiri-kōsaku*, peace negotiations with the Chiang Kai-shek government, but the operation began to falter in September and was finally called off on 8 October.[28] With the Tripartite Pact out of the way, Matsuoka moved to launch a new peace initiative towards China. He attempted to work through the leader of the Zhejiang financial group, but his efforts failed to produce the desired result and the talks were terminated at the end of November.[29]

There were, however, successes in China. A Japanese puppet government was formed in Nanjing led by Wang Chao-yao, Chiang Kai-shek's most trusted lieutenant. While the government was established in March, Tokyo postponed recognition until the *Kiri-kōsaku* had run its course. Once the operation's demise became apparent, Tokyo promptly recognized Wang's regime on 30 November. The Japanese government and the IJA initially had planned to reduce the number of troops occupying China by ceding control to the Nanjing government,[30] but this plan was shelved when that government's instability became clear and the British reopened the supply route to Chang through Burma on 17 October.[31] At this moment Japan lost a key opportunity to conclude the Sino-Japanese War.

The Japanese-Soviet situation was the second challenge. On 30 October, Matsuoka offered the Soviet Union a non-aggression pact without reservations.[32] Matsuoka's predecessor Arita Hachirō had proposed a neutrality treaty on 14 August, but the Soviets had conditioned its acceptance upon Japan's relinquishing rights to northern Sakhalin.[33] Although Arita could not accept such a condition, Matsuoka was willing to make concessions to enable his southward advance policy; it was imperative that the Soviets not threaten Japan from the north.

Speed was of the essence in bringing the Soviets in line, as Matsuoka was aware the British government had approached Moscow with a proposal for a joint attack against Germany.[34] Washington also made overtures to the Soviet Union to enter the war on the Allied side.[35] Matsuoka's intent was to deflect Anglo-American enticement and eliminate Soviet opposition to Japan and Germany. The aim was not to bring the Soviet Union into the Tripartite Pact, but to prevent Moscow from joining the Anglo-American camp. On this point the German foreign minister Joachim von Ribbentrop and Matsuoka were in agreement.[36] But the Soviets were not easily induced, and the Soviet-German talks in Berlin on 12–13 November ended in failure.[37] The German government then decided for war against the Soviet Union in the following spring. This decision, however, was concealed from Japan and Italy.[38] As Matsuoka was kept in the dark, he continued to work towards an agreement between Japan, Germany, and the Soviet Union. Unknown to him, the shift in German strategy had bankrupted his southward advance policy.

As for restructuring relations with Southeast Asia, Matsuoka dismissed Chief Representative Kobayashi upon the conclusion of the Tripartite Pact and appointed Yoshizawa Kenkichi, a former foreign minister, to continue negotiations with the Netherlands East Indies.[39] Following the stationing of IJA troops in northern French Indochina, Matsuoka entered negotiations with its colonial authorities on 22 October. Beginning in Hanoi and later moving to Tokyo, their purpose was to strengthen Japan's economic ties with the region.[40] Matsuoka did not believe Japan should control French Indochina; his posture was never hostile. Although he had proclaimed the creation of the Greater East Asia Co-Prosperity Sphere as a new regional order, he confined the sphere to economics, intentionally leaving out political considerations.

The US government responded with an economic embargo in 1940 to contain Japanese advances in the region. Washington had abrogated the 1911 Treaty of Commerce and Navigation earlier in the year, and in June placed oil and scrap iron under the president's export licence system. After the formation of the second Konoe Fumimaro cabinet, Washington added further items to the embargo list.[41] This, in part, prompted Matsuoka to strengthen Japan's economic relations with the Netherlands East Indies and French Indochina. He was also careful not to provoke the United States and Britain while waiting for the German invasion that would remove Britain from the equation. This concluded the second stage of Matsuoka's diplomacy.

The Third Stage: The Japanese-Soviet Neutrality Treaty

The movement to improve US-Japanese relations began with an unofficial civilian initiative from both countries at the end of 1940.[42] Since his appointment as foreign minister, Matsuoka's goal had been the dissolution of the British Empire while avoiding a head-on collision with the United States. One of the first things he did as foreign minister was to inform US ambassador to Japan Joseph C. Grew and US ambassador to the Soviet Union Laurence A. Steinhardt that war with the United States was out of the question.[43] The conclusion of the Tripartite Pact nevertheless strained US-Japanese relations, while the ensuing embargo was crippling the Japanese economy.[44]

By January 1941, the civilian-led US-Japanese peace mission had evolved into official negotiations.[45] Although Matsuoka at first had allowed them to languish, he came to recognize their importance and decided to play an active role upon the conclusion of an agreement with the Soviets.[46] Coinciding with this policy shift was a border dispute between Thailand and French Indochina that escalated into armed conflict on 28 November 1940.[47] Thailand had lost territory to the French and British in the nineteenth century and was intent on recapturing it by taking advantage of France's defeat in the European war.

Tokyo promptly involved itself as mediator in the dispute. By offering mediation, Matsuoka was able to thwart an IJA plan to conclude a military alliance with Thailand and then place more troops in the newly acquired Thai territory to prepare for the attack against British Malaya and Singapore.[48] Matsuoka took a hard line against the French to demonstrate Japanese leadership in the Greater East Asia Co-Prosperity Sphere. Britain also offered to mediate but was rebuffed by Thailand.[49] On 27 January 1941, Japan gained the position of sole arbitrator, and negotiations commenced on 7 February.[50]

Once the issue had been settled (unsurprisingly, in favour of Thailand), Matsuoka turned his attention to the United States.[51] Anxious not to further aggravate the Americans, he refused to entertain suggestions of a military alliance with Thailand or to acquire a military foothold in southern French Indochina for Japan; his desire was for Washington to understand his peaceful intentions.

Such actions, however, placed Matsuoka in direct conflict with the IJA, which continued to believe Germany would launch its British offensive in the spring of 1941. The IJA wanted to take advantage of the mediation and obtain a military presence in both Thailand and southern French Indochina by March.[52] As Matsuoka knew the US reaction would be harsh, he did not allow the IJA to drag him into its agenda.[53] Due to his firm resistance, Matsuoka was able to rein in the IJA and to conclude on 11 March a Thai-French Indochina agreement that included no Japanese military gains.[54]

The following day Matsuoka left for Europe. His first stop was Moscow, where he sounded out Stalin on a non-aggression pact.[55] He then travelled to Berlin and Rome. It was in Berlin that he realized Hitler had already decided to go to war with the Soviet Union.[56] With this shocking realization, Matsuoka visited Moscow on his return trip and again pressed Stalin for a neutrality pact – a vital diplomatic card to negotiate with the Americans.

The negotiations with the Soviets were difficult from the outset. In the end, Matsuoka got what he wanted on the condition that Japan would dissolve its rights in northern Sakhalin within months of the pact's conclusion.[57] As Matsuoka believed the German-Soviet war would break out soon, Japan would have to cede nothing to the Russians. After concluding the neutrality treaty with Moscow on 13 April, Matsuoka devoted his attention to reaching an accord with the Americans. This marked the end of the third stage of Matsuoka's diplomacy – his strategy was working brilliantly so far.

The Fourth Stage: Matsuoka's Failure and Resignation

Matsuoka returned to Japan on 22 April. During his trip he had spoken with Laurence Steinhardt, the US ambassador in Moscow, to prepare for the upcoming US-Japanese negotiations.[58] By this time Matsuoka had abandoned the southward advance policy. He was startled, however, to discover upon his arrival that the two countries had already discussed a Draft Understanding (*Nichi-bei Ryokai-an*).[59] The result of an unofficial civilian initiative, the Draft Understanding had been officially sanctioned by Prime Minister Konoe, who had kept Matsuoka in the dark.[60] Incensed and humiliated, Matsuoka opposed the Draft Understanding even though it provided a splendid opportunity to secure an agreement with the United States.[61]

Matsuoka's diplomatic strategy further unravelled when negotiations with the French Indochina government bogged down. In the end, an agreement was concluded only on 6 May.[62] Economic negotiations with the Netherlands East Indies also faltered, the Dutch government having exiling itself to London after the Netherlands' surrender to the Germans, thereby placing the colonial possession under British influence.[63] Since Japanese economic conditions were worsening by the day, time was of the essence. Matsuoka hoped that the Japanese-Soviet neutrality treaty would apply pressure on the Netherlands East Indies government, but this hope was illusory, as on 6 June the Dutch authorities rejected any concessions.[64] On 11 June Matsuoka broke off negotiations.[65]

The IJA now changed its strategy in favour of a new, autonomous southward advance policy, moving troops to southern French Indochina despite the vehement objections of Matsuoka, who feared it would ignite a war with the United States. Then, on 22 June, Germany invaded the Soviet Union, prompting a re-evaluation of the southward advance policy. There were three different views. Konoe insisted on halting the southward advance and reaching a compromise with the United States. The military, in contrast, regarded the German-Soviet war as an opportune moment to continue its modified southward advance policy. Matsuoka's view, however, was extraordinary: he insisted on immediate entry into the war against the Soviet Union based on the Tripartite Pact, and he requested the military and Konoe to support his plan.[66] Matsuoka now championed discarding the southward advance policy in favour of a northward advance policy (*hokushin seisaku*) to crush the Soviets in coordination with Germany.

The logic behind this *volte-face* was that Matsuoka had concluded that the German-Soviet war had completely demolished his plan of negotiating a settlement with the United States. He had believed that only an alliance with *both* Germany and the Soviet Union would provide enough pressure to persuade Washington to compromise towards Japan. Now, thanks to Hitler's actions, a tripartite pact consisting of the United States, Britain, and the Soviet Union had been created. Moreover, if the Germans and Italians were to lose the war in Europe, this new alliance evidently would next seek to destroy Japan. Thus, Matsuoka felt it prudent to cripple the alliance by attacking the Soviet Union while Germany was still formidable. And once the Soviet Union had been defeated, Japan would once again have leverage over the

United States at the negotiating table. In this way, Matsuoka's seemingly bizarre about-face was actually underpinned by a certain rationale that was quite logical if one did not factor in the issue of strategic materials: what Japan needed most in the face of the US embargo were all located in the south.

But Matsuoka's bellicose attitude alarmed even the IJA hardliners, who saw the plan as militarily difficult and lacking economic benefit. Even Konoe thought Matsuoka had gone mad. It was only a matter of time before the completely isolated Matsuoka would be sacked. Now seen as the chief obstacle and troublemaker, Matsuoka was finally expelled from the cabinet on 18 July.[67]

Conclusion

Japanese diplomacy in the 1930s aimed to establish autarky in East Asia. This was clearly seen in the 1935 campaign to separate north China from China proper (*kahokubunri kōsaku*) and in the construction of the New East Asia Order (*Tōashinchitsujo*) in November 1938. A showdown with the United States and Britain was carefully avoided in both cases. Matsuoka's strategy followed a similar pattern. He aimed to use Germany to build the Greater East Asia Co-Prosperity Sphere while avoiding direct confrontation with the Anglo-American powers. Matsuoka's diplomacy hinged heavily on German planning and military successes. He was, however, prudent enough to hedge the risks of such speculative diplomacy, and strove to halt the deterioration of relations with the United States through a mutually agreeable compromise.

With Washington unwilling to concede anything to Japan, Matsuoka gave up on reaching a compromise. Instead, he decided to negotiate with the Soviets to safeguard northern Manchuria, a necessary condition for the implementation of the southward advance policy. By taking a bold move southwards, Matsuoka was confident that Washington would be forced to become more flexible. The hope fizzled with the outbreak of the German-Soviet war. Although Matsuoka tried to manoeuvre Japan in the complex game of power politics, he was constrained by his own diplomacy, which depended on German diplomatic and military success. This was a fatal weakness.

Another flaw of Matsuoka's diplomacy was his misreading of the United States. After the First World War, the Anglo-Americans had tried to put a brake on Japanese expansion, which led to the perception in Japan that the they were blocking Japan's rightful development.

Matsuoka used this to his full advantage to garner public support. In the summer of 1940, Japan was in a position to choose a more favourable partner, Germany, but Matsuoka did not want to enter into a war with the United States. He therefore proposed the northward advance to improve Tokyo's diplomatic position vis-à-vis Washington. The plan was attractive because it did not require Japan to compromise with the United States, and it would have reduced tensions.

Although Matsuoka practised ambitious diplomacy, he hedged his risks with the principle that Japan would not go to war against the United States. From this perspective, changes in strategy – renunciation of the plan to compromise with the United States and the northward advance – were logical. These actions, however, helped to isolate Matsuoka within the Japanese government. In the end, the cabinet came to see him as an obstacle and forced him to step down.

Ultimately, Matsuoka could not manage both Japanese diplomacy and domestic politics. He counted on a German victory that never materialized. It would now be the task of the next foreign minister, Toyoda Teijirō, to undo the damage inflicted by Matsuoka and try to avert war with the United States.

NOTES

1 Shiozaki Hiroaki, "Gaimushō kakushin-ha no genjō daha ninshiki to seisaku," in *Nenpō: Kindai Nihon kenkyū 7: Nihon gaikō no kiki ninshiki* (Tokyo: Yamakawa Shuppansha, 1985).
2 Arita (1936–37, 1938–39, 1940); Hirota (1933–36); Shigemitsu (1943–45).
3 Tobe Ryōichi, "Shiratori Toshio to Manshujihen," *Bōei Daigakkō Kiyō* 39 (September 1979): 77–140; idem, "Shiratori Toshio to kōdō gaikō," *Bōei Daigakkō Kiyō* 40 (March 1980): 77–143.
4 Tobe Ryōichi, "Gaimushō kakushin-ha to Shin chitsujo," in *Nihon no kiro to Mastuoka gaikō, 1940–1941*, edited by Kimitada Miwa and Ryouichi Tobe (Tokyo: Nansōsha, 1993).
5 Sanbōhonbu, ed., *Sugiyama Memo*, vol. 1 (Tokyo: Fuyōshobō, 1994).
6 Matsuoka Yōsuke denki kankōkai, ed., *Matsuoka Yōsuke* (Tokyo: Kōdansha, 1974).
7 Ibid., 419–526.
8 Ibid., 527–620.
9 Kase Shunichi, *Sensō to Gaikō*, vol. 1 (Tokyo: Yomiuri Shimbunsha, 1975), 15; Hosoya Chihiro, *Sangoku dōmei to nisso shuuritsu jōyaku*, in *Taiheiyō*

sensō eno michi, vol. 5, edited by Nihon Kokusai Seiji Gakkai (Tokyo: Asahi Shimbunsha, 1987); Miwa Kimitada, *Matsuoka Yōsuke* (Tokyo: Chuōkōronsha, 1971); Miyake Masaki, *Nichidokui sangokudōmei no kenkyu* (Tokyo: Nansōsha, 1975); Yoshii Hiroshi, *Nichidokui Sangokudōmei to Nichibeikankei* (Tokyo: Nansōsha, 1977); Nomura Minoru, *Taiheiyō sensō to nihon gunbu* (Tokyo: Yamakawa Shuppansha, 1983); and Mori Shigeki, "Matsuoka Gaikō ni okeru Taibei oyobi Taiei-saku," *Nihonshi Kenkyu* 421 (1997): 35–62.

10 Miwa Munehiro, "Nichidokui sangoku dōmei teiketsuIJNi okeru nichidokuiso kousou eno gimon," *Nihondaigaku Seisankougakusu Kenkyu Houkoku* 25, no. 1 (1992): 21–39.

11 "Sekaijōsei no Suii ni tomonau Jikyoku-syori yōkō (July 27, 1940)," in *Nihon gaikōnenpyō narabi ni shuyobunsho,* vol. 2, edited by Gaimushō (Tokyo: Harashobō, 1967), 437–8.

12 Komatsu Keiichiro, *Origins of the Pacific War and the Importance of "MAGIC"* (New York: St Martin's Press, 1999).

13 Suzuki Akira, "Nihon Senji Keizai to Amerika" *Kokusai Seiji* 97 (1991): 103–18.

14 Nagaoka Shinjiro, "Nanpō shisaku no gaikōshiteki tenkai," in *Taiheiyōsensō eno michi,* vol. 6.

15 Hatano Sumio, "Nanshin eno Senkai: 1940," *AJIA Keizai* 26, no. 5 (1985): 30–1.

16 Bōeichō Bōeikenshujo Senshishitsu, ed., *Senshisōsho daitōa sensō kaisenkeii,* vol. 1 (Tokyo: Asagumo Shimbunsha, 1973).

17 Hatano, "Nanshin eno Senkai," 37–47.

18 Nagaoka, *Nanpō shisaku,* 29–35.

19 Hatano, "Nanshin eno Senkai," 30–1.

20 Hosoya, *Sangokudōmei,* 231–61.

21 Ibid.

22 Nagaoka, *Nanpō shisaku,* 29–35; and Hatano, "Nanshin eno Senkai," 30–1.

23 "Kihon Kokusaku to Gaiko nikansuru Matsuoka Gaimudaijin Danda (August 1, 1940)," in *Gaimusho kōhyō shu,* vol. 19, 127–8.

24 Nagaoka, *Nanpō shisaku,* 86–9.

25 Ibid., 51–9.

26 Hosoya, *Sangokudōmei,* 181–97.

27 Hata Ikuhiko, "Hutsuin shinchu to gun no nanshin seisaku (1940–1941)," in *Taiheiyōsensō eno michi,* vol. 6.

28 *Senshisōsho daitōa sensō kaisenkeii,* vol. 3, 1–32.

29 Ibid., 102–18.

30 Ibid., 38–102.

31 "Matsuoka – Cragie Ei-Taishi Kaidan Yōroku (October 8, 1940)"; "Shina-jihen kankei-ikken kakkoku buki kyoukyuu kankei Biruma narabi-ni honkon keiyu enshō-busshi yusō kinzetsu kankei," in Foreign Ministry Diplomatic Records Office [hereafter cited as DRO], Tokyo.

32 "Tatekawa Taishi no teian-seru Hushinryaku-*jōyaku an* (October 30, 1940)"; "Nisso churitsu-jōyaku kankei-ikken," in DRO.

33 Akino Yutaka, *Itsuwari no dōmei* (Tokyo: Keisōshobō, 1998), 11–18.

34 Ambassador in Bucharest Miyazaki to Foreign Minister Matsuoka (#9381), 19 July 1940; Matsuoka to Ambassador Washington Horinouchi (#9441), 30 July 1940; Ambassador in Rome Amau to Horinouchi (#9435), 31 July 1940; "Japanese Diplomatic Messages, 1940–1942," in Records Group 457, National Archives, College Park, MD [hereafter cited as RG 457: Japanese Diplomatic Messages]. Ambassador in Soviet Union Tōgō to Matsuoka (#1088), 7 August 1940, and Tōgō to Matsuoka (#1092 and #1255), 8 August 1940, "Beiso tsushō kankei-ikken," in DRO.

35 Hattori Satoshi, "Matsuoka gaikō to nanshin seisaku," *Kobe Hōgaku Zasshi* 48, no. 4 (1999): 927–88.

36 Horionouchi to Matsuoka (#10112), 21 August 1940; Horionouchi to Matsuoka (#11017), 22 August 1940, RG 457: Japanese Diplomatic Messages.

37 Miyake Masaki, *Starin Hitora to nisso-doku-I rengo koso* (Tokyo: Asahi-shinbun-sha, 2007), 153–96.

38 Hosoya, *Sangokudōmei,* 283–4.

39 Nagaoka, *Nanpō shisaku,* 92–3.

40 *Senshisōsho daitōa sensō kaisenkeii,* vol. 3, 159–69.

41 "Beikoku no Tai-nichi Keizai-sochi oyobi Ensho-sochi Ichiran-hyō (February 10, 1941)"; "Shina-jihen kankei-ikken Nichi-bei-kankei Dakai-kōsaku," in DRO [hereafter, DRO: Kōsaku].

42 Sudō Shinji, *Nichi-bei Kaisen-gaikō no Kenkyu* (Tokyo: Keiō-tsushin, 1986), 1–9.

43 Ambassador Grew to Secretary of State Hull, 24 August 1940, *Foreign Relations of the United States, 1940,* vol. 4, *Far East* [hereafter cited as *FRUS: Far East*] (Washington, DC: US Government Printing Office, 1955), 973–4.

44 "Beikoku no Tai-nichi Keizai-sochi oyobi Ensho-sochi Ichiran-hyō (February 10, 1941)," DRO: Kōsaku.

45 Sudō, *Nichi-bei Kaisen-gaikō no Kenkyu,* 9–11.

46 Ibid.; and Iguchi (New York) to Gaimudaijin (Tokyo) (#14208), 25 January 1940, RG 457: Japanese Diplomatic Messages.

47 E. Bruce. Reynolds, "Kōkatsu naru Shō-koku Gaikō," in *Dai-niji Sekai-taisen,* edited by Gunjishi-gakkai (Tokyo: Kinsei-sha, 1990), 149–51.

48 *Senshisōsho daitōa sensō kaisenkeii,* vol. 3, 182–5, 286–310; Tanaka Shin-ichi, *Sakusen-bucho Tōjō o Batō su* (Tokyo: Fuyō-shobō, 1986), 133.

49 *Senshisōsho daitōa sensō kaisenkeii*, vol. 3, 174–81; Reynolds, "Kōkatsu naru Shō-koku Gaikō," 152–4.

50 *Senshisōsho daitōa sensō kaisenkeii*, vol. 3, 204–15.

51 Ibid., 68–75.

52 Sanbō-honbu, ed., *Sugiyama memo*, vol. 1 (Tokyo: Fuyōshobō, 1994), 158–61, 165–8, 173–6; Tanemura Sataka, *Daihon-ei kimitsu nisshi* (Tokyo: Fuyō-shobō, 1985), 66–8.

53 Hatano Sumio, *Bakuryo-tachi no Shinju-wan* (Tokyo: Asahi-shinbun-sha, 1991), 61.

54 *Senshisōsho daitōa sensō kaisenkeii*, vol. 3, 210–14, 226–48; *Sugiyama memo*, vol. 1, 178–89.

55 Okamura Niichi, "Nisso Churitsu Jōyaku to Matsuoka Yōsuke," *Chuōkōron* (July 1964): 202–10; Hosoya, *Sangokudōmei*, 286–7; Boris Slavinsky, *Nisso churissu-jōyaku* (Tokyo: *Iwanami*-shoten, 1985), 86–92.

56 Kase Shunichi, *Sensō to gaikō*, vol. 1 (Tokyo: Yomiuri-shinbun-sha, 1975), 24. Memorandum by an official of the foreign minister's secretariat, 31 March 1941, record of the conversation between the Reich Foreign Minister and Japanese Foreign Minister Matsuoka in the presence of Ambassadors Ott and Oshima in Berlin, 27 March 1941, *Documents on German Foreign Policy, 1918–1945*, series D, vol. 12 [hereafter cited as DGFP] (London: Her Majesty's Stationery Office, 1962), 376–83; unsigned memorandum, 31 March 1941, record of the conversation between the Reich Minister and Japanese Foreign Minister on 28 March 1941, DGFP, 405–9; unsigned memorandum, 31 March 1941, record of the conversation between the Reich Minister and Japanese Foreign Minister on 29 March 1941, DGFP, 413–20; memorandum by an official of the foreign minister's secretariat, 4 April 1941, record of the conversation between the Führer and Japanese Foreign Minister Matsuoka in the presence of the Reich Foreign Minister and State Minister Meissner in Berlin on 4 April 1941, DGFP, 453–8; memorandum by an official of the foreign minister's secretariat, 7 April 1941, record of the conversation between the Reich Foreign Minister and Japanese Foreign Minister Matsuoka in Berlin on 5 April 1941, DGFP, 469–74.

57 Slavinsky, *Churissu-jōyaku*, 99–127; "Nisso churitsu jōyaku (13 April 1941)," *Nihon gaikōnenpyō narabi ni shuyobunsho*, vol. 2, 491–2.

58 Ambassador in the Soviet Union (Steinhardt) to the Secretary of State, 24 March 1941, *FRUS: Far East*, vol. 5, 921–4; Ambassador in the Soviet Union (Steinhardt) to the Secretary of State, 8 April 1941, *FRUS: Far East*, vol. 5, 932–4; Ambassador in the Soviet Union (Steinhardt) to the Secretary of State, 9 April 1941, *FRUS: Far East*, vol. 5, 934–5; Ambassador in the Soviet

Union (Steinhardt) to the Secretary of State, 11 April 1941, *FRUS: Far East*, vol. 5, 936–7.

59 "Nichi-bei ryōkai-an," *Nihon gaikōnenpyō narabi ni shuyobunsho*, vol. 2, 492–5.

60 Sudō, *Nichi-bei Kaisen-gaikō no Kenkyu*, 11–59.

61 *Sugiyama memo*, vol. 1, 199–215. Foreign Minister Matsuoka to Ambassador Nomura (#190, 191), 3 May 1941; Foreign Minister Matsuoka to Ambassador Nomura (#206), 12 May 1941; Foreign Minister Matsuoka to Ambassador Nomura (#216), 13 May 1941, in Gaimushō, ed., *Nichi-bei Kōshō shiryō* (Tokyo: Harashobō, 1978), 31–7, 48–59.

62 *Senshisōsho daitōa senso kaisenkeii*, vol. 3, 169–72.

63 Nagaoka, *Nanpō shisaku*, 92–3.

64 "Batavia nite Yoshizawa Daihyō no wagahō dainiji youkyu oyobi rangawa kaitō," *Nihon gaikōnenpyō narabi ni shuyobunsho*, vol. 2, 516–21.

65 Nagaoka, *Nanpō shisaku*, 94–9.

66 *Sugiyama memo*, vol. 1, 248–269. Foreign Minister Matsuoka to Ambassador Nomura, 1 July 1, *Nichi-bei Kōshō shiryō*, 100–2.

67 Gerhard Krebs, "Matsuoka Yōsuke to taisei yokusankai," in *Nihon no kiro to Mastuoka gaikō*, 80–91.

10 Dissembling Diplomatist: Admiral Toyoda Teijirō and the Politics of Japanese Security

PETER MAUCH

Admiral Toyoda Teijirō was by any standard an anomalous figure in Japan's pre–Pearl Harbor challenge to the international system. He served as vice navy minister from 6 September 1940 to 4 April 1941, and then as foreign minister from 18 July to 18 October 1941. In the former position, Toyoda led in overturning the navy's long-standing opposition to an alliance with Nazi Germany, an alliance which was, as a contemporary noted with more than a hint of apprehension, "a treaty of alliance with the United States as its target."[1] He secured the latter position by convincing Prime Minister Konoe Fumimaro that he was "enthusiastic" about the "American problem."[2] In other words, although his actions as vice navy minister set Japan on a collision course with the United States, Toyoda himself designated diplomatic rapprochement with the United States as the defining issue of his tenure as foreign minister. Crucial to this effort was Toyoda's determination to extricate Japan from alliance obligations he had embraced as vice navy minister.

Surprisingly few historians have turned their attention to the ideas, beliefs, and assumptions that informed Toyoda through this period. Tsunoda Jun established a negative image of Toyoda's actions as vice navy minister: he was "a schemer, an opportunist, skillful in adapting to circumstances, but unencumbered by any consistent principles or policies."[3] In a separate work, Tsunoda was no more positive in his appraisal of Toyoda's actions as foreign minister – even allowing that the admiral was caught "between a rock and a hard place." Distinguishing Toyoda's approach from that of his audacious predecessor, Matsuoka Yōsuke, Tsunoda nonetheless reckoned that the admiral's foreign policy was "nothing more than an opportunistic policy of getting by on a case-by-case basis."[4]

Dean of Japanese diplomatic history Hosoya Chihiro disagreed with this portrayal. Although quiet on details, Hosoya suggested that Toyoda "recognized the need to make concessions and work toward goals gradually."[5] Writing in 1986, Sudō Shinji went a step further by arguing that Toyoda assumed the foreign minister's post convinced of the necessity of both reducing the Tripartite Pact to a dead letter and withdrawing troops – albeit conditionally – from China. Sudō concluded that, in the end, Toyoda's (and Konoe's) efforts amounted to naught because of the "extreme mistrust" that Japan's recent advance into southern Indochina engendered in Washington.[6]

This chapter hopes to build on existing scholarship in two ways. First, no single work has yet attempted to analyse, as I do in this chapter, Toyoda's policies as both vice navy minister and foreign minister. Perfunctory mention has been made of his incongruous stance towards the Tripartite Pact – embracing it as vice navy minister and then openly suggesting its virtual abrogation as foreign minister – yet the admittedly less obvious *consistencies* in the admiral's actions remain uncharted waters. The identification of consistencies in his actions points to the second essential way in which this chapter departs from existing scholarship: I offer a more complete understanding of Toyoda's perceptions of both the world situation and the domestic political scene than has previously been attempted.

In short, I argue that the admiral's understanding of Tokyo's political dynamics induced him to embrace policies that could not but be construed as a challenge to the international system. At the same time, he drew from that policy strain within the Imperial Japanese Navy that railed against war with the United States and Britain – the two nations whose interests were most closely tied to the existing international system. The result was an uncomfortable compromise in which Toyoda willfully adopted policies that challenged the international system, all the while seeking to delimit that challenge so as not to unduly provoke the Anglo-American powers. As the title says, he was a *dissembling* diplomatist.

Appointment as Vice Navy Minister

It should come as no surprise that, when Toyoda assumed the vice navy minister's post in September 1940, he could rightly claim to possess great familiarity with international affairs. A native of Wakayama Prefecture, Toyoda graduated top of his Naval Academy class in 1905.

In a sure sign that his star was rising, the navy sent him to Oxford University in 1911. He returned to Japan three years later, and graduated top of his Naval War College class in 1919. Having established himself as one of the navy's best and brightest junior officers, Toyoda served from 1923 to 1926 as attaché to the Japanese embassy in London. He subsequently accompanied Admiral Saitō Makoto to the Geneva Conference of 1927, and was a member of Japan's delegation to the First London Naval Conference of 1930. Recognizing that Japan did not possess the wherewithal to challenge the Anglo-American nations' maritime preponderance, Toyoda emerged as a supporter of the naval ratio system agreed at the London Conference – and by extension the limits originally agreed at Washington in 1921–22. He was, to borrow the words of Sudō Shinji, part of the "elite within the navy's elite."[7]

If by 1930 Toyoda had considerable grounding in Great Power politics, he remained a relative novice in the treacherous waters of domestic Japanese politics. He soon learned his lesson. In the messy aftermath of the London Conference, Toyoda found himself in opposition to majority opinion within the navy, which violently opposed the international system of naval arms limitation. He also had the temerity to criticize one of the leading opponents of naval limitation, Chief of the Navy General Staff Prince Fushimi.[8] He immediately found himself removed from – and for the better part of the 1930s remained away from – the navy's political nerve centre in Tokyo. This was a frustrating decade for Toyoda, whose obvious abilities were matched only by his ambitions. He was a far shrewder individual for this experience when in early September 1940 he emerged from the wilderness to be appointed vice navy minister.

Before discussing Toyoda's actions as vice navy minister, one should briefly examine the circumstances – both international and domestic – surrounding his appointment. In the spring and summer of 1940, Germany's blitzkrieg seemingly had turned the existing international system on its head. The German army in quick succession overran Denmark, Norway, the Netherlands, Belgium, and – most shocking of all – France. Only Britain, which German forces were busy assailing from the air and sea, stood between Hitler and mastery over western Europe.

A concomitant upheaval was taking place in Tokyo. After some twelve months of studied neutrality in the European war, the Japanese government's years-old debate over whether to align itself militarily with Germany resumed with shrill urgency. Leading the way was the second Konoe cabinet's foreign minister, Matsuoka. A German alliance, he argued, would facilitate an end to Japan's ongoing war in China. He maintained that Germany's war against Southeast Asia's colonial masters had paved the way for Japan's advance into that resource-rich region. He also proposed to use a German alliance to bring about a turnaround in Japan's uneasy relations with the Soviet Union. Finally, he trumpeted that it would present the United States with an anti-democratic double front – in both the Atlantic and the Pacific – which would freeze that nation into the isolationist shell that had hamstrung its policy-makers throughout the 1930s. Underlying his diplomatic vision was the confident expectation of a total German victory in Europe.[9]

So far as the Japanese government was concerned, the navy presented the only remaining obstacle to the German alliance. From the inauguration of the Konoe cabinet in July until his resignation in early September 1940, Navy Minister Vice Admiral (later Admiral) Yoshida Zengo remained steadfastly opposed to the alliance. Two interconnected assumptions, both previously established by former navy minister Admiral Yonai Mitsumasa, informed this opposition. First, a German alliance would place Japan perilously close to war with the United States and Britain. Second, the Japanese navy – which would bear the brunt of the fighting in such a war – could neither expect assistance from its relatively small German counterpart nor hope to emerge victorious over its Anglo-American rivals. "From first to last," Yoshida quipped, "I will oppose this Japan-Germany-Italy Tripartite Pact which will make enemies of [the United States and Britain]."[10] Yoshida's opposition, however, generated heated dissent from within his own ranks. His subordinates clamoured for a German alliance, all the while training their sights on the Dutch East Indies' oil, which carried with it the tantalizing prospect of ending the navy's dependence on the United States for that precious resource. "Why can't we use it?" the leading pro-German admiral Suetsugu Nobumasa asked rhetorically.[11] The pressures literally broke Yoshida, who succumbed to a debilitating physical and nervous breakdown. He resigned his post on 3 September. Two days later, Admiral Oikawa Koshirō replaced Yoshida as navy minister and promptly appointed Toyoda as his deputy.

Vice Navy Minister Toyoda and the Tripartite Pact

As vice navy minister, Toyoda was afforded unusual freedom of action. His direct superior, Navy Minister Oikawa, is widely regarded as having "lacked any authority whatsoever" and been "at all times

indecisive."[12] Certainly, few scholars would disagree with the assertion that Toyoda played the leading role in overturning his service's
traditional opposition to a German alliance. His reasons for doing so
provide the first clear instance of responding to domestic pressures to
challenge the international system while seeking to keep that challenge
within limits that conformed to his *weltanschauung*.

The newly appointed vice navy minister viewed the domestic scene
on two levels: politics within the navy and at cabinet level. Neither lent
itself to maintaining opposition to a German alliance, as Toyoda feared
being bestowed the ignominious title of the shortest-serving vice navy
minister in history. With regard to politics within the navy, it is easy
to conceive of Toyoda – mindful of his bitter experiences of the 1930s –
as wanting to avoid the rancorous dissent that undermined the previous navy ministry leadership. At the cabinet level, Toyoda believed that
maintaining the navy's opposition to the alliance could cause the army
to withdraw its support for – and bring about the downfall of – the
Konoe cabinet. As he freely admitted to Prime Minister Konoe, the "domestic political situation" rendered the navy's continued opposition
to the alliance "impermissible."[13] (In another curious admission that
smacks at best of failed number-crunching and at worst of blithe buck-
passing, Toyoda later told Konoe he had expected the Policy Planning
Board to oppose the alliance on the grounds that it would yield little in
the way of "procurements.")[14]

In this way, Toyoda might appear to have shared the fatalism regarding the German alliance expressed by his politically adept subordinate,
Captain Takagi Sōkichi: "It cannot be helped."[15] This, however, would
underestimate Toyoda, for his worldview differed significantly from
Foreign Minister Matsuoka's. Whereas Matsuoka was convinced that
a "firm stand" on the part of the Tripartite Pact signatories would contain the United States to the Western Hemisphere, the navy had long
stressed the "inseparability" of the United States and Britain.[16] Unless
and until he saw evidence to the contrary, Toyoda was not ready to dispense entirely with that strategic perspective, especially given the US
Congress's appropriation of funds for almost two hundred and fifty
additional warships in June and July 1940 amidst talk of a "two ocean
navy."[17] Toyoda was thus not prepared to accept at face value Matsuoka's confident predictions of a total German victory in Europe. His embrace of the German-Japanese-Italian Tripartite Pact amounted instead
to a *gamble* on the *possibility* of German victory.

At the domestic level, Toyoda expected immediate and handsome
dividends. Months earlier, in making his case for the Tripartite Pact and

a concomitant advance into Southeast Asia, Matsuoka had asserted that Japan would "resist armed intervention by the US related to [Japan's] establishment of the New Order in East Asia."[18] Since armed intervention by the United States could not but come from across the Pacific, it stood to reason that the Japanese navy – long squeezed by the army's need for materiel to prosecute its war in China – would receive a large slice of the budgetary pie.[19]

By no means, however, did Toyoda envision the Combined Fleet's sallying forth and engaging its US counterpart on the expanses of the Pacific. He had, as he confided in Prime Minister Konoe, "no confidence" in the navy's ability to wage a victorious war against the United States.[20] At the international level, then, Toyoda looked to hedge his bets. It is well known that he parted ways with Matsuoka (and the German government) insofar as he stressed Japan must retain the right to decide independently when and whether to enter hostilities. When Matsuoka secured from his German protagonists a letter that provided the understanding demanded by the navy, Toyoda concluded that "the reason for the navy's opposition [to an alliance with Germany] was completely cancelled."[21] Still, when the Tripartite Pact was signed on 27 September, it explicitly committed Japan, Germany, and Italy to "assist one another with all political, economic, and military means when one of the three contracting parties is attacked by a power at present not involved in the European War or the Sino-Japanese conflict."[22]

Just as significantly, Toyoda was convinced that Japan should not in any way aid or abet Germany in its quest for European dominance. Although his vision was fluid and essentially reactionary to the exigencies of the war in Europe, this meant that unless Germany subjugated Britain – thereby prompting Washington to review both its trans-Atlantic commitments and its stance towards Southeast Asia – the British colonies of Hong Kong, Singapore, Malaya, and Burma were off-limits to Japanese expansion. So long as this remained the case, an advance into the Dutch East Indies was militarily unfeasible. And for obvious reasons, US possession of the Philippines was not to be challenged. This left Indochina, whose colonial master had already surrendered to the Germans.

Disillusionment with the Tripartite Pact

Just days before the Tripartite Pact was concluded, Japanese troops began marching into northern Indochina, the first step in Japan's southward advance. The administration of President Franklin D. Roosevelt responded on 26 September by imposing a virtual embargo on aviation gasoline, high-grade iron, and scrap steel.[23] Whether this reprisal conformed to Toyoda's estimates is unclear. What does seem certain is that soon thereafter Toyoda confronted the vacuousness of Japan's Tripartite Pact diplomacy. At issue was US policy, which, in the aftermath of Roosevelt's November 1940 election victory, proved more creative and more forthright in its opposition to Germany than anything Toyoda had foreseen.

Roosevelt elucidated the foundation of US policy at a press conference on 17 December 1940. "The best defense of Great Britain," he asserted, "is the best defense of the United States." Suggesting that the United States lend Britain the materials necessary to win its struggle for survival, he compared his proposal to lending a garden hose to a neighbour to put out a fire that otherwise might spread to one's own house. Then, in a fireside chat on 29 December, Roosevelt denounced the "unholy alliance" of Germany, Japan, and Italy, and held up a picture of the United States as the "arsenal of democracy." In his message to Congress a few days later, Roosevelt officially proposed what would result in the Lend-Lease Act, by which America's commitment to Britain – and conversely its opposition to Germany – was declared immutable.[24] Against this backdrop, the counselor to the US embassy in Tokyo, Eugene H. Dooman, warned Vice Foreign Minister Ōhashi Chūichi that, if Japan attacked Singapore, the "logic of the situation would inevitably raise the question" of a Japanese-US war.[25]

From this early date, Toyoda began wondering when – and under what circumstances – Japan might end its Tripartite Pact commitments. His gamble had not paid off: the United States would not allow Britain to fall, and hence Germany could not win. This left Southeast Asia off-limits to Japanese expansion, for Toyoda had no intention of allowing anything beyond a mopping-up of those colonies whose masters Germany had already subjugated. It was also hard to see what Germany, with its attention squarely on the war in Europe, could offer to bring Japan's war in China to an end. This meant that Japan had nothing to gain from its alliance partner. At the same time, the risks inherent in the alliance were growing – principal among them a war in which the Japanese navy would be pitted against its more powerful US and British counterparts.

Foreign Minister Matsuoka, however, was dancing to a different tune, preparing for a headline-grabbing trip to Berlin and Moscow through February 1941. Piqued, Toyoda warned the foreign minister on 26 February that, in his estimation, such a trip would "invite the unwanted opposition of the United States and Great Britain."[26] He was of course correct. With no conceivable way of stopping Matsuoka, however, Toyoda reverted to a characteristic effort to limit the fallout. He pressed Matsuoka for assurances that the foreign minister would make no commitments regarding a military advance into the colonial regions of Southeast Asia; that he would seek Germany's commitment to avoiding war with the United States; and that he would press Germany to assist Japan in its efforts to effect peace with China and diplomatic rapprochement with the Soviet Union.[27]

When Matsuoka returned from Europe in late April 1941 replete with the Japanese-Soviet Neutrality Pact, Toyoda had been removed from the vice navy minister's post. Evidently, Oikawa had grown exasperated with the fact that, within navy circles and without, people made only half-joking reference to "Navy Minister Toyoda" and "Vice Minister Oikawa."[28] As early as December 1940, Oikawa had complained of Toyoda's "political intrigues" to Commander-in-Chief of the Combined Fleet Admiral Yamamoto Isoroku, suggesting it would be better if the vice navy minister were relieved of his post sooner rather than later.[29] It took longer than such a complaint might suggest, but in one whirlwind day in early April 1941 Toyoda was promoted to admiral, placed on the navy's reserve list, replaced as vice navy minister, and appointed to the commerce and industry minister's post.

Toyoda's cabinet-level appointment suggests that he had in no way fallen out with Konoe. Indeed, the appointment probably reflected the prime minister's concern with – and desire to compensate for – Navy Minister Oikawa's taciturnity. Nor does it stretch the imagination to picture Toyoda himself making the case to Konoe. But if this were so, Toyoda's and Konoe's aspirations were disappointed. The commerce and industry minister was too far removed to exert any real influence on foreign policy-making, and Toyoda's voice subsequently carried little weight in the debates that arose when in late April Ambassador Nomura Kichisaburō presented Tokyo with a proposal for diplomatic rapprochement vis-à-vis Washington labelled the Draft Understanding between the United States and Japan.[30] Nor was Toyoda party to the decision to occupy the entire Indochinese peninsula following the outbreak of the German-Soviet war on 22 June. Originating within the army and navy, several factors informed the decision. First, it was seen as the way for Japan to break through the encirclement strategy of the ABCD (American-British-Chinese-Dutch) powers. As Commander-in-Chief of the Navy General Staff Admiral Nagano Osami put it in late July, there was "no way other than to break this iron chain [around our neck] before it is complete."[31] It was also hoped that the Indochinese occupation would sever an important supply route to Chiang Kai-shek, thereby facilitating an end to the festering war in China. Finally, it was hoped to pressure the Netherlands into providing access to Dutch East Indies' oil.[32]

An analysis of Washington's likely reaction was conspicuously absent in the decision to occupy southern Indochina. Matsuoka, who bewildered his colleagues by dropping his earlier insistence on the southward advance to argue for an assault on the Soviet Union's Far Eastern territories, sought to bring the American factor to his colleagues' attention. He warned them on 27 June that "if we advance into French Indochina we might have to fight Britain and the United States."[33] Matsuoka's spirited opposition notwithstanding, the issue was decided at an Imperial Conference on 2 July: the army and navy would acquire bases in southern Indochina, and in so doing would "not be deterred by the possibility of being involved in a war against the United States and Great Britain."[34] Despite their belligerent tone, the army and navy leadership convinced themselves and Prime Minister Konoe that "the occupation of Indochina would not affect our negotiations with the United States too adversely."[35] Indochina was, they reasoned, a French colony whose status was not vital to US national security. They also anticipated an agreement with France's Vichy regime providing for Japan's acquisition of bases in southern Indochina, which would allow the advance to be presented not as a military occupation but as the product of diplomatic agreement.[36] Matsuoka alone remained convinced that the Indochinese advance left no room for compromise with the United States. Yet, in making his case, he lost the confidence not only of the army and navy but also Prime Minister Konoe. The cabinet resigned en masse on July 16, and when the third Konoe cabinet was inaugurated two days later, Admiral Toyoda was announced as Matsuoka's successor.

Foreign Minister Toyoda and the Indochinese Advance

Toyoda clearly played no role in the decision to advance into Indochina. Germany's assault on the Soviet Union, moreover, had strengthened his doubts concerning the efficacy of the Tripartite Pact. Now that Hitler's focus had shifted away from Britain to the east, Germany's war was no longer the Japanese navy's war. Yet the domestic political scene required that he move cautiously. The army and navy general staffs had made clear that their support for the third Konoe cabinet – and, by implication, Toyoda's diplomacy – was contingent upon both the successful completion of the Indochinese advance and the continuation of a stance in Japanese-US negotiations faithful to the "spirit" of the Tripartite Pact.[37]

The admiral revealed himself to be well disposed to the Indochinese advance. "Although there has been a reshuffle of the cabinet," Toyoda notified Japan's ambassadors on 19 July, "there is no change in any way with existing policies."[38] On the same day he presented a note to the Vichy regime in France, giving a deadline of 23 July for its acquiescence to Japan's demand to station troops in southern Indochina.[39] Toyoda then reassured his Liaison Conference colleagues on 21 July that, "even though there had been a change in foreign ministers, there was no change in the attitude of the Imperial Government."[40]

Toyoda might more accurately have stated that there was no change in the attitude of the former vice navy minister-cum-foreign minister. It will be recalled that, as vice navy minister, Toyoda believed that unless and until Germany subjugated Britain the southward advance must stop at Indochina's borders. His acquiescence in this latest advance in no way contradicted that belief; on the contrary, it might be seen as its logical outcome. To return to this chapter's central theme, Toyoda was responding to those domestic political pressures that trumpeted the need to challenge the international system, while seeking to delimit that challenge so as not to unduly provoke the United States.

In retrospect, Toyoda's belief that the advance into southern Indochina was compatible with a turnaround in diplomatic relations with the United States seems implausible, if not fantastic. Yet at the time he was convinced that the Roosevelt administration would acquiesce in the Indochinese occupation to concentrate its attention on Germany. After all, the US Navy had begun escorting British lend-lease goods as far as Iceland.[41] Even a layman – let alone an admiral from one of the world's largest navies – could see that such non-belligerent activity would soon lead to clashes with German submarines. Toyoda hardly needed reminding, moreover, that the United States had entered the First World War in response to German submarine warfare. In a word, Toyoda reckoned that the Roosevelt administration was unlikely to antagonize Japan in the Pacific when it was challenging Hitler in the Atlantic. He also wondered whether he might not encourage the Roosevelt administration to focus its attention on the Atlantic by convincing his government colleagues to drop Japan's Tripartite Pact commitments.

Toyoda was not, however, naive enough to believe that the United States would leave this latest round of Japan's southward advance unanswered. In considering Washington's likely reaction, Toyoda expected expressions of moral indignation and, quite possibly, economic retaliation. His most immediate concern, therefore, was to pre-empt the hardliners in the army and navy who would presumably pounce on the US response to argue the necessity of further advances into Southeast Asia. "The occupation of Indochina will exert an influence on the United States," Toyoda warned his Liaison Conference colleagues on 24 July. "They will adopt a policy of putting an embargo on vital materials, freezing Japanese funds ... etc." He also pointed to the likelihood of a partial embargo on the export of oil.[42]

At this juncture, President Roosevelt proposed to neutralize Indochina, thereby throwing an unforeseen – and entirely unwelcome – spanner into the works of Toyoda's diplomatic vision. On 25 July Toyoda received through Ambassador Nomura a warning from the president that Japan's advance into Indochina might prompt an "oil embargo." Nomura's communication also conveyed the following: "The President said that if we were to withdraw our troops from Indochina, he would seek to have many countries guarantee its neutrality (much like Switzerland), and also to put in place a law which allows for the free and fair procurement of materials from Indochina ... However, I have the impression that [should we not take up the proposal] somehow or other economic pressures are very close to being realized."[43] Toyoda for his part had no intention of asking his colleagues to rethink the Indochinese advance. He had assumed the foreign minister's post convinced that, although the advance might complicate matters, it was by no means incompatible with Japanese-US diplomatic rapprochement. Now he was confronted by a presidential proposal not only clarifying Washington's opposition to the advance, but also offering a way out of the impasse.

Thrown by Roosevelt's proposal, Toyoda chose not to respond. In lieu of a response, Washington froze Japanese assets in the United States on 25 July; the British and Dutch followed suit. The following day Roosevelt called General Douglas MacArthur out of retirement to head a projected Philippine army command to reinforce the colony against possible Japanese attack.[44] From Washington, Nomura informed Toyoda on 25 July that "influential" members of the Roosevelt administration were now convinced of the "meaninglessness of continuing negotiations for Japanese-American understanding."[45] Perhaps more troubling for Toyoda, opinion in the Japanese navy was fast moving towards the same conclusion. Even as Japanese troops moved into southern Indochina, Captain Takagi noted on 29 July: "Many are of the opinion that, as a result of the U.S.-British asset freeze war plans vis-à-vis the United States must be reconsidered."[46] Vice Chief of the Navy General Staff Kondō Nobutake was more forthcoming, telling a sceptical Vice Navy Minister Sawamoto Yorio in late July: "Now is the time to decide on war against the United States and Great Britain."[47]

Toyoda had been foreign minister for less than two weeks but events were spiralling out of his control. Meeting with the US ambassador, Joseph Grew, on 27 July, he made a desperate attempt to retrieve the situation. When Grew raised Roosevelt's neutralization proposal, Toyoda stunned the ambassador by asserting that "no report" on the proposal "had been received from the Embassy at Washington."[48] In other words, Toyoda painted his silence not as a product of disinterest or as an act of duplicity, but as an unfortunate result of the ambassador's stupidity. He was, in effect, trying to buy time to allow cooler heads to prevail in Tokyo.

The Roosevelt administration, however, was not forthcoming. On 1 August it slapped an embargo on high-octane gasoline and crude oil. As Japan imported most of its oil from the United States, this had far-reaching implications for the Japanese navy, for, to borrow the words of naval historian Ikeda Kiyoshi, "battleships without oil cannot move."[49] The oil embargo pushed those naval officers already leery of a negotiated solution towards a more hardline stance. The Navy General Staff as well as the navy ministry's middle echelons argued vociferously that, unless there was a sudden change, Japan's oil stocks would dwindle and the nation would face "total surrender [before America's demands] or a hopeless war."[50] On 3 August the navy ministry's influential First Committee drafted a policy paper stressing that war should be opened by the end of October if rapprochement with the United States had not been realized by that time.[51] The First Committee had a powerful supporter in Commander-in-Chief of the Navy General Staff Nagano, who thundered: "If we don't act now, we will be driven to ruin."[52]

The Roosevelt-Konoe Summit Proposal

For Toyoda, this belligerence on the part of the navy – later joined by the army once it realized its vital interests in China were at stake – posed an ultimately insurmountable obstacle. Through August, he was given to wondering aloud whether the anti-war but ever-vacillating Oikawa might not be replaced by Admiral Yamamoto Isoroku, whose steely-headed appreciation of US power could be expected to steer the navy away from war.[53] In so doing, Toyoda was giving expression to his own irresponsibility: he had, after all, convinced Konoe that his naval background would enhance his presence as foreign minister.[54] Whatever the case, Toyoda over the ensuing weeks made no attempt to confront the advocates of war. Instead, he hoped to *offset* his hawkish colleagues by inducing the United States to offer an olive branch. Specifically, he hoped for a return to normal economic relations, in particular renewed access to US oil. This, he reasoned, ought to allow for renewed effort at diplomatic rapprochement. In this, Toyoda was operating on the same principle throughout the period under review: his policies were geared first and foremost to the prevailing political winds in Tokyo and secondarily to his reading of the world situation.

Toyoda's diplomacy in the aftermath of the oil embargo continued to overemphasize the United States' desire for a settlement in the Pacific to enable it to focus its attentions on Germany. This basic misreading of US policy first became clear on 5 August when he transmitted to Ambassador Nomura an ostensible (and belated) response to Roosevelt's Indochinese neutralization proposal. Among its terms was the restoration of normal commercial relations, although the root cause of the impasse remained untouched: Japan pledged to withdraw troops from Indochina only after the war in China had ended – itself on undefined terms.[55] Having submitted the document to Secretary of State Cordell Hull, Nomura warned Toyoda on 6 August that Hull had showed "no interest" in it. He then went to the core of the issue: "So long as Japan does not dispense with a policy of conquest by brute force, there is no scope for talks."[56]

Washington's rebuff met its mark. Konoe walked away with the impression that the United States was prepared for "any eventuality."[57] So too did the army, and its War Guidance Office began grasping for ways to forestall war with the United States. The key issue was whether Japan could regain access to US oil without "surrendering" diplomatically, and the office went so far as to question whether it was possible "at this late hour to secede from the Axis." Opinion was divided as to whether this concession alone would satisfy Washington, while Roosevelt's meeting with British prime minister Winston Churchill in the Atlantic only fuelled perceptions of a "harder-line [Anglo-American] stance toward Japan."[58]

Toyoda was pleased that even the army's middle echelons had begun to reconsider the Tripartite Pact. At the same time, he declined to force the issue. On the one hand, he feared a domestic backlash, deeming it wiser to allow the idea of abrogation to gain currency in Tokyo. On the other hand, he was unconvinced that the Roosevelt administration was preparing to adopt a harder line. Holding fast to the notion that Washington might yet prove willing to pay a price – with French and perhaps Chinese coin – for a settlement in the Pacific, Toyoda chose not to immediately broach the issue of abrogating the Tripartite Pact. It could be used later, to clinch a deal that bypassed Hull's obstinately moralistic diplomacy and instead relied on Roosevelt's supposed propensity for *realpolitik*. Toyoda thus instructed Ambassador Nomura on 7 August to "sound out" US policy-makers on the possibility of a summit meeting between Konoe and Roosevelt.[59]

The details of the summit proposal are well known. The basic idea was that Konoe would reach agreement with Roosevelt – on what terms is necessarily a matter for conjecture – and then cable the agreement directly to the emperor. The emperor, for his part, would approve the agreement before the army and navy could register their opposition. Once the emperor had signed off on any agreement emanating from the summit, the armed services would be confronted with a *fait accompli* and war would be avoided.[60] From a domestic political perspective this was a good plan. Its principal flaw, however, lay in its presumption of Washington's forbearance, which, in the aftermath of the Indochinese advance, was singularly unforthcoming. Ambassador Nomura dutifully raised the idea of a summit meeting in his 8 August meeting with Hull, but the secretary of state's response was resoundingly negative.[61] Undeterred, Toyoda instructed Nomura to float the idea of a summit in his forthcoming meeting with Roosevelt. In short, Toyoda was clinging to the hope that Roosevelt would override Hull's scepticism and instead gamble on a summit meeting in the Pacific.

Toyoda felt his views were vindicated when Roosevelt met with Nomura on 17 August. Fresh from his meeting with Churchill and the proclamation of their goals in the Atlantic Charter, Roosevelt handed Nomura two documents. The first put Tokyo on notice that, should it undertake any further aggression, the United States would "take immediately any and all steps" necessary for "insuring the safety and security of the United States." Having wielded a stick, Roosevelt then offered the Japanese government a carrot. The second document suggested Washington "would be prepared to consider resumption of informal exploratory discussions." In accordance with Toyoda's in-structions, Nomura at this point raised the possibility of a summit meeting between Roosevelt and Konoe. Relaying the gist of the meet-ing to Toyoda, Nomura reckoned Roosevelt was receptive to the idea and had gone so far as to suggest Juneau, Alaska, as a possible meeting place. It was now, as Roosevelt put it to Nomura in a judicious turn of phrase, Japan's "turn to open the door."[62]

Toyoda, however, chose to ignore this last remark, as it implied the need to exact concessions from the army and navy to realize the summit meeting. This was due in part to Toyoda's (and Konoe's) fundamental misreading of Roosevelt. Toyoda chose to believe that Roosevelt was responding in kind to Konoe's purported statesmanship, rather than – as seems likely – keeping his options open while allowing his mind, as was his wont, to "roam all over" the summit proposal, considering it "in its relation to past, present, and future."[63] Whereas Roosevelt had left the door to a summit slightly ajar, Toyoda clung to the hope that the president had all but approved the proposal.

In this way, Roosevelt's receptivity to the summit proposal might have had the unfortunate effect of convincing Toyoda and Konoe of the basic soundness of their efforts to realize a meeting without first con-fronting the army and navy with the need for meaningful concessions. This in turn ensured that the armed services were afforded a virtually free hand in determining their own response to the Roosevelt admin-istration's oil embargo. The belligerency of that response was striking. Taking a leaf from the aforementioned First Committee study, on 16 August the navy leadership surprised the army by proposing that di-plomacy and war preparations be "advanced simultaneously" until the end of October. "In the event that Japan and the US have not reached a settlement by mid-October," the navy asserted, "steps to exercise our power will be taken."[64] The army had no quibble with the deadline, but wanted a more concrete commitment for war from its sister service. After considerable debate, the army and navy agreed on 30 August to "complete preparations for war, with the last ten days of October as a tentative deadline, resolved to go to war with the US, UK and the Neth-erlands if necessary."[65]

Feeling as though he was "being put under pressure in everything," Toyoda was given to grumbling that matters of state policy were being "controlled by the military."[66] Committed, however, to using the sum-mit meeting as a means to bypass the armed services, he did not try to rein them in. If this was not already apparent, it became so on 26

August when Toyoda cabled two documents to Nomura with instructions to submit them to Roosevelt. The first document, the so-called Konoe message, was addressed directly to Roosevelt. It proposed a meeting in which the two leaders might discuss problems from a "broad perspective," to explore all possibilities of saving the situation. It addressed no particulars. The second document was by far the more revealing. It expounded at length on Japan's reasons for advancing into Indochina and asserted Japan would withdraw its troops from the colony "as soon as the China Incident [was] settled." The jury is out on whether Konoe would have gone further than this at a meeting with Roosevelt. So far as Washington was concerned, however, Tokyo had declared that withdrawal from Indochina was *not* a bargaining chip; Konoe's position would simply affirm that Japan's "present action in Indochina [was] not a preparatory step for military advance into neighboring territories." "In a word," Toyoda explained, "the Japanese Government has no intention of using, without provocation, military force against any neighboring nation."[67]

Despite Roosevelt's initial mild receptivity to these documents, Secretary of State Hull was less than sanguine. When Roosevelt handed Nomura his official response on 3 September – which stated Washington's desire to have an agreement on basic principles *before* the proposed summit meeting – it became clear that the president had accepted Hull's basic contention that he "should look before he leaped."[68] So far as Toyoda was concerned, Roosevelt had pulled the rug out from under his feet. He would now have to gain the armed services' acquiescence in meaningful concessions prior to a summit meeting, precisely what he had hoped to avoid by floating the summit proposal in the first place.

Toyoda nonetheless clung to the hope that the Tripartite Pact – or more precisely, allowing its virtual abrogation – might prove to be the ace up his sleeve. Partly a response to Roosevelt's insistence on an agreement of views prior to any summit, Toyoda's hope was also aided by the growing consensus within the Japanese government that saw the alliance as having outlived its usefulness.

In a series of meetings with German ambassador Eugen Ott through late August and early September, Toyoda gave full vent to his dissatisfaction with Japan's alliance partner. He dismissed Ott's assurances that the German-Soviet war would end before the year was out, arguing that military success – if attained – would be confined to "European Russia." The admiral turned on Ott, arguing that, until the

Trans-Siberian railway was reopened, Japan would remain totally isolated from its alliance partners in Europe. Noting that "this was not foreseen at the time of the conclusion of the Tripartite Pact," he put the ambassador on notice that he considered the alliance a virtually dead letter unless Germany was able to provide Japan the materials it could no longer procure from the United States.[69] Toyoda's forthrightness no doubt startled Berlin. Whether he had it in him to similarly shake Washington, however, was an altogether different matter.

Foreign Minister Toyoda and the Tripartite Pact

By early September Toyoda had drafted a new proposal designed to facilitate a Roosevelt-Konoe summit meeting. Japan would pledge not to attack the Soviet Union. It would further pledge not to advance beyond Indochina. In the event that the United States opened war against Germany, Japan would interpret its Tripartite Pact obligations "independently." Once peace with China was restored, Japan would "quickly" withdraw its troops there as well as from Indochina. Japan would undertake no actions that impaired US economic interests in China, and the principle of "non-discrimination" in trade would apply equally to the Southwestern Pacific. For its part, the United States would "suspend" all military measures in the region and "abstain" from any measures prejudicial to Japan's efforts to end the war in China. Most important, it would agree to restore normal economic relations with Japan.[70]

On 3 September an ebullient Toyoda gained the war and navy ministries' acquiescence to the proposal. Ignoring the army and navy general staffs, he cabled the draft to Nomura on 4 September, triumphantly announcing: "We expect that all provisions to which Japan promises and for which it is responsible, and in particular our position regarding the Tripartite Pact, will be sufficient to gain the US side's consent."[71] He handed the draft to Ambassador Grew in a similarly confident tone. Toyoda's expectations were unrealistic. Besides more directly addressing Washington's concerns over Japan's Tripartite Pact responsibilities, his terms offered little that was new and asked for much in return. The promise to withdraw troops from China hinged upon Japan's ability to bring Chiang to terms that remained undefined. Toyoda's seeking a pledge from Washington to act as little more than a disinterested observer towards the war in China was bound to arouse the Roosevelt administration's suspicions. Most astoundingly, Toyoda had not budged from his earlier assertion that the United States should end its trade embargo, even though Japan had no intention (for now) of pulling its troops from Indochina. On this score, it is difficult to escape the conclusion that Toyoda was engaging in a classic case of having one's cake and wanting to eat it too: he acknowledged that the Tripartite Pact no longer met Japan's interests but at the same time asked Washington to acquiesce in the spoils of that alliance.

In the meantime, the army and navy general staffs had begun pressing the government to adopt the late October deadline for war. "Ultimately, when there is no hope for diplomacy, and when war cannot be avoided," Commander-in-Chief of the Navy General Staff Nagano told his Liaison Conference colleagues on 3 September, "it is essential that we make up our minds quickly."[72] Immobilized by their long-standing refusal to confront the armed services, neither Toyoda nor Konoe took issue with the deadline. Accordingly, it was ratified three days later in an Imperial Conference: "In the event that there is no prospect of our demands being met by the first ten days of October through ... diplomatic negotiations," the Imperial Conferees agreed, "we will immediately decide to commence hostilities against the United States, Great Britain and the Netherlands."[73]

The deadline appeared all the more imposing when Washington's official response to Toyoda's latest proposal arrived on 10 September. It focused its criticisms on Tokyo's seeming supposition that "the government of the US would not be concerned with the character of the terms of peace which Japan intends to propose to China." Most troubling, however, the response trumped Toyoda's Tripartite Pact ace, criticizing his supposedly groundbreaking position on the grounds that it "left Japan free to interpret independently any commitment on this score." The summit meeting was off unless the Japanese government undertook "some further initiative" that did not "pass over or ignore the intention of the US government."[74]

The End of Foreign Minister Toyoda's Tenure

Toyoda had four weeks to break the impasse. To do so, he would have to confront his colleagues with unpopular policy choices *and* carry his arguments in the face of their anticipated opposition. Just as the proverbial leopard never changes his spots, Toyoda proved utterly incapable of altering – let alone overturning – his existing *modus operandi*. He was, from first to last, a dissembling diplomatist.

Upon receipt of Washington's unexpectedly harsh communiqué, the beleaguered foreign minister made a last, futile effort to secure Roosevelt's assent to a summit. The army, however, was having none of it. The War Guidance Office had been surprised – not at all pleasantly – to learn that Toyoda had submitted his last summit proposal to Washington "without any contact with the Supreme Command." It stuck to the army's long-standing position that Japan must make no "new arrangements" regarding China, meaning that even after the war had been concluded, Japan would insist on its right to "station troops in China in accordance with existing arrangements."[75] Toyoda's draft was subsequently shelved, and in its stead a new draft – written in large part by the army – took centre stage. It offered no more concessions than did previous Japanese proposals, while delineating the army's demands that troops remain in Inner Mongolia and north China for the "suppression of Communism," and that Japan be given preferential economic treatment in its dealings with China.[76] Toyoda failed to raise a single objection, and the document was adopted as state policy.[77]

Toyoda then took the curious step of withholding this latest proposal from both Grew in Tokyo and Nomura in Washington. No doubt he recognized it would do nothing to promote the prospects for a summit. Yet his refusal to argue against it meant Toyoda was in a trap of his own making and the army, for one, was not about to let him out. When Chief of the Army General Staff General Sugiyama Hajime reproached Toyoda on 25 September for his reticence, Toyoda meekly replied: "It will be wired this afternoon." That same day, the army and navy chiefs of staff insisted on 15 October as the absolute deadline for negotiations. The foreign minister assured them that he "fully understood" the need for the deadline.[78] He wired the latest proposal to Ambassador Nomura that afternoon.[79]

Washington's response was, as Toyoda plainly anticipated, stiff. On 2 October Hull demanded that Japan withdraw its troops from China and Indochina immediately.[80] In so doing, he took the last breath out of the sails of Toyoda's diplomacy. As if to underline the point, on October 4 Commander-in-Chief of the Navy General Staff Nagano stated: "There is no longer time for discussion. We want quick action."[81] Admiral Nagano also had accomplices in both the war ministry and the army general staff, who agreed on 6 October that there were "no prospects for the Japanese-American negotiations." The leadership in the navy ministry, however, baulked at the impending deadline for war. "If thought is given to the stationing of troops [in China]," it maintained, "then there are prospects [for the Japanese-American negotiations]." Infuriated, the army asked whether the navy ministry "at its own convenience" was "seeking to change" the decision reached at the 6 September Imperial Conference. Nagano stepped into the fray on 7 October, forcefully explaining to Navy Minister Oikawa that there were "no prospects for the Japanese-American negotiations" and that it was "not possible to extend [the deadline for negotiations] beyond October 15." Oikawa, however, continued to insist that prospects for diplomatic rapprochement still existed.[82]

Konoe brought matters to a head on 12 October when he invited Toyoda, Oikawa, Army Minister Tōjō Hideki, and Planning Board president Suzuki Teiichi to his Ogikubo residence. The idea was that the prime, navy, and foreign ministers together might be able to wean Tōjō away from the army's demand for war. Toyoda opened the proceedings by claiming that there was "ground for agreement in the Japanese-American negotiations." He refused, however, to push the army to reconsider its insistence on the post-war maintenance of troops in China, stating instead that the addition of "a few words" to existing proposals should be enough to gain Washington's acquiescence. Oikawa was too weak to state openly that the Japanese navy would not fight its US counterpart, instead suggesting that the decision for war or peace ought to be reached by the prime minister. "If the decision is to give up on war and instead to pursue diplomacy, that too is OK," he stated. Tōjō was having none of it. "There are no prospects for agreement," he stated baldly. "The yardstick for the armed services' actions is the [6 September] Imperial Conference decision." Toyoda then stunned the war minister with the following rejoinder: "To be frank with you, the Imperial Conference decision was rash." Konoe chimed in, stating that he had "no confidence" in Japan's ability to wage war successfully against the United States. It seems likely that at this point both Toyoda and Konoe were attempting to draw Oikawa into an outright refusal of war. What they got instead was a flabbergasted Tōjō, who pointedly asked why these issues had not been raised at the Imperial Conference. Fearful of the consequences of his earlier actions – and no doubt recognizing the logic in Tōjō's words – Konoe resigned as prime minister on 16 October. By this action, he erased the deadline for negotiations and brought an end to Toyoda's tenure as foreign minister.[83]

Throughout the period under review, Admiral Toyoda Teijirō consistently sought to strike a balance between domestic pressure for an overt challenge to the international system and US pressure to maintain the status quo. In this pursuit he was driven first by his own personal ambitions and second by the notion of security for his nation. With regard to the former – namely, his personal ambitions – Toyoda can be seen to have achieved qualified success. He did, after all, receive both his service's highest promotion and a cabinet portfolio (he would return to a cabinet portfolio in April 1945 under Admiral Suzuki Kantarō). With regard to his secondary goal – namely, security for his nation – Toyoda's efforts were a conspicuous failure. Underlying this failure was Toyoda's colossal misreading of US policies and intentions. When Washington proved less than amenable to his conception of a limited challenge to the international system, he was left with no tangible evidence with which to refute the growing consensus in the armed services – a consensus his policies had helped forge – that regarded war with the United States as "historically inevitable."[84] His vision shattered, Toyoda during his final days as foreign minister struck a hapless figure: buffeted from one side by the increasing belligerence of Japan's armed services and from the other by foreboding awareness of the power the United States could bring to bear on Japan. The question confronting his successor, the dour career diplomat Tōgō Shigenori, was whether he could cut through this tangled skein. The answer would come less than two months later at Pearl Harbor.

NOTES

1   Nobutaka Ike, ed., *Japan's Decision for War: Records of the 1941 Policy Conferences* (Palo Alto, CA: Stanford University Press, 1967), 9.
2   Konoe Fumimaro, "Dainiji oyobi daisanji Konoe naikaku ni okeru nichibei kōshō no keika," in *Konoe nikki henshū iinkai*, edited by Itō Takashi (Tokyo: Kyōdō Tsūshinsha Kaihatsukyoku, 1968), 222.
3   Tsunoda Jun, "The Navy's Role in the Southern Strategy," in *The Fateful Choice: Japan's Advance into Southeast Asia, 1939–1941, Selected Translations from Taiheiyō sensō e no michi*, edited by James W. Morley (New York: Columbia University Press, 1980), 268.
4   Tsunoda Jun, "Leaning toward War," in *The Final Confrontation: Japan's Negotiations with the United States, 1941, Selected Translations from Taiheiyō sensō e no michi*, edited by James W. Morley (New York: Columbia University Press, 1994), 150–2.
5   Hosoya Chihiro, "The Role of Japan's Foreign Ministry and its Embassy in Washington," in *Pearl Harbor as History: Japanese-American Relations,*

1931–1941, edited by Dorothy Borg and Shumpei Okamoto with Dale K.A. Finlayson (New York: Columbia University Press, 1973), 158.

6 Sudō Shinji, *Nichi-bei kaisen gaikō no kenkyū: Nichi-bei kōshō no hatan kara Haru nōto made* (Tokyo: Keiō Tsūshin, 1986), 164, 190.

7 Ibid., 164.

8 Sugimoto Ken, *Kaigun no shōwashi: Teitoku to shimbun kisha* (Tokyo: Bungei Shunjū, 1982), 141.

9 See Satoshi Hattori, in this volume.

10 Hoshina Zenshirō, Ōi Atsushi, and Suetsugu Masao, *Taiheiyō senso hishi: Kaigun wa naze kaisen ni dōi shita ka* (Tokyo: Nihon Kokubō Kyōkai, 1987), 19.

11 Suetsugu Nobumasa, *Nippon to nachisu doitsu* (Tokyo: ARS, 1940), 91.

12 Nomura Minoru, *Tennō, Fushiminomiya to nihon kaigun* (Tokyo: Bungei Shunjū, 1988), 173.

13 Konoe, "Dainiji oyobi daisanji Konoe naikaku ni okeru nichi-bei kōshō no keika," 184.

14 Itō Takashi and Nomura Minoru, eds., *Kaigun taishō Kobayashi Seizō oboegaki* (Tokyo: Yamakawa Shuppan, 1981), 178.

15 Itō Takashi et al., eds., *Takagi Sōkichi nikki to jōhō*, vol. 1 (Tokyo: Misuzu Shobō, 2000), 443–4.

16 For Matsuoka's "firm stand," see *Japan's Decision for War*, 10. For the naval perspective on Anglo-American inseparability, see *Takagi Sōkichi nikki to jōhō*, 454.

17 Stephen E. Pelz, *Race to Pearl Harbor: The Failure of the Second London Naval Conference and the Onset of World War II* (Cambridge, MA: Harvard University Press, 1974), 210.

18 Nihon Kokusai Seiji Gakkai, ed., *Taiheiyō senso e no michi: bekkan shiryō-hen* (Tokyo: Asahi Shimbun, 1963), 319–20.

19 Asada Sadao, "The Japanese Navy and the United States," in *Pearl Harbor as History*, 248–50.

20 Konoe, "Dainiji oyobi daisanji Konoe naikaku," 184.

21 Shinmyō Takeo, ed., *Kaigun Senso Kentō Kaigi Kiroku: Taiheiyō Senso Kaisen no Keii* (Tokyo: Mainichi Shimbunsha, 1976), 78.

22 *Foreign Relations of the United States* [hereafter cited as *FRUS*], vol. 2, *Japan 1931–1941* (Washington, DC: US Government Printing Office, 1944), 165–6.

23 Ibid., 222–3.

24 David Reynolds, *From Munich to Pearl Harbor: Roosevelt's America and the Origins of the Second World War* (Chicago: Ivan R. Dee, 2001), 105–10.

25 *FRUS*, 137–43.

26 Awaya Kentarō et al., eds., *Tokyo saiban shiryō: Kidō Kōichi jinmon chōsho* (Tokyo: Daitsuki Shoten, 1987), 328.

27 Yokoyama Ichirō, *Umi e kaeru: Kaigun shōshō Yokoyama Ichirō kaikoroku* (Tokyo: Hara Shobō, 1980), 102.

28 Sugimoto, *Kaigun no shōwashi*, 142.

29 Takagi Sōkichi, *Yamamoto Isoroku to Yonai Mitsumasa* (Tokyo: Bungei Shunjū, 1950), 70.

30 Peter Mauch, "A Bolt from the Blue: New Evidence on the Japanese Navy and the Draft Understanding between Japan and the United States, April 1941," *Pacific Historical Review* 78, no. 1 (2009): 55–79.

31 *Kaigun taishō Kobayashi Seizō oboegaki*, 92–3.

32 Bōei Kenkyūjo Senshishitsu, ed., *Senshi sosho: Daihon'ei rikugunbu*, vol. 4, *Daitōa sensō kaisen keii* (Tokyo: Asagumo Shinbunsha, 1973).

33 *Japan's Decision for War*, 66.

34 Ibid., 78–9.

35 Arita Hachirō, *Hito no me no chiri o miru – Gaikō mondai kaiko roku* (Tokyo: Kōdansha, 1948), 141.

36 Satō Kenryō, *Daitōa kaikoroku* (Tokyo: Tokkan Shoten, 1966), 148.

37 Sanbō Honbu, ed., *Sugiyama memo*, vol. 1 (Tokyo: Hara Shobō, 1967), 276.

38 Gaimushō, ed., *Nihon gaikō bunsho*, vol. 1, *Nichi-bei kōshō 1941* (Tokyo: Gaimushō, 1990), 163–4.

39 Gaimushō, ed., *Nihon gaikō nenpyō narabi jūyō monjo, 1840–1945*, vol. 2 (Tokyo: Hara Shobō, 1965), 153.

40 *Japan's Decision for War*, 105.

41 Ernest J. King and W.M. Whitehill, *Fleet Admiral King: A Naval Record* (New York: W.W. Norton, 1952), 343.

42 *Japan's Decision for War*, 107–10.

43 *Nihon gaikō bunsho*, vol. 1, 169–70.

44 Waldo Heinrichs, *Threshold of War: Franklin D. Roosevelt and American Entry into World War II* (New York: Oxford University Press, 1988), 131.

45 *Nihon gaikō bunsho*, vol. 1, 175–6.

46 *Takagi Sōkichi nikki to jōhō*, 548.

47 Itō Takashi, Sawamoto Norio, and Nomura Minoru, eds., "Shinshiryō – Kaisen ka hisen ka (Seigun shunōbu no kuchiku): Sawamoto Yorio kaigun jikan nikki: Nichi-bei kaisen zenya," *Chūō Kōron* 1230 (January 1988): 443.

48 *FRUS*, 535.

49 Ikeda Kiyoshi, *Kaigun to nihon* (Tokyo: Chūō Kōronsha, 1981), 121.

50 *Takagi Sōkichi nikki to jōhō*, 550.

51 Hatano Sumio, *"Daitōa sensō" no jidai: Nicchū sensō kara nichi-ei-bei sensō e* (Tokyo: Asahi Shuppansha, 1988), 207–8.

52 "Shinshiryō," 445.

53 *Kaigun taishō Kobayashi Seizō oboegaki*, 101.

54 Konoe, "Dainiji oyobi daisanji Konoe naikaku," 222.

55 *FRUS*, 546–50.
56 *Nihon gaikō bunsho*, vol. 1, 197.
57 Konoe, "Dainiji oyobi daisanji konoe naikaku," 226.
58 Gunjishigakkai, ed., *Daihon'ei rikugunbu sensō shidōhan: kimitsu sensō nisshi* (Tokyo: Kinseisha, 1998), 143–5.
59 *Nihon gaikō bunsho*, vol. 1, 199–200.
60 Yoshitake Oka, *Konoe Fumimaro: A Political Biography* (Tokyo: University of Tokyo Press, 1983), 139–40.
61 *Nihon gaikō bunsho*, vol. 1, 202–6.
62 Ibid., 223–37.
63 Robert E. Sherwood, *Roosevelt and Hopkins: An Intimate History* (New York: Harper and Brothers, 1948), 5.
64 Tanemura Sakō, *Daihon'ei kimitu nisshi* (Tokyo: Daiyamondosha, 1952), 77.
65 Ibid., 80–1.
66 *Japan's Decision for War*, 121–4.
67 *Nihon gaikō bunsho*, vol. 1, 252–7.
68 Robert J.C. Butow, *The John Doe Associates: Backdoor Diplomacy for Peace, 1941* (Palo Alto, CA: Stanford University Press, 1974), 251; *FRUS*, 347, 588–92, 600–1; and *Nihon gaikō bunsho*, 281–5.
69 "Toyoda daijin kaidan yōryō, 1. Otto doitsu taishi to no kaidan, Shōwa 16. 9. 13," Diplomatic Records Office, Ministry of Foreign Affairs, Tokyo, A-1-0-022.
70 *Nihon gaikō bunsho*, vol. 1, 304–8.
71 Ibid. Regarding the war and navy ministries' acquiescence in the draft, see Matsumoto Shigekazu, "Nichi-bei kōshō to chūgoku mondai: Terasaki gaimushō amerika kyokuchō no shūhen," *Kokusai Seiji* 37 (1967): Nihon saikōshi no shomondai, 83.
72 *Japan's Decision for War*, 126–9.
73 Ibid., 135.
74 *Nihon gaikō bunsho*, vol. 1, 323–7.
75 *Daihon'ei rikugunbu sensō nisshi*, 154–5.
76 *Nihon gaikō bunsho*, vol. 1, 371–7.
77 Daihon'ei rikugunbu sensō nisshi, 157.
78 *Japan's Decision for War*, 176–8.
79 *Nihon gaikō bunsho*, vol. 1, 367–77.
80 Gaimushō, ed., *Nihon gaikō bunsho*, vol. 2 (Tokyo: Gaimushō, 1990), 2–8.
81 *Japan's Decision for War*, 179–81.
82 *Daihon'ei rikugunbu sensō nisshi*, 163–4.
83 *Sugiyama memo*, 345–7.
84 *Japan's Decision for War*, 152.

11 "No choice but to rise": Tōgō Shigenori and Japan's Decision for War

TOSH MINOHARA

I was shocked to the point that I was blinded by utter disbelief … In the end, [the United States] completely disregarded the many years of sacrifice made by Japan, forcing us to forgo the great nation status that we had striven so hard to establish in the Far East. To do so for Japan, however, would only mean suicide. We had no other choice but to rise.[1]

– Tōgō Shigenori

The memoirs of Tōgō Shigenori vividly reveal the immensity of the blow that struck the foreign minister upon reading the diplomatic cable that arrived from the Japanese ambassador in Washington, Admiral Nomura Kichisaburō. Attached to the telegram was a note from US Secretary of State Cordell Hull flatly rejecting the latest Japanese proposal – *Otsuan*, or Plan B[2] – to attempt to resolve the ongoing US-Japanese impasse. The message of the so-called Hull Note[3] was unmistakable: Japan needed to initiate the first step and withdraw its troops from China[4] before Washington would even begin to consider lifting its stifling embargo. It was, in effect, simply a restatement of the original principles the United States had steadfastly maintained from the beginning of negotiations with Japan during the spring of 1941.[5]

If there ever was a point of no return in the long and winding road to Pearl Harbor, that day would certainly be 26 November 1941, when Tōgō, a leading member of the Tōjō Hideki cabinet and staunchly opposed to war with the United States, lost all hope of attaining peace and finally succumbed to the wishes of the hardline military. Of course, Tōgō was not a pacifist. As a seasoned career diplomat, he was unmistakably a realist who acted on behalf of pursuing and maintaining Japanese national interests.[6] As such, Tōgō could in no way support a war against a nation that was vastly more powerful both economically and militarily. But this logic creates a paradox in the foreign minister's actions that can be resolved only by providing an answer to the following question: what led Tōgō to ultimately conclude that Japan had "no other choice but to rise"? Was it, as most Japanese historians claim, because the nature of the Hull Note was so uncompromising that it essentially amounted to an ultimatum?[7]

The inherent problem with this argument is that the Japanese leaders never expected the United States to accept Japan's diplomatic proposal in *toto*. Hence Tōgō was not only perfectly willing, but also expecting, to negotiate further with Washington upon receiving a counterproposal. More significantly, it is inexplicable that Tōgō remained a member of the war cabinet, as his utmost objective had been to avert a disastrous conflict. By resigning, Tōgō could have gained valuable time for peace to prevail while also extricating himself from responsibility for the war.[8] But in the end, Tōgō not only decided to terminate the negotiations; he also chose not to resign. Further perplexing is the foreign minister's utter dismay and contempt over the Hull Note. Tōgō's emotionally charged words that fill the pages of his memoirs indicate an individual who was clearly taken aback by the note, seemingly as if he had been expecting a starkly different reply from Washington. What history does show us, however, is that, upon receiving the Hull Note, Tōgō underwent a metamorphosis.[9] In a complete *volte-face*, the foreign minister – the last bastion of peace – was now an ardent supporter of war with the United States.

With this as a backdrop, this chapter examines the period just prior to Pearl Harbor, which was to become the culmination of the events of the tumultuous decade of the 1930s. More specifically, the chapter presents a more coherent and logical reason behind Tōgō's *volte-face*, an understanding of which is critical in that Tōgō's reversal of position removed a significant obstacle standing in the path of Japan's fateful decision to go to war. Primary documents uncovered at the National Archives in College Park, Maryland, and the Diplomatic Record Office of the Ministry of Foreign Affairs (*Gaimushō*) in Tokyo dispel the prevailing understanding that the Hull Note – a product of the United States – was the final straw that forced Japan's hand in support of war.

Forming the Tōjō Cabinet

Just five weeks prior to receiving the Hull Note, Tōgō had been chosen to become the next foreign minister in the newly formed cabinet of Prime Minister Tōjō.[10] Severely handicapped by the steadfast refusal of the Imperial Japanese Army (IJA) to provide a realistic compromise in resolving the current diplomatic imbroglio with Washington, the ongoing US-Japanese bilateral negotiations led by the *Gaimushō* had reached a critical impasse.[11] The IJA stubbornly stood behind its hardline position that it would never acquiesce to withdrawing troops from the territory gained in the ongoing Sino-Japanese War. As the war had exacted a heavy price upon Japan in terms of both money and lives, the IJA could not simply extricate itself from the war without suffering a humiliating loss of face. Therefore, while it was undeniable that the situation in China had become a quagmire, the IJA could not accept any US demands that failed to offer sufficient compensation.

Ostensibly to accept political responsibility for the diplomatic deadlock, but in reality to escape from an increasingly untenable situation, Konoe Fumimaro had abruptly resigned as prime minister.[12] It was all too clear that his quest of leading the nation towards alternative internationalism – the infamous New Order for Greater East Asia – had utterly failed. However, the timing of Konoe's resignation could not have been worse. It occurred at a critical juncture when US-Japanese relations were severely strained. Japanese assets in the United States had been frozen and a total oil embargo had been in effect since 1 August 1941. As such, a new prime minister had to be chosen and a new cabinet formed without delay to prevent a lapse in the negotiations to repeal the US embargo, which was slowly asphyxiating the Japanese economy.

No one wanted this onerous task, and at the same time the task was not just for anyone. A strong and able leader who possessed solid domestic support and could rein in the military was *sine qua non*. Only a few men met this criterion, and in the early stages Higashikuni Naruhiko, an imperial family member, was viewed as the most promising candidate.[13] Selecting an imperial court member to lead the government would be an unprecedented move. However, considering the volatility of the situation, Higashikuni, a first cousin to the emperor, was seen as the only individual who possessed the moral leadership and authority to suppress the ambitions of an increasingly rebellious army.[14]

Unfortunately, the plan failed to materialize. Senior members of the imperial household, led by Kido Kōichi, vehemently objected to any direct involvement in politics by any member of the imperial family.[15] The logic behind this was that in the event Higashikuni failed to subjugate the military and war ensued, the emperor himself would have to shoulder part of the blame.[16] This in turn would blemish the image of the imperial court and inflict serious damage upon the legitimacy of imperial rule. Furthermore, how could a living deity ever be held accountable? At crucial moment, when the fate of the entire nation was at stake, the imperial court's decision was driven solely by the instincts of self-preservation.

With the prime candidate eliminated, the elder statesmen were now forced play a risky hand: they would turn to their greatest nemesis, General Tōjō. Tōjō had been the hawkish war minister in the previous Konoe cabinet, and it was his uncompromising attitude that had led to the complete paralysis and eventual collapse of the government.[17] At this critical juncture, however, Tōjō was only one of a few select individuals with enough clout and influence to rein in an increasingly recalcitrant IJA. If he became prime minister, would he be able to succeed where Konoe had failed? For the senior leaders in Tokyo, this question was based on a calculated risk, akin to fighting fire with fire. Moreover, there was always the possibility that Washington would interpret such a political manoeuvre as evidence that Japan was now firmly committed to confrontation with the United States. In fact, upon learning that Tōjō had been chosen to lead the next Japanese government, President Franklin D. Roosevelt simply concluded that control of the army over the civilian government had finally manifested itself in the open.[18]

In reality, however, "Prime Minister" Tōjō was no longer the same person as "War Minister" Tōjō. In what Japanese historians refer to as the *Tōjō hensetsu*, or Tōjō *volte-face*, upon coming to power the general completely altered his earlier bellicose stance towards the United States.[19] One reason behind this drastic reversal was that, as prime minister, Tōjō was no longer bound to represent only the interests of the IJA. But an even more profound reason was that the emperor himself had asked Tōjō to avoid war with the United States and to seek a diplomatic resolution to the crisis. Tōjō deeply revered the emperor – after all, he would willingly sacrifice his own life rather than incriminate the emperor during the Tokyo War Crimes Tribunals – and he had given his word.[20] This was more than sufficient for Tōjō to reconsider his hitherto hardline attitude towards Washington.

Tōgō's Efforts to Avert War

True to his word, Tōjō wasted no time in reversing the imperial edict of 6 September 1941 that called for immediate war preparations, followed by war in early October if no significant progress had been obtained in the ongoing US-Japanese negotiations.[21] Reversing the edict would not have been possible had it not been for Tōjō's firm grip on the IJA. With one stroke, the stage was set for Japan once again to seek a diplomatic solution to the present crisis. At the same time, Tōjō was keenly aware that he needed to assuage concerns about him on the part of President Roosevelt and Secretary of State Cordell Hull. Through various confidence-building measures, Tōjō sought to redefine his former image and show his eagerness to reach an agreement with Washington. Thus, a key component of this plan was to bring in a foreign minister who would be able to convey such a message clearly. With this in mind, Tōjō decided to seek the assistance of a highly experienced career diplomat, Tōgō Shigenori.

By this time, Tōgō was one of only a handful of remaining pro-American and pro-Anglo individuals – the so-called *kokusaikyochou-ha*, or internationalist faction – within the *Gaimushō* that had survived the vicious purges conducted by the fervently nationalistic foreign minister, Matsuoka Yōsuke.[22] Tōgō, who had been a vocal opponent of the Tripartite Alliance, felt strongly that Japan's place in world affairs was with the Anglo-American camp. He also was firmly convinced that entering into an alliance with Germany would only further alienate London and Washington.[23] Such differences over Japanese diplomacy were the primary reasons behind Matsuoka's deep-seated resentment of Tōgō. Hence, as a way of prodding Tōgō to resign from the *Gaimushō*, Matsuoka had recalled him from his post as ambassador to the Soviet Union. Despite his being forced to return to Tokyo, Tōgō nevertheless steadfastly refused to resign from the ministry.[24] It was, however, his firm support of traditional internationalism that made Tōgō the ideal candidate as foreign minister in the Tōjō cabinet.

When Tōgō was first approached by Tōjō, his initial inclination was to decline the appointment, as it was all too evident that the task on hand would be an overwhelming one.[25] At the same time, Tōgō possessed a burning desire to guide the nation safely through perilous waters. He thus informed Tōjō that he would accept the position under three conditions.[26] First, the highest priority of the new government must be to avoid war with the United States, to which end all diplomatic channels and solutions must be exhausted. Second, the navy minister to be appointed must not be a hardliner[27] – that is, Tōjō would appoint the navy minister upon consultation with Tōgō. Finally, Tōgō would be authorized to implement a major reorganization of the *Gaimushō* to remove any pro-German or other *kakushin* [renovationist] diplomats[28] from key policy-formulating positions within the ministry.[29] Tōjō accepted these terms, and with Tōgō now onboard as the new foreign minister, the initially sceptical policy-makers in Washington were now prompted to re-evaluate their earlier assessment that Japan was no longer committed to seeking peace in the Pacific.

Tōgō's Diplomatic Initiative: Plan A and Plan B

Foreign Minister Tōgō wasted no time in revamping the *Gaimushō*, re-assigning three ambassadors, five section chiefs, and many more mid-level diplomats.[30] Furthermore, he formulated two separate peace proposals – *Kouan* [Plan A] and *Otsuan* [Plan B] – that mandated significant compromises on the part of Japan. The comprehensive and detailed Plan A sought an all-encompassing solution to the existing points of contention between Japan and the United States; its primary objective was to seek a definite resolution to the Sino-Japanese War, which had been dragging on for four years.[31] However, since the plan also stipulated that the United States would permit Japan to occupy Manchuria for another twenty-five years (Tōgō initially insisted on five years, the IJA demanded ninety-nine), it was clear that the proposal would require further negotiations to iron out the differences. Hence, Tōgō drafted a second note, the less ambitious Plan B,[32] which sought simply to alleviate the immediate source of friction between the two nations – namely, Japan's recent military advance into southern French Indochina. The plan proposed the immediate withdrawal of all Japanese troops from the southern half of Indochina in return for the suspension of the US oil embargo for a period of three months. In that sense, Plan B was a significant departure from previous Japanese policy, and immediately met fierce resistance from key elements of the IJA.[33] But Tōgō's resolve was firm: he would resign if the plan were not approved.[34] He also did not fail to remind the prime minister that, should the plan be defeated and war became unavoidable, the IJA alone would have to accept the blame. Faced with a determined foreign minister, Tōjō grudgingly agreed to support the plan, which was then formally approved by the IJA and the Imperial Japanese Navy (IJN).[35] Tōgō was now able to submit his proposal to the Americans; the ensuing US-Japanese negotiations began on 20 November 1941.[36]

Around the same time, a group within the US State Department was putting the final touches on a US proposal, the so-called *modus vivendi*.[37] Although portions of *modus vivendi* were very similar to Japan's Plan B, most of it had been drafted before the receipt of the Japanese proposal. The details of the US proposal will be touched upon later in the chapter, but it is important to keep in mind that Tōgō mistakenly believed the *modus vivendi* was a direct counterproposal to his Plan B. In reality, the US plan had been formulated completely independent of the Japanese plan, a seemingly innocuous error that later would bring forth severe repercussions.

On 22 November, Secretary of State Hull secretly revealed the contents of the *modus vivendi* to the ambassadors and ministers from Australia, Britain, China, and the Netherlands[38] and instructed them to transmit its contents to their respective governments. The ambassadors, with the notable exception of China's Hu Shih, were generally pleased with the US proposal since it provided a realistic means of averting a two-front war. Clearly, however, peace was to be attained at the cost of China. Perturbed by the sellout, Hu quickly transmitted the details of the US proposal by telegram to Chiang Kai-shek.[39] The proposal would see a few more revisions before being dropped altogether from the Hull Note. The 22 November version of the proposal – which in the end never saw the light of day – actually was extremely conciliatory towards Japan,[40] a fact that would also have a significant impact upon Tōgō's decision-making.

Pre-war Japanese Sigint and the Intelligence War

Scholars on both sides of the Pacific have long accepted the view that Japan suffered a lopsided defeat in the *johosen*, or intelligence war, even before the first bombs were dropped on Pearl Harbor on 7 December 1941.[41] It also has long been assumed that a technologically inferior Japan did not possess the ability to effectively amass and assess intelligence, particularly in using the "scientific method" of decoding and decrypting. The basis for this assumption is grounded in the findings of several official assessments conducted by the US government and in the lack of archival evidence that suggests otherwise.

Of the existing reports, two are particularly revealing of the typical evaluation of Japanese intelligence capabilities. The first, dated 1 November 1944, was authorized by the US Army's Signal Security Agency. It concludes that "the history of Japanese methods of obtaining intelligence *is not brilliant* [emphasis added]." It further states, "what little progress [the Japanese] have made was mainly with the help they received from Germany. Tokyo's policy was to bleed others of cryptanalytic information and code books ... But when Germany agreed only to furnish information on a reciprocal basis the relationship was terminated since Japan had nothing to offer in return."[42] The second report, dated 4 September 1945 and authorized by the US Military Intelligence Service, reaches a similar conclusion: "the quality of Japanese intelligence was generally poor at best, and most of the time, inaccurate spy reports comprised the core Japanese intelligence."[43] Due to the lack of availability of more recent intelligence reports, most mainstream scholars generally have supported this view.[44]

In stark contrast to Tokyo's supposedly dismal intelligence capabilities, Washington maintained a highly sophisticated code-breaking operation aimed at Japan known as MAGIC;[45] a similar operation aimed at German codes and ciphers was called ULTRA. Many books have examined the enormous successes of these two operations and the role they played in altering the course of the war. For example, MAGIC was successful in breaking the high-grade Japanese diplomatic traffic known as PURPLE (messages constructed by the Type 97 European Alphabet Printing Machine).[46] Since the *Gaimushō* was convinced that its most sophisticated cipher could not be broken, PURPLE was used extensively to transmit highly confidential information between the *Gaimushō* in Kasumigaseki – the Tokyo location of Japan's government ministries – and its thirteen key embassies. This meant that, even before Japan's decision to enter the war, Washington possessed substantial insight into Japan's foreign policy motives and objectives throughout the US-Japanese negotiations. This is not to say that the United States knew in advance of the attack on Pearl Harbor via PURPLE – the *Gaimushō* and Tōgō himself were intentionally left in the dark regarding this ultra-secret military operation.

Less known is that, although the US code-breaking operations excelled at collecting and decrypting Japanese diplomatic messages, they encountered significantly more trouble in translating the documents into English.[47] The problem was exacerbated by the fact that Japanese Americans were prevented from assisting in the task until well after the war had begun. As a result, many small errors crept into the translations. For example, *gozenkaigi* [imperial meeting] was translated as "morning meeting," since the Japanese term *gozen*, meaning "in the presence of the emperor" was a homophone for *ante meridian*.[48] Errors of this nature and magnitude are relatively harmless and thus can be disregarded, but in some cases a simple mistranslation can alter the meaning of a diplomatic correspondence completely.

An unfortunate example of this occurred when Tōgō transmitted a note describing Plan B to Ambassador Nomura. In the note, Tōgō brought Nomura's attention to the fact that the compromise plan should be regarded as a *saigoteki jouhoan* [a final-like compromise plan], and therefore he was not to make any changes to the plan no matter how slight.[49] Through MAGIC, Washington was successful in intercepting and decrypting this message even before it was received by the Japanese embassy in Washington.[50] Unfortunately, a serious error was made in the process of translating the note: Plan B was translated as an "absolutely final proposal" – in other words, an ultimatum – when in fact that was the farthest thing from Tōgō's mind.[51] All that Tōgō wanted to avoid was a situation where Nomura, out of his personal zeal to secure peace, would disobey instructions and revise the agreement himself.[52] This, of course, would have confused the ongoing negotiations, as it would not have been sanctioned by the Japanese government.

As he anxiously awaited a formal reply from Washington, Tōgō had no way of knowing about the grave error made in the translation. He was keenly optimistic since he had gained a major concession from Tōjō: the prime minister would suspend all military operations currently underway, including naval operations of the combined fleet, if the United States offered a serious counterproposal to Plan B. This was the critical breakthrough that Tōgō had long been awaiting – a peaceful resolution to the crisis now seemed within his grasp.

Unknown to Tōgō, however, Washington had misinterpreted Plan B as a flat-out ultimatum,[53] a serious error that would start a vicious cycle that would end as a tragic failure of diplomacy. One could reasonably argue that Tōgō should have been more prudent in drafting the note, but the note had never been meant to be read by a third party – indeed, the top secret [*kancho fugo*] cable had been intended for Nomura's eyes only; not even the code clerk was permitted to get near the message. More important, however, Tōgō did not have the faintest clue that the Americans were reading his dispatches.

Tōgō had good reason for using such an ambiguous phrase as "final-like" in his note. Ambassador Nomura – a former admiral, not a professional diplomat – on many prior occasions had deviated from instructions sent from Tokyo and instead had presented his private peace plan to the secretary of state.[54] This created substantial confusion since Washington could not discern if Nomura's proposals had the official sanction of the Japanese government. The MAGIC decrypts certainly implied that they were merely his own private proposals, but it was difficult to imagine that the ambassador would act on his own accord without at least some form of tacit approval by Tokyo.

The truth was, however, that no such approval had been given. Frustrated by Nomura's repeated transgressions from official instructions, Tōgō wanted to be absolutely certain that he would not make even the slightest of changes – whether inferred or otherwise – to Plan B. It had required painstaking effort on the part of Tōgō to persuade Tōjō and the other cabinet members to agree to the plan. If any unapproved changes were made, it would present the IJA with a convenient excuse to raise objections and attempt to derail the entire peace initiative. This is also why, as a precautionary measure, Tōgō sent the veteran diplomat Kurusu Saburō to act in the capacity of second ambassador to Washington; he arrived on 20 November.[55] This was an extraordinary diplomatic manoeuvre, but a necessary one in order to keep a watchful eye on the unpredictable Nomura.

Despite Tōgō's enlarged expectations, his plan began to fall apart the moment the United States interpreted Plan B as an ultimatum. From the US perspective, it then no longer made any sense to submit a counterproposal that fell short of Japanese demands. Such gesture would not only appear to appease the Japanese and thereby cause injury to US prestige; it would also damage Sino-US relations without gaining anything in return. This sealed the fate of the *modus vivendi*. The United States concluded that Tokyo's leaders were now firmly committed to war and thus it was no longer possible to reach a compromise. Secretary Hull was keenly aware that, by striking the *modus vivendi* from his note, war would be a near certainty. When meeting with Australian ambassador Richard G. Casey – who asked if Australia could act as a mediator – a clearly uninterested Hull retorted that the "diplomatic stage was over."[56] In this way, the gross misinterpretation of Japanese intentions would set in motion the diplomatic chain of events that ultimately would lead the United States on a collision course with Japan.

Herein exists the justification by Japanese apologists of why Japan was forced to attack: the United States had decided on war *before* Japan. At the root of this argument – used also by the defence during the Tokyo War Crimes Tribunal – is the unwavering belief that, if the United States had not read and misconstrued Japanese diplomatic cables, peace might have prevailed. But is this really a tenable argument?

With the wealth of new evidence now available, one can conclude that Japan was also equally susceptible of misreading diplomatic messages obtained through signals intelligence. A recently declassified

1967 US Central Intelligence Agency (CIA) document discovered at the National Archives in Washington[57] and an entire folder of actual decrypted diplomatic messages found in the Diplomatic Record Office in Tokyo that until recently was not known to exist[58] reveal a startling fact. Japan had been extremely successful in establishing a highly competent joint decoding/decrypting operation between the *Gaimushō*, the IJA chief of staff, and the IJN Staff Office. The archival materials clearly indicate that Japan was able routinely to intercept and read high-grade diplomatic messages by China, Britain, and the United States.[59]

In addition to the archival material, interviews with former cryptanalysts reveal the following story. Relatively unsophisticated Chinese messages were decoded in a matter of hours and were circulated to a small group of decision-makers by the next day;[60] for other countries, the procedure took on average about four to five days.[61] The CIA report initially theorized that Japan had obtained the diplomatic notes simply by stealing a copy of the original, a reasonable conclusion since the preconceived belief even in the late 1960s was that Japan never possessed such capabilities. This hypothesis was shattered, however, when a CIA analyst noticed that intercepted British cables had been typed with US spelling[62] – for example, "cipher" was written with an "i," not the "y" usually used by the British Foreign Office. Furthermore, the presence of garbled message groups followed by an approximate word in parenthesis clearly indicated that Japan most likely did not steal the content of the messages via the direct method.[63] It was now an indisputable fact that Japan had been able to read US and British diplomatic cables systematically, not just the four cables the CIA discovered in its reassessment of captured pre-war Japanese diplomatic records.[64]

The Tōgō *Volte-face*

For historians of the period leading up to Pearl Harbor, the ramifications of this revelation are enormous. Although academic research into Japanese intelligence studies is still in its infancy, recently discovered archival material already sheds light on why Tōgō decided to support war at a critical juncture while also choosing to remain in and support the Tōjō cabinet when hostilities commenced. This *volte-face* has long baffled historians, since Tōgō was committed to peace and had entered the Tōjō cabinet to steer the nation away from a collision course with the United States. He could have simply resigned from the cabinet if he did not concur with its policies, particularly as they related to war with the Americans, and he undoubtedly would have created considerable political havoc by doing so – effectively paralysing the Japanese government until a replacement foreign minister could be appointed. Such action also would have been completely in accord with Tōgō's own philosophy, as he had been steadfastly determined to resort to any possible means at his disposal to avert a catastrophic war. One should not forget that he had already threatened to resign over Tōjō's unenthusiastic attitude towards his Plan B. And yet he chose to become an integral member of the war cabinet; how does one explain this paradox?

The fact that the Japanese were reading most, if not all, of the Chinese diplomatic traffic provides a logical explanation to Tōgō's *volte-face*. It was a process that involved two stages. The first stage began when Japan intercepted the aforementioned 22 November telegram sent by Ambassador Hu to Generalissimo Chiang in Chongqing. The note had carefully outlined the precise details of the *modus vivendi* as presented by Hull. The cable, stripped of its cipher and decoded, was rushed to the foreign minister since it was believed that it contained Washington's initial response to Plan B.[65] Since the US draft proposal of 22 November (slightly revised on the 24th and the 25th) contained many significant concessions, such as allowing Japan to maintain troops in Manchuria, it is not difficult to imagine how elated Tōgō must have been. Washington was now finally backing down from its hitherto stubborn insistence on upholding its firmly established set of principles and taking a more flexible approach by submitting a reasonable and workable counterproposal to Japan's Plan B. It was the moment when Tōgō felt that his efforts were finally paying off. All he had to do now was to wait patiently for the actual *modus vivendi* to be presented formally to the Japanese government through the usual diplomatic channels. The problem, and a major one at that, was that Tōgō had grossly misinterpreted Washington's course of action. The final decision to submit the proposal had not yet been made by President Roosevelt; Tōgō merely had a sneak preview of a proposal still under consideration.

The second and final stage of the *volte-face* occurred on 26 November. Tōgō was anxiously awaiting the US reply to his Plan B, most of which he believed he already knew in advance from Japanese SIGINT (signals intelligence).[66] To his "utter disbelief," when the actual note was received, there was absolutely no mention of the *modus Vivendi*[67] – it was as though it had simply vanished. Making matters worse, the Hull Note did not make a single reference to Tōgō's Plan B. It was painfully clear to Tōgō that Washington had not only rejected his plan outright; it had also dismissed the idea of submitting a counterproposal. In the end, what was presented was the same set of basic principles: the United States would not negotiate with Japan unless Japanese troops were first withdrawn from China proper.

To return to the quote at the beginning of this chapter, the reason for Tōgō's bitterness can now be finally and fully understood. Furthermore, we now know why, after reading the Hull Note, Tōgō was convinced beyond any doubt that Washington had decided on war, leading to his conclusion that Japan now "needed to rise." Considering the alternatives in the face of this perceived reality, not even Tōgō could find any rationale to oppose war. Moreover, taking into account Japan's dwindling strategic oil reserves, the opportunity to strike a devastating first blow against the United States was now or never. Although the odds of emerging victorious in such a conflict were undeniably slim, it was a much more appealing alternative than capitulating without a fight. Besides, Japan had gone up against the odds and successfully defeated a formidable and much stronger foe during the Russo-Japanese War of 1904–05. Who was to say that history would not repeat itself, and, as before, perhaps a favourable truce could be obtained after the enemy was struck a quick and decisive initial blow.

Of paramount importance, however, is that, at the very moment Tōgō gave up on peace, the final obstacle standing in the way of Pearl Harbor effectively had been removed: Japan had crossed the Rubicon, and the gears of the war machinery were now set in full motion. As a result, *Niitakayama nobore* ["Climb Mt Niitaka"], not *Tsukubayama hare* ["The weather is fine on Mt Tsukuba"], would be the phrase etched forever in the memories of the Pacific War. The "day that will live in infamy" was now less than a week away, as the IJN's mighty combined fleet, commanded by Admiral Nagumo Chūichi, steamed towards the North Pacific.

Conclusion: The Fog of Diplomacy

The relationship between raw intelligence and the policy-maker is oftentimes a difficult one. Accurately assessing the significance of information contained in an intercepted diplomatic correspondence is never a simple undertaking, particularly since none of the messages is intended to be read by a third party. As such, these communications are oftentimes ambiguous, allowing for a greater margin of error when extrapolating their precise meaning and relevance. Moreover, such errors can lead to fallacious interpretations that, in turn, can contribute to flawed conclusions. In many cases, these errors can be relatively inconsequential, but when two nations are on the brink of war, even the minutest of errors can have a profound impact.

The case examined in this chapter came at a critical juncture in US-Japanese relations. The unfortunate amalgamation of mutually mis-interpreting each other's intentions – the US misperception of Japan's Plan B and Tōgō's misperception of the Hull Note – was a key factor that led Japan down a path that ultimately would seal its fate. Hence the new knowledge of Japanese pre-war successes in deciphering US diplomatic messages is a mixed blessing. Although the discovery is sig-nificant, it does not minimize the tragedy that contributed to the turn of events in autumn of 1941. If anything, it further reinforces the tragic history of Japanese foreign policy vis-à-vis the United States.

Furthermore, despite the long underestimation of the successes of pre-war Japanese signals intelligence operations, one fundamental fact remains unchanged: Japan was unable to avert a catastrophic war that would end only after its major cities had been utterly devastated by the incendiary bombing of B-29s, not to mention the dropping of the atomic bombs on Hiroshima and Nagasaki. Could all of this have been avoided if Tōgō had correctly assessed the available intelligence and steadfastly maintained his staunch opposition to the war?

Perhaps this is too much blame to place upon the shoulder of one in-dividual. However, with our new knowledge that the Japanese knew a lot more than previously had been believed, this merely emerges as one out of many important and unresolved issues that still need to be con-templated by scholars examining the *kaisenki* period of Japanese his-tory. In time, future research will further expand our understanding of pre-war Japanese intelligence, and the information uncovered will in turn allow us to better grasp the motive and rationale behind the deci-sions Japanese leaders made in 1941. Eventually, future historians may be able to present a much more comprehensive and holistic picture of US-Japanese relations just prior to the Pacific War.

Kimi no tame yo no tame no koto wa nashitogenu
[I failed to accomplish my duty for the Emperor and for the people]
Ima wa shishitemo sarani oshimaji
[Now, even upon death, the regret will not escape me]

This is the poem that Tōgō wrote on 28 January 1950 while incarcerated in Sugamo Prison.[68] He would be dead a mere six months later due to an illness. Was he perhaps reflecting upon his fateful actions of Novem-ber 1941?

NOTES

1 Tōgō Shigenori, *Jidai no Ichimen: Tōgō Shigenori gaiko Shuki*, vol. 1 (Tokyo: Hara-shobō, 1985), 251, 253.
2 For the contents of the plan, see Ministry of Foreign Affairs, ed., *Nihongaikō nenpyō narabini shuyō bunshō* [hereafter, cited as *NGNSB*], vol. 2 (Tokyo: Hara-shobō, 1965), 555.
3 The term "Hull Note" is not commonly used in US literature; in contrast, in Japan it is the accepted term for the 26 November 1941 note from Hull to Tōgō.
4 The Hull Note did not specify whether "China," indicated in the note, included Manchuria; however, an earlier draft of the note clearly stated, "withdraw from China (excluding Manchuria)." This phrase was later stricken by US State Department Special Advisor Stanley K. Hornbeck.
5 The negotiation officially began on 14 April with the Hull-Nomura conversations; Tōgō, *Jidai no Ichimen*, 167. The US principles were known by the Japanese as *Halu yon-gensoku*, or "Hull's four principles." Contrary to the Japanese Foreign Ministry, the US State Department preferred to refer to the diplomatic talks as a "conversation" rather than a "negotiation." I use "negotiation," as it more accurately reflects the nature of the ongoing discussions.
6 An important biography of Tōgō is Hagiwara Nobutoshi, *Tōgō Shigenori: Denki to kaisetsu* (Tokyo: Hara-shobō, 1985). Another biography was written by his grandson, Tōgō Shigehiko, *Sofu Tōgō Shigenori no Shōgai* (Tokyo: Bungei-shinju, 1993).
7 This is the standard interpretation presented in most Japanese texts dealing with the outbreak of the war. For example, see Iokibe Makoto, ed., *Nichibeikankei-shi* (Tokyo: Yuhikaku, 2008), 136.
8 Tōgō's resignation would not have led directly to the collapse of the government, unlike that of a war or navy minister, but it certainly would have created chaos coming at a critical juncture in the US-Japanese negotiations. For details of the Meiji cabinet system, see Momose Takashi, *Showa Senzeki no Nihon: Seido to jittai* (Tokyo: Yoshikawa-kobunkan, 1990), chap. 5.
9 Tōgō, *Jidai no ichimen*, 257–9.
10 Fukushima Shingo, "Tōjō naikaku: Rikugun no yokoguruma wo tsuranuite kuni wo horobosu," in *Nihon naikaku shiroku*, vol. 4, edited by Hayashi Shigeru and Tsuji Kiyoaki (Tokyo: Daiichi-hoki, 1981), 328–9.
11 Gaimushō Hyakunenshi Hensaniinkai, ed., *Gaimushō no hyakunen*, vol. 2 (Tokyo: Hara-shobō, 1969), 598–9.
12 Miyake Masaki, "Dai sanji Konoe naikaku: Wasen no kantō," in *Nihon naikaku shiroku*, vol. 4, edited by Hayashi Shigeru and Tsuji Kiyoaki (Tokyo:

Daiichi-hoki, 1981), 308. For the latest biography on Konoe, see Tsutsui Kiyotada, *Konoe Fumimaro: Kyoyou shugiteki populisto no higeki* (Tokyo: Iwanami Shoten, 2009).

13 Masumi Junnosuke, *Nihon seijishi*, vol. 3 (Tokyo: Tokyo Daigaku Shuppankai), 296.

14 Miyake, "Dai sanji Konoe naikaku," 308.

15 Tsunoda Jun, "Nihon no taibei kansen," in *Taiheiyō sensō eno michi*, vol. 7, edited by Nihon Kokusai Seijigakkai (Tokyo: Asahi Shimbunsha, 1963), 296–8.

16 Togawa Isamu, *Showa no saisho: Tōjō Hideki to gunbu dokusai* (Tokyo: Kodansha, 1982), 152.

17 Tōjō Hideki kankōkai, ed., *Tōjō Hideki* (Tokyo: Fuyō-shobō, 1974), 57.

18 Fukuda Shigeo, "Amerika no tainichi sansen," in *Taiheiyō sensō eno michi*, vol. 7, edited by Nihon Kokusai Seijigakkai (Tokyo: Asahi Shimbunsha, 1963), 433–4.

19 Sudō Shinji, *Nichibei kaisen gaikō no kenkyu* (Tokyo: Keiō-tsūshin,1986), 238–9.

20 For further details, see Kamei Hiroshi, *Showa Tennō to Tojo Hideki* (Tokyo: Kojinsha, 1988).

21 For the content of the edict, see *NGNSB*, 544–5.

22 Tōgō, *Tōgō Shigenori*, 219. Tōgō was considered to be among the three elite disciples of Shidehara Kijūrō, along with Saburi Sadao and Shigemitsu Mamoru.

23 Hagiwara, *Tōgō Shigenori*, 259.

24 Tōgō, *Tōgō Shigenori*, 230.

25 Ibid., 251.

26 For an overview of Tōgō's approach to foreign policy, see Bōeichō Bōeikenshujo Senshishitsu, ed., *Senshisōsho daitōa sensō kaisenkeii*, vol. 5 (Tokyo: Asagumo Shimbunsha), 189–99.

27 Admiral Shimada Shigetarō, a crony of Tōjō's, was appointed navy minister.

28 For further details on the so-called renovationist diplomats, see Shiozaki Hiroaki, "Gaimushō kakushin-ha no genjō daha ninshiki to seisaku," in *Nenpō: Kindai Nihon kenkyū 7: Nihon gaikō no kiki ninshiki* (Tokyo: Yamakawa Shuppansha, 1985).

29 In the end, four senior diplomats were forced to leave the ministry; Shiozaki Hiroaki, *Nichieibei senō no kiro: Taiheiyō no yuwa wo meguru seisenryaku* (Tokyo: Yamakawa Shuppansha, 1984).

30 Tōgō, *Tōgō Shigenori*, 255–6. According to the prominent historian Tobe Ryoichi, most of those pressured to resign from the foreign ministry were from the pro-Axis renovationist camp, of whom the most prominent were diplomats such as Matsumiya Jun, Nimiya Takeo, Fujimura Nobuo, and

Shigematsu Nobuo. Research presented at the Kobe University Diplomatic and Political History Seminar, February 2010.

31 For the content of Plan A, see *Gaimushō no hyakunen*, 604–7.

32 Tōgō, *Jidai no ichimen*, 220–2.

33 Ibid., 222–5. From the perspective of the IJA, see *Senshisōsho daitōa sensō kaisenkeii*, 256–7.

34 Tōgō, *Jidai no ichimen*, 227–8. Tōgō discussed his resignation with former foreign minister Hirota Kōki, who persuaded him to remain to wrap up the US-Japanese negotiations successfully.

35 Ibid., 228–9.

36 Sudō, *Nichibei kaisen gaikō*, 268.

37 Ibid., 267. For details of the *modus vivendi* (final draft), see *Foreign Relations of the United States, 1941*, vol. 4, *Far East* [hereafter cited as *FRUS: Far East*] (Washington, DC: US Government Printing Office, 1956), 661–4.

38 Memorandum of conversation by Secretary of State Hull, 22 November 1941, ibid., 640.

39 For the details of Hu's reactions, see Paul Hyer, "Hu Shih: The Diplomacy of Gentle Persuasion," in *Diplomats in Crisis: United States-Chinese-Japanese Relations, 1919–1941*, edited by Richard Deans Burns and Edward M. Bennett (Santa Barbara, CA: ABC-CLIO, 1974), 164–6.

40 *FRUS: Far East*, 637–40.

41 For an overview, see Bessatsu Rekishdokuhon, ed., *Taiheiyō sensō jōhōsen* (Tokyo: Shinjinbutsu Ouraisha, 1998).

42 Signal Security Agency, "Japanese Signal Intelligence Service," 3rd ed., IS-3-01605, 1 November 1944.

43 Military Intelligence Service, "The Japanese Intelligence System," 1471–1, 4 September 1945.

44 For example, Iokibe Makoto, Sudō Shinji, and Hata Ikuhiko.

45 The decrypts have been published as Department of Defense, ed., *The "Magic" Background of Pearl Harbor*, 8 vols. (Washington, DC: US Government Printing Office, 1977).

46 Ronald Lewin, *The American Magic: Codes, Ciphers and the Defeat of Japan* (New York: Farrar Straus Giroux, 1982), 36–7.

47 This point has been highlighted by Komatsu Keiichiro, *Origins of the Pacific War and the Importance of "MAGIC"* (New York: St Martin's Press, 1999), as well as by Sudō, *Nichibei kaisen gaikō*, 295–309.

48 For a thorough examination of the technical difficulties of translating intercepted Japanese cables, see Komatsu, *Origins of the Pacific War*, 247–69.

49 Tōgō, *Tōgō Shigenori*, 232–3.

50 David D. Lowman, *MAGIC: The Untold Story of U.S. Intelligence and the Evacuation of Japanese residents from the West Coast during WWII* (New York: Athena Press, 2000), 60–1.

51 Tōgō, *Tōgō Shigenori*, 228. Tōjō agreed that he would permit further compromises if the United States showed an interest in either Plan A or Plan B.

52 Kase Toshikazu, *Nihongaikōshi: Nichibei kōshou*, vol. 23 (Tokyo: Kashima kenkyujo-shupankai, 1970), 75–82.

53 *FRUS: Far East*, 640.

54 For Nomura's shortcomings as a "communicator," see Hilary Conroy, "Nomura Kichisaburō: The Diplomacy of Drama and Desperation," in *Diplomats in Crisis*, 298.

55 Tōgō, *Tōgō Shigenori*, 235–6. In his memoirs, Tōgō laments that Kurusu betrayed his expectations by acting just like Nomura upon arriving in the United States. One also has to wonder about the wisdom of sending a diplomat who had been the signatory to the Tripartite agreement.

56 Memorandum of conversation by Hull, 29 November 1941, *FRUS: Far East*, 687.

57 "Reports on items based on material contained in the Archives in the Japanese Ministry of Foreign Affairs, 1868–1965," Herbert O. Yardley Collection, RG457 NARA II, College Park, MD, 38 November 1967 [hereafter cited as HOY Coll., RG457].

58 "Tokushu jōhō tsuzuri," Diplomatic Records Office, Ministry of Foreign Affairs, Tokyo; this contains a sample of the actual Japanese decrypts.

59 Ibid.

60 Interview conducted with former IJA codebreaker Kamaga Kazuo (now deceased) at his residence in Yokohama, Japan.

61 Ibid.

62 "Memorandum for SUKLO," HOY Coll., RG457.

63 Ibid.

64 "Reports on items based on material contained in the Archives in the Japanese Ministry of Foreign Affairs, 1868–1965," HOY Coll., RG457.

65 The actual decrypt of this cable unfortunately does not remain in the existing records, as most of it was burned by the Japanese on the eve of surrender. However, cables from nearby dates do exist, and considering the ease with which the Japanese were able to read Chinese codes, it is illogical to surmise that they had not been able to intercept this particular cable.

66 The content would have been the following: Australian Minister to the US Casey to Prime Minister John Curtin and Minister for External Affairs H.V.

Evatt, 24 November 1941, cablegram 1021, Australian Department of Foreign Affairs and Trade online archives.

67 Tōgō, *Jidai no ichimen*, 251–3.

68 Ibid., 433.

Contributors

Jessamyn R. Abel is a historian of modern Japan at Pennsylvania State University. She received a BA in Politics from Princeton University and a Master's degree in International Affairs and a PhD in History from Columbia University. She has held post-doctoral fellowships at Columbia's Weatherhead East Asian Institute and Harvard University's Program on US-Japan Relations. Her recent publications include articles on the 1940 and 1964 Tokyo Olympiads in *International History Review* 34, no. 2 (2012) and *The East Asian Olympiads 1934–2008*, edited by William M. Tsutsui and Michael Baskett (Global Oriental, 2011). Her essay on Japanese whaling culture appeared in *JAPANimals: History and Culture in Japan's Animal Life*, edited by Gregory M. Pflugfelder and Brett L. Walker (Center for Japanese Studes, University of Michigan, 2005). She recently completed a book manuscript on Japanese internationalism in the twentieth century. Her new project examines the bullet train in the context of the global development of high-speed rail.

Cemil Aydin is Associate Professor of History at the University of North Carolina at Chapel Hill. He studied at Boğaziçi University, İstanbul University, and the University of Tokyo before receiving his PhD from Harvard University in 2002 in the fields of history and Middle Eastern studies. He was an Academy Scholar at the Harvard Academy for International and Area Studies, and a post-doctoral fellow at Princeton University's Department of Near Eastern Studies. He is currently working on a book manuscript on the intellectual history of the idea of the Muslim World (forthcoming, Harvard University Press). Dr Aydin's publications include *Politics of Anti-Westernism in Asia: Visions of World Order in Pan-Islamic and Pan-Asian Thought* (Columbia University Press, 2007);

and "Critiques of the West in Iran, Turkey and Japan," in *Comparative Studies of South Asia, Africa and the Middle East* 26, no. 3 (2006).

Evan Dawley is a Historian at the Office of the Historian, US Department of State, and Adjunct Professor of East Asian Studies at Georgetown University. He received his BA in History from Oberlin College, an MA in East Asian Studies from Harvard University, and his PhD in Modern Chinese History from Harvard University. He has been a Visiting Professor of History and Humanities at Reed College and a Professorial Lecturer in History and East Asian Studies at The George Washington University. His current research interests include Taiwanese identity, Japanese settlers in Taiwan, ethnicity, and colonialism. His publications include "Changing Minds: American Missionaries, Chinese Intellectuals and Cultural Internationalism, 1919–1921," in *Journal of American East Asian Relations* (2003); and "The Question of Identity in Recent Scholarship on the History of Taiwan," in *The China Quarterly* (June 2009).

Yuka Fujioka is an Adjunct Lecturer of International Politics and History at Kwansei Gakuin University and Kobe College in Nishinomiya, Japan. She received her BA in English Literature from Kobe College, an MPP in Public Policy from the John F. Kennedy School of Government at Harvard University, and an MA in Political Science from The George Washington University. Having served as a television newscaster in Japan, she is currently working towards her PhD in History at Kobe University and is also preparing to publish a monograph that examines the relation between Japan's public diplomacy and its immigrants in the United States. Her past publications include "Japan's Postwar Settlement in U.S.–Japan Relations: Continuity of Prewar Ideology in Domestic Politics," in *Journal of Washington Institute of China Studies* (2006); and "Are Explanatory and Normative Analyses Rivals in the Study of International Relations?" in *International Political Economy* (2009).

Rustin Gates is Assistant Professor of History at Bradley University, Peoria, Illinois. He received his BA in History from Occidental College and holds an MA and a PhD from Harvard University in Modern Japanese History. His most recent publications are "Pan-Asianism in Prewar Japanese Foreign Affairs: The Curious Case of Uchida Yasuya," *Journal of Japanese Studies* 37, no. 1 (2011); and "Solving the 'Manchurian Problem': Uchida Yasuya and Japanese Foreign Affairs before the

Second World War," *Diplomacy & Statecraft* 23, no. 1 (2012). His new project examines Japan's Self-Defense Forces in the context of U.S.-Japanese relations during the Cold War.

Satoshi Hattori is an Adjunct Lecturer of Diplomatic History at Osaka University. He received both his BA and MA from Niigata University and his PhD in Japanese Political History from Kobe University. The topic of his doctoral dissertation was a re-evaluation of the so-called Matsuoka diplomacy, which was recently published in Japanese as *Matsuoka Diplomacy* (Chikurashobo, 2013). His current research interest is in Japanese diplomacy and economic policy during the interwar period from the standpoint of national strategy.

Masato Kimura is Director of the Research Department at the Shibusawa Eiichi Memorial Foundation in Tokyo and Adjunct Professor of International Studies at the Department of International Communication, Kanda University of International Studies in Chiba, Japan. He holds a BA and MA in Economic Theory and a PhD in Political Science from Keio University in Tokyo. His current research interests include trilateral relationships among Japan, China, and the United States. His major publications (in Japanese) are *US-Japan Non-Governmental Economic Diplomacy-1905–1911* (Keio Tsushin, 1989); and *Zaikai Network and Japan-United States Diplomatic History* (Yamakawa Shuppansha, 1997). He has written several papers, including "Specifying 'Interests': Japan's Claim to the Northern Territories and Its Implications for International Relations Theory" (with David A. Welch), *International Studies Quarterly* 42, no. 2 (1998).

Peter Mauch is Senior Lecturer of International History at the University of Western Sydney, Australia. He received both his BA and PhD from The University of Queensland, Australia. He has taught at Kyoto University, Doshisha University, and Ritsumeikan University. His publications include *Sailor Diplomat: Nomura Kichisaburō and the Japanese-American War* (Harvard University Asia Center, 2011), as well as essays in *Pacific Historical Review* and *Diplomatic History*.

Tosh Minohara is Professor of US-Japan Relations at the Graduate School of Law and Politics, and also holds a joint position with the Graduate School of International Cooperation Studies, Kobe University. He received his BA in International Relations from the University

of California, Davis, and his MA and PhD in Political Science from
Kobe University. He has had various visiting appointments with such
universities as Harvard University, University of Oxford, Leiden University, and Seoul National University. His major monographs include
(in Japanese) *The Japanese Exclusion Act and US-Japan Relations* (Iwanamishoten, 2002), which was awarded the 2003 Japanese Association
for American Studies *Shimizu Hiroshi Prize*; and *The Anti-Japanese Movement in California and US-Japan Relations* (Yuhikaku, 2006). He is also
the editor of *Japanese Foreign Relations and National Security during the
2000s* (Kashiwashobo, 2011); *Another History of US-Japan Cultural Relations* (Chuokoron Shinsha, 2012); and *Examining a Century of American-Japanese Relations* (Asahi Shimbun Press, 2012). In addition to numerous
newspaper and journal articles, he has also contributed to the following edited publications: *The Emergence of the 20th Century World* (Seiunsha, 2000); *Twenty Debates of Showa History* (Bungeishunju, 2003); *From
Marco Polo Bridge to Pearl Harbor: Who Was Responsible?* (Yomiuri Shimbun Press, 2006); *World War Zero: The Russo-Japanese War in Global Perspective*, vol. 2 (Brill, 2007); *International Politics in East Asia during the
Interwar Period* (Chuo University Press, 2007); *The International Political
History of East Asia* (Nagoya University Press, 2007); *A History of US-Japan Relations* (Yuhikaku, 2008); and *Reconsidering the Showa Era* (Asahi
Shimbun Press, 2010).

Sumiko Otsubo is Associate Professor of History at Metropolitan State
University in St Paul, Minnesota. She received her BA in Hispanic
Studies from Sophia University, Japan, and her PhD in History from
Ohio State University. She spent a year as a post-doctoral fellow at the
Reischauer Institute, Harvard University, while teaching at Creighton University in Omaha, Nebraska. Currently, she teaches Asian and
world history courses at Metropolitan State University. Her research
focuses on the body, gender, and medicine in Japanese history. Her
publications include "Toward a Common Eugenic Goal: Christian Social Reformers and the Medical Authorities in Meiji and Taisho Japan,"
Kenkyū Sōsho 86, *Dōtoku to Kagku no Intāfēsu* (Konan University Sōgō
Kenkyūjo, 2006); "Engendering Eugenics: Feminists and Marriage Restriction Legislation in the 1920s," in *Gendering Modern Japanese History*,
edited by Barbara Molony and Kathleen S. Uno (Harvard University
Asia Center, 2005); "The Female Body and Eugenic Thought in Meiji
Japan," in *Building a Modern Nation: Science, Technology and Medicine in
the Meiji Era and Beyond*, edited by Morris Low (Palgrave Macmillan,

2005); "Women Scientists and Gender Ideology in Japan," in *A Companion to the Anthropology of Japan*, edited by Jennifer Robertson (Blackwell, 2005); and "Between Two Worlds: Yamanouchi Shigeo and Eugenics in Early Twentieth Century Japan," *Annals of Science* 62, no. 2 (2005).

Jun Uchida is Assistant Professor of History at Stanford University. She received her BA in History and International Relations from Cornell, her MA in History from the University of California at Berkeley, and her PhD in History from Harvard University. Her first book, *Brokers of Empire: Japanese Settler Colonialism in Korea, 1876–1945* (Asia Center, Harvard University Press, 2011), tells the story of Japanese settlers in Korea, who formed one of the largest colonial communities in the twentieth century, focusing on their overlooked but dynamic interactions with Koreans on the ground. As a supplement to the book, she also published her oral history research on young settlers who grew up in wartime Korea in "A Sentimental Journey: Mapping the Interior Frontier of Japanese Settlers in Colonial Korea," *Journal of Asian Studies* 70, no. 3 (2011). Taking a regional approach to the study of empire, her current book project explores the lives and activities of merchants from Ōmi Province and their offspring across Japan's transpacific diaspora in pre-1945 Asia and America.

Index

ABCD (American-British-Chinese-Dutch) powers, xvii, 241–2
Abe Yoshio, 132
Addams, Jane, 126n40
Akamatsu Katsumaro, 60
alcoholism. *See under* eugenics
Aldrich, Winthrop W., 10–11
Ambaras, David, 128n55
Anesaki Masaharu, 21, 22, 39
Anglo-Japanese Alliance (1902), 50, 51, 191
anti-Westernism: in Japan, xix–xx, 26, 36, 45, 61, 62; and pan-Islamism, 45, 48–9, 62. *See also* East–West dichotomy; pan-Asianism
Anzako Yuka, 157n107
Aoki Setsuichi, 21, 22, 30, 80
Arai Kinta, 175
Arakawa Gorō, 73
Araki Sadao, 58, 199, 204–5, 207, 208
Arita Hachirō, 216, 223–4; and Uchida, 192, 196, 208, 209
Arsène-Henry, Charles, 222
Ashida Hitoshi, 207
Atkins, E. Taylor, 69
Ayukawa Yoshisuke, 7, 13

Bentz, Nathan, 184n87
Bose, Rash Behari, 58–9, 67n49
Britain: 1902 Anglo-Japanese Alliance, 50, 51, 191; ABCD powers, xvii, 241–2; Anglo-Japanese relations and Matsuoka, 209, 221, 222, 224–5, 228, 242; Anglo-Japanese relations and Toyoda, 235, 239, 240–1, 243, 244–5, 251; Anglo-Japanese relations and Uchida, 190, 191, 197, 201–3, 205–6; Anglo-Japanese trade relations, xv, 25, 201, 202–3, 206, 244–5; British colonialism, 54, 58, 66n41, 103; and the financial panic of 1929, xiv, xv; International Economic Conference in London (1933), xvii, 9, 203; and Germany, xvi, 12, 216–17, 220, 222, 223, 236, 242, 243; Japan's attack on the naval base in Singapore, xvii, 225, 240; and Japan's attack on Shanghai, xv; and Japanese intelligence, 268; and Japanese pan-Asianism, 54–5, 58–9, 216–17; and leprosy, 85; and the Tripartite Pact, 215, 237, 238; and the US, 227, 238, 240–1,

Yutaro Tomita, 5

JAPAN AND GLOBAL SOCIETY